LYONEL FEININGER

HANS HESS | LYONEL

FEININGER

HARRY N. ABRAMS, INC., NEW YORK

On the binding: *Toy City* (drawing), 1955

Library of Congress Catalog Card Number: 61–9389

TABLE OF CONTENTS

ACKNOWLEDGMENTS

This monograph is based on the wealth of material, for the most part unpublished, that has been preserved by Feininger's family and friends and in archives in the United States and Germany. The source material for the details of Feininger's life is not only rich but is also clear and noncontradictory; and, since the dates of Feininger's paintings are also clearly established, it has been possible to treat the artist's life and pictures together. Feininger's paintings and Feininger's development as a painter are the subject of this book.

I wish to express my sincere gratitude first to Mrs. Julia Feininger, without whose great knowledge and unshakable confidence this book could not have been written. I am equally grateful to her for entrusting me with rich and valuable original material. The oeuvre catalogue, a model of accuracy and acumen, is her personal contribution to this volume. I am very grateful for the friendly help and interest taken by the artist's sons – Andreas, Laurence, and particularly Theodore Lux Feininger. To Mr. Bernard Karpel and Dr. Annemarie Heynig, whose bibliographical contributions complete this volume, and to Mr. R. N. Ketterer, who first suggested this monograph, I wish to express my sincere thanks.

Mr. Alfred H. Barr, Jr., of the Museum of Modern Art, New York, has in the most generous way allowed me to use the original material that he has collected. I also wish to thank Dorothy C. Miller and William S. Liebermann of the Museum of Modern Art, New York, and Henry S. Francis of the Cleveland Museum of Art. Miss Leona E. Prasse, also of Cleveland, who is working on the catalogue of Feininger's graphic work, has kindly allowed me to study the documentation she has assembled. Thanks are due Perry T. Rathbone, Museum of Fine Arts, Boston, and Charles Kuhn, Busch-Reisinger Museum, Harvard University, for their help, and to the late Professor W. R. Valentiner. For most valuable help in the Archives of American Art, Detroit, I wish to thank Edgar P. Richardson, Miriam Lucker Lesley, and Virginia Harrison. Dr. Ernst Scheyer, Wayne State University, has, since the completion of the manuscript of this monograph, sent me his own study of Feininger's early life. I was able to express my gratitude for placing Feininger's letters at my disposal to H. Francis Kortheuer, the friend of Feininger's youth, during Mr. Kortheuer's lifetime. I also wish to thank Mrs. Dayrell Kortheuer, Mint Museum of Art, Charlotte, North Carolina, as well as Mrs. Margaret Spicer-Simson, for allowing me to see the letters of Theodore Spicer-Simson; Dr. Helene Frank, for her communications; Dr. Kurt Otte of the Kubin Archiv, Hamburg, for permission to use material preserved there; and the archivist of Marburg University, for making available Feininger's letters to Herwarth Walden. To Dr. Lehmann-Brockhaus, and particularly to Mr. Hans Beilhack, I wish to express my thanks for assistance in the library of the Zentralinstitut für Kunstgeschichte, Munich.

For valuable information I am in debt to Professor Erich Heckel, Professor Karl Schmidt-Rottluff, and Dr. Walter Kaesbach. I am grateful, too, for the communications of Professor Walter Gropius. For permission to see and use letters from Feininger I wish to express my gratitude to Gerhard Marcks, Karl Schmidt-Rottluff, Erich Heckel, Mark Tobey, Stefan Pauson, Erlo van Waveren, Marianne Noack, and many others. I would also like to thank Rudolf Probst, Mannheim; P. Josserand, Bibliothèque Nationale, Paris; W. Nachbaur, Stuttgarter Kunstkabinett; H. Adler, Galerie Änne Abels, Cologne; Gutekunst und Klipstein, Zurich; Dr. Elisabeth Speer, Staatliche Galerie Moritzburg, Halle; Edith Hoffmann-Yapou, New York; Keith Andrews, National Gallery of Scotland, Edinburgh; Willi Apel, Indiana University, Bloomington; G. van den Rydt, Collège St.-Servais, Liège; Professor E. Finlay-Freundlich, University of Mainz; Werner Haftmann, Gmund-am-Tegernsee; Dr. Clemens Weiler, Städtisches Museum, Wiesbaden; Douglas Cooper, London; Alexander Goehr, London; Dr. Herbert Kunze, Anger-Museum, Erfurt; Karl Heinz Janda, Nationalgalerie, Berlin; and especially Mrs. Marian Willard Johnson, New York, for their help.

To all private collectors, as well as to all curators and directors of public collections in the United States, Great Britain, and Germany who were of assistance, I wish to express my thanks. In the actual work on the book itself I owe most to the active assistance of Lillie Hess.

Pictures mentioned in the text are indicated by the page number if the illustration is a full-page color or black-and-white plate; otherwise indication is by the number in the oeuvre catalogue, where the illustration can be found. All translations, unless otherwise stated, are by the author. The footnotes are arranged under chapter headings and are at the back of the volume; since the notes contain only the source reference and no additional information, they may well be disregarded during reading of the text. The most important sources are: correspondence between Lyonel and Julia Feininger; Julia Feininger's diary; Feininger's letters to his sons — Andreas, Laurence, and Theodore Lux; letters to H. Francis Kortheuer, from the years of the artist's youth, and to Alfred Vance Churchill, his older friend, from his years of study; correspondence with Alfred Kubin from the years 1912 to 1919; letters to Alfred H. Barr, Jr., and Feininger's answer to a Museum of Modern Art questionnaire; and letters to Alois J. Schardt, from Feininger's late years.

All owners of paintings and all friends of the painter have given me their assistance for this book in the firm hope that Lyonel Feininger's work may take its rightful place in the literature of the history of art of our time.

York, England, 1959   Hans Hess

The artist's grandfather,
Alois Adolph Michael Feininger
in 1861, age 51

Kronenstrasse 13, Durlach (Baden),
the business card of Adolph Michael Feininger,
lithograph by Feininger und Compagnie

Karl Feininger,
father of the artist;
Elizabeth Cecilia
Feininger, née Lutz,
mother of the artist

Feininger, age 12

Young Feininger with his father and an unidentified
man, August 1885

Lyonel Feininger, 1896

At the Baltic coast, Graal 1905

In 1907

Julia and Lyonel Feininger, 1905/6

X

Julia and Lyonel Feininger at Ettersberg near Weimar, July 17, 1906

Julia, Graal 1905

Feininger at the harmonium in his studio, Weimar 1922

top: The houses of the Bauhaus masters at Dessau (architect, Walter Gropius)

above: Feininger's studio at Dessau

opposite page: Lyonel Feininger, Dessau (photograph by Josef Albers)

XII

XIII

The Bauhaus masters, from left to right: Albers, Scheper, Muche, Moholy-Nagy, Bayer, Schmidt, Gropius, Breuer, Kandinsky, Klee, Feininger, Gunda Stölzl, Schlemmer

Julia and Lyonel Feininger, 1929

XIV

New York, 1951
(left: photograph by
Kosti Ruohomaa)

(below: photograph by
Andreas Feininger)

Toy houses and figures carved in wood and painted by Feininger, before a woodcut by the artist (photograph by Andreas Feininger)

XVI

CHILDHOOD IN AMERICA

1871–1887, New York, Sharon

Like all Americans, Lyonel Feininger was the child of a new country and of a European ancestry at the same time: he was born in New York City on July 17, 1871, at
85 St. Marks Place; his ancestors came from Germany, France, and Italy. His father,
in registering the birth, named his son Charles. Later, the child was baptized Charles
Léonell. The artist's father, Karl Friedrich Wilhelm Feininger, was born in Durlach,
Baden, in 1844, the son of Alois Adolph Michael Feininger, born in 1810, and Lena,
née Brennioni, born in 1819, who came from an Italian family that had arrived in
Baden about 1750.[1] Adolph Feininger had a shop in Durlach. His business card,
which showed his house in the Kronenstrasse, was lithographed by Feininger und
Compagnie of Durlach. Who that lithographer Feininger was is not known, but it is
possible that he was a practicing artist as well as a commercial printer. Feininger's
paternal grandfather left Germany after the failure of the Revolution of 1848.
Together with many other German democrats of that time, among them Carl Schurz,
he came to America. The artist's mother, Elizabeth Cecilia Lutz, was born in 1849
in Elizabeth, New Jersey, the daughter of Captain B. Lutz and his wife Maria Eva
Gutting, whose mother came from Arles in France. Lyonel's father and his mother's
father both fought with the Union army in the Civil War. His grandfather Lutz
became a captain; Karl Feininger served in the 2nd Brigade Band of the 10th New
Hampshire Volunteers.[1a] Both of Feiningers's parents were musicians. The father,
Karl, was an eminent violinist, a virtuoso performer but also a fine musician,
who, by his precept and presence, impressed upon the young son the seriousness,
devotion, and hard work that are the making of an artist. The mother, Elizabeth
Lutz, was a singer and pianist of merit, highly respected as a teacher throughout
her life.

The artists of the period felt themselves closer to the aristocracy than to the middle-
class milieu from which they had come and which most of them despised for its
philistine prejudices. Such aristocratic aloofness was part of Feininger's heritage and
remained one of the lasting elements in his makeup. His parents appeared to him
"very rare and exceptional persons; my mother the most beautiful lady, my father
the greatest violinist in the world."[2] They were celebrated artists, and remote. Such
remoteness made it necessary for the child, early in life, to identify himself closely
with his own inner life, and made him see other people at a slight remove. That
feeling of "estrangement," which he retained in all the human figures that later
appeared in his paintings, goes back to his first impressions. To grow up as the child
of artists makes for loneliness. For the artist is concerned first of all with himself
and his art, and devotes more time to his work than do other people. If father and
mother are musicians who have to practice, teach, and tour the world, the home of
the child becomes a lonely place indeed. Surrounded for some time of the year by
love and splendid activity, only to be abandoned for long periods by both parents, the

1

child turns inward to himself. Great moments of experience are followed by voids. "I remember very well, when I was quite a little boy, of four or five years – in our house in New York (we had a whole house, basement, ground floor, and two upper stories) I sat in the big dining room at dusk – the door of the large stove, which also heated the music room above through a grate in the floor, was opened, so that I could hear better – and there I sat, enchanted while my parents played violin and piano – Bach, Beethoven, Mendelssohn, Schumann, Schubert – a shudder went through me, I think no one knew what happened inside me."[3]

Then, when his parents were away on one of their frequent concert tours, the boy was sent to a family of farmers, the Clapps, in Sharon, Connecticut. There he found a warm and human family life. "The good farmer folk in Sharon were much closer to us than our almost hypothetical parents."[4] A roaring stove, which he describes vividly, gave the imaginative child visions of spooks and ghosts. "As children in America in the country, we roasted apples every night during the winter ... there we sat ... my sister Helen and I on a plaid, in front of the dear, small, cast-iron cathedral stove (the fire was visible through the Gothic tracery of the doors, and we called the stove the 'cathedral'). . . . Behind us sat the farmer's family . . . and told ghost stories."[5] Léonell's parents occasionally came to Sharon to visit their children. His two younger sisters, Helen Bartram and Elsa, were very close to him. He spent much of his youth in Sharon, and grew up free and independent; he remained aware of and grateful for this freedom throughout his life. The farmers in Sharon, the Clapps, had two daughters. Ida Clapp painted in a ladylike fashion. One day when she daringly put an orange spot of color on a window in her picture, to indicate light, the young Feininger was enchanted. One need not make too much of a roaring stove or an orange spot in the window, but a child remembers what is significant; and what he recognized as belonging to him, even the ghost stories, left their impression on the child. The country around Sharon remained with Feininger as the landscape of his imagination. "Connecticut hills against a westering late afternoon sky, with broad valleys spotted with homesteads, barns and high old trees among which the village church nestles, came into my life right from the first impression I could receive,"[6] he wrote much later. Roaming the country around Sharon and sitting by the fire were a healthy counterpart to the severer life in New York but there, too, he found things to interest him. In the city he watched the building of the El on Second Avenue, not far from his home. "In the late 70s, I saw the Second Avenue 'L' built, from the first, when the heavy cast-iron pedestals were brought from somewhere uptown by drays and deposited on the sidewalks ... followed by the pillars, girders, and finally the mounting and connecting of the structure, extending for as far as the eye could reach, downtownwards in a terrific row. I watched the entire process of construction. . . . How I watched the locomotives and studied the peculiar scissors-motion of the driving rods."[7] He was fascinated, like any boy, by engines and cranes, rattling machinery, workmen, steam, and noise, but also by the scissorlike contradictory motions and the perspective of the structure. Rivers and ships fascinated Feininger early; the shores of the Hudson and the East River were his playing grounds. "The waterfront of Manhattan was a magnificent spectacle: tall ships, forests of masts and yards, long slanting-up bowsprits, reaching

2

from above fantastic figureheads right across West Street almost to the buildings opposite, stood side by side for many hundreds of yards along the shore. The Hudson, the East River, each crawled with sailing sloops, schooners, brigs, ships and paddle-wheel steamers."[8] He used to stand on one of the long footbridges over Fourth Avenue, crossing the tracks of the New York Central Railroad, and watch the incoming and outgoing trains. At the age of five he already drew, from memory, trains seen from above and in accurate perspective.[9] His later pictures are full of the nostalgic love for old locomotives, with their brass domes and bright colors, for the viaducts of the Elevated, the masts of ships, and the wide expanse of the river.

When Léonell was nine, his father began to teach him the violin. Karl Feininger was a strong and capable master, who probably demanded more of his son than of his other pupils. Possibly because he felt that his frequent absences left Léonell in need of discipline, and in accordance with the Victorian precept that children never should be idle, he had Léonell copy music for him. A few years later the boy was already playing in concerts. At the age of twelve, Léonell contracted a severe illness, and was sent to his grandfather's home in South Carolina to recuperate. He retained the impressions of his visit to the South, but little shows in his later paintings. When traveling with his father along the St. Lawrence, the boy was more interested in the ship's engines than in the wide expanse of water with its thousand islands. On one excursion he and his father were joined by a perfect stranger, and a photograph was taken of the three sitting on stones in the middle of the rapids (page ix).

He went to school in New York, P. S. 69, and there formed a friendship with H. Francis Kortheuer that lasted to the end of his life. The letters of this boyhood friendship were preserved by Francis Kortheuer to the end of his days. From them we learn much of interest about the young Feininger. He had early drawing lessons from Francis Kortheuer's Aunt Hilda, who was a gifted lady and taught the two boys "still life," but little influence can have remained from that well-meant effort — except proof that young Léonell liked to draw. "At one time," his friend relates, "we used to attempt caricatures that we called 'concert' drawings. They were scrawls showing violinists in the orchestra holding their instruments upside down or in some impossible way"[10] — the parents of both boys were musicians. The young Feininger was most concerned, however, with mastering technical problems; he built model boats and engines, and made drawings and perspective studies for his models. His father thought, in the best Greek tradition, that manual occupation was unbecoming to an artist — the boy was meant to become a violinist — quite forgetting that the artist is himself a craftsman who works with his hands as well as his mind. The young boy may not have known that, either, but his temperament was such that the practical solution of a theoretical problem fascinated him — and his instinct proved correct. His sailing boats and models were tried out on the pond in Central Park. There is no better way to experience the relation between design and performance than by sailing a boat. The very shape of the boat determines its speed and its resistance to water and wind. If one wants to study the visible effects of invisible forces, a sailing boat, which traces in the pattern of its course the sum of its conflicting forces, is just the right thing. The smallest change in proportion and design is reflected and magnified in the course taken by the boat in the water. Beyond the joy of making things, young Feininger's enthusiasm for model yachts gave him an early lesson in the dynamics of movement.

His great days in Central Park were those "when the three captains (Arvidsen the Swede, truest old salt of the group, poor as a churchmouse, silent, scraggly-bearded and gray, and with the weather-wise eyes of an old experienced seaman; Capt. Grant, the American, . . . and, so to speak, the engineer and scientist in the construction of models; and lastly, Tarleton, the Englishman and gentleman yachtsman who brought along his deep and narrow cutters) came to the pond." "In those times there was something to look at indeed, and when the 'captains' (sometimes all three of them at once) brought out their newest creations, the three-foot class, there was no end of excitement for the boys at the pond. The models were exquisitely designed, built, and rigged, with housing, topmasts, and automatic steering gear. Among them were schooners of exceeding beauty, copies in miniature (exact in all measurements) of the celebrated big yachts. . . . In the forenoon we (the captains and I) would generally have the pond to ourselves. I was in constant attendance, for at that time I had been taken out of school, being thought to be delicate in health, which I surely was not (I was only skinny and light-weight)."[11]

Railroads and steamboats are part of the American heroic saga — recorded and glorified by the lithographers Currier and Ives, whose prints entered every American household between 1840 and 1890. Naïve and gruesome, romantic and factual, these lithographs depicted, and shaped as well, the mood and vision of a whole generation. Within the collective saga of a nation, children have their own secret dream world. They have, like Feininger and his friend Kortheuer, whole countries in their dominion. Feininger's was called "Colonora," his friend Kortheuer's "Columbia"; their dream world had coasts and rivers and strange railways, streets, and parks; it was the secret world to which only they had the keys.[12] Of that country of Colonora Feininger was to paint pictures later in his life, pictures of that distant coast — the "Coast of Nevermore" — that island beyond the icebergs, the strange land that borders a reality which lies within one's grasp but which can never be reached by an ordinary boat. He never lost his dream world, he never lost his innocence; it was from this secret world that he draws his strength and his images. He remained jealous about his secrets, never allowing anyone to enter his world; the coast is unpeopled, and, if there are figures, they are not real people who can come and go as they please, but unreal people, and he is the magician who has them in his power.[13] When he was fifteen, his parents went on a long concert tour to Europe, and the boy remained alone in New York. The story now takes us unexpectedly to Wall Street. He was put by his father into the banking house of a friend of his. There Léonell Feininger earned as much as seven dollars a week as an errand boy. Three years later, referring to this, he wrote his friend Alfred Vance Churchill that he could always go back to Wall Street.[14] He remained an errand boy for less than a year, but he never spoke as Dickens did of his days in the bootblack factory. When his sisters were sent to a convent in Belgium he felt more lonely than ever, living in Plainfield, New Jersey, with a landlady who had little understanding of his youthful imagination and who made his life rather miserable.

The young Feininger had already discovered his ability to draw and went occasion-

Locomotive
watercolored drawing, 1884

ally to the Metropolitan Museum. Of all that he saw there, the only paintings "to make a deep impression ... were from a very early period; they represented Gothic architecture with figures bright and beautiful in color and clearly silhouetted."[15] In his early days in New York and in the country, memories were stored on which he drew throughout his life. He relived time and again his American youth; and, among the sources of his art, the humble lithographs as well as the Gothic paintings in the Metropolitan have their rightful place. The jumble of houses that is New York, the multitude of ships in the harbor, the landscape of Connecticut, the men in top hats in Wall Street, the lonely world of childish bewilderment and wonder — his whole American youth formed the artist who was to emerge later.

THE YEARS OF STUDY

1887–1893, Hamburg, Berlin, Liège, Paris

At the age of sixteen, alone and very young for his age, he was called by his parents to Germany, and sailed in November, 1887, on the Boston steamer *Gellert* — a steamship of under 3000 tons and still carrying sail — to Hamburg. On board he enjoyed reading his favorite *Yachts and Yachting*,[1] but the actual sea on which he found himself he did not like at all, and the thirteen days seemed long and miserable. This journey brought the young violinist to Europe, where he had gone to complete his musical education but where, in fact, he became a painter. When he arrived, he stayed with a friend of his parents, "Aunt" Prealle in Hamburg. When he learned that his teacher in Leipzig, where he was to go, was absent at the time, he decided to stay where he was and, during a short visit to Berlin, obtained his parents' permission to study drawing at the Kunstgewerbeschule in Hamburg.

There is no documentary evidence to throw any light on the young boy's decision to change from music to drawing. But there is sufficient indirect evidence to show that the idea of his becoming a violinist was his father's and that his own inclination was always strongly toward drawing. He had drawn from his earliest childhood, mainly locomotives, boats, maps, and caricatures. (A drawing of a locomotive, made when he was thirteen, is reproduced on page 5.) In the many letters preserved from this and the following years, he only once mentions the violin; but the letters are full of drawings and talk of his progress and his hopes as an artist. These early drawings on his letters are fine pen-and-ink studies or comic illustrations to the stories in his letters. American and English caricaturists of the day had an influence on his style. His first German drawings are reminiscent of the work of Wilhelm Busch. At the Kunstgewerbeschule he attended the drawing class and the painting class. But it would be wrong to assume that at that period a young student was allowed to paint;

*Northern End
of Navy Island*
pen drawing, 1889

NORTHERN END OF NAVY ISLAND.

even the painting class was essentially a drawing academy. There — in his own words — he studied "drawing and copying watercolors in watercolor."[2] He wrote that he drew for eight hours each day but that it did harm to his eyes, and that he had to reduce his hours to six. His teacher appreciated his work and soon promoted him to the higher class. That Feininger had decided to become a painter is clearly shown in a letter dated February 27, 1888, from Hamburg: "I love it [painting]

6

Fantasy
wash drawing, 1889

and am so determined as to my future calling, that Life would seem not worth struggling through if I could not follow this calling."[3]

Although his formal education had been neglected, he had observed well and had read all the right stories, from *Gulliver* to *Crusoe*, Mark Twain's *Life on the Mississippi* to *Don Quixote*, as well as technical books. He had collected pictures of locomotives and all sorts of mechanical contraptions and he had seen engravings after Turner. "I knew [of] Turner from a big book of steel engravings — a classic work — when I was a mere boy not yet in my teens."[4] In a letter to Churchill he spoke of his "Turner worship." In the Metropolitan Museum he had discovered his love of Gothic architecture. He discovered in Europe the continuity of history; and the impression was all the deeper for being new and unexpected. The newly arrived student from America "was very lonely and very homesick,"[5] and spoke only English — or, rather, American — and little German. He was a typical child of the New World. He had the unspoilt and questioning curiosity of Mark Twain's *Innocents Abroad* (published some twenty years before he made his journey). There was little prejudice in the boy, but there was seriousness of purpose and the full knowledge that to be an artist meant hard work and constant application. He knew that art demands all of a man, whether musician or painter; and, if he was young, in that respect he knew more than many young men. He did not give up music. He played the violin and taught himself to play the piano. Music played a part in his life second only to his chosen art.

In 1888, when Wilhelm II became emperor of Germany, Feininger left Hamburg and arrived in Berlin, where he was admitted to the Academy under Ernst Hancke — a man whose painful endeavors nearly ruined a gifted artist and might have deprived the Kaiser of one of his most eminent caricaturists. The old Berlin was a cheerful city. The errand boys still whistled their "Gassenhauer"; illustrated comic papers were on sale at the street corners. The chimney sweeps and apprentices with

7

their famous Berlin wit were remembered by Feininger in his later years. The Christmas Fair in the snow outside the Schloss he liked most, and he never forgave the new Emperor for banning it from the Schlossplatz. Feininger's first published drawing appeared during his first year in Berlin; it is the title page for a "Festzeitung" issued for a students' ball. Influenced by the style of Wilhelm Busch, it is dated "14. 11. 88." and signed "Léonell C. Feininger." The name Léonell he used throughout his student days; he later changed it to Lionel (Lionell), and eventually to Lyonel because he liked the sweep in the "y." On June 29, 1889, he wrote to Kortheuer that he had passed his examination brilliantly and that it had taken him only a week whereas it had taken the other students five, and that only nine out of ninety candidates had been admitted. On July 24, 1889, he reported from Harzburg, where he spent his holidays, that some of his drawings were to be shown in the big Academy exhibition of that year. One of his earliest drawings survives, dated May 27, 1889, in bistre (below). It is a carefully observed drawing of the rudder and stern of a barge. The division of the object into clearly defined planes and the marked angularity in the reflection of the boat's bow in the water show an early independence of mind and a tendency toward clarification of light and space.

As early as 1889 and 1890, Feininger was already working as a cartoonist for the humorous weeklies. At nineteen he was becoming a regular contributor to a weekly magazine. He felt, even then, that a great loss of freedom was entailed in working for publishers, and complained that he usually had to do "pen work" and very few "fantasies," although "I am getting to be a regular storehouse of the most vivid, horrible, drastic chiaroscuro effects man ever saw or dreamed of."[6] He hoped to make himself independent and thus be able to return to America. But this dream of returning to America and, with it, his boyhood, ended abruptly for a trifling reason. He had pawned an old watch, "which wouldn't even tick," to help a friend.

Rudder and Stern of a Barge, sepia drawing (bistre), 1889

8

His father sent him into "exile" to a college at Liège in Belgium. "My word, I was treated like a lost sheep. When I went to the railway station to board the train for Brussels, my father never even said good-by to me. I left home unaccompanied. Well, I never again saw my father."[7]

The Collège Saint-Servais at Liège was a Jesuit college. Feininger found the fathers and students likable. His time at the college was valuable to him; he learned French and German, completed his education, and continued to draw. He was not older than the other boys in school, but was already more experienced; he had worked on his own and was even "famous." To Churchill he wrote, "Oh! I feel already the misery of celebrity! I am plagued all day long for drawings, drawings, drawings, from every one of the several hundred boarding scholars."[8] Though such fame was local and limited, it was nevertheless a form of recognition of his talents and a source of self-confidence.

The French illustrators were not without influence on his early style. He wrote from Liège to Churchill, October 7, 1890, that he had read "several splendidly *illustrated* books of Jules Verne, illustrated principally by 'Riou'[9] . . . fantastic enough, and *just* in my taste." Feininger illustrated *A Ship of '49* by Bret Harte for his friend Fred Werner. The drawings have been preserved. Among the German illustrators he liked Vogel and Richter most of all.

Like all young artists of the period, Feininger hoped to go to Paris one day, and he wrote to Churchill that he was learning good French at the college, which "will be of use to me in . . . Paris, where I will most probably go."[10] In the same letter he reported to Churchill, "I was a week in that most beautiful old city, Brussels!! . . . Then the quaint old houses, three and four century old, some of them, with their huge chimneys and quaint gables, give existence in their darker recesses to monstrous shadows." He found "a great choice of subjects . . . both in ancient streets and wondrous old walls, buildings, etc., and human caricatures, or, rather, character studies in the working class, and the peasants, in their blue blouses and velveteen pantaloons and sabots and the inevitable meerschaum pipe."[11] It was in Belgium that he had his first encounter with the old Europe. The gabled houses and crooked streets, the Belgian peasants and the Jesuits themselves were to become subjects of his paintings. An artist finds in nature whatever corresponds to his own inner aim. Feininger discovered his love of old buildings.

Drawings of this period are preserved in the Archives of American Art in Detroit,[12] among them *Sunset After Rainy Afternoon.* A drawing dated September 19, 1890, shows a hilly street inscribed on the back by Feininger, "I make the houses pretty much to suit the picture, but still they are very interesting naturally." A drawing of roofs seen from above shows Feininger's early interest in new viewpoints. In another drawing he is concerned with the problem of space and perspective. Spooky houses, and a strange feeling for the *spiritus loci* are early indications of later developments. He decided to "direct more attention to landscape, and . . . draw from nature"[13] and recalled his outdoor sketching in 1888, which he described as the "first taste of air and freedom from the musty Hanckian temple."[14] He had come to realize that his own observations were of greater importance in his development than the teaching at the Academy. He wrote to Churchill, "I had the misfortune to be too much under Hancke's realism to be able to see where my fault, one of too much realism without proper bounds, lay . . . until I had left the academy."[15] The teaching of the Academy of "ideal" art barred the way of the young artist in whatever direction he might have wished to develop. It made observation and understanding of everyday reality as impossible as the free exploration of his own fantasy. The question that occupied him was the linking of his own "fantasy" with the observation of nature. He wrote to Churchill that his teacher Hancke demanded "nonfantasy,"[16] whereas his own mind was full of the most fantastic inventions. What Feininger saw in nature contradicted the teaching of the Academy; wanting to express his own fantasy, he found his way toward the illustration of fairy tales and caricature.

Just then, when the personality of a young and independent artist was beginning to develop, his father informed him that he intended to put him "into business." Fortunately, it was possible to persuade him to change his mind, and Feininger could report on May 14, 1891, "my father seems to be inclined favorably toward my pursuing an artistic career."[17] He was allowed to return to Berlin, where he went to study in the atelier of Schlabitz. Later he wrote to his friend Fred Werner, "I had been 'in exile' (at school in Liège, Belgium) no longer than 8 months, but I came back . . . grown to young manhood, with a different outlook on life than before."[18]

Schlabitz took his class "sketching" every Saturday. The Barbizon school and French *plein-airisme* made itself felt in Berlin, at least on Saturday afternoons. Feininger was pleased with his new teacher, who had given him quite a new direction, for he insisted upon much simpler and stronger working of light and shade. The young artist accepted with gratitude any support for the inclination that was his own. But the school organized by Schlabitz was short-lived, and Feininger returned to the Academy during October, 1891, where he worked under Professor Woldemar Friedrich. Friedrich had a high opinion of Feininger's talent and inventiveness and was pleased to have him in his class as a "stimulus."[19] Feininger's ideas were different from those of the Academy. He demanded of a picture that it have "meaning" and "inwardness," and wrote that to those elements in a picture "not a single thought" was paid at the Academy. "Leo will never win . . ." Feininger wrote of himself, "any recognition at all at the hands of the Academy, for he is no academician." As soon as he could make an "independent [selbstständiges] work at home I am as free and sure . . . as can be."[20] He wrote that only in the life class could he learn anything, because there was no professor "to kill one's own natural instincts."[21] It would be wrong to stay at the Academy because "here is only risk of confirming one's errors."[22]

Feininger had reached the end of his years of study. His teachers had recognized his talent, but more important for him was the growing feeling of his own strength. "I have lately acquired a vast deal of power in drawing."[23] He recognized that he could be an artist and expressed it in a sentence where he links this knowledge with the statement that with work alone can art be developed: "and am become a truer artist in my sentiments and heart with each day's honest effort."[24] When he could write this he was well on the way to being an artist. He decided to leave the

Drapery Study
pencil heightened with white
1891

Academy and go to Paris; if his parents would not let him go, he would "elope."[25] But there was no need for that. To enable him to travel he accepted some commissions, including hundreds of cigar-box labels and illustrations for a novelette for the *Berliner Illustrierte Zeitung*. He complained mildly that he had to do violence to his imagination, but a visit to Paris would be well worth it. In November, 1892, he reached Paris, where he worked at the Atelier Colarossi. He was now on his own, and could develop with greater independence. Only one letter is preserved from Paris, dated May 17, 1893, from No. 9 Rue Campagne Premier: "My great wish has been realized, and I have been in Paris to study. I have been here 6 months. ... My stay has been wonderfully beneficial to me — *wonderfully*, the only time I have ever been seriously at work, and I have been happy in my work."[26] From Berlin, shortly after his return, he reported that he had been the most sedate "student that . . . ever went to Paris. Besides, on 80 marks a month there is no great show for a rakish existence"; at no time did he have "enough money to study to my heart's content," and often went hungry to bed. Yet he was happy "to have made the experiment," and "content to build up my own art for a while."[27]

After his return he wrote to Churchill, "I spend one or two hours daily in making notes of all sorts of passers-by on the street, from our windows. And out of doors I do the same; also in restaurants, etc. It is of the greatest value to me to . . . seize instantly the character of an object whether animate or otherwise."[28] The plaster cast had been replaced by the observation of real life in motion. Paris had held its promise of liberation from the teaching of the Berlin Academy. Paris had become for him the city of his liberation. On two more occasions in the future his road will take him to Paris at the crucial points in his development, and in each case he will find there what he hopes to find; Paris, to him, will always be the turning point in his art. Now Feininger was content to wait and work in Berlin. "I shall hire a small studio here in the winter, and the comic papers shall be flooded with my drawings."[29] At the age of twenty-two he began his life as a professional illustrator and caricaturist.

11

THE CARICATURIST

1894–1904, *Berlin*

The year 1894 marked the beginning of Feininger as an independent person. The relations between his parents had reached the point where separation had become inevitable — all the more reason for him to make his own life as independent as it could be. He wrote to Churchill on April 6, "My prospects are of the very brightest."[1] Later he told his friend Fred Werner in a letter, "In 1894 I began to have regular work for the 'Ulk' through the kindness of Manzel the sculptor, who was on the staff as a political cartoonist. That was the real beginning of me as a wage-earner."[2] From that time until 1906 he worked regularly for the Berlin satirical weeklies — the *Ulk*, supplement to the *Berliner Tageblatt*, and the *Lustige Blätter*. At the time, however, he considered his stay in Berlin to be only temporary. On January 8, 1894, Feininger wrote to Kortheuer, "I am yearly expecting to be back in N.Y. but somehow it doesn't happen. It was a great and splendid thing for me to be able to study in Germany and France. ... I have become more attached to old-world refinement and influence than I possibly can realize until they are once out of my grasp. As a beginning to come back 'home' I sent a number of drawings to Harper Brothers in N.Y. and just this morning received a notification from them that they have accepted 5 drawings out of 9!" A few months later he wrote to Kortheuer, "I have had great encouragement from Harper and Bros. in N.Y. and

Don Quixote
Caricature from *Lustige Blätter*

sold some more works to them a few days ago," and that they had asked for some sketches of fairies, goblins, and gnomes, "just the sort of thing I want to do."[3] Feininger contributed some "small fantastic drawings" to *Harper's Round Table*, and John Kendrick Bangs wrote "nonsense stories" around them. On May 8, 1895, he contributed four drawings, "Sister Sue's Dream about Brother Tommy," to the same paper. When, at the end of the year, he was offered a permanent appointment on the staff of one of the Berlin satirical weeklies, he was quite undecided if he should accept the appointment, since it meant giving up his work for Harper's and, with it, the hope of an early return to America. After some hesitation, he accepted the appointment in Berlin.

Within a few years Feininger became Germany's foremost political cartoonist.

He was given the front page of *Ulk* and *Lustige Blätter*, usually in two, three, or four colors, which he used in a manner comparable only to Toulouse-Lautrec. The majesty of the planes of deep green and mauve contrasted with white and black, in *Pleistocene Man* (page 18), a cartoon on the Prussian election law (which at the time still divided the electorate into three classes with different franchises), or later, the monumental design of *Der Zar* with the Russian ruler set against a high wall in different greens and yellow, shows Feininger not only as a master of the conception of caricature but as a colorist and draftsman of a power unequaled in his day. In composition, in color, in content and monumentality, his pages for the humorous Berlin papers are pictures in the full sense of the word.

The ideas expressed in the political and satirical cartoons were not necessarily of his own choice. The topic of the day was discussed by an editorial board, and the task of illustrating the idea was given to one of the artists. What Feininger made of his subjects and how he dealt with his task graphically and pictorially reveal him as a draftsman and painter. The figure is transposed from the real world of politics into the unreal world of history. Feininger takes his figures out of their time and places them in their abstract position, transposing topical comment to the plane of historic necessity. He was soon recognized as the leading cartoonist of his day. Georg Hermann, the historian of German caricature, in his *Die deutsche Karikatur des 19. Jahrhunderts*, wrote as follows: "The first of the Berlin draftsmen is Lionell Feininger . . . [he] is equal to every task; he creates political drawings of monumental effect in strong contrasts . . . he possesses an extraordinary gift of drawing, an extraordinary perception of form."[4] The fact that Feininger did not submit his talent to the service of any one political tendency was noted and praised by Hermann at the time.

There is little doubt that the editors' opinion and Feininger's own coincided in that they were both altogether critical of the Kaiser's reactionary regime. Indeed, a conformist satirical publication would not make sense; satirical journals express the critical and enlightened thought of their time. The statement of an unconventional truth not only gives scope to the caricaturist but remains the only worthwhile task for an honest man. Outside the political field, society offered further material for irony and caricature.

The turn of the century brought with it a spate of speculation about the future. The twentieth century had from its beginning a mystique of unending technical progress; it had inherited that mystique from the nineteenth century, from the social Utopians as much as from Jules Verne. With the end of the second millennium coming within measurable distance, the technical wonders of the future became the subject of many books and illustrated articles, and the twentieth century developed its own peculiar form of megalomania. For the comic journals this was a welcome theme; they began to parody the more incongruous and absurd speculations.

To Feininger especially, such ideas came naturally, from his own love of machinery (preferably old-fashioned) and his love of the fantastic, with its speculative quality of discovering new possibilities. Two such drawings had already appeared in a *Studenten-Fest-Zeitung*, in the winter of 1891—92, revealing the spirit of the years

before 1900. The issue of the *Fest-Zeitung* had as its theme "Berlin A.D. 2000," and Feininger contributed two drawings foreshadowing the future, that of the world as well as that of his own art. One, a cartoon (shown at left) only 1½ inches wide and running the whole height of a page 11½ inches long, depicts the Friedrichstrasse; it is signed and "dated" *L. Feininger 2000*. It is a skyscraper town with concrete roads at many levels, with deep lights and shadows in the canyon of the endless straight-lined street, with airships floating — fantastic now only in that it was an accurate prediction. The second drawing is a pure and strikingly modern science-fiction cartoon, signed in full, "Léonell Feininger," and again "dated" 2000. The subject is the Mars Express, complete with all the necessary science-fiction devices of rotor blades, rockets, cylinders, and a text on the "re-entry problem." In "Die Insel der Blödsinnigen," published by the *Lustige Blätter* in 1901, drawings by Feininger and other illustrators appeared. In 1902, for *Ulk* of Dec. 5, he invented something like the tank (page 15), inspired by a news report that King Leopold had had a bulletproof automobile built for him. But Feininger's imagination went far beyond the necessary, and he forecast the future all too accurately. The term "futurist," used later in a strict art-historical sense, arose from the same nostalgia for the future that had possessed the youth of the beginning of the century. The adoration of the machine not only was the basis of Futurist art but is an integral part of the myth of the twentieth century. How closely this is connected with a romantic conception of the machine age, and how Feininger reacted, will be seen later.

Apart from his work for *Ulk* and *Lustige Blätter*, we know that Feininger had become popular as the cartoonist of the bicycle, and was himself an enthusiastic cyclist. He had developed a craze for bicycling comparable only to his earlier crazes for boats and railways. He bought the latest model Racer every year. His letters to his friend Kortheuer are now as full of bicycle lore and technical facts as they had formerly been of yachts and trains. In one year he reported that he had bicycled over 10,000 kilometers.[5] The feeling of speed, of freedom, of mechanical wonder appealed to him. Georg Hermann even went so far as to say, "His best work he has done in the caricature of the bicyclist. He is the psychologist of the bicycle and the sportsman; he has evaluated this modern cultural factor [Kulturfaktor]. How he understands the bicycle! It is not a simple machine made of steel; it is seen almost as a living being."[6] This is perfectly correct; and Hermann proves himself

farseeing when he observes that in Feininger's art the animate and the inanimate
world are treated as possessed by the same
spirit and force. Feininger's relation to
the objects is often more personal than
his human figure, where he remains detached.

To James Laver goes the credit for
having first understood the importance
of the bicycle in the social history of
manners and morals. The bicycle at that
time was not really a means of transport
but a vehicle for escape — the escape
from parental control. It changed the outlook of a whole generation. As the illustrator of the bicycle, Feininger became,
without knowing it, the spokesman of
the younger generation. The bicycle was

The Mars Express, A.D. 2000, 1891–92

modern but in an odd way old-fashioned; it appealed to Feininger for its quaintness
as much as for its modernity.

In January, 1898, he was invited by the *Narrenschiff* to send as many contributions
as he could, with a guarantee to print all he sent. Feininger wrote to Kortheuer,
January 30, 1898, that it was the best-printed publication and that everybody tried
to have his work published there. "I myself admire much that is in the modern
direction but am distinctly individual in my work, so that I am coming in demand
as *modern* and yet as *original.* Others copy me much, tho' I would never pretend

Bulletproof, pen-and-wash drawing heightened with white, 1902. Drawing for the print in *Ulk*

15

to be able to create followers in the strict sense. I crave after *serious* work and that is what I mean to turn to when I can properly study."[7] He goes on to say that he hopes to return to Paris if the Dreyfus Affair permits it.

During February his contract with *Ulk* was suddenly terminated but the *Lustige Blätter* and *Narrenschiff* made him new and favorable offers. Feininger never worked for the *Jugend*, a Munich publication, but he studied it and, sending some issues to Kortheuer, he mentioned Rudolf Wilke as one of the most gifted German caricaturists and also mentioned Bruno Paul.[8] Bruno Paul's work is quite similar to Feininger's own early caricatures.

For *Das Narrenschiff* he illustrated almost single-handed a special issue, "Das Narrenrad." He also contributed light-hearted drawings in a parody of Biedermeyer to *Licht und Schatten*, a serious publication devoted to graphic art and poetry. When he first took a studio, to flood the comic papers with cartoons, as he put it,[9] he hoped to devote his time to book illustration and fantastic drawings. He had written to Churchill, "I have chosen a certain distinct field . . . book illustrating is my aim . . . for the present at least, illustrations for fantastic subjects as fairy stories, *nonsense* stories . . . and children's books. . . . I find in this field everything to call out my powers and feel happy in my work."[10] The fantasy, which he had then thought would express itself in book illustration, is the same fantasy that pervaded his early paintings and also his drawings, watercolors, and woodcuts of later years. The elements of his art can be found in his caricatures and his early drawings. Fantasy and a sense of the comic are so much at the root of Feininger's being and art that their nature deserves investigation.

For the deliberate choice of nonsense and the fantastic there are two very good reasons. The first and most important is to be found in the artist's own temperament. From early childhood he had seen good-natured fantasies. He discovered mysteries in the recesses of buildings and strange figures walking on the roofs and in the streets. The darkness was not frightening; it was only more alive than the day. The daylight did not consume all mystery; it brought it into sharper relief. Feininger's haunting figures do not come from a different world; they are only slightly different people, or, if they are quite normal people, their world is just slightly out of joint. This playing on the minute difference with as slight a distortion as necessary is typical of Feininger as a caricaturist. All his fantasies border on the realm of the possible; they are indeed highly probable, just a little bit more probable than plain reality. There is no gruesomeness, but there is a belief in the possibility of the natural's taking a different shape. Nonsense can arise only from that wisdom of innocence that has not yet learned to place events into firm and, therefore, false categories. It is a floating perception, which refuses to recognize any borderlines. Though fantasy and nonsense are closely linked, the idea of the comic is inherent only in nonsense. The reversal of the expected, the turning of one thing into its opposite, the reappearance of the same thing on a higher level — these laws of dialectics are also laws of the comic. The comic results from the antithesis of the sense it contradicts. Nonsense is the exact opposite of sense; so each sense has its nonsense. Fantasy has no counterpart: it does not live in the world of sense or nonsense; it lives in the cracks between.

June 17, 2004! Race Around the World
From *Ulk*, June 17, 1904

Hennig as Disciplinarian (A rooftop training course for policemen).
From *Ulk*, February 23, 1906

Balance. From *Sporthumor*

Around 1840. From *Sporthumor*

Der Diluvialmenſch.
„Ach Gott wie komiſch, das ſtammt ja noch aus meiner Zeit!"

Pleistocene Man (referring to the Prussian Constitution before World War I): "Good Lord, that's funny! It's still the way it was in my time!" From *Lustige Blätter*

Nonsense and fantasy must not be mistaken for one and the same. Nonsense has its basis in the recognition of the opposite possibility; fantasy has its basis in the hope that a new possibility may appear. The two are thus separated by the entire gap between perception and hope; they do not always coexist in the same mind. In Feininger's mind they did coexist, and he used his dual gift with wonderfully surprising results. Indeed, his most serious work is induced by the thought: "How would the world appear if it were slightly different?" It is not the scientifically logical approach that tempts him to move the overlapping planes of his picture by a slight degree; it is the hopefulness of the fantastic artist who expects and, therefore, finds revelations with every slight change of perspective — suspecting that behind every house front, if it could only be moved, there would wait a world of surprises. Nonsense and fantasy are united in the grotesque.

The idea of the continuity of existence, the fluidity of life, the boundless and borderless nature of the universe — all this the painter understood without benefit of science. The stern system of order and category that was the nineteenth century's contribution to science had resulted in a mechanical conception of the world, which assumed that, once an object had been classified and given its number and place in the order of things, it was thereby known and determined. People and things, once they had their name and their place, could not change their position or provide any surprises. The artist was the first to sense that each thing has not one place but many and that it fools one less often if one expects it to be somewhere else than if one expects it to behave in accordance with the established order of the Prussian philosophers. Voltaire had fought Leibniz with the same wit with which Feininger and Klee, Morgenstern and Lewis Carroll reduced that hopeless philosophy. The victory of nonsense became the victory of sense, the victory of living matter over dead matter, the triumph of dialectics over logic. Modern physics confirmed it.

It is as interesting to observe how far an artist conforms to the style of his time as it is to observe how far removed he is from the current mode. The fashion of the *avant-garde* of the 1900s was *art nouveau* (in German "Jugendstil" after *Die Jugend*, which began publication in Munich in January, 1896). *Art nouveau* was proclaimed as the style of the new movement that was fighting against the eclecticism of the nineteenth century. Feininger was well acquainted with the style of *Die Jugend* through two of his colleagues, Ernst Stern (b. 1876), a pupil of Stuck, who had worked for *Die Jugend* before coming to Berlin in 1905 to join the *Lustige Blätter*, and Gino von Finetti (b. 1877), who had also worked for *Die Jugend* in Munich and who was now an illustrator for *Ulk* and *Lustige Blätter*. Feininger studied the work of other illustrators with great interest. In his letters to Kortheuer he asks to be sent copies of American magazines with the work of the illustrators he liked best. A. B. Frost and F. B. Opper were his favorites. He also appreciated the work of Howard Pyle, E. A. Abbey, W. T. Smedley, and C. S. Reinhard.[11]

There are several reasons why Feininger did not respond to Jugendstil. The first was his temperament; the idealizing of natural form was alien to him. The emphasis on the languishing form and the lascivious eroticism of Beardsley did not belong to his mode of feeling. The purely decorative use of line was not his intention. He did, however, benefit from some of the new possibilities opened

by *art nouveau*. Like Beardsley, he used large planes of contrast, and, again like him, created a new monumentality on a small scale — without, however, destroying it with ornamentation of the drawing. Feininger's feeling for scale and proportion was extremely sensitive. He wrote later to Julia, in 1906, "The slightest difference in relative proportion creates enormous difference with regard to the resulting monumentality and intensity of the composition. *Monumentality* is not attained by making things larger! how childish! but by contrasting large and small in the *same* composition. On the size of a postage stamp one can represent something gigantic."[12] He saw the possibility of using "unnatural" color in his cartoons, colors that were being used by the architects and decorators of *art nouveau*. The olive, pale green, mauves, and pinks in Feininger's cartoons are colors that correspond to the feeling of the time. That he used them expressively shows his strength, but the possibility of using them at all was suggested to him by the current mode. His escape from all the vices of *art nouveau*, however, is based on his own feeling for form and his entirely different attitude toward life. He was not a *fin-de-siècle* figure, nor did he, like Whistler, who was truly expatriate, have to prove himself more decadent than those Europeans with some excuse for decadence. He did not suffer from *ennui* — he was still the "innocent abroad." His humor was not elegiac but nonsensical, and nonsense is the best antidote to languor and morbidity.

One entirely new element had made its appearance in modern art; its effects are well known, but its significance has to be stated. In 1854, the first treaty with Japan ever to be signed by a foreign power was signed by the United States. From then on the entirely new world of Japanese art became known in Europe. Whistler painted his first "Japanese" pictures in 1863. The Japanese woodcut opened the eyes of European artists to the possibilities of nonperspective space and the great strength of open planes. The fact that a plane in white or color could contain the illusion of recession, that the spectator was capable of feeling perspective without the eye's seeing it or the mind's working it out along carefully calculated lines of recession, was a new discovery. In the unsuspected depth of the Japanese woodcut, the value of planes was enhanced. No more were they destroyed or pierced by perspective; they could stand next to or above each other and play a sensitive game of values. The outline, too, was a revelation to the Western artist. It was to be debased in Jugendstil, where the ornamental quality was overstated, but it was fully understood by Toulouse-Lautrec, whose line had the expressiveness and coldness of the Japanese. Feininger's own feeling for line and space was not so much influenced or awakened by the Japanese mode; it corresponded to a feeling for rightness and proportion that was innate in his own person. It is a spiritual rather than a visual penetration of space that Feininger shares with the Eastern artists.

In Feininger's early caricatures the value of the unfilled plane is fully understood. The use of line is very personal, in intention antidecorative; it is never used aesthetically, in the sense of the period, but expressively. The probing line, which feels its way around his figures and gives them their outline, is a nervous, sensitive line, registering the vibrations of his hand and mind. By leaving something indeterminate, it conveys the feeling of a floating rather than a fixed position in space. The form that thus arises appears all the firmer. Feininger's line is fastidious, like his handwriting and his person. It is a witty and a wise line, occasionally bizarre and always unmistakably his own. In the color printing of the comic journals, usually done by lithography, the choice of color could be left to the artist, but the number of colors used was limited by economy. The illustrator had, thus, to learn how to obtain varied effects with as few colors as possible. Feininger not only developed a very subtle and personal choice of colors outside the obvious range, but also learned how the selection of two unusual colors in partial superimposition could produce

The Merchants Before the Temple of Peace
From *Lustige Blätter*, 1907

surprising results when the top color was allowed to modify and play within the ground color. This experience he later used in his paintings when he developed a use of color nearest in conception to that of the Divisionist painters. His own sense of color had from early days been bizarre; he had a very personal feeling for the mood of a color. In one of his cartoons[13] the colors range from yellow through orange and deep bluish green to violet. The many gradations made possible by the process of lithography and the modification of a light color by the use of a darker but different color are first experienced in his pictorial caricatures.

A complete inversion of colors is used in the *Temple of Peace*[14] (page 21), where the page shows the same drawing twice. In daytime the sky is blue, the square yellow — at night the sky yellow and the square blue. With this complete reversal of day and night the relativity of color is demonstrated to perfection. Such reversals and inversions of color values will play an important part in Feininger's use of color in his painting. Here it is only foreshadowed, proving that his mind was occupied with such dialectical possibilities. But also in the pure black-and-white range, lithography allowed many shades and degrees of light and dark. Feininger possessed a hypersensitive feeling for nuances; he could thus learn early to develop his natural gift for gradations of tone. Feininger's preoccupation with the perspective of roofs and gables makes his drawing of the rooftop training course for policemen, 1906 (page 17), not only highly amusing but worth studying as a composition. Quite fantastic is his man about town (page 23) who escapes being swept away by Berlin's early mechanical streetcleaner at 5 A.M. Here the mechanical monster has taken on a soul, and the man about town has become a ghost.

Thus Feininger's personality already found expression in line, color, mood, and perspective in the early period of his life when he was a caricaturist and illustrator. That the experience and discipline gained was later used to greater purpose is no reason to neglect his years of practical apprenticeship in the world of the illustrated papers. Feininger himself has never denied the importance of this period. That his years as a caricaturist were not wasted Feininger admitted in 1924, when he wrote to his old publisher, Dr. Eysler, "Far be it from me to underrate those important years of development as a 'comic draftsman' [Witzblatt-Zeichner]; they were my only discipline."[15] As early as 1896 he had written to Churchill, "I am continually experiencing the gratification of knowing myself to be gradually becoming a popular artist, who is sure of finding both appreciation and gratitude for his endeavors! and it is after all a sweet sensation to know that one is in touch with so great a portion of humanity."[16] This statement is worth recording. Later, when he ceased working directly for the public, the thought of being "in touch with humanity" remained in his mind. Feininger was never other than a humanist in his art.

In the same letter he wrote to Churchill, 1896, again after a long interval, about "landscape motives" and reports, "I do not paint at all; but let not that grieve thee! For I have all the old love and appreciation for color, and am only biding the time when I shall be able to devote myself to it as I shall wish." Some drawings of landscape motives date from these years.

In September, 1892, he went to the Baltic Sea. From the island of Rügen he rowed to Seedorf and found the wreck of the *Triton*, a schooner that had sunk many years

Größenwahn
Megalomania

(Zeichnung von Lyonel Feininger)

„So'n Kavalier bin ich noch lange: ich fahre Auto, bin um fünfe noch auf der Straße
und springen lassen kann ich auch was".

"I'm the same kind of sport he is — I drive a car, I'm still on the streets at five in the
morning, and I can make quite a splash too." From *Lustige Blätter*

The Road to Oranienburg, pencil drawing, 1898

24

before. The drawings he made exist, and in his recollections the wreck of the *Triton* recurs as one of the first strong impressions of the sea. He returned to the Baltic in 1893; and later in his life, the Baltic coast became for him a place of rest and inspiration.

Some drawings of the year 1898 are preserved; *The Road to Oranienburg*, dated July 3, 1898 (page 24), already contains the summary conception of form and a special interest in space recession and interval. The solid mass of foliage is treated architecturally. The idea of progressive space and movement is already sensed but not fully developed. The sketch of people in a Berlin café dates from January 1, 1899 (below). From the year 1901 we have an astonishing drawing of *Göhren, Rügen* (page 26). In its vastness and simplicity it is a mature work. It may be considered Feininger's first known drawing of the Baltic Sea.

One reason why Feininger did not return to America was the serious illness of both his sisters. Helen and Elsa suffered from consumption and the family needed him. He had promised to hold himself responsible for the cost of the treatment of his sister Elsa, and he worked as much as he could to help. He wrote to Kortheuer on May 12, 1899, "There is no question of my coming to New York. I shall never get there, I suppose ... there is no spark of life or interest in me." [17] After their final separation in 1896, Feininger's father returned to America and his mother remained in Berlin with her two daughters. In the winter of 1898–99 Feininger lost both his sisters within the space of a few months. He had been very much attached to them and had spent not only his youth but much of his early life in Berlin in their company. The elder, Helen, had married Dr. Berson, and Feininger had lived in their house for a while; the younger sister, Elsa, had been engaged to one of his friends. With their sudden deaths, Feininger felt more alone than ever before. He withdrew completely from the world but his friends thought it right to bring him out of his loneliness and took him to see some people. During the year 1900 Berson introduced him to the house of Gustav Fürst (1840–1918), a painter who had studied in Berlin and Paris and was known for his decorative murals.

Fürst's daughter Clara (b. March 15, 1879) was a gifted pianist. She and Feininger were married early in 1901, and had two daughters, Lore (b. December 14, 1901) and Marianne (b. November 18, 1902). Feininger continued to work for the humorous weeklies; he had a regular income and could make his family comfortable.

At the Café, pencil drawing
Berlin 1899

Göhren (Rügen), pencil drawing, 1901

During the winter of 1903–1904 Feininger exhibited for the first time at the eighth exhibition of the Secession (Zeichnende Künste). He was represented with two watercolors and a drawing. In 1904 he exhibited at the Grosse Berliner Kunstausstellung (Landesausstellungsgebäude) at the Lehrter Bahnhof, as a member of the Association of German Illustrators (Verband Deutscher Illustratoren). Feininger and Gulbransson were given pride of place with the largest number of exhibits. Very few letters have been preserved from this period. In 1903 Feininger wrote to Kortheuer that he is "sitting almost constantly over the worktable . . . and aside from the question of homesickness I am very happy. I guess though I sometimes think that I've lost the ability of feeling free from sadness."[18] At the end of the year he wrote, "If I had been left to have my choice of a calling I should have turned to some engineering or constructive calling for dead sure. Well, here I sit, a success in a way but just for that reason unable to leave the scene of my success since I should have to begin all over again. . . . I've been over 16 years here, and am $32^{1/2}$ years old; it will soon be $^{1}/_{2}$ of my life; and consider me, after all these years, still a typical American, with 'American' oozing from every pore, so that on the streets I continually am pointed out by passers-by as 'ein echter Amerikaner.'"[19]

In spite of his success and the esteem in which he was held, his life as a caricaturist did not satisfy him. He had never liked the dependence on publishers and editors. His most personal work was hardly understood and often rejected. His own ideas and aims were shared by no one. His creative and constructive gifts were unused. Life continued without much hope and with no prospect of development. Feininger felt not unhappy but empty.

26

THE EMERGING PAINTER

1905–1908, Berlin, Weimar, Paris

In March, 1905, Feininger met Julia Berg, née Lilienfeld, a young painter. They fell in love, and decided to remain together; they never returned to their former homes. Feininger's new existence as an emerging painter is linked with his life with Julia. He needed the strength and courage of at least one person who firmly believed in him. The time had come for a new existence, and Julia made it possible and became part of it. In letters to Julia and in their conversations Feininger attempted to clarify his own position. "I am barely an artist. Certainly not in the 'clowneries' the world knows."[1] He continued the debate "because I have such fantasies I have become a caricaturist, a man who feels everything more strongly than the prescribed norm; even, yes above all, beauty! What grotesque thought to be condemned to create in eternal travesty. Inside one sees a heaven of beauty, which the philistines who carry the word beauty eternally on their lips, can never experience. Small wonder, that we the professionals, who are caricaturists from inner necessity all turn melancholic."[2] When Feininger sent his famous caricature *King Edward of England* to Julia he wrote, "I should like to compose a picture like that — life size. ... Everything I now do is just like the stroke of an axe; how can anything mature and differentiated arise? But I *could* do it *if!* And one day we shall see. Not from ambition, not by any means, but from an inner knowledge of conviction I can say that. Pouf! Boum! as the French say when someone uses big words."[3] Thus the great caricaturist draws himself — his humor saves him from melancholic despondency but the problem has to be faced and he is serious about it.

He wrote to Julia in answer to a letter from her, "For the first time in my life I have

Windspiel, wash drawing for a lithograph, 1902

not been taken to account why and for what reason the water is violet instead of *blue!*"[4] and told her that she was the first person who had not asked him. It seems a simple and sensible enough question not to have been asked, but in 1905 a person who failed to ask it was an exceptional person.

Julia was the first to recognize the painter in Feininger. How much Feininger needed her confidence and understanding in those days of inner searching he expressed in a letter to her. "About your judgment of my work I can only say: you ... confirm me even there; but how could it be different.... It is only curious, that I needed such confirmation; for years I have longed to hear once what you said to me today."[5] On October 30 he wrote, "I feel again the strength to work better. ... I am growing young again, and my fantasy is coming back. I begin to feel more simply and naïvely again, and wish to work at *my* art once more."[6] Feininger intended to free himself from the "serfdom [Frohnarbeiten]" of the caricaturist's life and devote himself to independent graphic work. "I should love to do lithography ... above all old towns ... a series of such motives and after that a cycle of locomotives."[7] One of the intended lithographs was carried out — *Windspiel*, an early locomotive, dates from 1906, based on the drawing of 1902 (page 27).

Julia had left Berlin to study at the Kunstschule in Weimar, where Feininger went to see her in 1906. There he discovered the many Thuringian villages that became the themes of his pictures. He made his first drawings of Gelmeroda in the summer of that year (page 63).

In a letter of November 2, 1905, he paints in words a picture that is recognizably his own. In this description we can see the earliest unpainted "Feininger." At "8 : 20 A.M.," the letter states, "I see the picture that I have before my eyes every morning. . . . I see the houses in front of me to the left and to the right as far as the view extends — below still cool in the tone of the shadow, getting warmer toward the top. *Reflecting windows* — below, yawning and dark; above, silvery; and on the very top, where they reflect the blue sky, they are deep blue. And the long cliff of the façades is, in the upper stories, illuminated so deeply golden by the sun, which then is reflected on my table; on this sheet, iridescent like an opal in gold and violet — and above the golden stripe of the upper story of the houses a sky in turquoise blue. . . . Reflecting windows. . . . As a little boy in the country, I used to love them. That will also be a series [of pictures]! Sunset all in gold and violet . . . two or three rows of windows facing west that throw the gold of heaven back like spears — the whole picture to be transposed into indescribably beautiful tones. In the already dying eastern sky — the 'good night' sky — there are suddenly pieces like precious stones out of the sun-drenched, glowing western sky, placed quite frankly and daringly — to me this forcible placing together of two skies always held some mysterious beauty."[8] Feininger felt the strength and the poetry of nature as a heightened reality. He understood the world as a force of opposites. Nature revealed to him her truth; he saw with his own eyes the diamonds, the spears of light, the dual sky, the power of opposites. He understood nature dialectically as an event arising ever new in the process of creation, not as a static reality. Feininger sees his paintings of natural events before he has found the pictorial forms that correspond to his thought and vision. During the years he will have to discover the pictorial forms, which are already alive in his thought.

Since Paris had become the city of his liberation, Feininger had always intended to return. Now that he was thinking of freeing himself from his work for the illustrated papers, he thought about going to Paris with Julia, as a good beginning for their new life together. To carry out the plan good fortune was needed, and that presented itself in the person of James Keeley of the *Chicago Tribune*, who had come to Berlin looking for new talent. He wanted to take Feininger back to the States as a contributor to the *Tribune*. The offer from Mr. Keeley confronted Feininger with a decisive question for his whole future. He commented on the irony of fate: often before he had hoped for an opportunity to go back to America; now, when it was offered, he did not want to leave. In the end, a most satisfactory arrangement was made. Feininger obtained a contract allowing him to work in Europe for the *Chicago Tribune*. On March 5, 1906, shortly after the contract was signed, he had already finished his first page for America and sent it to Keeley. With the contract from the *Tribune*, Feininger and Julia were able to go to Paris and to stay there for some years.

The first page of the "Kin-der-Kids" in the *Tribune*[9] announced, "Feininger, the famous German artist, exhibiting the characters he will create." His characters are small figures on strings; the most fantastic is the tall man in the center, who is as unreal as his creations. The magician who manipulates his figures is the projection of himself; the artist is coming to life in the pictures he inhabits (page 30). The

terrible catastrophes that happen to the balloons and ships in the Kin-der-Kids when a whole church steeple falls on a ship are never designed to hurt anyone or anything. There is no pain, no glee over disasters, no evil thought in any picture. The football matches, the ju-jitsu fight, scenes in prison or bird cages, all spring from a fantasy devoid of all unkindness; yet they are not sentimental or whimsical. They are realistic in terms of another world. This effect is achieved by the artist in the same way in which the political cartoons of his Berlin days were conceived pictorially. By the relation of scales, with overlong trees or figures; the cutting of the picture into unexpected proportions; an extension of planes almost beyond their capacity; and a use of color so subtle and clear that, with the play of the scale of the planes, another play within the tones of color and shape is played. It is not a complete harmony that is created but a near harmony, which lives by its very slight divergence from the expected.

Most personal of all is the inner feeling of the figures, as if Feininger, a tall, angular, and boyishly jerky man, had felt his way into them. They move and act as if animated not only by the spirit but by the body of their maker. In his pictures we shall often find a tall, straggly man going through the world; and that man is always Feininger. It is as if he had painted that world to live in it, as if he had created a world of fantasy to be inhabitated by himself. He has no intention of taking us into this world; it remains his own and we remain the spectators: there is no entry into it. It is so personal that it defies any attempt to take part in the game. His pages for children play a game for children, not with them.

"The Kin-der-Kids" was followed by another series, "Wee Willie Winkie's World." The world Feininger created for these pages of the *Chicago Tribune* contains landscapes with trees and clouds in humanized shapes and expressive features, seascapes with birds, and rocks with human faces — the whole world is shown as human. In fairy tales animals speak and stones have thought. In Feininger's pages this is more than an anthropomorphic device. It contains the essence of the comic, where the object is aware of its own consciousness. In Wee Willie Winkie's world a puddle spits and splutters in astonishment when a stone is thrown in. A noisy railway engine, Willie declares, was "just showing off." Things have not only character but self-knowledge and will. Life has taken hold of the whole inanimate world. A strange *genius loci* pervades each drawing. The loneliness of the houses in their isolation is enhanced by the emotive quality of the color and its effects of removing the toy houses not only from our world but even from the world in which they are depicted.

Wee Willie Winkie's World. From *Chicago Tribune,* 1906

The loneliness of childhood pervades this world, but it is a loneliness without despair. In the drawing of Wee Willie Winkie watching the sun disappear (page 31), the time sequence is expressed in the relative changes of all elements — the line of the horizon, the color of the boat, sea, sky, and foreground, the interrelation of space, time, and light are given, as well as the mood of the sun and Wee Willie Winkie. It is only a strip cartoon, but it contains the problems of modern art in a pure form and it contains Feininger's knowledge and the solutions that he has found and will later develop.

Feininger and Julia arrived in Paris on July 24, 1906, and rented a studio at 242 Boulevard Raspail. The studio had formerly belonged to Sinding, a Norwegian sculptor; later, Picasso had a studio there in 1911. They furnished it in the usual manner with pieces picked up in antique shops. Feininger was in one of the happiest periods of his life. He was freed from his work for the Berlin periodicals, living in Paris, setting up his first home with Julia. He returned to the Atelier Colarossi, where now Matisse and his circle were working. He made friends with the German artists of the Matisse circle, Hans Purrmann, Rudolf Grossmann, Oscar Moll, Rudolf Levy, all early disciples of Matisse. The friends met at the Café du Dôme, and later became known as the Dôme circle.

Suddenly Feininger found himself in a new world. He had known Paris as a young and modest student. Now that he had returned, he lived in the center of the world in which the new art was developing. Wilhelm Uhde was the *doyen* of the Dôme circle; Hans Bondy, the publisher, was a frequent visitor. For him Feininger illustrated *Nordische Volksmärchen*. A member of the group was Wil Howard, a painter from Leipzig who claimed succession to the English throne and, more important in this context, was one of the founders of *Le Témoin*.

The artist's friendship with Richard Götz was possibly the most important; in conversation with him Feininger clarified his mind. He wrote much later about these conversations with Götz, "I began to observe works of art and the paintings of the artists with whom I was acquainted in Paris (the Dôme group especially) began to acquire new meaning for me. Also the postulate that the artist should be an experimenter, seek out logical and constructive solutions — create *synthetically pure* forms." [10] In Paris Feininger learned to recognize new possibilities that he had already thought of but had not dared to apply. Of his caricatures, those in which he had attempted fantastic and daring solutions had always been returned to him. In Paris Feininger learned to understand that daring was now the order of the day and he found encouragement to follow his own convictions.

In Paris he made notes wherever he went. Rue Saint-Jacques, Rue de la Gaieté, Montparnasse — rarely Montmartre, the Panthéon, Sainte-Geneviève and the quays — were his main places of interest. The subjects he observed and the pictorial notes he made are used later in his paintings. Throughout his life Feininger stored memories, which reappear in his pictures after many years.

From this period many drawings exist, almost all of single figures observed at the café, at the street corner, at work, anywhere. They show great speed of perception and the trained caricaturist's eye for the essential characteristics, but they are not so much caricatures as character studies; they are close observations of people.

Regulars at the Café du Dôme, pencil drawing, 1908

Crayon sketches, Paris 1908

From *Le Témoin*, 1907

34

35

L'Impatiente (La Belle). From *Le Témoin*, 1907

36

One of Feininger's closest friends and probably, next to Götz, the best company, was Jules Pascin, whom Feininger drew at the Café du Dôme (page 43). When the contract with the *Tribune* was coming to an end, Feininger worked mainly for *Le Témoin*, a short-lived but extraordinary paper that Paul Iribe, himself a brilliant designer, had founded. Juan Gris was also one of the contributors. The first number appeared in October, 1906; it was edited by Iribe only for the first issues until April 27, 1907.

For *Le Témoin* Feininger was not obliged to illustrate ideas that were not his own. He was free to make his own drawings, for which Iribe found titles. *L'Impatiente* (page 36) later appeared as the painting *Lady in Mauve* (page 95). In this first drawing for *Le Témoin*, the high houses, the angular tall figure, are conceived as in his later painting. In *Exactitude* (page 38), the huge figures are striding with an inner speed, hitherto unknown in drawing, with a feeling for haste as only the Futurists conceived it; yet there are no devices to give the illusion of speed; it is inherent in the stride of the figures. Iribe's title: "Où allons-nous? Je n'en sais rien. Alors pressons." In *La Doute* (in *Le Témoin*) two workmen ask, "Premier mai? Premier avril?" with the well-founded scepticism of the working class. What breadth of conception Feininger could achieve then is shown in the greatest of all his cartoons, *L'Exode* (pages 34–35), a double page for *Le Témoin* on the occasion of the expulsion of the Jesuits. He had known the Jesuits well at the Collège Saint-Servais. Without rancor and without love, they are shown as they leave, and the first to leave with them is Feininger himself.

Many of the drawings for *Le Témoin* could later reappear as paintings (*Newspaper Readers, Diabolo Players*) because as drawings they were already pictures and not illustrations. The liberating step from pictorial journalism to independent picture-

Diabolo Players, pencil drawing, 1907

Exactitude. From *Le Témoin*
1907

making came with the drawings for *Le Témoin;* once these had been conceived and executed by Feininger in accordance with his own ideas, the independence of his work was established in his own mind.

The importance of his stay in Paris he described later in a mainly autobiographical letter to Kubin.[11] "Then suddenly came the liberation! A contract with Chicago made it possible to move to Paris, and at long last get to know the world of art! I could think, feel and work *for myself.* . . . Only during the last five years did I learn *what* art *could* and *had to be* for me! Since that time my awakening and development went quickly and strongly forward — I have never formed myself consciously on others, but still won from them the knowledge of art and everything in my *intuition,* which for decades had withered (nay, *suppressed* because of the publishers) began to develop."

Feininger had reached the real turning point in his life. He was beginning to paint. Although he was already thirty-six, he considered himself — and we must consider him — a young painter.

Wölfflin has recognized two essentially different approaches toward painting: that of the artists who conceive a picture as drawing — among these Wölfflin includes Holbein and Dürer — and that of the artists who conceive their pictures as pure painting — among these he counts Rembrandt and Velázquez. The fundamental conception underlying a picture designed by a linear temperament is conceived in lines, with color serving form, whereas the "painterly" painter conceives his work as consisting of volumes expressed in color, with line emerging as the shape emerges from the paint.

Feininger's temperament was linear, and the natural conception of his work was in lines and planes, with color as tone playing a vital and often independent part but never preceding the definition of volume by line. He himself had written, "Drawing is the soul of art,"[12] echoing Ingres' famous dictum. Faced now with the medium of paint, he tried at first to do exactly what came least naturally to him — to build up his pictures by brush strokes alone. His first two paintings were still lifes painted on April 21 and 22, 1907. They were followed by six small pictures painted on board. Of these, three are Parisian subjects after nature, interesting because, even in their very small size, they are monumentally conceived. A certain influence of the Matisse school seems evident (compare a strikingly similar painting of 1902 by Matisse: *Notre-Dame in the Late Afternoon*, in the Albright Art Gallery, Buffalo[13]). These studies in oil are astonishingly mature, broadly painted, and spatially well organized. The other three paintings, a still life on a table, a country church, and a farmhouse, show no sign of immaturity; they show, indeed, an easy mastery of the medium (cat. 3, 4, 5, 6, 7, 11).

What Feininger had to overcome was not his tradition as a draftsman but his mental image of himself as a caricaturist. He attempted two separate ways out of this *impasse*. The first, obvious way was to paint still lifes and landscapes without figures, thus avoiding any resemblance to his caricatures. The other way, less obvious, was more difficult: to take compositions that had appeared as drawings and

Pencil sketches, Paris 1906

as caricatures, and to develop them into paintings. In this process he had to come to terms with his own past and build greater, more lasting works with the material of former experience. It is a remarkable sign of honesty to himself that he did not deny his past, that he continued to keep it alive and to grow with it. In the paintings that still bear the visible traces of his caricatures Feininger is taking greater risks — but also achieving greater gains in terms of his own maturity — than in his still lifes and landscapes. These were exercises in the use of paint and, since they were done by a maturing and gifted man, were also pictures of sensitivity and merit. But, in his paintings of figures, he overcame his old self, and found a secure base and inner assurance to build further.

He appears to us in one of his first paintings, *The White Man*, shadowing his counterpart, a small, dark man. There he stands, as high as the Tour Saint-Jacques, hands in his pocket, an American in Paris, a painter looking at his world. The picture is unsigned and undated; in his mind it is not even there — it is an attempt to find himself, to project himself into the new world of painting. His whole development had tended toward this self-realization. The caricaturist "Uncle Feininger" from the *Tribune* had become the painter Feininger in *The White Man* (page 173).

In his first year as a painter, 1907, he had done most of his pictures "before nature," and three, as he called it, "out of his head." During the summer of 1906 he had visited Normandy — Ouville, La Rivière, and Quiberville. During the summer of 1907 he spent some weeks in the Black Forest at Freiburg, where he painted three oil studies after nature (cat. 11—13). During the autumn of the same year he returned to the Baltic, to Lobbe on the island of Rügen. He now had to come to

Longueil, pencil sketch, 1906

40

At the Atelier Colarossi
pencil drawing, Paris 1907

terms with nature within the new context of painting. Two paintings of farmhouses from Lobbe on Rügen show his preoccupation with the new medium, a thick *impasto* in broad brush strokes builds up a solid painting. There is more freedom of handling in his landscapes and townscapes than there had been in his first still lifes, but they are still exercises in the current mode of painting, with the aim of mastering the medium.

The way to clear his vision from all residue of the routine he had acquired as an illustrator was through observation of nature. His letters of the period speak of his struggle and of the new discoveries he made for himself alone. He wrote from Lobbe, "there I observed such a striking effect of contour that I did not hesitate to paint it, although I have never seen anything like it in a picture. Namely: to the left of the objects the contours were blue, to the right a warm green, and this appeared to transpose itself from the object to the adjoining sky. That is why in the warm gray sky I painted on the left a broad blue stripe next to the already dark blue contour and a broad light green stripe in the sky on the right. In this manner, not only the roof and the other objects reaching into the air have their colored outlines [Kontur] but vice versa also: the sky has its colored contour." [14]

This fundamental discovery of the unity of the object and the space in which it stands was to become a determining factor in Feininger's painting. It was his vision of nature and the transposition of his observation into a new form of painting, which was beginning to develop in his mind. His process of work and thought is best expressed by himself. "I am painting naïvely what I learn to see. For a few days now I have been in harmony with the means, but thought [Überlegung] is not excluded — it is wonderful, this newly developed faculty." Next day he wrote, "On what I now am painfully learning I shall build . . . [the work] must become *more charged*,

41

pulled apart, and newly created. . . . A good sign for my work: nobody likes it!" "I can visualize already quite different values of tone and luminosity — other possibilities of *transposition* than hitherto — but it is almost impossible to get away from *accustomed* reality. What one sees must undergo an *inner transformation*, must be crystallized." [15]

Feininger's development progressed rapidly. He is quite aware that he had begun as a painter rather late in life. He wrote to Julia, "I have to do still so much ground-work [Roharbeit] . . . not for nothing does one start to paint at thirty-six as a cheer-ful old man and then paint with a locomotivelike passion eight or ten hours daily. But hope dawns on me." [16]

During October, 1907, he returned to Paris with Julia and took a new studio at the old address on the Boulevard Raspail. With one exception — a still life — all paintings of the winter of 1907–1908 are grotesques. The *Wedding Trip*, an old crazy *Locomotive* (cat. 25), and the *Newspaper Readers I* (cat. 34) are the outcome of his old desire for the fantastic. Caricature here becomes independent; it is his second alternative of freeing himself from his past experience by finding for it a painterly expression. Later Feininger wrote about his early attempts, "When I started back in 1907, my first paintings I was but a caricaturist and my intentions regarding oils were vague. . . . My ideal was to build up pictures formed of silhouetted ob-jects. . . . I had seen shooting-gallery figures [Schiessbudenfiguren] of cut sheet iron, and painted in a simple array of more or less violent colors, with no modeling. This

Ladies at an Exhibition
pen and colored ink, Paris
1908

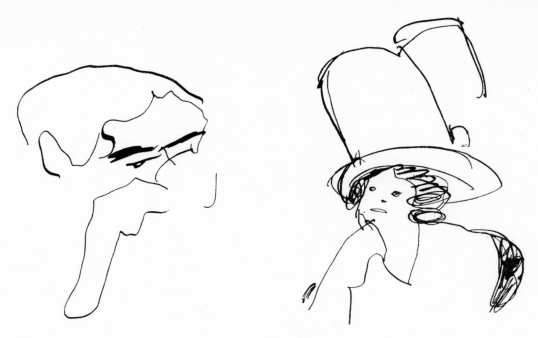

Pen-and-ink sketches, 1908. Left: *Pascin with a Cup;* right: *Lady with a Hat*

was in Paris, and after I had definitely given up caricatures for the Chicago Tribune, and was at last working entirely 'on my own.'"[17]

In May, 1908, the last money from the *Tribune* contract had been spent and Feininger's years in Paris came to an end. During the spring of that year Julia and Feininger went to London, where he saw for the first time the Turners that he had admired in steel engravings since his childhood. During his short stay in England, he visited the mother of his friend Theodore Spicer-Simson in the Chilterns and made drawings of London characters. On the way to Berlin the couple passed through Paris and took leave of their friends. During the autumn of the same year, they returned to London and a marriage was concluded on September 25, 1908. The family, which now included their first son Andreas, could settle down in Berlin. The Feiningers liked Zehlendorf, then still a rural section outside Berlin, and they took an apartment there, at Königstrasse No. 32. The family was installed there during the last months of 1908, and they remained there for the next eleven years.

NEW PERSPECTIVES

1908–1912, *Berlin-Zehlendorf*

In Zehlendorf Feininger for the first time had his own painter's studio in Germany, a large room with windows to the east and north, and was happy in his new surroundings. His friends were Ernst Stern, then stage designer for Reinhardt; Francis Christophe; Bruno Paul; the painter Scheurich; Galanis of *Assiette au Beurre*; Pascin, illustrator of the German weeklies; Ernst Heilemann, a painter of fashionable women, and his American wife. His family was growing. Laurence, his second son, and Lux, his third son, were born in 1909 and 1910. The summer months were spent on the shore of the Baltic resort of Heringsdorf.

From a well-known illustrator he turned himself into an unknown painter. At nearly forty years of age, he began a new life, striving for the realization of his art. The years 1909–13 were the years of struggle and lack of recognition; the real achievement of those years was the growth of his confidence in his own work.

That his work was not understood by others needs little stressing — that aspect of the history of modern art is too well known and it is as true of Feininger as of any of the other innovators. He even feared that making a present of one of his pictures would be unacceptable. He wrote to Julia, considering whether his father-in-law might be pleased with one of his pictures as a birthday present, "It is almost as if I were trading with elephants and crocodiles — and, when I give away such a nice animal, I only embarrass the recipient who has to feed and house it."[1]

Every artist who makes a new contribution to art suffers from two forms of difficulties: one arising from his inner condition, the other from the world around him. From the ignorance of the outside world the painter can remove himself by a stubborn disdain and a firm belief in his own aims. But the inner doubts are more difficult to overcome; the more critical and hard the painter is with himself the more he seems to impede his own advance. Never — so he thinks — is any work so great as he had hoped to make it. Yet, the further in fact the work is advanced, the more difficult it becomes for the artist to recognize it, because in the process of creation he himself and his vision have undergone changes and advanced in step with the work. The painter who sees the finished picture in front of him is not the same man who began it. The finished work fails to satisfy the higher demands now made upon it and a feeling of powerlessness takes hold of the creator. The greater the advance — the greater the doubt. From this conflict arise the sudden hope and the growing desperation. Doubts and hopes alternate from day to day. Feininger could write, "A future dawns on me — I shall not have lived in vain,"[2] and four days later, "I search in vain for *a single work* of mine which could last."[3]

The first picture completed in the new studio at Zehlendorf was *The Manhole I*, originally called "The Infanticide" (page 49). It groups five figures as in a dance of which none of the participants is aware. The eccentric focus of the picture is the manhole, hiding its tragedy. The workman's long tool gives one line of the triangle,

Aufruhr

Emeute, pen-and-ink drawing, 1909

Arbeitslose

Unemployed, pen-and-ink drawing, 1910

46

completed by the line of the street sweeper's brush with the meeting point in the manhole. In the world of this picture, the five figures are lonely as people, and connected only by the fate of their placement together. The bright red of the railing and the strange mauves and greens of the figures remove the picture further from the known recognizable world. The view is from above, as it might be seen by a huge, towering figure of a man who remains invisible and yet is part of the picture. The painter forces one to take his own view and makes the traditional comfortable role of the spectator impossible. Traditional perspective has not been quite overthrown but has been modified: the scale of the figures does not correspond to their place in perspective; the ground and the objects obey conventional perspective laws, enhancing the oddity of the figures in this painting.

In the paintings of this early period Feininger was essentially concerned with the use and meaning of color. This period of his paintings can be classified as "the figurative period," in which, apart from a few still lifes and landscapes, the human figure is an essential part of the composition. His studies as a draftsman and his observation of character and movement served as the basis from which he developed his paintings.

Feininger's use of color is as direct as that of the Fauve painters, but his choice of colors is subtle and strange. The color disharmonies are softer and the mood created more dreamlike. A mauvish pink predominates, countered by strong blues and greens. The colors live by the subtle violence of their disharmonies.

In his pictures of this period the human figure plays a dominant part, but neither the figures nor the settings in which they move pretend to be real. The degree of dreamlike fantasy varies. From the slightly removed *Sunrise* (cat. 47), an old town with toy houses and dark figures going their unexplained ways, to the wild absurdity of *Émeute* (page 175) and the carnival pictures, the whole range is traversed from the almost possible to the plainly absurd. In *Street in Paris (Pink Sky;* page 174) traditional perspective is "bent" to suit the artist's purpose but not abandoned. The figures in silhouette reveal Feininger's preoccupation with the outline as the sum of all possible views of an object. The silhouette contains the body in all its movements. The great strides made by the figures show the summary experience of bodies in movement. Each figure contains not only its present "step," but the last and the next as well; here Feininger foreshadows the aims of other painters of the time: to present visible movement (as opposed to the illusion of movement) in the picture. The spectator can calculate when exactly the fat woman behind the lamp post has crossed the road or when exactly the tall gentleman in the middle of the road will have overtaken the large man in the front. What the spectator cannot estimate is any figure's intention. The picture excludes emotional participation; it is a painting of movement and place. It is a comic scene, but essentially a study in space and speed.

The same observations hold true for the *Green Bridge* (cat. 44), where, however, a mysterious relationship is created by the spectators on the bridge watching the same spectacle from another viewpoint. The viaduct, the high bridge, echoing experiences from the artist's childhood in New York and from his visits to Arcueil, assumes in Feininger almost symbolic importance. It is as if his own feeling for height, the projection of his own slim angular figure, found an echo and identification in tall structures. He seems to have projected his feeling of height not only into the movement of his figures but also into the movement of buildings.

Émeute (page 175) of 1910 is probably the greatest of the grotesque pictures. In a village, painted with expressive truth and with a deliberate normality, plain lunacy has been let loose — a revolt by a body of people whose class interests can, clearly, in no way be reconciled. A deadly serious man with a red flag tied to a pitchfork is led by an entirely unreliable representative of Bohemianism followed by a crowd of gentlemen with top hats shouldering sticks or flails, some irate workmen, and a crowd of women. The flagbearer is given as a counterweight an equally tall gentleman dancing diagonally to the marching hero. The whole procession is preceded by a woman in evening dress, who seems to have just walked out of a picture by Toulouse-Lautrec. The whole village could not in actuality have harbored nearly so many elegant revolutionists. This is a picture of romantic irony from the *Tales of Hoffmann,* an episode from a dream world.

The *Carnival in Arcueil* of 1911 (cat. 63) is stagier, more artificial, and quite sinister. The tall trumpeter in the center seems to let the figures move to his tune. Has the artist once more taken his place in the picture, and has he created a world to inhabit it himself? In an odd way, one can see the figures almost from the back, from the viewpoint of the tall trumpeter. Some magic has been wrought; the picture plane goes on, but one does not enter it from outside; one is in the middle of events and takes part in the inner perspective of the picture.

Feininger is approaching, in a burlesque and carnival mood, the most serious problem of modern art — the discovery of new perspectives. Looking at the fun of Arcueil one might not think so. The underlying seriousness, however, can be shown unmistakably; it will seem that in this grotesque Feininger had taken the first steps toward new perspective possibilities.

In the first years of the twentieth century, Picasso painted his circus people — buffoons and harlequins. The transposition of reality was possible to the artist only in the allegory of disguise. To remove the human fate from the trappings of ordinary life, it had to be translated, elevated, or debased beyond the everyday experience of ordinary reality. Feininger called his carnival pictures "Mummenschanz" paintings. There is more in this word than just disguise; there are the sinister overtones of a different life and disparate identities. Ensor expressed this insight in his pictures of masks. It was a new awareness of the many forms a *persona* can take; it was an enlargement of life beyond the bourgeois establishment. It was a protest against the belief that man is no more than a member of society. To illustrate this, the artist had to choose the outcasts, the circus,

Woman's Figure, first sketch for *The Manhole*

1 The Manhole I, 1908 (31)

the mask, the Mummenschanz, the living reality on the edges of society. The other way out, chosen by Picasso and by the German Expressionists — the mask of the primitives, the frightening other alternative to the civilized mode of life — was closed to Feininger, whose whole temperament was opposed to the savage in imagery as well as in experience.

The overtones of a life other than ours given by the heightened reality of the carnival, the possibility of a dreamlike independence of the spirit, yet dependent on human values, expressed Feininger's awareness of forces that society could not utterly control. Feininger's other world is still controlled by man. The trumpeter holds his figures on invisible strings, as "Uncle Feininger" had held his marionettes on the first page of the *Chicago Tribune*. With the figurines in his dreamland Feininger came to terms with the "human condition." As in his political caricatures he makes the fate of men appear as a spook, in the carnival pictures Feininger could express the fantastic side of his imagination. He had yet another problem to solve in terms of painting; that was his relation to nature. He had made nature studies from his early days, sketches of landscapes and houses, trees, bridges, fences, sky, and sea, but he had not yet transformed his observation into paintings, though he had made a beginning with oil sketches after nature in the previous years.

During the summer of 1910, Feininger was painting at Neppermin; it was there and then that he resolved not to paint directly after nature. He wrote, "How hard it is to paint anything but the most tedious naturalism, which, when painted, is not naturalistic at all, but only *langweilig;* I mean to keep right at each study until I have it where I want it. It is so strange, how free and good and strong my drawings are after nature, compared to my painting, but I am *sure* I shall get to it yet."[4] A few days later he wrote, "Sometimes I hate and despise 'nature'! I like *my* pictures so much better!"[5] For a while he was tempted to give up, and then decided, "I am beginning to get the better of that darned nature I scolded so much, and when one gets *so* far, one likes her very much indeed and is correspondingly grateful to her for her good help."[6] He wrote about his oil sketches a few days later, "I do not find my studies at all good. . . . I can find no *Reiz* in them at all, and am only happy that I can at least paint better 'out of my head'! I could cheerfully burn every one of the studies and never feel that I had lost anything at all. I shall paint the pictures I see here in the landscape from *Notizen* and memory, when I get back to Zehlendorf — and they will be good . . . I shall go walking about and make many notes."[7]

This was to be one of Feininger's most important decisions. The attempt of painting out of doors was completely abandoned; all his later pictures were to be painted in the studio. Once removed from the direct observation of nature, the process of transformation and clarification could begin and the picture be developed in accordance with its own laws. The evolution of the forms he found in which to express his vision of nature is the real history of Feininger's painting. He was never to deny nature as the source of all reality. His transposition of nature into his art became the process of his development as an artist.

In two still lifes of 1911, Feininger attempted to come to terms not so much with nature in the landscape sense of the word, with light, atmosphere, and space, but with the solid objects of the still life. In these two paintings he is testing for himself

50

Sketch after nature for *Village Neppermin* (1919), Conté crayon, 1910

the validity of Cézanne's discoveries. The pictures added nothing new to the art of his time but were necessary for him; he had to investigate once the solid object in space, the painting of volume. The solid object was not his central interest in painting; he did not really explore its world. As a restatement of Cézanne his *Still Life with Lemons* (cat. 65) of 1911 can be compared to Juan Gris' *Les Œufs* of 1912. The similarity is greater than one might have expected in view of the quite different aims of the two artists after that point. Feininger was more interested in space than in objects, less concerned with volume and weight than with movement. The "thing itself" was never his aim.

Feininger joined the Berliner Secession in 1909, and in 1910 for the first time exhibited one painting, *Longueil, Normandy* (cat. 48). In 1911 he was represented with two paintings. As an illustrator he contributed drawings to *Licht und Schatten;* a *Mardi Gras, The Monster* (a locomotive), and a title page with the *Rathaus at Swinemünde,* which was to appear later as a painting (cat. 70). He continued to work for the humorous weeklies — his caricatures still appeared in *Lustige Blätter* and *Sporthumor* — because his family could not live on his unsalable pictures. Julia's father could help and did so in a generous way — but the more necessary such help

51

was, the less Feininger liked accepting it — and he suffered acutely under a feeling of "uselessness," as he expressed it.

Until now Feininger had attempted to find a way toward his pictures through caricatures and his observation of nature. His own ideas were richer and more mature than the pictorial means as yet at his disposal. What he wanted to achieve he knew; how to express it had not yet been solved.

A short visit to Paris in 1911 was to be decisive for his future development. In a letter written in 1913 to his old friend Churchill, Feininger relates his own progress step by step. "Having never painted before 1907 ... it chanced that I never had fallen into Impressionism at all! My first pictures, after I commenced in oil, in April 1907, were caricatures ... after my *drawings* of such fantastic subject[s], made from time to time ... in 1908, I came to have the opportunity of drawing out of doors all summer and made very many notes ... and experimenting with *colored outlines* & contrasting surfaces"; he goes on: "1909 I first commenced to sketch landscape, still decorative, worshipful of Van Gogh. 1910 I had attained to greater rhythm, somewhat neglecting color, of which I felt perfectly sure. 1911 my studies had brought me to the critical state where imitation of Nature is imminent, but in that Spring I had gone to Paris for 2 weeks and found the art world agog with Cubism — a thing I had never heard even mentioned before, but which I had already, entirely intuitively, striven after *for years*."[8]

From Paris Feininger went one day to Meudon with his friend Götz, and sent a post card to Julia on which Götz entered the postscript, "Leo experienced in Meudon the greatest sensation of his life, a viaduct with two locomotives."[9] He had gone out specially to revisit the viaducts. The interplay of the works of man with the natural surrounding, architectural form reaching high into the sky with locomotives in the air like toys, was an event out of his own world.

The accidents of time and space, the interrelations of disconnected events, were recognized as serious problems by the artists of the time. It has been noted earlier that, in his carnival pictures, Feininger approached the problem of new perspectives, which is the problem of the relation between the event and the standpoint of the observer. Exactly as the connection among the comic, the fantastic, and the real world always raises the question of reality — so in the connection of events, coincidence alone makes them real. The new artists had done with the "expected." All that art and science could do had been done. The artist and the scientist were looking out for the unexpected — and found it. Modern art arose not only from a new mode of seeing but from a new mode of thinking, which included the acceptance of every manifestation of reality.

In his letter of the next day, Feininger described the viaducts crossing each other high above the roofs of the houses, and added, "If I could have shown them to Mr. Scheffler [an art critic in Berlin], he would of course have said, 'juggling with possibilities.'"[10] That, then, was the unforgivable sin of the modern artist. Like the clerics in Galileo's time who refused to look through Galileo's telescope and trusted dogma more than their own eyes, the public of the day refused to recognize any new view of the world as valid.

"Juggling with possibilities" — that was the aim of the artists of the time. This aim was not understood by the majority of men, to whom the unshakable world picture was sacrosanct and to whom every new possibility appeared as a threat to their own security. The artists, like the scientists, discovered from observed reality the secrets hidden in complex reality. The discovery coincided with the development of the actual pictorial forms that could express the new knowledge. Art, like society, only sets itself the problems that it can solve at any given state of development.

The most important event of the year 1911 was the Salon des Indépendants, where the Cubists exhibited their discoveries for the first time. At the Salon des Indépendants Feininger showed six of his paintings. Matisse, Delaunay, and Chirico were represented; it was an occasion that brought many names of the future together.

Feininger had made the acquaintance of Delaunay, whose interests in the exploration of light and color were parallel to his own. The preoccupation with light as a force that alters visible reality Delaunay and Feininger had in common; also the careful study of color values and contrasts. But, where Delaunay wanted to establish laws, Feininger never intended to go beyond what his eye could extract from light and observe in the way it transformed the world. Apollinaire, who had given the name of "Orphism" to the movement founded by Delaunay, described it as "the art of painting new structures out of elements that have not been borrowed from the visual sphere but have been created entirely by the artist himself" — an aim Feininger never made his own.

What mattered to the artists was the possibility of daring that had come into the world of painting. The break-up of form, the break-up of light, and the freedom to treat each picture as a new reality were common to all, and one pioneer gave courage to the others. What Feininger gained in Paris was new hope for his own endeavors. The year 1912 thus became a year of further experiments for Feininger. From the conflict of experiences that had come to him from outside as well as from his own searching, a style was emerging. Once he had gained the knowledge of the new world of art in which he felt at home, to which he belonged, he realized that he was not alone and that other serious artists were now "juggling with possibilities."

The new possibilities even followed him in his sleep. He wrote to Julia, "Recently I dreamed I was a 'Cubist' and had to shade nothing but squares diagonally from top to bottom." [11] He had discovered new possibilities for himself, and now he also saw new possibilities revealed by other painters. He had contributed his carnival pictures with their inherent new perspective from the center of events; the Cubists were exploring new perspectives by penetrating the solid object. The world of the still life, of volume and spatial relation within the object, was not Feininger's concern; the perspectives of space and the interconnection of events were his main interest. The Futurists succeeded in finding pictorial forms for the simultaneity of events, which is another way of saying that time had become a dimension in painting. This Feininger approached in his drawings and paintings of the summarized movement of the figure. The interpenetration of events is a Futurist discovery, the revelation of simultaneous view is a Cubist discovery, and the summary presentation of the sequence of events is Feininger's contribution. All three have in common the inclusion of the time sequence in the pictorial event.

In 1912 Feininger abandoned the carnival pictures. A development of new forms becomes more clear when it takes place in the known world and not in one already removed from reality. The human figure returned to the real world. Feininger began to compose pictures with strollers and bathers at the seaside, unifying the movements of waves and people, the sky and boats, in one angular rhythm. In the first of these pictures, *Angler with Blue Fish II* (cat. 68), the carnival people once more come back into a picture; large figures on the shore are silhouetted against the sea. As a painting of space relations outside formal perspective the picture contains new thought. The anglers' rods form a big triangle declaring the interrelation of men and space and give shape to a new order arising from the accident of their meeting. The human fate of the lucky fisherman with a fish and the one without, meet in the prolongation of their personality — the overlapping rods. Behind them life goes on, as always unaware of the success or failure of men. *Bathers at the Beach I* (cat. 71) is further advanced, and the relations of shore and sea and sky, with their contradictory movements, are expressed firmly. The figures in silhouette contain the experience of movement and are the forerunners of later bathers. This experiment is carried much further in the *Bicycle Race* (page 176) and the *Trumpeters* (cat. 78), two paintings that have caught the Futurist aim of bringing noise and speed into the painting. The summary forms given to the cyclists and trumpeters contain within their silhouettes the succession of movements in which speed is contained. As compositions these paintings are beautifully balanced; and the unity of space and speed is complete. The air has begun to take solid form, almost as the material force that a cyclist encounters.

In the *Bicycle Race* Feininger reached a point where he had taken hold of all that had been developing within him, where his old knowledge and his new language of forms came together to make one of the key pictures of modern art.

In the same year appeared two more paintings that laid the foundation for Feininger's contribution to the art of his time. In *High Houses I* (cat. 85; Paris), and *Teltow I* (cat. 86) he created for the first time his architecture of space uniting the tectonic masses with the surrounding air and achieving the monumentality and solidity for which he had been aiming. With these paintings, Feininger entered the new phase of his development — a striving for unified monumentality.

High Houses I dates from the same year as Delaunay's *Towers of Laon*.[12] The pencil drawing for this picture dates from 1908 in Paris — Feininger's notes and sketches predate his paintings by many years; time had to pass after the first impression before the final transformation became possible. The painting, the first Feininger ever sold, was acquired in 1913 by Bernhard Köhler, the great collector and patron of the Blaue Reiter. It was burned in the Second World War.

Teltow I was acquired, also in 1913, by Paul Poiret, then at the height of his fame. It was possibly through Paul Iribe, a friend of both Feininger and Poiret, that the collector's attention was drawn to the still unknown painter. That picture has not been traced and may also have been lost in the war.

To create his pictorial world, Feininger had to re-create the picture space. His own discoveries as well as the possibilities revealed by the Cubists combined to make a new space conception possible. Linear perspective had been replaced by Seurat and

Cézanne, who created a new perspective of tone and planes, forming a receding space of aerial perspective, firm and, at the same time, more transparent than the linear perspective of the Renaissance. But Seurat's and Cézanne's pictures were still seen from one viewpoint. The Cubists abandoned the viewpoint outside the picture and entered optically into the picture space itself, seeing the object there from many viewpoints. Feininger had also entered his pictures, and, by taking his place in the picture space, he could explore the picture from within. Feininger was himself aware of this desire, which one can so clearly perceive in his paintings. "I am now trying to formulate a *perspective of objects*, quite new, quite my own; I would like to place myself into the picture and there observe the landscape, the objects, that are painted." [13] In this autobiographical article for *Les Tendances Nouvelles*, Feininger stated for the first time his artistic aims: "I believe firmly that every picture that deserves the name must be an absolute synthesis of rhythm, form, perspective, and color; and even all that is not good enough if it *is not expressive!*" [14]

Having achieved mastery of pictorial form, Feininger could face the encounter with nature with greater confidence. The summer of 1912 was spent at Heringsdorf. With his newly found assurance, so different from his feeling during the summer at Neppermin, he knew he would not be enslaved by nature but could master her. Between nature and the picture now stands the mature painter. "I am finding my own form of expression for nature." [15] "What I can use from nature, I take with enthusiasm." [16] His many drawings after nature, which he called "nature notes" [Naturnotizen], were executed with great rapidity, almost immediacy. Most of his paintings are preceded by nature notes. He said once that at the moment of "looking away" from the subject, he comprehended its form.

The importance of Feininger's nature notes must be fully understood; there exist

Fishing Boats, pencil sketch, 1912

several thousand such drawings, all rapid sketches that contain, however, as his studies of character had formerly contained, a summary of space and form. The note itself already contained the spirit of the future picture. Thus it is not so much that the painting is based on a drawing as that the same vision as in the drawing later finds expression in the painting.

In 1912, at Heringsdorf, Feininger made the notes that would lead to the compositions of *Steamer "Odin," Benz,* and *Zirchow,* all of which appear in several versions. From his notes he developed his compositions mostly in charcoal; these compositions were transferred to canvas. Up to this point the pictorial conceptions had already undergone several stages of clarification. The final solution of the pictorial problems was found in the process of painting.

In the letter to Churchill mentioned before, Feininger continues to trace his development: "1912 I worked entirely independently, striving to wrest the secrets of atmospheric perspective & light & shade gradation, likewise rhythm & balance between various objects, from Nature. My 'cubism,' to so miscall it, for it is the reverse of the french cubists' aims, is based upon the principle of monumentality, *concentration* to the absolutest extreme possible, of my visions. . . . My pictures are ever nearing closer the Synthesis of the fugue." He then proceeds to give a name to his own art form. "My 'cubism' (again, falsely so-called); call it rather, if it *must* have a name, 'prism-ism.'"[17] As Feininger himself implies, it is not necessary that every form of pictorial expression must have a name. We thus hope to act in his spirit if we suggest that we do not employ the term "prism-ism" that he coined and used only once, and thus spare the history of art one more "ism."

During 1912 Feininger made the acquaintance of the artists of the Brücke. With Schmidt-Rottluff, who painted Feininger's portrait in 1915,[18] a friendship was formed that lasted throughout his life. He wrote in a letter to Heckel[19] that he remembered their "first meeting in 1912, and the 'Brücke,' which then opened a new world for me." He did not join the group. His own aims were different and he was not a person to join any group or to formulate a program. Marsden Hartley was in Berlin at the time and knew Feininger. Many years later the work of the two artists was united at a joint exhibition in New York at the Museum of Modern Art.

In the same year, a friendship with Alfred Kubin developed. The first step was taken by Kubin, who had sent him his novel *Die Andere Seite* and asked Feininger for some of his drawings. In his reply Feininger wrote, "I too live a little in your mysterious country [Die andere Seite], it is very real to me. I too have my own world."[20] In *Die Andere Seite* Kubin described the dress of the dream people, "old-fashioned curved top hats, colored dress coats, mantles with capes, that was the dress of the men. Ladies promenaded in crinolines with strangely old-fashioned curls, with bonnets and wraps — it was all like a masquerade."[21] The description written by Kubin in 1908 fits Feininger's "Mummenschanz" pictures of the same period. Both artists found the Biedermeyer just sufficiently removed to be outmoded and sufficiently near to be still plausible. But here the similarity ends. Kubin's gruesome and tormented imagination was different from Feininger's vision of a weird but human world.

2 Harbor Mole, 1913 (113)

During 1912 Feininger exhibited two paintings at the Freie Secession: *Strasse*[22] and *Velocipede Riders,* as they were described. From this fact one cannot conclude that the important pictures mentioned before had not yet been painted when the exhibition opened, because, as Feininger stated in *Tendances Nouvelles,* "In Germany I prefer to exhibit only the less frightening pictures ... the best of my works are always sent back."[23]

In America the interest in the new movements in European art found its most important expression in the Armory Show.[24] Feininger had been invited to exhibit at the Armory Show, but for reasons not known he did not send any pictures. The one letter preserved from the Armory Show Committee to Feininger may throw some light on the absence of so many artists from Germany in the exhibition. The letter to him reads in part, "You must give the American public an opportunity of seeing some of your work; I enclose some literature of a newly organized society under whose auspices you could make your debut. – The date of the first exhibition will be early in 1913. (Jan. or Feb.). . . . Present indications lead us to believe this exhibition will be the biggest event in New York's art history. . . . The co-operation of some of the really big men in art – of Germany – England – France and Spain, is looked for. Perhaps you could give us some idea of the situation in Berlin . . . and possibly knowing some real, 'new blood' you could put us on the track of. We did get a glimpse of 'official' German art – a few years ago; we felt certain it was not representative. . . . Mr. Leon Sabo may possibly be the associated representative in London, Paris and Berlin. I had a little talk with him about you. . . . If you have any suggestions to make, I should be most happy to present them at the next meeting of the Association."[25] Perhaps it was that Feininger failed to advise the committee; perhaps it was due to Sabo's resignation; the fact remains that neither Feininger's work nor that of many other artists then active in Germany was shown. Feininger, however, did contribute to an exhibition in America. Die Photographische Gesellschaft in New York exhibited drawings and graphic work in the winter of 1912–13. He remained, as much as he could, in touch with America, and was in regular correspondence with his father, who showed great understanding for the art of his son.

THE MATURE PAINTER

1913–1918, *Berlin, Weimar*

By 1912 Feininger had laid the foundations for his future work and in three paintings had made a big step forward. In 1913 he painted twenty-one pictures in all,
and every single one has its place in his development. Two are devoted wholly to
the human figure, *Sleeping Woman (Julia)* (cat. 112) and a *Portrait Study of Julia*
(cat. 106). All other compositions point the direction in which Feininger was to
develop. They are paintings of ships and the sea, inspired by the Baltic, and paintings of Thuringian villages and churches.

The human figure was gradually disappearing from his work except in some great
compositions with figures as symbols. The disappearance of the large human figure
cannot be wholly explained by stressing Feininger's preoccupation with spatial composition. There is a deeper significance in its absence. The more Feininger was
concerned with the breaking up of form, the more hesitant he became to include
man in this process. His respect for the human person prevented him from dissecting
the human body. A further reason is that Feininger himself filled the picture
completely. He entered into it and took possession of it so entirely that there was
no room left for others. His own thoughts so possessed the picture that no intrusion
could be tolerated. He was searching between the forms that he laid bare for the
truth that escaped and had to be captured and bound. Like one possessed, he was
groping through the destruction he had wrought, dissecting the forms that were
the reflection of his mind. The search in the painting is a self-searching process;
the relation between his paintings and himself was that of a living identity. He had
written, "My paintings are the battlefield on which I try to find clarification for
myself."[1] The picture was himself, and all he inflicted upon it he suffered, and
all he released from it he released from himself.

"Human subjects [Menschliches] in the usual sense I shall never represent in my
pictures — though I am moved by the human [Menschliches] in everything and
cannot do anything without a warm human feeling,"[2] he wrote to Julia. The word
Menschliches comprises more than the human figure, but neither tragedy nor
comedy can be presented without it, and, in that sense, the human condition disappeared from Feininger's pictures. But that man as a human figure disappeared
from his pictures does not mean that man disappeared from his work. In every painting of Feininger's, man is present. The humanism and universality of Feininger's
pictures make them great. All formal discoveries must finally serve a purpose,
greater than a mere juggling with formal possibilities. In inventing his pictorial
means Feininger often omitted the human figure, but he never omitted man himself. Choosing his subjects for compositions, he searched for the meaningful, for
the spirit. When he turned to the painting of architecture, the spirit of man was
included. He painted the *spiritus loci*, the genius of the place. The total reality of

In the Town at the End of the World, pen-and-ink drawing, 1912

his subjects includes their meaning. He painted the relation between architecture and space, between the man-made and the eternal.

Each building has its own inner law; the spirit of its form is revealed as an active force. In the many different versions of the same subject, the fundamental unity of the subject is preserved. The changes are not those of different views or different illuminations, as are the changes of Monet's *Cathedral of Rouen*. With different emanations of the essence of the subject, a new comprehension of its spirit is taking shape. The pictures included hitherto invisible aspects of reality. Forms are found

60

for hidden relations; lines of perception in thought and feeling assume shapes and colors, gaining for the first time the power to be visible. It was as if a magic cap had been taken off reality, revealing its hidden shapes.

There are towns and places with which a man has an affinity, where his destiny is to be fulfilled. Feininger was very sensitive to such feelings. His life was linked with Weimar. Ever since he had lived there in 1906 with Julia, he had been in love with the place. "Then," he wrote to Kubin, "it was a fairy tale, and the old magic still lives in us."[3]

In April, 1913, Feininger returned to Weimar and stayed until September. He had to be alone and secluded in order to come to terms with his art. Julia understood the need and always made it possible for him to go away. We owe to these frequent separations the many letters that have been preserved. Feininger wrote almost daily to Julia about himself and his work. "Weimar," he wrote, "always has been and always will be the town of the miracle of my life. . . . How difficult it was to bring my inner life into harmony with my mode of creation."[4]

The hundred villages of Thuringia, in their spiritual isolation, became the subjects of his work. All summer he went on foot or on his bicycle to the villages around Weimar, discovering new places and new possibilities. "And lately, here, in Gelmeroda, in Vollersroda, Mellingen, Taubach, and in many places, greater, more daring pictures dawned on me, I shall soon start on them. That I can absorb and create at the same time I hardly dared hope until now, but it is so, and will grow stronger. This is probably the *first period of maturity* in my life as an artist. Only in drawing had I been capable of such intensity [Steigerung]. When working out of doors during the last days, I became quite ecstatic; by the end of the afternoon I had become pure instinct and ability. I stood in one place and drew the same motif three or four times — until I grasped it exactly as I felt it."[5] Feininger had found his way of transforming his knowledge into terms of art. He wrote that his work had gone "beyond *observation* or *statement*" and had reached the point of "magnetic fusion, the liberation from all fetters."[6] "In the afternoon I went out . . . to Gelmeroda; I drew there for an hour and a half, always around the church, which is wonderful."[7] The church of Gelmeroda was to Feininger what Mont-Sainte-Victoire was for Cézanne, the subject of a lifelong search for new discoveries of hidden meanings, waiting for formal expression. With Gelmeroda Feininger remained in loving communion throughout his life; there are thirteen compositions for paintings and many drawings and watercolors devoted to this church — the last lithograph of his life returns again to Gelmeroda.

With *Gelmeroda I* (page 177) Feininger emerges as himself. The church rises from the ground, stately, mysterious, natural; it asserts itself and its presence. The picture is painted in solid color, merging into one great tonality of strength. The church is in slate blues, the pine tree in a dark, nearly black mauve, and the sky, in the light of the dark Thuringian forests, a mauvish green which even in its lightest parts is somber, yet bright compared with the many green strokes in the sky. The front of the church is in a warm golden color, with an inner intensity reflecting the light foreground. Solid as it appears in geometrical forms, it is tender and cruel in pale pink, bright green, and black. The sinister pine tree dances in the wind; the steeple reaches into the sky, piercing the picture; next to its dull slate blue, a streak of light blue from an invisible sun carries into the height. It is a very robust picture. One feels how it has grown strong and direct through power of vision: the spirit of place finds form and color, as lyric poetry of a manly and unsentimental nature finds expression. There is a murmuring of pine and stone and slate, in a dark mood and yet triumphant, a monumental darkness in its own right.

Gelmeroda II (page 180) is a slow movement in the suite of Gelmerodas. If the first version established the theme triumphantly, the second version takes a calmer look at a different view of the same church. The steeple divides the world in a harmonic scale of greens and pinks. The complementary colors are used to resolve the harmony into disharmony. The measure of the distinct vertical sections of the sky is weighted finely, and the tonal gradations of space are firmly enclosed by an inner frame creating a rectangle in the sky, equal to the rectangle that holds the church. A quiet group of figures composed along an invisible triangle is echoed by the triangular porch of the church. The houses to the left and right play their own rhythm.

This picture may serve here as one in which to elucidate some of Feininger's aims and how they are achieved — always remembering that a great painter does not create consciously after a formula or a program, not even his own, but that the totality of his being responds to the picture as he creates it. The painting *Gelmeroda II* could be analyzed mathematically — measuring spaces, distances, proportions, and colors — and it would prove nothing beyond the sensibility of the artist; but it is worthwhile seeing and feeling the rhythmic proportions, the inversions of light and dark, the stately movements in the planes of the picture. He can weigh form and color and place them against each other so that each form makes its counterpart, and each color sings its echo. It is a sonority of glass, a reflection of mirrors, the penetration of space by tones of color. The vibration that the firm geometrical forms set up in their interplay creates a static harmony that in all stability has the semblance of movement. The secret of that movement lies in the vibration of tones at play with the forms. In Picasso the forms unite in violent combat; in Feininger they produce a majestic edifice of organlike sound.

Bridge I (page 179) is almost unique in Feininger's work — unique only for purely formal reasons. For the first time he succeeded completely with an architecture of curves in which every line is bent by one all-pervading force. The ground, the arches of the bridge, and the trees form themselves in one complete rhythm. Everything seems swept upward, firmly held in place by the meeting point of the arching lines. The structure of the bridge, its very own static necessity, has made the arching necessary; and in some later bridge compositions Feininger will again succeed with the rhythmic curve. But it was the curve of actuality, not the curve of his temperament, that determined the picture.

His temperament did not express itself by the sweeping curve. When Feininger tried to impose curves on a subject that from its own nature did not demand them, his attempts were artificial and unsolved. Feininger's curves remain structural and unemotional, sensitive but not obsessive. The danger of a purely decorative use of rhythm

Gelmeroda
Sonnt. d. 15 Juli 06

First drawing of the church at Gelmeroda, pencil, 1906

Pencil sketches, 1913. Above: Benz; below: Park at Weimar

was avoided by his temperament; his line never felt the independent decorative urge of Jugendstil. Feininger's complete freedom from any affinity to Jugendstil made it impossible for him to use lines other than structurally. He attempted, quite consciously, to master the free curve. The philosopher Knoblauch went so far as to renounce his friendship with Feininger because, he wrote, Feininger had "betrayed" the curve.[8] For Knoblauch the curve held a metaphysical meaning; for Feininger it held a physical meaning. The geometric curve is a more self-willed thing than is the free emotional curve. The mathematical curve obeys its own laws and subdues the intention of the painter. It wills its own completion and perfection, opposed to the aim of the artist. The geometric curve is a useless vehicle, and Feininger abandoned it very soon. The very deadness of the geometric curve was its merit in the eyes of the abstract painters. It contained nothing of man, and personified its own abstract law and order.

During the spring of 1913 Feininger worked on three paintings. It was his habit to develop several pictures at the same time. He said once, much later: "It has always been my wish to have a great long studio with about six easels standing, each bearing a work in progress of developing."[9] The three paintings were *Bridge I* (page 179), *The Beacon* (cat. 116), and *Gelmeroda I* (page 177). *The Beacon* and *Gelmeroda I* have a strong similarity. The steeple in the one and the tower in the other stand silhouetted against the light; the acuteness and direction of the angles are in both paintings very much alike. The whole composition is at the same time centrifugal and centripetal, fleeing away and rushing into the center of the composition. What all three pictures show clearly — and it is worth observing once — is the painter's way of attack; this comes from the sides of the picture, whence the forces are pressed inward, and from below and above. The picture seems the result of the pressure of forces from the four sides. The center of the composition seems to arise forcibly and necessarily as the result of the pressure applied; the forms spring forth as a result. They do not give the illusion of dynamism; they are the result of actual dynamic forces. It is not a dynamic *design* but a dynamic *event* that has actually happened in the process of painting. We are in the field of modern art, far removed from the art of illusionism and illustration. We are in the field of energy of modern art, in the realm of the magicians Klee and Picasso, where reality takes shape in the process of creation. The reality of modern art is its existence; the proof of its creation is its being.

Two paintings of this year go back to compositions originally conceived in 1908. *High Houses II* (page 178) is a reminder of old houses in Paris destined for demolition. It is based on a composition done in 1908 at Heringsdorf for the first time, and then again in 1910. It is closely related to *High Houses I*, the same Paris subject in a different mood, and is in a strong blue and grayish tonality — an almost gay picture in spite of the doom upon the houses. The second version (1913) of *The Manhole* (cat. 103) is compositionally very close to the earlier picture: it retains the same organization of space and figures as before. The figures are not motivated by a will of their own but are tied together by a now visible structural necessity. Here, too, a tragedy is hidden, as the original title of the painting implies. It is the secret of a place with sinister associations. The colors are as sharp and bitter as the shapes.

Gelmeroda III (cat. 102) reverts to the view of *Gelmeroda I*. Its excitement is more controlled; it is further removed from nature than *Gelmeroda I;* and it needs all its force to withstand the tremendous pressure from the left. Yet it remains firm and strong under the impact, almost like a ship with flags flying. With its prismatic sky and wildly fleeing forms, this picture is related to *Harbor Mole* (page 57). In *Harbor Mole* and *The Beacon* Feininger chose a theme that occupied him often — the place where land and sea meet, where two great forces face each other. In his picture a man-made edifice stands lonely among the breakers — an outpost at the end of the world. This conflict Feininger solves dramatically in the interpenetration of the great spaces. The seashore, the line between the land and the sea, held a strange fascination for Feininger. It was the end of one world and the beginning of another. It was neither quite here nor quite there; it was an edge — and every edge is a precipice with lurking danger. In such a world the figure of man takes on a new proportion. The subject of the bathers on the shore occupied his mind and recurs in his work. He wrote about it, "Today I have composed on the canvas a seaside bathing picture and tried to divest the process of everything familiar, to represent it in *such* a way in form and rhythm as I have always felt it at Heringsdorf — nether worldly and monumental."[10] A few days later, "I am painting . . . the bathers on the beach in front of the black water — now the intuition [Ahnung] that I had one-and-a-half years ago finds expression. It will be a strange picture and, I believe, very beautiful. But melancholy and somber."[11] This picture, called *Bathers I* (cat. 109), is a calm, rectangular composition of broad solid planes, divided equally between the sea and sky, with sailing boats on the one hand and land and people on the other. The movement of the ships and people is in constant relation. The separate events form a pattern too great for the participants to understand, two separate worlds becoming one. The unity of opposites is a recurring aim in Feininger's work. Be it the dual sky, the sea and the seashore, or the boats and the onlookers, such separate entities are united in one all-embracing vision. From such pictorial dialectics he created his poetry of man in the universe.

Not until Feininger had established his identity as a painter in his work and in his own mind was it possible for others to recognize him as a painter making an independent contribution to the art of his day. The heroic years of modern art before World War I were marked by some great exhibitions. Such exhibitions were intended as demonstrations; they were recognized as weapons with which the new art fought for recognition. Artists who had founded groups and movements, like the Brücke or the Futurists, fought in closed ranks, arranging their own exhibitions. For individual artists who were not attached to any group, room was found in some of the large exhibitions, together with the organized groups. To the first important event of that kind, the Salon des Indépendants of 1911, Feininger had sent six pictures.[12] To the Blaue Reiter exhibitions in Munich in 1911 and 1912 and the Sonderbund exhibition in Cologne of the latter year, Feininger had not been invited, for the simple reason that he was still unknown as a painter. For the next exhibition, the Erste Deutsche Herbstsalon of 1913 arranged by the Sturm group, he was invited. At this most decisive event in the history of modern art in Germany, Feininger established his identity as a painter in the eyes of the more perceptive sponsors of the new art.

66

Franz Marc had written to him from the Blaue Reiter, in an undated letter,[13] that, at the suggestion of Kubin, he would like to invite him to exhibit at the Erste Deutsche Herbstsalon and added in a postscript, "You did not receive an invitation earlier because no one in our circle had known about your pictures until Kubin drew our attention to them." The invitation arrived on Feininger's forty-second birthday, Juli 17, and appeared to him the "most promising present."[14] In a letter to Kubin he states how happy it would make him to show his work in the company of the Blaue Reiter.

The Herbstsalon was a demonstration against the Neue Secession, which had broken up during that year. Feininger refused to be drawn into the conflict being fought out in public. He was, however, in sympathy with the modern group, and did not exhibit in the Secession again until the Freie Secession had been founded. The Herbstsalon was organized by Herwarth Walden, the most courageous and perceptive protagonist of modern art.

The exhibition created the expected outburst of hostile criticism. The *Vossische Zeitung* wrote, "Not worth a visit," the *Deutsche Tageszeitung*, "All those without talent are exhibited," and the *Frankfurter Zeitung*, "The impression has been created that in this exhibition something could be seen of progress in development. Never has a pretension been more arrogant, never less well founded."[15]

Bernhard Köhler, the collector and friend of the Blaue Reiter artists, had helped generously to make the exhibition possible. He bought *High Houses I* at the exhibition. "You don't know," Feininger wrote to Julia, "how this offer encourages me and gives me a different inner *security*. I have been pining away under the constant feeling of my *uselessness*, wrong as this idea may have been."[16]

He was content to have found some recognition, and, happy to exhibit in the company of artists whose aims he respected, he wrote, "Through the present connection with other real creative artists [Gestaltern] I can see in my own work for the first time both weakness and my own manner. To 'take sides' has always been abhorrent to me — but to know that one acts together with others who, each in his *own* way, want to achieve an inner expression, gives one strength."[17] At the same time he realized that close identification with any movement, and the battles and publicity this might bring in its wake, would be dangerous for his own development. "Those circles, to which the Sturm belongs ... have hitherto been a bit strange to us and maybe *too* 'stormy' and I cannot help feeling certain misgivings with what values, possibly quite superficial and vainglorious ones, we shall have to reckon! One thing I know *for certain:* it will not alter anything in my working life. On the other hand, I cherish the hope that I can work with more gusto — now that people are positively concerned with me and might perhaps hold high hopes."[18] During the Herbstsalon Feininger met Walden and the artists and poets of the Sturm circle for the first time, and remained their friend.

The exhibition had made a great impression on Feininger, and his comments on the artists of his day are important and revealing — not least the comment on Delaunay, which might help to destroy the legend of Feininger's dependence on Delaunay's theories. "There is a great wealth of beautiful pictures, truly stimulating. For *one* of them I have, however, little understanding, and I can see in the work of Delaunay only sterile, stubborn, and not even well-clarified experiments with purely physical problems of light. An *instrument* can make a much clearer and more valuable analysis of the spectrum. One recognizes [in Delaunay] a pretentious manner and a poverty of creation, which makes one conclude that there is a very mechanical inner life. Possibly what he strives for in theory might be productive in others who have enough strength to create. That is just the good thing today, that there are so many possibilities to make art."[19] In the same letter to Kubin he wrote that the exhibition represented a great moment in the history of art in Germany. Kubin had asked about Feininger's views on Marc, Kandinsky, and Klee. Feininger replied: "Think of my hardness, and, as you wrote: coldness, clarity, order, and, then, the complete freedom from all fetters of a Kandinsky! I should be wrong to form today a final judgment; for the time K. gives me a lot to think about; what he expresses is exactly the opposite of what I intend. I admire him ... as one admires something totally strange." Of Marc he wrote that "his Tower of the Blue Horses is of otherworldly beauty."[20] The last letter of that year contains the answer on Klee. "*Quite wonderful!* Prickling and exciting, of staggering expression and novelty of form, as I felt it — the force which is sometimes hidden in children's drawings and which makes one very sad, that we, as adults, cannot reach it consciously. Does Klee *paint?* I should like to know! That he plays the *violin* is *certain*, if to conjure up a world of sounds from four strings is equal to conjuring up a world view with penlines, crosses and triangles!"[21]

Feininger was in sympathy with the new painters, who all sensed a new world picture and tried to give it expression. He recognized their personalities and their new vision. But Feininger was not engaged in a battle of styles and theories. And even the question of whether his own art was "modern" was of no interest to him. His art was his own. The most revealing statement is contained in a letter to Kubin. "I, for instance, *could* not [paint] differently from the way I am doing quite regardless of whether others paint in a similar way or not, whether my works are 'modern' or 'new art' or not. . . . Since my childhood I see and feel in a certain way [Richtung] . . . . I try to fathom the laws in nature, but nature itself is excluded and done with as a goal at the moment when I have deciphered these laws. The *outer* form matters little; 'new art' exists only with the arising of a distinct undeviating personality."[22]

Feininger had no theory of painting; he had that sense for contemporary reality that makes a painter an artist of his time. His thought was as much involved in his work as were his eyes. He was trying to obtain clarity, and he analyzed his own work, but he was not working in accordance with a theory, either his own or borrowed. The laws he obeyed were the laws of the picture as it revealed its structure, the laws of nature as he transposed them into his art. He did not impose a law of his invention; he transposed the laws that he observed. He revealed patterns; he did not invent them. In a letter to Kubin he wrote, "I could not ... choose the purely abstract form, because then all progress ceases ... one has only to refine one's eyes, study *intensively* problems of light, problems of the volume of light and color; and then one sees that the laws of nature are as strict as any mathematical law that man can formulate."[23]

Four charcoal compositions from the years 1912 and 1913 that illustrate his thought are reproduced in this volume. In the drawing *Bicycle Race* (page 69) preliminary to the painting (page 176) and in the composition (page 69; without title) with a

Bicycle Race
charcoal, 1912

Feininger 1912   RADRENNEN

Untitled composition
charcoal, 1912

Feininger   October 1912

69

Reflected Sunlight
charcoal, 1913

Railroad Bridge
charcoal, 1913

crowd of men in the street, the process of elimination of any detail except for lines of force is clearly brought out. In the composition, planes of different light intensity indicate in what way the intended picture (never executed) was to develop. In the composition *Railroad Bridge* (page 70), which Feininger later inscribed "Inversion of Values," and in *Reflected Sunlight* (page 70), the process of Feininger's thought can again be studied clearly. The light and dark alone and their varying degrees of force establish, in the points of intersection and penetration, the pattern of space, which is the reality of the picture.

Here an investigation into the nature of reality is indicated.

Reality is a constellation of events; it becomes actual when it forms a pattern that can be apprehended. The pattern of events that manifests itself as reality arises from the encounter of the events in the intersection of space and time. Actual reality is only one of many possibilities; unrealized possibilities remain unperceived, potential reality. By "juggling with possibilities" the painter discovers potential realities. In the picture, lines, angles, and planes become visible by the very fact of their encounter. In the interpenetration of planes, color interpenetrates form. The structure and tonality of the picture arise in the process of the encounter of color and form and in the process create the new reality of the picture. There is no difference between the reality of the picture and the reality of the events of this world. From the sum of all possibilities that one could call total reality man at every stage becomes aware only of those events that, separating themselves from the endless realm of possibilities, manifest themselves as existent. Actual reality arises on the meeting points of perception when events take on forms that we can apprehend. Thus the "crystalline form" in Feininger's pictures explains itself as the precondition of visible reality. Only those lines, planes, and colors that meet and interpenetrate become visible and by their meeting determine mutually their own existence. By understanding the nature of reality one understands the reality of nature. What formerly appeared as a duality reveals itself as a unity. From his understanding that the creative process reveals valid reality the painter draws the strength of his conviction. Whatever he forms becomes real, because the forming of reality in the picture is identical with the process of the formation of actual reality. In the picture the painter forms his vision of the universe. The mystery of creation becomes comprehensible in the creation of a human order, in the refusal to recognize chaos as anything but lack of poetry.

In 1913 Feininger, as he thought himself, had reached his "first period of maturity" and was finding the forms of his art. With this he also found understanding and recognition, at least in a small circle in Berlin. At the beginning of 1914 Feininger considered moving to Weimar with his family. No decision was taken but he spent the summer of 1914 in Weimar in his old studio in the Kurthstrasse. At first he occupied himself with etching and spent much time drawing out of doors in the Thuringian villages.

A few days after his arrival at Weimar on April 11, 1914, he had begun work on *Nieder-Grunstedt*. There are two versions, Nos. *IV* and *VI* (cat. 122, 123), of this year; both deal with the new problems of spatial organization. On June 9 he wrote, "I am *painting again* . . . the slanting houses of Nieder-Grunstedt. . . . I am 'myself' again; I am again in touch with the cosmos [Weltall] of the great forms, the great rhythms, which alone ... satisfy me."[24]

Umpferstedt I and *II* (cat. 119, page 73) are, at the same time, both Cubist and Futurist in approach. A simultaneity of events creates a multitude of shapes, but remnants of observed reality remain. These are pictures of a transitional stage in which the past has not been overcome and the next step has not been taken. The solution for Feininger did not lie in the destruction of form but in the finding of new form. Forms of observed and newly developing reality coexist in the picture. The most revolutionary composition of that year was achieved in *Benz VI* (page 181). This explosive picture is composed in two diagonals in the shape of an "X." Here Feininger was able to play the two opposing diagonals against each other, creating a tension and a counterplay of forces. The lines of the new perspective go inward and outward at the same time; they are no more the lines of flight of traditional perspectives nor the pyramidal composition of classical painting. They hold a complete inversion of forms and colors, a balancing and counterbalancing of tensions, spaces, and directions. The centrifugal and centripetal forces of the picture hold it in active balance, as opposed to the passive balance of tradition.

In *Street of Barns* (cat. 125) another form of balance is achieved with the same means. Every shape is poised on the tip of a triangle, like a complex mobile come to perfect rest.

The *Country Road to Nieder-Grunstedt* (cat. 118) is one of Feininger's rare attempts to make organic nature obey laws of architectural monumentality. The trees are given sculptural unified shapes, linked with the direction of the road, in one rhythm.

In the summer of 1914 an epoch came to an end. Those living then could not have known it and it is an accident of history that at that moment Feininger expressed his hopes and conviction in a prophetic sentence. "One thing I know already now: I shall give to mankind a new perspective of the world; I hope to live until I have formed it in a hundred pictures."[25]

When war broke out in August, 1914, Feininger left Weimar and returned to Zehlendorf. His personal reaction to the events of the war was even greater seclusion from the outside world, even deeper withdrawal inward.

As a foreigner in Germany Feininger tried to remain as unprejudiced as possible and to stay above the warring parties. In letters to his father in New York he attempted to do justice to the German viewpoint. During that period he contributed some drawings to *Wieland* for the benefit of the German Red Cross. These drawings are sarcastic and not exactly favorable to the Allies. During the progress of the war he changed his views. The war itself appeared to him abhorrent and terrible.

In 1915 Feininger completed one of his few large figure compositions of the period, *Jesuits III* (page 183), following *Jesuits II* (cat. 114), painted in 1913. In the new picture, the sardonic subject of a Jesuit watching a lady of great elegance pass in the street has been modified. The colors are strong—cardinal mauve, red, and yellow—on green ground; the geometrical curves flow freely and rhythmically. The picture remains a rarity in Feininger's work: an attempt to master the curve. In the new picture there is much sarcasm and doubt, much irony and distance.

72

3 Umpferstedt II, 1914 (120)

The *Girl with Green Stockings* of 1915 (page 182) is one of Feininger's few paintings to which the term "Expressionist" could be applied. It might well have been meant as an essay in an idiom that was not his own. The presence of the figure is strong and direct. This painting remains unique in his work until the *Portrait of a Tragic Being* of 1920 (page 93) reveals this unexpected side of the artist's possibilities.

Gross-Kromsdorf I (page 185) also of 1915 is a monumental composition of great serenity, which in its formal simplicity will recur again as *Gross-Kromsdorf III* (cat. 219), with enhanced luminosity.

Gelmeroda IV (page 184) returns to the viewpoint of *Gelmeroda I*. The mauve pine tree on the left, having gained in stature, fights for dominance in the picture with the church itself.

The *Self-Portrait* of 1915 (page 75) is a monumental picture. A yellow face with green eyes looks out from a light blue background under dark arches, in a mood of self-irony and disguise. Feininger himself later spoke of these qualities, at the time when the picture was being shown at the Sturm exhibition of 1917. He told how the public streamed toward the painting — where "the diabolical face grinned at them! Wonderful! I enjoyed it. What is better?" he asked, "a beautiful idealized portrait [of the artist], or self-irony?" He preferred the latter, and described it as "the incognito of a mask."[26] It was not the first time that he had entered a picture in disguise, but it was one of the few occasions that he admitted it.

During 1915 there are several grotesque pictures, among them *Locomotive with the Big Wheel* (cat. 138), *Sailboats with Black Sails* (cat. 141), and *Promenade* (*Arcueil II*; cat. 144). They show a necessity for Feininger to give vent to his fantasy. One would have a very one-sided impression of Feininger if one thought of him as a painter only of complex and demanding compositions. In his life and in his painting he could be lighthearted, irresponsible, and happily unconcerned. The grotesque themes of his earliest paintings, which derived from his caricatures, return. He wrote to Knoblauch, not without some malice: "God protect us from those 'soulful' artists. You must have seen in my work some viciousness — I always let myself go on some scurrilous composition after having painted a serenely felt picture ... besides, for the very sensitive artist sarcasm is like a protective, prickly skin toward the outside world."[27]

In the *Green Bridge II* of 1916 (cat. 163), which is composed of curves, houses and people play a counterrhythm with the regularity of a pendulum; it is toylike and dancing, and the scene is held firmly together by the bridge itself. The picture has the accuracy of dreamlike reality.

An important work of the year is *Behind the Church* (also called *The Square*; cat. 155), a picture of mysterious luminosity in dark brown and blues in which space has been completely freed by being completely enclosed. The peace of mathematics seems to have descended, and a perfect harmony has been established. *Vollersroda III* (cat. 164) is similar in construction. The two compositions *Zirchow V* and *VI* (page 77; cat. 162) are conceived in bolder planes than previous paintings. These pictures have greater density in composition and color and a static monumentality. The Futurist element of conflict has been removed; an approach

4 Self-Portrait, 1915 (137)

nearer to Cubist aims was his endeavor at this time. "Where before I aimed at movement and unrest I have now felt the eternal calm of objects and even the air surrounding them, and have attempted to express that. *The world*, which is furthest removed from the *real world!!*" he wrote to Kubin on January 15, 1915.[28]

How the paintings of the monumental period arose from the state of the world, and the painter's reaction to the happenings of the time he recalled in a letter to Alfred Barr. "There is an aloofness in the work of those dreadful years, not to be obtained through any conscious effort of aspiring for an ideal — it was suffering and horror of the Soul that made my visions so 'final.' So I think that 'Zirchow,' No. 5, 6 and 7, and 'Vollersroda III' and a few others of that period, have stood over all my other endeavors — not technically, but in monumentality of sentiment and conception."[29]

Although during the war years traveling was difficult and a foreigner needed special permission, Feininger spent part of the summer of 1916 in Wildpark near Potsdam, in a house belonging to his wife's family. In 1917 the family obtained special permission to spend some time in the Harz mountains at Braunlage, where he made many studies, none of them leading to paintings, but all consciously attempting a formalization of nature, testing the Cubist experience on natural forms (pages 80 and 81).

The painting *Head in Architecture* (page 186) may be seen as one stage of this preoccupation with Cubist forms; but it is not a Cubist picture, for it does not disrupt the form of matter. As a painting it remained experimental. It had acted like a catalyst, speeding the process that was developing. A related painting is *Woman's Head (Julia)* (page 187) in which Cubist forms are resolved. He does not break the structure of matter; he reassembles the forms, creating a new likeness.

The human figure as a figurine reappears in a strange painting, *Behind the Church II*, 1917 (page 189), which can be compared to a ballet scene. Here the figures perform a dance, and the architecture takes part as well. It is a scene in which the instability of men is set in a world of instability and all relations to the real world are placed in doubt. Though fantastic and comic, it is nevertheless the expression of a tragic moment, the same tragedy that was cruelly revealed by the Dadaists and, more gently, by the Blaue Vogel cabaret a few years later. The instability of the world in its physical and social sense became clear to the artists, and each one expressed it in his own way; Feininger's way is ironical, according to his nature. It is a new act in the *comédie humaine* — a masquerade of lost souls, stepping through the mirror cabinet of the tricks and illusions of a world that no longer provides any stability to men. Everything is in doubt: the place, the space, the road. If the figures were only ghosts, it would be undisturbing; if the whole were a fairy tale, it would be comical — but it is 1917, and the time for laughter has long gone from the world.

This painting can be understood as a reflection of the artist's own position of instability — he is an alien without animosity in a breaking world, belonging and not belonging at the same time — and as a forecast to a future state of being which became almost normal for the floating inhabitants of Europe during and after the wars — the suspension of reality.

Later Feininger was often asked if he had designed the sets for *The Cabinet of*

5 Zirchow V, 1916 (153)

Dr. Caligari. He had not had anything to do with the film, and was only shown it, at his own request, many years later at the Museum of Modern Art. On several occasions, however, he had been invited to design for the stage, which he always refused, being probably well aware that the order of space he created in his pictures would, on the stage, take on a new and false reality.

Bathers II of 1917 (page 79), related to the first composition of this subject, is a picture of two worlds, with the sky and the boats in the upper half and the people in front of the sea, like emblematic figures. The figures are modeled like sculpture; they appear almost metallic in their rigid hardness, with reflecting surfaces. The rhythm is mechanical, like a forerunner of the Triadic Ballet. The figures turn their backs, retreating from this world. The entry into the sea is like an entrance into the nether regions lost in darkness. The light colors of the figures — silvery gray, blue, white, orange, and golden yellow — contrast with the almost black sea. The boats are light and somber at the same time — brown, white, and gray; they stand freely in space and form a counterrhythm to the grouped figures that is equally mechanical but follows its own laws. It is an enigmatic picture suggesting the realm of shadows — the entry into Hades in bright sunlight. Willi Wolfradt has expressed the same thought in the short sentence, "Karneval am Acheron."[30] In spirit it is related to *Behind the Church II* — there, all is a spectral, floating dance in the cabinet of mirrors; here, all is static and at rest — yet the uncertainty of existence is the same.

Bridge III (page 190) resembles in composition and clarity *Behind the Church*, 1916 (cat. 155). A still, almost colorless tonality of blue and brown, an equal perfection in structure, and the same great calm relate the two paintings.

It was a necessity for Feininger to have to break through the balanced perfection of his forms because no way leads beyond perfection and rest; therein it resembles death. He wrote March 14, 1917, to Knoblauch, "Therefore the strong swing of the pendulum; between final rigidity and returning liberating movement; between colorlessness and colorfulness; these are states of the soul and not a program." He goes on: "The terrible events in the world weigh on us and leave dark traces in my work. But what is more natural than my always recurring struggle for gaiety in a picture that strives for the exact *opposite* — movement and color? Liberation? But the man behind such different works is always the same. In the gayest as much as in the most resigned pictures the aim is *ultimate form* for the thought. Always: *ultimate form!*"[31] To overcome such perfection, arrested at the point of no return, Feininger painted *Markwippach* (page 83), one of his gayest pictures, painted with joyful abandon. The world seems to fall apart and come together of its own accord; the church and the houses dance; the colors are bright and direct. It has something of the spirit of Chagall's Russian villages. Markwippach in Thuringia must have appeared quite irresponsible to Feininger. He called the picture his "peacock" picture, for it shines in all the colors of the bird. He had once in a Thuringian village met a peacock and that encounter may have found its transformation in the picture. He had been so impressed that he had written about it to Julia, "Quite mystical — I shall never forget the impression."[32]

78

6 Bathers II, 1917 (181)

Pencil drawing, 1917

In the great series of the Gelmeroda church, *Gelmeroda VII* (page 188) comes next; Nos. V and VI were never painted. The numbers stand for compositions in charcoal, which were not all executed as paintings. There are thirteen Gelmeroda compositions, of which eleven became paintings. No. X was painted but destroyed by the artist. The numbering is his own, followed here and in the *œuvre* catalogue.

This seventh composition, with the steeple firmly enclosed in a diamond shape, has a tremendously dramatic and monumental sky. In mood it is almost sinister. A dark reflection comes from the pine trees, which are not visible except through the darkness they exude. The painting is held in tones of reddish-yellowish browns and moist greens. The entrance to the church, like a tomb, ranges from grayish white to grayish blue, dark blue, and black. The steeple of the church is dark blue; it takes on the green and yellow light of the air. The barns and houses of the village have become glowing crystals. A deep romantic feeling for stone and slate and earth and for the folklore of the Thuringian forest, with its precious stones deep in the mountains, has found expression in this dark sonority. This most mysterious of all monumental paintings has surpassed the dark mystery of *Gelmeroda I.*

Feininger's paintings are the final achievement of his inner vision, the materialization of a state of awareness, or "inwardness," as he called it. What distinguishes Feininger from the Expressionists is their desire to project their whole personalities into their paintings, not to enlarge the world within themselves but to enlarge themselves in the world. Feininger's urge was not for self-realization but for the realization of the image that he carried in himself. His pictures are the outcome of his spiritual condition, created in joy or pain.

They are decidedly not the archetypal images of the primitive mind, archaic or modern; they are the images of contemporary reality filtered through the spiritual awareness of his mind. His point of departure is nature; the distance from nature in the painting is determined by the power of the process of transformation. He finds in nature as much confirmation of his inner vision as nature can yield to him. When Feininger speaks of his life it is in the terms of a romantic: "But I conceive life as a constant yearning for the eternally unfulfillable."[33] When he speaks of his work it is in the terms of the classic. "I *know* ... that in the whole world, in *all* worlds, there can be nothing lawless, nothing accidental, nothing without *form* and *rhythm*, nor could there be. Why, then, in art? Should not art, which reveals man's *creative will*, be filled with form, law, and spirit?"[34] A

Braunlage, pencil study, 1917

81

classical striving for completion goes through a romantic agonizing process of creation. Romantic in Feininger is his nostalgic yearning for fulfillment, his longing for the grasp of the ultimate. Classical is his knowledge that the ultimate can be attained because it is not formless. The emotional content of his work is often romantic; the form found for the content is classical in order and law. Measure and proportion, rhythm and movement, sonority and echo, are locked together in a firm framework of structure, determined by the force of necessity. There is no romantic doubt left, once the forces of the picture have been locked with the key of necessity. Classical order has been established; a new law has been laid down; and romantic lawlessness banished from the picture.

Ever since Walden had become aware of Feininger at the Herbstsalon, he had been firmly convinced by his work. Feininger had become part of Walden's circle, the Sturm Kreis, and had made friends with the poets, painters, writers, and philosophers who were Walden's friends. Feininger had an equal gift for friendship and solitude; he could be attached and detached at the same time.

The terrible years of the war made it necessary for those who shared a common belief in a brighter future to act together for the liberation of art and man. The longer the war lasted, the clearer it became that the old Imperial order was doomed to destruction. To build a better world on the ruins of the old — this was the hope that kept men sane. The revolution that was in preparation was not only a political and social upheaval but a revolt of the injured spirit of man. Revolution meant liberation, and only the illiberal were not revolutionists.

The aims of the artists of the Sturm were decidedly antiaesthetic. The degradation of art to the sphere of luxury and voluptuousness was one of the accusations these artists leveled against the bourgeoisie. The puritanical flavor of the Sturm polemics against the "epicurean" in art, against the "consumer's" approach to the picture, was the underlying ethos of Walden's attitude: "Art ... is not a *luxury* but a *necessity!*" as Feininger had written to Kubin.[35] To Julia he had once written the aphoristic sentence: "*Need* produces the artist — it can also ruin him. But luxury produces the *aesthete*."[36] The artists of the Sturm had a missionary approach to their work. Walden was aiming at the regeneration of the world through art. Those were to be the aims of the Bauhaus as well.

If Feininger, both at the Sturm and at the Bauhaus, stood aloof from the battle of the day, he nevertheless shared the same hopes and tried to realize in his art his visions of the harmony of the world.

Herwarth Walden was the permanent revolutionist of modern art. His interest was not in any movement but in movement as such. He supported the Expressionists and the Futurists, the Cubists and the Blaue Reiter, and various individual artists as long as they were shattering old conventions. Walden was a remarkable judge of value and integrity. To mention all the names of the artists that he first exhibited would make a selective dictionary of modern art. His programmatic courage in keeping the flag of international solidarity flying by showing the work of Italian, Russian, and French painters, and the one outstanding American in wartime Berlin, deserves political as well as artistic recognition.

Walden had arranged an exhibition in 1916 that Feininger shared with Felix

7 Markwippach, 1917 (168)

Müller. Feininger's drawings appeared in the Sturm, and some of his pictures could always be seen at the gallery. In 1917 Walden arranged at the Sturm the first comprehensive exhibition of Feininger's work. Feininger described in a letter exactly how his pictures were hung and how Walden became more and more excited in the process of hanging them. With great skill and understanding he arranged one wall after the other, and Feininger observed how the rhythms and sonorities of his pictures began to live together. The exhibition became alive and exciting. Walden himself bought *Marine* (cat. 121) before the exhibition opened. Feininger did not go to the opening, but he was delighted to hear of the big crowds that attended and of the impact that the pictures made. A few days after the opening, he went to see the exhibition and in a detached way enjoyed his own work.

Walden had told him that, with that exhibition alone, Feininger would come through. Walden had not only good judgment in pictures but also a sense of the spirit of the time. Walden was right. With that exhibition Feininger's name was established. In a letter to Julia he called the exhibition "the turning point in our life [unsere Welt-wende]."[37] Until their "Welt-wende," Julia alone had believed in Feininger's future. When, in 1906 in Paris, she had given him her palette and encouraged him to paint, she had given up her own work, which, judging by her drawings for *Le Témoin* under the pseudonym "Regninief" (Feininger spelled backward), showed accomplished talent and a feeling for space not unrelated to Feininger's own. She alone had recognized in Feininger the potential painter; ten years had passed since he had turned to paint. The Sturm exhibition marked the end of the unknown and the beginning of the known painter.

The last and worst year of the war increased the material difficulties of the artist. Paint was either unobtainable or of such poor quality that it gave no effect. The days were filled with chasing the unobtainable; Feininger was weakened by persistent undernourishment, and every small task became an exhausting enterprise.

The work of 1918 bears traces of the hardships suffered; there are fewer paintings than in former years. In *Teltow II* (page 191), which was later bought by the National Gallery in Berlin, Feininger stands at equal distance from the world of nature and the world of formal abstraction. Every shape is reduced to its essential necessity; the rhythms are repetitive and logical; the aim is static.

In *Mellingen V* (cat. 187) the static quality has been overthrown. As in all Feininger's village pictures, the composition is not too formal and a spirit of gaiety and recklessness seems to prevail.

Both *Yellow Street II* (cat. 186), a Parisian subject, and *Bridge IV* (cat. 191) appear as contrasts. The bridge seems to come out of "Wee Willie Winkie's World" of the *Chicago Tribune* days. In the picture the tragic and the comic live closely together. It might have been a deliberate return to happier thoughts that made the picture a necessity. As we know, in Feininger's work a serious painting is often followed by a lighthearted, bizarre work.

The strongest composition of the year 1918 is *Zirchow VII* (page 192), a powerful dynamic structure in dark colors with glowing planes. Power has been compressed, potential energy firmly enclosed. Feininger does not paint the volume but the force that binds matter together.

Woodcut, 1919

In 1918, Feininger began to make woodcuts; from the winter of 1918–19 alone there exist over one hundred plates. The woodcut had been rediscovered by the Expressionists of the Brücke and the Blaue Reiter as a forceful and direct way of making a statement. Feininger's woodcuts are not charged with the violent emotion of the Expressionists. On a small scale he achieved the same monumentality that he achieved in his paintings. He used black and white as opposite forces in terms of planes creating space; he used, dialectically, opposition of contrast of weight and area, achieving stability of movement or dynamic force.

His work in woodcuts was of great importance: it helped him to simplify the issues of spatial organization; it was a new discipline. The woodcut makes it possible to manipulate planes without designing their outlines. Each plane determines the other by the process of subtraction, the void becomes a force, the untouched a reality. It was this magic in woodcutting that appealed to Feininger. In his woodcuts he expressed all sides of his temperament — his seriousness, his playfulness, his love of the grotesque.

Small woodcuts, printed on thin, colored paper, blue, green, yellow, pink, as the mood demanded, began to decorate his letters (pages 316–317). He was a wonderful letter writer both in form and in content. His written page is a pure aesthetic pleasure, and his style, in German and in English, beautifully direct and very descriptive. His letters have a great literary and art-historical value and should one day be published.

He loved woodcarving, and made for his sons whole villages, occupied by figures of Belgian peasants or Americans — with churches, houses, bridges, viaducts, and railroad engines. A whole fairy-tale world can be found in his toys, as serious and as grotesque as his cartoons had once been and as his woodcuts were now. Whatever he touched he transposed into his own world.

The comic figures in Feininger's toy world are the memories of his childhood. The men in top hats are the grown-ups whom the child cannot comprehend. They have become toys; their seriousness and their importance is taken away from them. The child has become the artist and treats the world of grown-ups as toyland. As the lonely boy once felt deserted and viewed a strange world that he did not understand and that no one explained to him, now the adults have become toys and remain lonely in the world that they inhabit.

In this irony there lies much pain and nostalgia — the wish to belong and yet to be excluded. Feininger shows the seriousness of life in the guise of its comic inversions.

Woodcut, 1918

THE BAUHAUS YEARS — WEIMAR

1919–1925, *Weimar, Deep*

On November 9, 1918, the revolt of the sailors of the German fleet signaled the end of a lost war and the end of the Kaiser's empire. It was the moment for action. Members of the old German Werkbund formed the Novembergruppe, and Feininger joined this group. The word "November" expressed all the hopes of the new era. The group's aim was the gathering of all progressive forces among the artists for the regeneration of cultural life. They had great hopes, great plans, and great people.

The manifesto of the Novembergruppe, entitled "Ja: Stimmen des Arbeitsrates für Kunst in Berlin," appeared in 1919 with a front page by Feininger (*The Town Hall in Swinemünde*). The program, an affirmation of support for everything new, contained the sentence, "Our voices say 'yes' to all that is growing and developing" ["Unsere Stimmen sagen 'Ja' zu allem Keimenden und Werdenden"]. The manifesto was signed by nearly every prominent artist in Berlin: Otto Bartning, Rudolf Belling, Lyonel Feininger, Walter Gropius, Erich Heckel, Mechtilde von Lichnowski, Gerhard Marcks, Erich Mendelsohn, Otto Müller, Karl Osthaus, Hans Pölzig, Christian Rohlfs, Karl Schmidt-Rottluff, Bruno Paul, W. R. Valentiner, and other architects, painters, and writers. The practical aims of the Novembergruppe followed the ideas of the Werkbund, which had been founded by Van de Velde (1863–1957). Van de Velde originated the workshops in Weimar in 1902. By 1906 these workshops had developed into the Kunstgewerbeschule. When Gropius and his friends discussed in Berlin the foundation of a new school, their thoughts turned to Weimar. At an afternoon party at Adolf Behne's when the plans were discussed, Feininger asked: "Can't you take us along?" and was told, "You are already on the list." The thought of working in close harmony with the men who had taken the regeneration of the arts to heart and the knowledge that he would return to Weimar meant much to Feininger, who accepted their invitation at once and became the first "master" (as the professors were called) at the Bauhaus.

The Bauhaus cannot be understood if one thinks of it only as an advanced school of design. The founding of it was in intention a moral act, a step in the reformation of society through the unity of the arts and technics, culminating in architecture. Its program was directed against the idea of *l'art pour l'art*, against the academic tradition, and against art as a luxury. The lost unity of the worker-craftsman and the creative artist was to be re-established. These ideas were based on those of Ruskin, William Morris, Van de Velde, and Peter Behrens. The ethics of the Werkbund, of the Sturm, and of the Expressionists found their logical continuation and application in the Bauhaus. In the accomplishment of these aims the practical training of craftsmen had the same value as that of the creative artist. Gropius did not want to abolish the distinction, but intended to unite artists and workers in the social and moral task of creating the buildings of the future.

Gropius understood the creation of space in architecture in the same way that Feininger understood the creation of space in his pictures. In "Idee und Aufbau des Staatlichen Bauhauses," Gropius wrote: "Man invents through his own intuition, through his metaphysical powers, which he draws from the universe, the immaterial space of semblance. But this space of vision aims at its realization in the material world; with spirit and work, matter is mastered."[1] Here, in these words of Gropius, Feininger's conception of space is summarized as completely as in Feininger's own statements. Feininger was the one painter of the time who in his work practiced what Gropius preached. His appointment as the first of the Bauhaus masters was natural and logical.

The Bauhaus was founded in the spring of 1919, and Feininger arrived in May. From Weimar he wrote, "but the most wonderful thing is the new *studio*. . . . The *good* man Gropius! He gave it to me straight away. . . . He went everywhere with me through the school. I saw the print workshop! Wonderful! . . . We shall be in a painter's heaven here! . . . Many of the pupils . . . have seen us too, they'll know by now. Well, they will have to get used to Papileo."[2] (Feininger's name in his family, from Papi—father, and Leo—Léonell.)

When Van de Velde had resigned in 1914 he had recommended Gropius as his successor. The old school had carried on throughout the war years but, in Feininger's words, "had fallen asleep like the sleeping princess [Dornröschenschlaf]." [3] Teachers and students were to be rudely awakened by Gropius, and very soon rumors spread in the town of the terrible revolutionists who were supposed to have arrived in Weimar to take over the school. An unholy alliance of reactionary artists of the old school and local political representatives began their first attempts to strangle the Bauhaus at birth. The attacks were mainly directed against Gropius. When it became known that Feininger was a Cubist, he, too, appeared for a time as the great danger to art and morality in Weimar, and attacks were directed against him as well — against Feininger, who, of all people, was least likely to be a "dangerous influence," who believed so firmly in the spirit of the individual that he even doubted the value of all art teaching. His horror of teaching a "dogma" was frequently expressed in his letters. To make his point that each artist has to develop on his own lines and that he must find his own way, he arranged an exhibition of several hundred of his own drawings in the school, to show the development from observation of nature toward personal expression. The exhibition impressed the students, who very soon gained confidence in their new teachers. Feininger was glad to note the students' independence of thought and their readiness to develop new ideas.

On May 30, 1919, Feininger attended his first Master's Council meeting and was ceremoniously welcomed. He was most impressed, but regretted the afternoon lost to painting. By July, Feininger had found a house and could bring his family to Weimar. He wrote on July 11, 1919, "Until we meet in our dear Weimar! the fairy tale part II begins!" [4]

The Bauhaus Manifesto appeared in 1919 with Feininger's woodcut *Cathedral of Socialism* on the cover. Never before had the words "cathedral" and "socialism" been combined in one title; it summarized perfectly the Bauhaus attitude. Based on the romantic illusion of the medieval "Bauhütte," the Bauhaus program hoped to emulate the spirit of devoted craftsmanship in the modern world. Medieval mysticism as well as modern political thought was the root of the Bauhaus ethics. The romantic idea of the medieval Bauhütte may be an illusion, but even illusions become powerful and effective when they are believed. The romantic conception of the Middle Ages was thus linked with the modern romanticism of the machine. The Bauhaus could become part of the myth of the twentieth century because it shared it.

The same romantic conception of the future that Feininger had expressed and satirized in his technical fantasies at the turn of the century, the same love of the machine as the harbinger of the future, dominated the Bauhaus.

The political antagonism that the Bauhaus encountered from its first days strengthened rather than weakened the spirit of loyalty and coherence within. A very happy mood pervaded the whole school and expressed itself as much in the seriousness of the work as in the famous Bauhaus festivities. But throughout all the years in Weimar, from 1919 to 1925, development was interrupted by political intrigues. Only the strength of character of the Bauhaus masters held it together. What saved the Bauhaus was the quality of its men.

The masters at the Bauhaus were Feininger and Marcks, who both came in 1919.

Itten came later in the same year; Muche joined in 1920; Klee arrived in January, 1921; Schlemmer, 1921; and Kandinsky, 1922; and Moholy-Nagy joined the Bauhaus masters in 1923.

Many of the Bauhaus masters were old friends of the Sturm days in Berlin. "Kandinsky and I remain good friends. Saturday I shall be together with Klee; they are all wonderful people, Muche, Schlemmer, and the other colleagues. I only now recognize clearly a cumulative force emanating from them, firmly rooted in their outstanding *human* qualities."[5] The value of the Bauhaus masters to the school was their very presence as a spiritual force. The contribution of the Bauhaus masters was found as much in their own paintings as in their actual teaching. They were not meant to influence their pupils but to enable them to take part in a life of creative activity. There is no Bauhaus school of painting; the separate masters, all strong personalities in every sense, did not formulate a program or influence one another. The friendship of Klee, Kandinsky, Feininger, and Schlemmer was based on personal sympathy and mutual respect, not on an identity of artistic aims.

The future of the school was in doubt from month to month. Feininger wrote, "We have to make heavy concessions at the Bauhaus, the planned exhibition will already be staged now, and we are all reluctant to make 'art policy.' . . . One thing is certain: if we cannot show 'achievements' to the outside world and gain the support of the 'industrialists' then hopes for the future of the Bauhaus are slender. It is necessary to aim at income and *production*."[6]

Feininger's work was concerned mainly with the graphic workshop. He was responsible for the editing and production of the portfolios [Bauhaus-Mappen]. His master printer was Ludwig Hirschfeld, who took care of all the technical work. On November 14, 1921, he wrote that he had finished the lettering for the inside cover of the portfolio, and on the following day he reported about the work, saying that he had "started it and must see it through, because the 'Mappe' of the Bauhaus masters . . . is also a creation for the glory of our cause [Denn die Mappe der Bauhausmeister . . . ist schliesslich auch eine Schöpfung zu Ehren unserer Sache]."[7]

The battle for the renewal of art and the recognition of the achievements of the new masters was not confined to Weimar. A new spirit pervaded the whole country. The removal of the Imperial government and the many small rulers in Germany had thrown new responsibilities on the national and provincial authorities who assumed power after the November Revolution. The lifting of the Imperial government restriction on the purchase of works of modern art (the Emperor had included Impressionism in this definition) gave a new freedom to the national and provincial museums. The directors of the German museums deserve recognition for their whole-hearted support of living art. At an exhibition of I. B. Neumann in April, 1919, the city of Stettin bought the first Feininger for a public collection, and fifteen more works were sold.

Through Dr. W. Kaesbach, who had known him and admired his work, Feininger became acquainted with Professor Ludwig Justi, the director of the Berlin National Gallery. When, in the spring of 1919, permission was given to the National Gallery to acquire works by modern artists, Justi appointed Dr. Kaesbach to organize the modern section of the National Gallery in the newly established Kronprinzen-Palais.

90

The National Gallery acquired *Vollersroda III* (cat. 164), later exchanged for *Teltow II* (page 191). When the Kronprinzen-Palais opened its doors for the first time, Marc's *Tower of Blue Horses* and Feininger's *Teltow II* and *Vollersroda III* were hung on the same wall. In the compositional dynamism of both artists there is indeed a similarity that some have traced to Delaunay; this view, however, appears unjustified, for both Franz Marc and Feininger had rejected Delaunay's theories. Marc, in an undated letter to Delaunay, had written, "Dear friend, many thanks for sending me your aesthetic treatise, I have sent it today to Klee. I have read it carefully, I hope you don't mind if I admit frankly that the manner in which you try to approach the mysterious laws of art does not seem to me very fruitful. I *love your pictures* and I do not deny that your philosophical and historical ideas may be necessary and reasonable for your own artistic development and for others, I suppose, but never for me. . . . I can even see the danger for you. It is not true, my dear, that 2×2 makes four, never."[8] Feininger's views are recorded in his letter to Kubin (pages 67–68). What Marc, Delaunay, and Feininger have in common is their preoccupation with light as a force. A similarity in Feininger's work to that of some American painters has also been observed. Comparison has been made with the "ray line" of Charles Demuth; in Demuth's pictures the light ray simplifies outline but does not gain independent force. The similarity between Joseph Stella and Feininger is greater –

again not through any influence or knowledge of each other's work but through a common origin in Futurism. The work of MacDonald Wright and Morgan Russell in their "synchromatic" period owes its origin to the influence of Delaunay. Actually, Feininger neither knew, influenced, nor was influenced by any artist working in America. Similarities have their ground in the common experience of Cubism, Futurism, and Orphism, from which each artist drew the inference nearest to his own aims.

In that first summer after the war, the persisting stimuli of Cubism and Futurism merged with Feininger's own discoveries into his mature style. If he was right to have spoken in 1913 of a first period of maturity, it is right for us to see in the Bauhaus period a second. In Feininger's art there was beginning a new phase, which, like all his others, had arisen slowly from his previous work and had been long in maturing. It is now that the large translucent planes appear and that the structure of his pictures loses some rigidity. The light that imbues every plane of the picture loses some of its self-willed dynamism. It plays in less violent shafts and penetrates the planes of which the picture is composed. From the illuminated plane Feininger advances to the luminous plane. The new phase may be called the transparent period.

In *Village Neppermin* (cat. 195) the light in the picture seems to originate inside the painting itself, with an interchange of light from plane to plane. An independent world of luminous planes has been created. More than anywhere in Cubism, light as well as form has become active. A new force in addition to form and color has entered the world of painting and is playing an active part in pictorial organization. Generated light has been added as a new element in the interplay of forces. From now on, Feininger's works have to establish an inner harmony involving one more factor than hitherto.

In *Church of Nieder-Grunstedt* (page 194), which is a less static composition, the conflict is resolved. With a near-Futurist vehemence, the composition achieves a strong balance. *Gothen* (page 193) has the rhythm of a steady triumphal procession, built up in tones of gray with blue and carmine accents against a sky of deep green in which the light is firmly held. *High Houses IV* (cat. 198) is a calmly composed painting with a golden tonality.

In two pictures of 1920, Feininger imparts monumentality to the human figure. *Beachcombers* (cat. 211) is the counterpart of the *Bicycle Race*. The picture forms a diagram of forces; the forward movement of the figures, countered by the weight of the burden, creates a formula of force and movement where the figures express the relation of inherent and active strength — painted with the same knowledge that revealed the diagram of forces in the *Bicycle Race* (page 176). In this formal analysis of the *Beachcombers* one must not overlook the human content of the picture. The *Portrait of a Tragic Being* (page 93), a portrait of one of his friends, the wife of a musician, remains unique in Feininger's work. Broadly painted, it is a wholly Expressionist picture, with a violent clash of red and yellow and a direct emotional impact. Both in conception and in manner of painting this picture shows that there were various possibilities for the development of Feininger's art. The road opened by this picture was not followed again.

8 Portrait of a Tragic Being, 1920 (212)

The paintings of the 1920s show a progressive development toward greater luminosity and transparency. The pictures are composed in large planes, which at first do not interpenetrate. In *Hopfgarten* (page 196) the world has regained its stability; in large planes a vast and peaceful architecture of space is constructed. The *Viaduct* (page 197), restrained in color, achieves a mannerist elegance. It is not far removed from observed reality, but is refined to the point of perfection. In this picture Feininger's aristocratic feeling has found an architectural expression for hauteur.

Gross-Kromsdorf III of 1921 (cat. 219) is as much a strict as a fanciful painting. The strictness of form is negated by wild and fanciful color, glowing from within; its chromatic abandon is firmly held in check by the rigid organization of planes. Feininger's predilection for negating form with color – giving a bitter form a sweet color, and, to reverse the process, giving a friendly form a harsh color – shows again and again in his pictures. To him the terms "heavy" and "light," "gay" and "sad," "tragic" and "comic" are dialectically related. Only in the interplay of contrasts does the picture as a whole reveal itself. Thus, every painting becomes an expression of his knowledge that joy and sorrow, calm and movement, harmony and disharmony determine each other. His pictures are not a representation but a presentation. They present the active process in which the picture and the observer take part. An event is caught in the picture – not an intention. A process – not a state of completion. The crystalline form, the mutual illumination and penetration of the planes change their relation in light, color, and form. They remain interdependent and become active.

Architecture II (also called *The Man from Potin*; cat. 221) is a departure from the mysterious luminosity of the pictures of this period. Feininger rebuilds a solid street in solid color with the lively figures of his Paris days.

original "note" to "Lady in Mauve"

Sketch, Paris, 1906

Related to *The Man from Potin* and, like it, a recollection of Paris, is the *Lady in Mauve* (page 95). Originally designed as a drawing for *Le Témoin*, it appeared as a painting in 1922. One of his few paintings with one large figure, the *Lady in Mauve* becomes a focal point, not a turning point, in his *œuvre*. Feininger, aged 50, looked back for a moment on an episode from the past. There is a fleeting compliment to Cubism and a slightly ironic remnant of Futurist speed in the movement of the lady's feet (shades of Balla's dog) with the whole of Feininger's architecture leaning backward to let her pass. An unexpected similarity can also be discovered by comparing this picture with Marcel Duchamp's *Nude Descending a Staircase* of the year 1912. The movements dissected by Duchamp are identical with the movements summarized by Feininger in 1906 in his *Témoin* drawing, then called *L'Impatiente* (page 36).

94

9 Lady in Mauve, 1922 (227)

Gaberndorf I (page 199), a composition of the church at Gaberndorf, dates from 1921; in monumentality it marks the highest point of Feininger's dramatic compositions. The tremendous triangle of light reveals a field of abstract forces in physical conflict.

Gelmeroda VIII (cat. 217) is a calm picture. In the suite of Gelmerodas, fast and slow movements follow each other. The houses are almost translucent; the steeple oscillates its blues, like a tuning fork, and the vibrations of the colors give a living note in time and space. Here the color sings. The square in the sky, bisected by the steeple, is mildly inclined, emphasizing the verticality of the structure. Feininger has developed the art of the interval to a degree unknown in painting before him. The intervals in planes and colors, the angles at which lines meet and are echoed or repeated, show a miraculous sensibility. The steeple re-creates its own outline as an echo or a shadow; the figures in the foreground echo in their intervals the rhythms of the whole.

The *Cathedral* of 1920 (page 195) appears rather surprisingly at that period. The Futurist intensity — the desire to use curves and spirals — remains mechanical. It has all the machine quality of the Bauhaus ideology but strays far from Feininger's own credo. There are no other paintings in his *œuvre* quite like this; he never returned to the literal presentation of sound in shape. To make the ringing of the bells visible was an aim of the Futurists, not his.

The sense of humor and absurdity that pervaded Feininger's early paintings he never lost. It recurs in pictures of this period, such as *Old American Locomotive* (cat. 246), which he had begun ten years before and which he completed in 1924. (In dating a picture Feininger always used the date of completion.) He also found an entirely new outlet for his sense of the absurd in drawings and watercolors: mysterious ships cross nonexistent seas; good-natured sprites hide in dark forests. Here all the formal preoccupations of his paintings are utterly abandoned, and a wild world finds expression in scraggly outlines. He referred to them as "children's drawings."

Moonlit Night
pen and wash, 1918

Some of these nervous, scraggly drawings are meant as pure fun and fantasy. But many others deal with the very subjects of his paintings, and reveal another side of the artist as much as another side of the subject. Such drawings do not outline and silhouette the structure of a building; they go tentatively around it; they vibrate on the surface that they create in approaching an imaginary outline of the building. In this drawing process, the contours retain their fluidity and never quite confine the shape — not unlike *sfumato*, Leonardo's unclear outline that leaves the observer in slight doubt about where the figure begins and ends and thus suggests life and movement. The buildings, trees, boats, or clouds retain their own will and mystery. They appear in the artist's work as a relaxation from the firm discipline that he usually applied to his pictures and to himself. This counterweight to the classical order that rules in his pictures appears as a necessary corrective to his own work. In these drawings, hesitancy rules over certainty, and freedom — anarchy almost — over order. The pictures have nothing accidental in them, but they appear accidentally achieved; all traces of effort are consciously blurred. A spontaneous growth of line and color makes these works, mostly on a small scale, as strange and otherworldly as the works of Klee.

During the late summer of 1921, Feininger and Julia visited Hildesheim, Lüneburg, Lübeck, and Riebnitz. The Brick Gothic architecture of these towns, so different from Thuringia, was reminiscent of the Belgian towns that were among his first memories of Europe. Lüneburg and its old gables appeared in many pictures painted later. The journey that summer went as far as the Baltic, to Heiligenhafen and Fehmarn.

The painting *The Bay* (cat. 234) owes its origin to drawings from that period. This picture, at first sight, might appear little else but a stylized form of naturalism; yet it is in actuality something very different. Its color is near and yet removed from natural color. The painting has reached that one possible point of balance where the conflict between nature and style has been resolved. Every shape has been abstracted until the picture contains the essence, the concentrated vision of a real world.

In the summer of 1922 Feininger returned to Lüneburg but, after the strong impressions of the previous year, was slightly disenchanted. He wrote, "When the first spell has passed a great emptiness remains in the place."[9] From Lüneburg he went on to Timmendorf, where Gropius' mother owned a house. There Feininger spent several weeks of the summer with Kandinsky and Gropius. Feininger was mainly occupied with making nature notes, particularly studies of cloud formations. The days in Timmendorf were quiet and gay in the company of his friends.

During the winter months in Weimar, Feininger held "open house" once a week, and many Bauhaus students came regularly. After one evening Feininger wrote, "They all wanted to hear music, so we had to sit down, B. and myself, and play. First Bach's Passacaglia, then the 'Russian' [Fugue].[10] Then B. and I played another prelude and the fugue, and *I* played the fugue because it was my favorite. . . .[11] While my playing was unsure and unconcentrated before when I accompanied, all the more assured and well did I play now so that we developed the fugue really well. What was most rewarding was that I could for once really show my conception of the fugue. B. said, it was remarkable that I with my innate feeling for Bach had not become a musician instead of a painter. But we agreed that the nature of Bach finds expression also in my paintings."[12]

Feininger had, as early as 1890, thought of themes for fugues, and had attempted to compose them with Fred Werner in their days of friendship in Berlin in the 1890s. In 1921 Feininger began to compose fugues. He was rarely without either a piano or harmonium in his studio. Music was a part of him that had to find expression. He wrote thirteen fugues altogether.[13] Some of them were performed by organists in various churches and at public recitals. The first to perform his work was Willi Apel. Later his compositions were performed on special occasions in Germany and in America. The sixth fugue was published in facsimile.[14]

It is a misconception to think of painting as music — or to explain it in musical terms. Feininger's music found its expression as music. In 1913 he had written, "I project my whole love and longing into my work, into music and seemingly crazy pictures."[15] The operative word here is the *and*. Feininger did not think of his painting as music; to him the fugal form and the dialectics of counterpoint were clear laws of thinking. Such laws were in accordance with his temperament and thought; they also became structural principles for the making of his pictures. It is not music we see but visible shapes that obey "fugal" laws.

Feininger investigated the possibilities of inversion, of mirror effects, of overlapping, and of the interpenetration and synchronization of events. These principles of fugal construction are all used in music to build a temporal order; Feininger applied them in his paintings. In this contrapuntal conception of painting he is an innovator. He might not have been able to make this contribution if the laws of counterpoint had not been alive within him. The Bauhaus days were rich, not only in artistic creation but also in musical experience and composition. As he worked in both fields, the laws of music became more important in his paintings — the laws, not the music.

In honor of Feininger's fiftieth birthday, Wilhelm Köhler, then director of the museum at Weimar, arranged an exhibition of the work of Feininger and Klee, together with Gothic paintings. Both artists were surprised to find that their own work harmonized in "sonority" [Klang] with the mystic mood of the Gothic artists. Similarity of color with the German Gothic masters can be observed in both Klee and Feininger — the sudden appearance of unexpected luminous areas of color arising from mystical dark surroundings, like stained glass in Klee and like facets of a crystal catching a ray of light in Feininger. These two painters develop a luminosity within the picture by different means. In Feininger's work, the choice of color itself is often Gothic. The strange pale yellows and distant bluish greens, which can be found also in Altdorfer and Bosch, are colors that deviate by only a slight degree from natural color, and, by their very slight departure from the observed, remove the whole scene into a world quite recognizable but unreal.

The sky in Gothic painting is the natural sky over the earth; its atmospheric depth is observed and, at the same time, translated into a symbol of eternity. The sky is real and unreal at the same time. The longing for eternity and fulfillment transposes the real world into a vision. This spiritualization is the alternative to the romantic

10 Town Gate-Tower II, 1925 (253)

attitude in which eternity is comprehended as unattainable. The development of the picture from the observation of nature, the transposition of natural color into pictorial color, the development of pictorial form from natural form, the creation of a new unity of rhythms are Feininger's aims in his art.

Every summer he stayed, for as long as he could, on the Baltic Sea. His whole being was refreshed; his whole life unwound after the winters of painting and struggle. He never painted in the summer, but made drawings and watercolors and observations; he collected notes, which were to grow into pictures. After one summer in Timmendorf he discovered, in 1924, Deep on the Baltic, where he returned every summer for twelve years. The months on the Baltic Sea were the happiest in Feininger's life. He usually stayed alone for a few weeks, and was then joined by Julia and his three sons. They took simple lodgings and enjoyed simple pleasures. Feininger relived his boyhood with his own sons. The model boats he built were raced against his sons' boats. He made long walking tours inland to Treptow, Greifenberg, Kolberg, and nearby small towns and villages. From all these places he brought back drawings and notes. With Laurence he went to the village church and listened to his son playing Bach, Buxtehude, and Feininger's own compositions.

The study of architectural space had given Feininger a new vision of the sea. The study of the space of the sea will in turn be reflected in his architectural paintings. If one compares the sea pictures of 1912 from Heringsdorf with the painting of 1923, *Clouds above the Sea II* (page 200), the vast step forward will be visible immediately. An entirely new feeling for the immensity of space has been expressed with a new discipline. Feininger created an architecture of space; he gave it form and substance. He imposed an order; yet it was an order derived from nature and not forced upon it. Above the line of the horizons that he shows us, the sky is built in tones and planes that owe their origin as much to nature as to the ordering mind. The mind at work here is a classical mind. The immensity of space is given form and human relation; it cannot dissolve or escape into a romantic world; it is commanded and held in place by its own laws. In composition this painting is strikingly similar to Caspar David Friedrich's *Monk by the Sea* (formerly in Berlin). The placing of the monk against the universe is echoed in Feininger's two figures. The spatial division of the two pictures is nearly the same, the mood of loneliness and longing identical. Both of these pictures of the Pomeranian shore have left the seascape far behind. Man and the universe is the subject of both pictures, not the sea. The spirit is the same but the sentiment is not. The German Romantic Friedrich paints an allegory, Feininger a state of mind. Feininger's sky is as eternal as Friedrich's; both artists see a mystery, but Friedrich sees the mystery of creation, Feininger the mystery of existence. The *Wreck of the Hoffnung* (in Hamburg) by Caspar David Friedrich, with its crystalline sharp shapes of ice hemming in the wreck, forecast the shapes of Feininger's own paintings. Feininger was quite unaware of a precursor; as he wrote to Barr, "paintings of C. D. Friedrich I only saw long after I had painted those pictures (*Bird Cloud, Dunes*, etc.) which brought about my reputation of having been influenced by him." [16]

A description by Feininger of a natural scene is already on the way toward its final transformation, which he accomplished later in a picture: "When I turned

100

11 The Bird Cloud, 1926 (268)

Sketch for *The Bird Cloud*, pencil, 1924

Cloud Study, pencil sketch, 1924

102

around, I saw, almost frightened, a tremendous double rainbow of incredible sharpness and clarity — stretched over the dune from its point in the east, right to the cutting in our beach, almost a complete semicircle, because the sun stood already opposite on the horizon. Added to this was an intensity of color, the uncanny coppery glow of the sunset hour. The bow stretched across a deep violet sky, and in its midst appeared ghostly cloudheads in stratified rows; on the east fringe they cut across the bow — a tremendous thunderstorm was coming up; toward the top this wall of cloud folded over the rainbow, turned from purple to copper, right to the top of the sky lemon yellow — but duller, paler than the yellow in the rainbow itself. For an hour Laurence . . . and I stayed and made notes and drew. Until the sun had set, the rainbow remained — at the end only its eastern leg on an almost midnight black sky. The copper-brown dunes and the beach, much lighter than the sky — it was almost eerie. In the west there were an equally frightening sunset, quite improbable in color — and the zigzag staggering of the clouds; through an opening a sword of flame reached across the whole sky." [17] The picture based on this experience is *Rainbow* (cat. 258). Unlike Caspar David Friedrich's *Landscape with Rainbow* (Weimar), Feininger's painting depicts physical forces of which the ordering mind of man is an integral part.

Feininger discovered in nature possibilities that lie hidden; when he invented a cloud that appeared even to him improbably daring, he one day found that cloud in the sky. "Last night on the beach there was a mirrorlike smoothness and strange cloud formation. I see colors here at the sea, indescribable. . . . The day before yesterday, all the colors of the rainbow were present in an incredible purity, a menacing sky, foreboding yesterday's thunderstorm! Last night I suddenly experienced *my* cloud . . . in exactly the same colors! And it is always like that. I can paint what I like — nature herself always confirms it." [18]

Both the *Blue Cloud* of 1925 (page 202) and *The Bird Cloud* of 1926 (page 101) are paintings in which the seemingly willful forms imposed by the artist are in fact forms that nature contained and revealed.

Feininger had discovered in early life his affinity with Turner. He went as far beyond Turner in his paintings of the sea as Cézanne went beyond the Impressionists. It is no longer the moment of light or the movement of the sea that is grasped as an impression; the majesty of its eternal space is formed to last. Like Cézanne, Feininger made "something solid" from the tradition of Impressionism. But classical form-giving is not all; there is in the classical tradition the dark power of the myth. *Blue Marine* of 1924 (page 200) is such a painting of dark mystery. The boats and figures are apparitions silhouetted in a different reality; time is suspended; the events are not connected, but belong to different spheres of reality. A revolution of the invisible spheres has brought them together — a world of shadows is revealed.

One cannot fully realize Feininger's understanding of the sea if one does not consider his watercolors. There are many more sea and marine pictures in that medium than in his oils. Some of Feininger's greatest visions find expression in his watercolors, which are monumentally large in conception. His watercolors are always based on a drawing that organizes space. Color is used as an emotional enlargement of space, transforming the planes and distances.

The peaceful but concentrated work on his watercolors was the necessary counterpart in his life to the hard-won struggles in his paintings. The medium obeys his directions; a complete harmony of intention and result arises simultaneously. Feininger's watercolors are like the gifts that the gods give without asking for payment or penance.

In the architectural compositions of the period one can observe a greater luminosity and a much stronger feeling for air. It was the experience of the sea that gave new breath to the painting of architecture. The small figures in Feininger's compositions of the sea and of architecture must not be regarded as mere figurines. They give to the composition of space the human scale, yet they are more than compositional elements that might be included or excluded at will. Their task goes beyond indicating scale – they enlarge spiritual space. They are subject to the forces of the composition and caught in the network of lines. These lines, which originate with them, extend to shape the space; the lines that meet to give the figures their shape originate in the structure in which the figures have their being. Man is included in the scheme of things. The paintings of the years before 1920 had striven for monumentality. In that process Feininger had gained a firm grasp on the picture's structure; he could now afford to lighten the structure without losing his firm hold on the pictorial form he had mastered. Air and light penetrate his pictures, and a new kind of aerial perspective is developed.

A forerunner of his development can be seen in *Troistedt* of 1923 (cat. 236), where the contour is no longer absolute and the colors of the planes interpenetrate. The space is kaleidoscopic – flooded by colored light – blues ranging from light to dark – golden yellow tones penetrating the solid, deep reds and blues.

The study of two subjects painted by Feininger in two versions each during these years will show his development.

The *Church of the Minorites* in Erfurt was painted in its first version in 1924. In 1923 a room had been placed at his disposal at the Museum in Erfurt, where he worked. The painting was completed the next year; it is a calm and poised composition of great delicacy and monumentality. Two years later, in 1926, a second version was completed, similar in composition but different in size and color. Both paintings have achieved a transposition of nature arrested at the fine point where form and content are one (cat. 248; page 205).

In both paintings Feininger succeeded with a transposition of nature, where idea and reality become one. The picture, aiming from the world of nature, meets the vision of the painter at the point of fusion and identity.

Town Gate-Tower I of 1924–26 (cat. 262) is based on drawings from Neu Brandenburg. It is more formalized than the second version of 1925 (page 99), which returned nearer to observed reality but which gained in luminosity and air.

In *Gaberndorf II* (page 201), shapes take on symbolic quality; the recurring theme of the upright-pointing arrow with its echoes and mirror images, although deduced originally from nature, may owe something to Klee's emphasis on the arrow as a directing symbol in art.

Gables I, Lüneburg (page 204), the first picture of Lüneburg, is very close to observed reality. Many more paintings entitled "Gables" or "Lüneburg" were to follow. They

104

seem, of all Feininger's work, the least resolved. Was this because he was fascinated by the architecture of the Brick Gothic, with its great natural charm, and was at first unable to free himself from the attraction of the original? His first Gables pictures are the least transmuted, least spiritualized works of Feininger. He needed to absorb an atmosphere over a long period of time before it could be distilled in his mind. The paintings of Lüneburg remain impressions until later, in *Architecture III* (also *Gables II*); the recollection arises in a clarified and transposed light. Since 1921 Feininger had been closer to nature again. But in his work the results of experience can be observed only after a lapse of time; the nearness to nature had its source in the more relaxed years immediately after the war, when a freer life had become possible. The monumental pictures, on the other hand, were the outcome of the experience of the war years. Writing to Barr, he said: "It seems to me that some pictures about '16–'17, up to '20, have a more monumental character than later ones. I ascribe this to my having, since 1921, recommenced my intense studies of Nature, which ceased entirely during the years of the War."[19] Nearness to nature, Feininger knew, held great dangers for him as well as great attractions. During the last years in Weimar a new phase of Feininger's art was maturing. "I am trying ... at least in one of the many half-finished pictures, to reach the state of transfiguration [Verklärung]. At the moment it's hard work; barely here and there a spot shines through in the process of dematerialization."[20] The pull of nature and the will to transmutation are the opposing poles that, in their conflict, release the energy that Feininger needed to create his pictures.

The conflict in his own creative process was fruitful, but the conflicts in the world surrounding him were not helpful to his development. The Bauhaus was in a permanent state of crisis.

What had attracted Feininger originally to the Bauhaus was the idea of an ethical approach to art, as well as the community and friendship with other artists. Within the Bauhaus, the different masters placed a different emphasis on the primacy of the separate — but, in Gropius' mind, united — aspects of Bauhaus activity. The Bauhaus masters held different opinions about the priority of technical as against spiritual values. Feininger had written as early as 1919, "Gropius sees the craft — I the spirit — in art. But he will never expect me to alter my art, and I shall assist him in every possible way, because he is such a faithful, honest man and a great idealist without self-seeking."[21] On this foundation of mutual trust they had worked loyally together. But Feininger's whole outlook was opposed to the mechanical in art. Coming from the station in Weimar one day in July, 1923, he saw a Bauhaus poster and wrote, "'Art and Technics' the new 'Union,' was the motto of the Bauhaus, proclaimed in posters at the railway station...."[22] "I reject it with all my heart — this misconception of *art* is a symptom of our time. The demand to couple the two movements is nonsense in every respect. A real technician will rightly reject every artistic interference, and, on the other hand, even the greatest technical perfection can never replace the divine spark of art."[23]

In 1924 Kandinsky and Jawlensky, the survivors of the Blaue Reiter, together with Feininger and Klee formed a new group to be known as the "Blaue Vier." The "Blue Four" never intended to formulate a program; their sole aim was the arrangement of joint exhibitions, because the artists felt in mutual sympathy and found that their paintings could live together in the same exhibition. Emmy Galka Scheyer represented the interests of the group in the United States and arranged many exhibitions, particularly on the West Coast. In 1923 W. R. Valentiner had already arranged the first show of Feininger's work in America, at the Anderson Galleries, New York, but there had been no response. When, in 1924, Feininger had to have his American passport renewed, he was asked for an assurance that he intended to return to America. In a letter he wrote about it, and added, "This is not impossible for the boys' sakes; they are all regular American citizens. But what I should do there, I could not say — because there are no ways of making a living. My art would be impossible there . . . a friend of ours [Emmy Galka Scheyer] has been working hard for the 'Blaue Vier,' without any financial success — in California, after New York and the East have failed, dozens of exhibitions, hundreds of lectures and articles . . . some enthusiasm, more curiosity, but no material success. Now I am here as an 'alien,' and have great hesitations about my home country — I cherish no illusions."[24]

Except for Jawlensky, all the members of the Blaue Vier were Bauhaus painters; they were in fact the Bauhaus masters who placed "the spiritual in art" above "the technical in art." The technical tendencies were represented mainly by Moholy-Nagy. An article by Moholy-Nagy in the catalogue of the L.J.A. (*Leipziger-Jahres-Ausstellung*, 1925) upset Feininger very much. "Nothing but optics, mechanics overcoming 'old' static painting . . . and all the time, cinema, optics, mechanics, projections, and movements and even of mechanically produced optical slides . . . in the most beautiful spectral colors that one can keep like gramophone records and . . . project with a lamp. . . . We can say that this is terrible, and the end of all art . . . it is technically a very interesting task — but why call this mechanization of optics art? and the only art of our time? and still more, the future? Is that an atmosphere in which painters like Klee and some of us could grow? Klee was quite paralyzed [beklommen] when we talked about Moholy."[25]

The paradox of this situation was that the Bauhaus had its two sides, both of which made history: the one, the spiritual in art, represented by Kandinsky, Klee, and Feininger; the other, the mechanical, constructive side, with Moholy-Nagy and Gropius. Both sides contributed to the development of art, architecture, and technology in Europe and America.

The rise and fall of the Bauhaus was symptomatic of a general trend, and can be understood only in context, not in isolation. The political attacks against the Bauhaus increased in proportion to its healthy influence. All over Germany the powers of reaction were consolidating their forces and campaigned to regain political and ideological power. The Bauhaus had already been accused of "cultural Bolshevism" in 1919; its end in Weimar was a foregone conclusion the moment its opponents gained power in the state of Thuringia. The new government terminated the Bauhaus contract. Early in 1925 negotiations were begun with the mayor of Dessau, and favorable offers were received. But we shall not trace the history of the Bauhaus. What concerns us is the problems faced by the Bauhaus artists. The issue to be decided was whether a collective or a personal decision would be made.

106

Klee and Muche had already accepted an invitation by Wichert to go to Frankfurt. Klee was reluctant to break his promises, though Wichert had assured him that he retained freedom of decision. Feininger hesitated, wishing to remain with the Bauhaus but feeling that his teaching obligations were a hindrance to his work. All felt the need for a collective decision, and in the end it was decided to move together to Dessau. Feininger agreed; he was granted the privilege of joining without teaching; his presence was felt to be desirable and important for masters and pupils alike.

Feininger was offered a professorship in Weimar at the art school there, which now had the architect Otto Bartning as principal, but he preferred to be with his old friends.

The importance of Feininger as a teacher has been beautifully expressed by Muche: "At the Bauhaus Feininger exemplified the mysterious process of creation of the artist contained within himself, drawing from his inner depth and giving out the essence. . . . In that sense Feininger could not have a 'pedagogic method,' no art teaching with laid-down concepts with which to convince. He taught without intentions by the precept of his presence as a man and a creative artist."[26] And Gropius says, "I would like to emphasize the extraordinary effect of Feininger's outstanding human qualities on his students in the Bauhaus. His remarkable attitude of modesty, even in front of a mediocre student, combined with his loving empathy for young people struggling to find their own way had a magnetic effect on them. The humility shown to them increased their courage and self-respect; they left in a state of stimulation which is the precondition for creativity and, after all, the best education can offer."[27] And Muche continues, "The Bauhaus . . . is admired today, one looks for the reason and believes to find it in its teachings and aims. . . . The secret of the creativity of the Bauhaus was the spirit that we can still feel in Feininger's words and his works — the spirit that linked him and his friends."[28]

On February 12, 1925, the masters held a meeting in Klee's studio, and in the afternoon the mayor of Dessau and his officials came to an agreement with the masters. "To all of us the thought that we can *remain together* is most important and consoling."[29]

Marcks went to Halle (Burg Giebichenstein); all others decided to go to Dessau. When Klee still hesitated, Feininger explained to him that, if he went alone to Frankfurt, he would be regarded there with a curiosity "usually reserved for fabulous animals."[30]

An exhibition of the Bauhaus painters seemed to have been planned for New York. "I talked with Klee about the exhibition of the Bauhaus masters in New York. Klee has refused, because he also is too short of works for the show. So I am not the only one of us, who stands aside."[31] On October 13, 1925, Gropius returned from Dessau with the news that building was proceeding, and that the new Bauhaus might be ready early in the new year.

When the Bauhaus moved to Dessau, the Feiningers remained for a time alone in Weimar, awaiting the completion of the houses that Gropius was building for the form masters (page xii). During July the family moved to Dessau, and, with the summer of 1926, a new period in the life of the painter began.

THE BAUHAUS YEARS — DESSAU

1926–1932, Dessau, Deep, Halle

On July 30, 1926, Feininger arrived in Dessau. *"Everybody* here is *charming! . . .* Reception at Klee's house . . . tea with Kandinskys."[1] The new house was a great success — good light, good rooms, and a feeling of space. The only drawback was that a multitude of Dessau burghers came to stare at the modern houses with flat roofs. Occasionally they stared into the windows. In Dessau, too, the Bauhaus was an alien intruder, but for the time being the difficulties of the last years in Weimar had been forgotten.

He was now much freer than he had been in Weimar, and his feeling of freedom found expression in his work. During the late summer Feininger returned to Deep. From 1926 on, his paintings, mainly pictures of the sea, became lighter, while gaining in formal strength.

The *Glorious Victory of the Sloop "Maria"* (a famous New York yacht of the 1840s; page 109) may serve as an example of Feininger's observations of what he called the "dual sky" [zweierlei Himmel]. This duality, observed in nature, is used with dramatic effect. The dual sky is presented in dual color: in the complementaries mauve and bluish green. The duality of sky and water is given by a mirrorlike but not identical reflection of shapes. The large, dark triangle in the water is reflected by an inverted triangle in the left sky; the planes of the right sky are echoed in the shapes of the left water. The picture is composed in the shape of a rectangular cross with each of the four sections playing against all the others. In this fugal formalization, true observation of boats and light is the actual basis for the formal construction. No system is imposed upon nature; rather, natural forces find formal expression.

In *The Bird Cloud* (page 101) it is again the light that orders the shape of the picture. If the *Sloop "Maria"* was based on division of horizontals and verticals, *The Bird Cloud* is based on the intersection of diagonals. The cloud, in the shape of a flying bird, becomes a constellation of light in the sky, with its shadow on the ground. The play of diagonals arises on a firm horizon, where, as often occurs in Feininger, the lightest color (here yellow) plays the strongest part.

It is quite characteristic of Feininger's contradictory or, as we have called it, contrapuntal approach to painting that he reverses the value of color. Thus, a light color can become the darkest point of a picture; a recession in color — which traditionally goes from dark to light — Feininger reverses. This continuous play between the expected and the unexpected, this reversal of laws and creation of a new logic of color and perspective, distinguishes his painting. Feininger's use of color is often paradoxical. He uses it sometimes to enhance the formal value of shape, at other times to negate it — a weak shape is given a strong color, a strong shape a weak color. In the same paradoxical way, he treats light color as strong, and dark color as light.

Within a picture Feininger used complementary colors as interchangeable. His

108

12 Glorious Victory of the Sloop "Maria," 1926 (265)

choice of complementaries was never the straight blue-yellow or red-green pair of opposites; he ranged over the whole scale of intermediate complementaries and achieved chromatic results that had never been achieved before. The glow — the luminosity — that he gives to his color is astounding. The luminosity of the colors arises from their contrast; the complementaries do not merge or cancel each other out — they sharpen the conflict. Every smallest part of the picture lives through the clash of colors. The glow arises from the interrelation of the colors themselves. Feininger developed a form of divisionism, which resembles Seurat's in that color is applied in small dots. These colors do not merge in one tonality but retain their own luminosity, contributing their share to the active tonality of the picture. Feininger has actually invented "new" colors in the sense that he has discovered chromatic possibilities not previously perceived. The similarity in approach between Feininger and Seurat was first noted by Eduard Trier[2] and recently by Alfred Hentzen.[3] The identity of aims appears twofold — in the monumental silhouette giving the summary of a shape, and in the development of a new aerial perspective, which is built with tonal values in firm, glasslike planes. Both organize space as receding in "quantum" steps, each step being separate and marked, as opposed to the fused aerial perspective of the Impressionists. The nearest forerunner can be seen in Poussin's clear, stagelike organization of receding planes in space.

In Feininger's sea pictures one observes a shadow play of light — as one can observe in his architectural paintings a play of shadows. The shadow reveals the possibilities which the object contains within itself. Distortion is not arbitrary but the projection of one possibility that the shadow can take from the original form. With the source of light in the picture itself in movement, acutely angled forms arise that owe their origin to the object. These projections, in their meeting and interpenetration, create new structures in space. In Cubism the viewpoint of the spectator and, with it, perspective entered the picture and began to move; in Feininger's pictures the source of light has entered the picture as well, and begins to move, illuminating objects from within and projecting new aspects of their form. The prismatic appearance of Feininger's pictures has, thus, different causes: the prismatic color arises from the refraction of colored shadows; the prismatic formations in space are the result of projected shadows, which, in their interpenetration with other shadows, organize themselves into new structures in which the projected image of their original form is contained and modified. The shadow projections of colors and shapes form the event of the picture arising as structure.

The year 1927 marked an important change in Feininger's work. He spoke of the liberation from the purely static, that will give him a new conception of "pictorial form" [Bildform].[4] In his development he had passed through a period of rigid organization of space. From his Cubist form he had reached a static picture form with space and light firmly organized, creating a new pictorial reality. This static form had exhausted its creative possibilities exactly as the Cubist still-life form had exhausted the inventive power of Picasso. Feininger's own inventions became for him a prison from which he had to break out. This breaking through the static form to freedom did not happen in one jump, but by a process of evolution from within

13 Marine (1927) (278)

the picture space itself. It was through the liberation of color that Feininger broke the firm yet too rigid structure of his forms. He was never to abandon order and clarity, but the severity that had possessed him was loosened from within. Equally well-ordered planes were to arise, to form less rigid pictures. He had to go through the discipline of severity before he felt free to abandon it on the level of achievement that he had reached.

Color took on new meaning in his work. He wrote, "Colors that once were only colorful [bunt] now become sonorous [klingend] again and subordinate themselves to the whole."[5] "I am attempting to 'paint' from the 'matière' [Material]."[6] "I have a picture on the easel now which really promises to arise from color. . . . Yesterday I understood the secret . . . planes and forms conceived as color."[7] As a means of liberation his new understanding of his charcoal compositions was the key. That discovery came simultaneously with the discovery of the independence of color. "Strange to say: my charcoal compositions are also 'things in themselves' — as drawings, no more than stimuli for the pictures which obey entirely different laws. To transfer such studies into color does not work."[8] By letting the structural problems solve themselves in the abstract black and white he could allow the color of the picture to arise from the spirit of the color alone. His colors came to act together as forces creating what he called "sonority" [Klang] in the same way that his forms act as forces or rhythms. Such sonority contains an element of time. The interplay of colors creates a living, vibrating process that is not static but fluid. To the dynamism of form the sonority of color has been added. There are, thus, more mobile powers to interact and enrich the sum of possibilities.

The paintings of 1927 show the first results of this development. Without established control of form the new freedom of color could not have been allowed to develop. Formal strength has become the self-evident framework within which color could now range freely.

Steamer "Odin" II (page 206) has, for this period, an oddly Futurist excitement; Feininger himself considered it to belong to an earlier period. A very similar composition is *Marine (1927)* (page 111). Color here has loosened; the planes are enlivened from within; the design is formal, even rigid; but the brushwork — and, for the first time since his earliest work, one can again speak of visible brush strokes — is free and painterly.

In three paintings of the sea Feininger reached a poetic simplicity and clarity that border on the abstract — not in the sense of nonobjective but in the sense of essential. These are *Dunes at Evening* (cat. 291), *Mouth of the Rega I* (cat. 283), and *Before the Rain* (cat. 288). Timelessness has been created with the suspension of time — the moment of eternity, which resembles eternity itself as a drop resembles the ocean. To the poet, "reality is translucent,"[9] and to Feininger the world dissolves into transparency. Not the romantic boundless universe, without end or beginning, but the classical universe of bounds and order. The poetry of the world is the content of Feininger's pictures. Silence is the precondition of harmony, stillness the void in which events find their resonance; and out of nothing appears the iridescence of the invisible made actual.

The architectural compositions of this period include *Dröbsdorf I* (cat. 301), which

14 Architecture III, 1927 (272)

has a lightness and looseness not achieved before. Color now plays the new vital part that Feininger had discovered for it. In *Yellow Village Church I* (cat. 281) the planes do not interpenetrate with a dynamically directed force but, in their transparency, create the intersections of their existence in space, removed in distance from the observer like a world transmuted behind a curtain of glass.

Wilhelm Boeck makes an interesting comparison between Picasso's approach to the painting of architecture and Feininger's: "Picasso's method of articulating the picture surface by radial planes is perhaps best clarified by a comparison with the related and yet entirely different methods used by Lyonel Feininger in his city views. Feininger too divides the plane by radial lines, but he invests the spatial layers and their complicated optical refractions with a disembodied transparency, beside which Picasso's scaffolding seems robust and material. Compared with Feininger's spiritual reflection of the external world, Picasso's picture is a rigidly organized, independent new creation, in which the original experience appears merely as *le souvenir d'un souvenir.*"[10]

Architecture with Stars (page 207) and *Architecture III* (also called *Gables II*; page 113) represent the highest point of spiritualization and abstraction in Feininger's work to date. Forms that retain the outline and meaning of their origin appear in a world of new order. *Gables II* glows in deep red and deep blue, opaque and solid within a mysterious translucency. Here the old Lüneburg that had captivated Feininger with its picturesque charm and had held him close to the subject, finds its first transformation. Comparing this with a picture of strange spiritual and formal kinship, *Green Orange Gradation with Black Half Moon* by Klee (Busch-Reisinger Museum, Harvard University, Cambridge, Mass.), one recognizes a similarity between the two artists and friends both in awareness and expression. There is no mutual influence, but a strong bond of sympathy.

The paintings of this short period are the most poetic of all Feininger's work, revealing a side of his spirit that was to find new expression in a different form twenty years later.

One painting unique in Feininger's work dates from that year (1927) – *Broken Glass* (page 115). This picture stands quite by itself not only in Feininger's work but in modern art. In its combination of real and unreal, substantial and insubstantial, order and accident, it is a synthesis of all the opposites with which Feininger's knowledge of the world was concerned. It is an epitome and an epitaph. It is one of the great moments and monuments of our century. Feininger once had said of himself, "Spatial Cubism will need one martyr."[11] We might say, this is his monument.

At the end of the year 1927, Feininger's connections with America were revived by a visit of two young Americans, one of whom was to play an important part in the history of modern art. He was so excited that he sat down immediately to write to Julia: "Now, think *why* I am writing in English? I have had almost two hours together with 2 charming young 'academic' Americans (Harvard University). . . . Yesterday all day they wandered about Dessau, saw the Bauhaus, were at the Church Concert in the evening, and are so enthusiastic about everything. One is a 'professor' but like a boy of 25, and intensely interested in my work. He saw it at

15 Broken Glass, 1927 (280)

115

the 'Blue Four' in California! and is going to write all about modern German Art, of which nothing at all has been written in England and America — and wants to know *all* my work. They both are coming again to-morrow and I shall have them eat a chop with us at $1^{1}/_{2}$ o'clock so that we have a good long time together. The 'professor,' Mr. Alfred Hamilton Barr, Jr., has bought an aquarell from 'Fides,' ... and I got the enclosed letter from Probst this morning, before the Americans came! where Probst says that the aquarell goes to America! And the other young man [12] was so interested to see my 'fugue XII' on the piano, that we played it together — and they both were delighted and full of wonder! We may try some other fugues tomorrow. How I wished you might be here to meet these young men! They are staying perhaps for a few days yet — tomorrow I bring them to Klee, whom they want to meet. They were at Moholy's and are now at Schlemmer's. Kandinsky is not well enough to receive them. You can imagine how much we talked!" [13]

From this meeting a lasting friendship developed, and when, not so many years later, Feininger returned to his native country, the young "academic" had become the founder and director of the Museum of Modern Art in New York.

In 1928 Feininger wrote to Barr [14] that he was concerned to get in touch with the United States, for it was necessary for him to return there "within a year or so"; he had received permission from United States authorities to remain in Dessau for some time, but would eventually have to return if he was to retain his nationality. At that time, it was not the political developments in Germany that made Feininger think of returning to the United States but his desire to retain his citizenship, which he had preserved throughout the war. His sentimental ties with his native country kept an American future alive in his mind. Danger signs on the political scene in Germany were not lacking, however. By the end of the first year of the Bauhaus in Dessau, a local election revealed that a new fight against the Bauhaus was in the making and that the same reactionary movement which was gaining strength all over Germany and which had been effective in Weimar was at work in Dessau also.

The whole question of why antagonism to modern art was an essential element in reactionary thought is worth considering. The reactionary political movements made use of the abhorrence of modern art, which was widespread, and in doing so were on the safe grounds of popular prejudice. They appeared as the defenders of common sense, and could count on the support of a majority averse to any new outlook. Animosity toward modern art, as a political platform, was important for the very reason that it had no political importance at all, serving as a uniting force for the heterogeneous elements of discontent, which had nothing in common but their prejudices.

Feininger's life was now fairly strictly divided into a winter half in Dessau and a summer half on the Baltic. Music — playing Bach and his favorite organ composers as well as his own compositions on his harmonium — occupied him much of the time. He still played the violin every day. During a visit to Dresden to see an exhibition of his work at Fides, he met Fritz Busch, Rudolf Serkin and Emil Nolde. Stokowski and other musicians visited him in Dessau.

During these years his fugues also received their first public performance. Willi

Apel had played Fugue IX in the Meistersaal at the Bauhaus on December 3, 1924, and again at a concert in Leipzig early in 1929. Fugue VI was played at the opening of the Blue Four exhibition in 1926 at Los Angeles. When Clarke of Stanford University played the fugue, Bloch commented: "No one in America could write such a fugue."[15]

In the years 1926 to 1930 exhibitions of living art held in German museums and in private galleries followed in rapid succession. Feininger was represented in most of them. He sometimes did not have enough paintings to meet all the many requests. He exhibited regularly at Probst's Fides in Dresden. His dealers were Goldschmidt and Wallerstein in Berlin, who, however, had no exclusive rights. Flechtheim at one time had wanted to take over Feininger's work, but through a misunderstanding this plan did not materialize. Feininger himself was much too withdrawn to seek exhibitions.

In Berlin, Justi had arranged a room at the Kronprinzen-Palais devoted to Feininger's work. A large retrospective exhibition was first suggested in 1927. During 1928 the Kronprinzen-Palais arranged an exhibition of modern works from private collections in Berlin in which Feininger was represented with twelve paintings. During the same year, Dr. Alois Schardt intended to acquire *Zirchow V* (page 77) for the Museum at Halle, which already owned *Zirchow VI* (cat. 162). These pictures as well as *Viaduct* (page 197) Feininger described as "irreplaceable pictures of former days"; he was delighted that "his strongest pictures would be together under municipal care, and be protected for posterity."[16] The Museum in Halle also acquired a number of graphic works to complete two rooms devoted entirely to Feininger's work.

His public renown increased, but he found that he had traveled to the end of a road and that he had to break through another barrier. Feininger could not rest comfortably on an established style. There was in him a desire equal to Picasso's, though far less easy to recognize, never to retrace a path that had already led to success. Although Feininger limited himself in his choice of subjects, he had a tremendous variety of approaches to the problem of the picture.

The city of Halle intended to commission an artist to paint one picture as a present for the city of Magdeburg. Schardt suggested Feininger, who accepted the invitation and from 1929 to 1931 lived for part of the year in Halle to paint not one but eleven pictures, all of which the Moritzburg Museum acquired. Those eleven paintings were all lost to Halle through the persecution of modern art; and only two have been restored to the city since the war. Of the others, four have again entered public collections in Germany – in Mannheim, Cologne, Hamburg, and Munich; one is in a private collection in the United States; one is in Germany; one was burned; and the whereabouts of the two other pictures remains unknown. Halle also lost all the other works by Feininger that Schardt had acquired.

Feininger had accepted Schardt's offer with confidence. His stay in Halle was made happy by the thoughtful arrangements made for his work. In the old tower of the Moritzburg a studio had been equipped where he could work in a monastic atmosphere of peace and concentration. He was encouraged by his friends Schardt and the sculptor Gerhard Marcks, who had left the Weimar Bauhaus for Halle, and was

117

often visited by Julia and Laurence from nearby Dessau and Wickersdorf. Andreas worked at the Museum, in the photographic studio. Feininger liked the city very much. He wrote from Halle "how colorful" the atmosphere of the city appeared to him, "most beautiful how I suddenly live in a whirl of color [Farbentaumel]! I am sure I could never be like that in Dessau! Here *everything* is colorful, alive and stimulating." [17]

Although the painting of the eleven pictures of the city spanned three years, we shall here consider them as a group. Pictures of other subjects from the same period of activity will be considered later.

As subjects for his pictures of Halle, Feininger selected the Church of St. Mary (Marienkirche), the Cathedral (Dom), and the Red Tower (Rote Turm).

St. Mary's consisted originally of two churches, one dedicated to St. Mary, the other to St. Gertrude. In 1524 these were modified, and the eastern pair of towers of the Church of St. Mary was joined by a bridge, hence the unusual structure. St. Mary's is also called the Church on the Market (Marktkirche). [18]

St. Mary's was painted in several versions. The side view, *Church of St. Mary I* (now in Mannheim; page 211) of 1929, though not translucent, has retained luminosity; the silvery sky is contrasted by deep blues, deep reds, and matte ochre browns, chromatically very rich. The paint surface is opaque and the paint enlivened by free brush strokes; form is built up by color in subtle contrasts. For the first time a white line appears as the definition of a shape. Much later in his work this white line will become a carrier of a new meaning; here it serves to confine a shape that is otherwise treated freely in color. It is a strong composition, monumentally conceived.

This composition was followed by the frontal view of the same church. In *Church of St. Mary* (now in Munich; cat. 327) of 1930, Feininger has taken a conventional view; this is a painting that is approachable from the ground, that the spectator can enter, that is less removed from ordinary vision than most of his paintings. Some elements of the composition have crystallized their form; others have not reached the same stage. In color and composition it is very strong, although not firmly resolved. *Church of St. Mary with the Arrow*, also of 1930 (now back again in Halle; page 212), is the most interesting of the Halle compositions. The transposition from reality has not produced an exploration of the recesses of space but has liberated the forms from their substance; the arrow introduced in the sky echoes shape and meaning of the emancipated architectural form. As in the Munich picture, the composition of the masses is built on a triangle of light. Here the similarity ends. The Munich picture clings to observed reality. In the *Church of St. Mary with the Arrow*, a new reality has been created; a self-willed structure has arisen, owing only a memory to actuality.

The final version, *Church of St. Mary at Night* of 1931 (now lost; cat. 340), goes back to the side view of the first conception.

The Cathedral (Halle; cat. 339) was painted in 1931; this picture is now again in Halle. *Cathedral Choir*, also of 1931 (cat. 335; now in Hamburg), is probably the least resolved of all the Halle pictures, though not without beauty and light. It clings closely to a conventional view.

118

16 Gelmeroda IX, 1926 (263)

Church of St. Mary and Red Tower II, Halle, charcoal, 1929

120

The Red Tower also gave rise to two compositions, both of 1930. *Red Tower I* (cat. 331) is now lost. *Red Tower II* (cat. 332) is in a private collection in America. Here, too, the view is conventional in the sense that it is one of the few paintings by Feininger into which the spectator could enter on the level of the foreground. The view is an extension of the spectator's view, which was alien to Feininger's conscious removal of the picture from the conventional viewpoint. In the process of bringing the picture down to earth, the intangibility of the autonomous picture has been lost. It is no more a flight of the imagination which adopts viewpoints from above, below, or within the picture; it is the everyday view of the man in the street, and the picture forfeits some of its independence and its mystery.

There are two paintings of Halle not devoted to the great architecture of the city. One, *Am Trödel* (an old market; cat. 317) of 1929, has all the virtues and all the faults of the picturesque.

The Bölbergasse (burned; cat. 338) of 1931 was, however, a daring and new composition with a huge light well of a sky enclosed on three sides in an irregular long polygon with firm and hard rhythms of rectilinear houses, in violent but resolved contrast with the inner part of the light sky.

The last of the Halle pictures, *The Towers Above the City* of 1931 (now in Cologne; page 213), shows the Marktkirche stretched out like a ship riding above the roofs, composed somewhat like one of Feininger's sea pictures with a vast sky ordered by the architectural shapes that penetrate it. Yet this picture, too, has not quite soared above its earthly station.

The Halle pictures caused Feininger great difficulties. With all their coloristic richness they are far less "transposed" than his previous work and they have not always found their pictorial completion. Two reasons can be found to explain why Feininger's Halle pictures, beautiful as some are, have fallen short of the high achievements he had reached in 1927. The paintings of Halle were commissioned, and for the first time in his life Feininger painted for a known patron. The temptation to be "understood" may have been strong and may have exerted a pull toward greater naturalism. A further cause must be seen in the fact that Feininger, for the first and last time in his life, made photographs of the subjects and used them for his compositions. That this made his work all the more difficult he realized very soon. In a letter to Schardt he wrote from Deep, "I have begun with the composition of some Halle pictures. It is at first very difficult to get away somewhat from the photographs . . . in *drawing* from nature a certain selection is made *immediately*. It is much easier to shape the impression into the pictorial form." [19] Feininger had learned by a long and hard process of self-discipline to translate his observations of nature into pictorial terms. That process of transposition, so painfully acquired, he had just brought to a new height of perfection. The Halle pictures have gone in varying degrees toward that final stage of rightness and spiritualization. Their final clarification was impeded by the intrusion of another reality, that of the photograph. A photograph is also a picture but there is no way of transposing a picture into another picture. Finally the artist succeeded in overcoming the obstacle that he had placed in his own way. At the end of the Halle period he wrote to Julia: "I am struggling with the Cathedral picture [Halle] . . . *never* again shall

I work after photographs; that is quite abominable and leads away from the 'pictorial' and [away] from painting altogether."[20] "Three times yesterday and a last time this morning I extinguished the Cathedral picture. Now it is completed, and the hopeless task of freeing it from the photographic has been achieved."[21]

Schardt himself, though very perceptive and thoughtful, had a tendency to "explain" modern art to an audience and to search for means to bring modern art nearer to the public. In an article in the *Jahrbuch der Denkmalspflege der Provinz Sachsen und Anhalt* in 1931 he reproduced photographs of the actual subjects painted by Feininger, taken from the same angle as the paintings and in similar light, to prove that the artist had not abandoned "truth to nature." In this instance the proof was not too difficult, for Feininger actually had based his compositions on photographs. This conception, however, devalues the significance of the autonomous picture. Schardt's merit to have called the Halle pictures into the world is by no means diminished, though his interpretation may have made Feininger's work more difficult and has not made the understanding of his work easier, contrary to what Schardt had hoped.

By the middle of May, 1931, Feininger had completed his task at Halle and was weary of it. "These last pictures do not make me happy. . . . I have no gift for mass production [Serienarbeit]. I could now see hundreds of more beautiful pictures of the town."[22] In describing the paintings of Halle, reference has been made to the spectator who could or could not "enter" the painting. To clarify this distinction, a brief excursion into the history of perspective becomes necessary.

Renaissance painting was based on the principles of rhetoric in the Ciceronian sense.[23] The aim of Ciceronian oratory and of Renaissance painting both was to please, to move, and to convince. This attitude toward painting makes the involvement of the spectator a necessity; it was for the spectator that illusionist perspective was introduced. The modern artist does not tell a story to please, to move, or to convince. The spectator is not addressed directly; he is excluded from the picture's conception. The most obvious change resulting from this new attitude is the abandonment of linear perspective, which had its source in the eyes of the spectator in a central position.

The end of the Renaissance tradition had finally been brought about by the Cubists; when linear perspective was abandoned, the spectator lost his firm point of view from which he could "step into" the picture. The modern picture was constructed from many viewpoints, even from within the picture space itself.

In Feininger's work one can distinguish different approaches to perspective. In his architectural compositions a multitude of viewpoints are used, and the spectator cannot find one position from which he could "walk" into the picture as he could with traditional paintings. Among Feininger's pictures there are several in which an overriding central perspective, from the spectator's point of view, is combined with the inner perspectives of the picture. Those compositions make an "entry" possible — and therefore remain nearer to nature and are comparatively "acceptable" because they involve a lesser degree of alienation. Feininger's most mysterious and removed compositions are those into which one can enter only spiritually. In his paintings of the sea, the conventional perspective is enlarged and summarized

Village in the Rain, pen-and-ink drawing, 1931

to such a degree that the spectator's viewpoint ceases to be actual and becomes imaginary.

The paintings of Halle are only one part of Feininger's work during these years; there are other paintings which carry on the history of his development.

Three paintings of 1928 are concerned with the forms of trees. In *Gelmeroda XI* (cat. 295) the pine tree has almost the same pictorial importance as the church itself. The architecture of man and of nature are placed side by side, revealing the identity of tectonic laws. The church and the tree have grown from the same soil in the same spirit; to the painter this union is revealed in his search for form.

Church in the Woods (cat. 298) carries this thought even further; here the shapes of the pines determine the shape of the church — a mystic marriage of form and meaning.

In *Edge of the Woods* (cat. 304) trees alone serve as architectural elements for the creation of the structure of space and light.

During 1929 and 1930 a remarkable group of yacht and sailing-boat pictures is added to Feininger's œuvre. *The Big Cutters* (cat. 305), *Skerry-Cruisers* (cat. 321), *X 54* (cat. 306), *X 21* (cat. 326), *Mouth of the Rega III* (cat. 318), *Sunset at Deep* (cat. 322), and *Yachts* (cat. 307) all belong to these years. The sailing boat, with its multitude of triangular shapes reacting to the movement of wind and sea, makes visible the forces that act upon it. The boat obeys a number of laws, changing its direction and its speed and, in that process, dividing the space in which it moves. Feininger understood boats and the sea; from his observation and experience he has created vast constructions of space, uniting the elements of air,

123

light, sea, and speed. He stands in the same relation to Turner as Cézanne stood to the Impressionists; he has made something "lasting" of the awareness of atmosphere and movement. He has found solid forms for the laws of change.

Calm at Sea III (page 125) is one of Feininger's greatest achievements of spatial organization. The boats are the interpreters of space. There is, however, more to see and understand than structural principles. In Feininger's work, the mystery that is inexpressible must be comprehended. Working on this picture he wrote, "I am working at the small painting 'Calm at Sea III' with utmost tenacity. It is no smooth sailing, but I'm getting into painting, and am not afraid to go ahead: placing color onto color, washing off again, energizing form, compelling the picture into supernature. Inch by inch, however, I have to struggle to transform the object into terms of picture-space."[24]

The *Pyramid of Sails* of 1930 (cat. 328) is remarkable for its depth and mystery. On the almost black sea two different sonorities, a violet-yellow and an ochre-blue, play with and against each other. Space is dissolved in color and organized by movement. The line of the horizon is broken, keeping the surface of the sea in flux. Light, matter, and movement interpenetrate, creating a poetry of space.

The sea gave to the painter greater freedom to express his awareness of the cosmos than did his architectural subjects, where he was by necessity bound to a given organization of form. His own vision of the order of the world could be more fully expressed in the empty space of the sea and the sky. The static element of architecture forced some of its own laws on the painter's vision; the transformation had to begin with a solid object. In his pictures of the sea, the laws of his imagination found form; in his architectural paintings, the forms had to find their equivalent in his imagination.

The process of thought and work is thus reversed. In the paintings of the sea he masters his vision; in the paintings of architecture he masters the object. In the one he imposes form; in the other he liberates form. In this dialectic of force and liberty, Feininger releases the form-giving and form-finding elements of his creative ability. In the present phase of his work, he found the task of the liberation of form from the object the harder task.

His letters describing the slow and painful process in the completion of *Gelmeroda XII* (page 209) have their place in this context, giving insight into the painter's mind while he was at work. "I had a lot of work to complete 'Gelmeroda XII'; the *over*completion [das *Über*fertige] of some parts I had to paint out — but now all is again atmosphere and I leave it as it is. In a few weeks I could still alter it."[25] He wrote on April 16: "'Gelmeroda XII', morning, noon, and night! That picture *must* go right [muss werden]."[26] On April 19, he wrote: "At eleven I went on the roof to lie down in the sun for an hour doing nothing — after I had ruined 'Gelmeroda' completely — and that was very wise. Afterwards I painted so well, that even I was pleased — some important divisions in the picture were corrected — with that the space suddenly gained in balance [Ausgleich] and significance [Bedeutung],"[27] and on April 22, he said: "I have tanned almost the color of a red Indian. . . and with the cunning of a red Indian I am weighing every new spot of color on 'Gelmeroda' . . . some things have altered, but now it's coming right."[28]

124

17 Calm at Sea III, 1929 (308)

The work that goes into the making of a work of art remains invisible. If one now sees *Gelmeroda XII*, with its calm poise and indisputable "rightness," one forgets (what normally one does not even know) the doubts and hesitations, the many possibilities from which the final work emerged. As it now confronts us in the perfection of a mirror fugue, divided by the steeple as the great caesura, a painting of almost mathematical perfection, one is tempted to measure the proportions, to find the echoes and the conflicts in color, the inversions in shapes, and so to establish a law of stabilized harmonies. But this would be wrong. No law ordained it; no rule commanded it. It is balance and perfection, achieved through wisdom arrested at one point of its existence.

The *Regler Church (Erfurt)* (cat. 324) is many steps further removed from observation than some of the Halle pictures. Here the essence of the structure is distilled. The towers rise as in a vision; they are substantial but spiritualized — suspended in "special space." The church rests firmly on this earth, but an incursion by the spectator is made impossible; the space has been organized as picture space, not our space. Within the colors a secret play between "dead" and glowing paint heightens the transformation from the real to the unreal. The fusion of planes in an interplay of forces creates stability through opposition.

The *Ruin by the Sea* (cat. 330, whereabouts now unknown) is one of Feininger's most interesting pictures. There are extant ten pencil studies after nature, all from July 11, 1928, for this painting. From these the "approachable" view has been excluded in favor of the "unapproachable" view (pages 126, 127). The subject has been removed from this world into the world of the autonomous picture. The motif in the painting itself contains all the memories and shadows of reality; it

Ruin by the Sea, pencil drawing, 1928

Ruin by the Sea, pencil drawing, 1928

projects its shape and its moods like a lighthouse of unreality. The romantic quality of the ruin as such has been transformed into a new order, weird but logical; the suffering ruin has become an active force. A painting of 1940, *Ruin on the Cliff II* (cat. 397), goes back to the same studies of 1928.

In *Gables III* (also called *Lüneburg II*, page 210), as in some Lüneburg subjects, the picture tends to remain more firmly fixed in the field of observed architecture. The new use of solid color is confined to the buildings; the sky retains its translucency. Yet, with all its solidity, it has its own mystery. The first use of "graphic" means in painting will be seen here appearing in the gables of the highest houses on the left. Those graphic elements we shall find fully developed in Feininger's late American period.

In 1929, the newly founded Museum of Modern Art in New York included Feininger in its first exhibition, entitled "19 Living Americans," with seven pictures, listing him for the first time as an American artist. Alfred Barr, who arranged the exhibition and wrote the catalogue, thus reclaimed Feininger for his native country. Feininger, in a letter of January 29, 1930,[29] expressed his own pleasure not only for being recognized in America but also for contact with a wider world than the ever more restrictive atmosphere of Germany. In 1930 the first news of sales in the United States arrived from Los Angeles, from Galka Scheyer's exhibition of the Blue Four.[30] At the time these first signs of recognition in America had no influence on Feininger's life and thought, but, a few years later, the fact that his name and his work were not entirely unknown in his own country was to be decisive for the course of his life and his art.

While Feininger was working in Halle during the winters, and at Deep during the summers, the Bauhaus was undergoing important changes. Gropius had left in

1928, to be succeeded by Hannes Meyer. Feininger's own contract expired in 1928 but he remained associated without any obligations. During Feininger's stay in Halle, his friends Gerhard Marcks and Alois Schardt had tried to persuade him to settle in Halle at Schloss Giebichenstein, the Art School where Gerhard Marcks worked. Though Feininger desired a change, the thought of leaving his remaining friends at the Bauhaus, Klee and Kandinsky, was too hard to bear.[31] The coming disintegration of the Bauhaus could already be perceived. The growing political tension, the depressed mood at the Bauhaus, all weighed on the sensitivity of the artist. In Thuringia, meanwhile, the National Socialists had formed the government. One of the first acts of the new party in power was the removal of modern works from the museum in Weimar, foreshadowing the events of later years. Feininger was very tired after the winter of 1930–31, and eager for an entire change of climate and impressions. His old friend, Theodore Spicer-Simson, the English portrait medalist (a medal of Feininger's head exists in bronze from the year 1927), had a country house in Bourron near Paris, and invited Feininger. On June 6, 1931, he arrived at Bourron. The change "liberates body and soul!"[32] he wrote. He made long tours on a bicycle through the countryside. During June, he revisited Paris. Outside his old studio at the Boulevard Raspail the trees had grown so much that the windows were now in the shade, but everything else remained as it had been before, and he spent his days in the happy recollection of the years in Paris when he had become a painter. At the end of June he joined his family at Quimper, and visited from there Concarneau, Benodet, Tréboul, Douarnenez, Audierne. Quimper, he wrote, "contains some wonderful old churches & entire streets."[33] There are many drawings and watercolors of Quimper and the Brittany coast, but no paintings were based on the drawings. The German bank crash of 1931 forced the family to return to Germany in August of that year. He returned to Deep for the remainder of the summer, and wrote, "I am making good drawings from Concarneau and Tréboul."[34]

In 1931 Feininger was sixty. It was his twenty-fifth year as a painter. Several exhibitions in honor of his sixtieth birthday were being held in Germany. Probst arranged a large show in Dresden that was also shown at the Folkwang Museum. Since his youth, Feininger's attitude to life and people had been one of withdrawal. He liked company, he loved birthdays and parties, but he remained within the circle of his family and friends. He never liked crowds, exhibitions, publicity. Anything that took his anonymity from him seemed to take away part of his personality. Like a man afraid to lose his shadow, he felt, when his name was mentioned, that he had lost something of himself. The possibility of a retrospective exhibition at the Kronprinzen-Palais (the building of the National Gallery in Berlin devoted to modern art) had been discussed. Feininger had been reluctant to agree to it. He thought that the time for the exhibition was either too late or too early. At fifty, he thought, he had been at the height of his power and, at seventy, he might have completed his work.[35] But his objections were overcome, and the exhibition was arranged for the autumn of that year.

The exhibition at the Kronprinzen-Palais became the most important exhibition of his lifetime. Never before or after were so many of his paintings brought together.

Eight galleries at the Kronprinzen-Palais were devoted to paintings, watercolors, and drawings. A letter written shortly before the opening reveals the artist's attitude. "Do you think the exhibition will be good? I have the feeling that the exhibition tears away my anonymity — there is almost a feeling of 'exhibitionism,' because the effect on the public of such strange work must be principally one of curiosity and unfamiliarity; 'Sensationalism.' I declare honestly, that if I could prevent it now, I would gladly do so. I don't think I care to see it, even!"[36] Two days later he wrote to Julia, "Yesterday your beautiful long letter from Berlin made me *so* happy . . . your joy about the exhibition makes me cheerful!"[37]

Justi had invited the American Embassy to the opening, which pleased Feininger, and he asked, "Will my compatriots be interested?"[38] History does not record the answer to the question. A friend, Mr. Emmanuel Benson, had written from New York that I. B. Neumann had told him that "thousands daily stream into my exhibition."[39] Feininger commented, "The world has a good news service." When he eventually visited the exhibition, he retained his anonymity by paying admission at the door.

The exhibition was beautifully and intelligently arranged, grouped according to the artist's creative periods, with paintings, drawings, and watercolors in orderly sequence in separate rooms. Thus, the exhibition gave a clear and logical outline of the artist's achievements in his twenty-five years as a painter. Feininger's whole *œuvre* up to that date was represented by his greatest works. With this exhibition, Feininger was recognized by a wide public as one of the great figures of the art of the time.

It was fortunate that this retrospective exhibition at the Kronprinzen-Palais was held in 1931. It was very nearly the last moment of the German republic, which had just one more year to live, or, rather, to die.

In the summer of 1932, the city council of Dessau, where the National Socialists had gained a majority, voted against the continuation of the Bauhaus. Feininger commented bitterly, "That the Social Democrats refrained from voting is only characteristic."[40] In that one sentence the essence of the political situation was clearly defined. The Bauhaus was only a minor local political question, but the same defeatism that let the Bauhaus go under without struggle brought down the whole edifice of the German republic. The Bauhaus could exist only within the framework of a liberal political system. It had begun its life in 1919 in Weimar when the National Versammlung gave Germany its democratic constitution. It had to end when the Weimar Republic ended and the democratic constitution was suppressed. The end came in 1933, when the National Socialists came to power and abolished all democratic institutions and, with them, freedom of thought and expression.

WITHDRAWAL FROM THE GERMAN SCENE

1933–1937, Berlin (Siemensstadt)

In March, 1933, when Feininger left Dessau, his pictures were stored at the museum in Halle, in the Moritzburg where he had worked for so long. Then he and Julia went to Deep to spend the summer, and friends offered them a house near Berlin for the winter of 1933–34.

Feininger the American was homeless in Germany. His main concern was for the future of his sons. Fortunately, they had all completed their training and were already successful in their work. In a strange way, the three sons had inherited separately the gifts of their father. Andreas had begun as an architect; he later became a famous photographer. Laurence was a scholarly musicologist. Theodore Lux, the youngest, was a painter. Thus architecture, optics, music, and painting, the essential interests of Feininger's life, found their reflection in the work of his sons. For Julia and himself, the future they had to face together, surrounded by the forces of hate that had changed the face of Germany, looked bleak. A time and a tradition had come to an end. The painter found himself face to face with a hostile world. He painted little. One cannot perceive a clear stylistic development in Feininger's work. Among the pictures of the years 1933–37 there are some important and beautiful paintings. These owe their form to the stylistic development of the past and belong in spirit and achievement to the forms he had previously created.

In one group of paintings, however, he explored new possibilities. These are closely related to his watercolors of the same period, beginning in 1933, where all transparency and atmospheric considerations were abandoned. He was preoccupied, as never before, with the "object." The object was becoming more independent; it poses itself as a riddle that cannot be penetrated but can only be apprehended. It was as if he held a toy in his hand — a sailing boat he had made himself — his eyes closed as he felt it. Removed from the real world, the painter has taken possession of a piece of wood and the recollection of its form. One has the impression that the painter asks: What is real? What am I? But, because he is a painter, he has to go on painting to be himself. A profound sadness speaks from these pictures of childlike greatness.

Two paintings, *Caravels* (cat. 356) and *Marine (after woodblock)* (cat. 355), based on his own woodcuts, are significant, because the objects, toy sailing boats on a fairy-tale sea, are apprehended as detached objects. The reality of the object in its isolation is at the same time denied, because the object, to start with, was a man-made toy. The whole picture is a dream with the magic of childhood.

In the drawings of the years 1933–34 Feininger created planes by a succession of parallel or near-parallel black lines; according to their intervals, the planes appear more or less solid, creating a shape and becoming gauges of space. Feininger's feeling for intervals and gradations had found a new pictorial outlet. The drawings, which either remained in black and white or were given strong, plain color, delib-

130

Pen-and-ink drawing, 1934

erately unsubtle and direct, represent his main work of the period. One can feel a conscious coldness and hardness. There is denial of "beauty" and an emphasis on logic and reason; yet the fine play of the parallel lines results in new beauty and reason enriches feeling. Feininger called these "flag pictures" because color was used in two or three clear bands divided like a flag.

In his paintings he was concerned with isolated objects in space. They are real objects, painted in solid planes, more removed than ever before in his work. It is a strange encounter between the thing and the mind. This tendency is developed in a painting of 1935, *Mill in Spring* (page 217), where the objects have become entirely static and the painting stiffly formalized. Forerunners of these pictures could be seen in the paintings of Heringsdorf from 1912; then, too, these paintings marked an intermediate period between the tragic-gay carnival pictures and the new experiments leading to new solutions — the construction of form and space. Now again, these paintings of striped planes are an intermediate stage in the development. New solutions of space will appear later in Feininger's work. Three paintings of sailing ships date from 1936 and 1937; *Barque at Sea* (cat. 378) and *Mid-Ocean* (cat. 385) belong to this group. In these pictures, Feininger's extension of spatial depth has been abandoned; a flat pattern of broad bands of color serves for the definition of planes. These are sad and lonely pictures, filled with a longing for something unattainable. The *Four-Masted Bark* (page 220) is a toy boat — rigid, wooden, geometrical, man-made.

But in *Ship of Stars II* (cat. 386) the painter breaks through the hard form of the preceding pictures, and, suddenly, a true magic quality appears, with a ship floating in a space of its own, holding its own secrets and releasing itself from the bounds of reality — a sailing boat as unreal as the Flying Dutchman. In the toy-boat painting the sea has taken hold of the boat; in the *Ship of Stars* the boat has taken hold of the sea. One boat is as shapeless as the waves; the other shapes the waves in its own reflection. Here in two pictures is the dilemma of the artist: Will the object run away from its maker, or will the maker impose his will on the object? For Feininger there is always a classical and a romantic answer.

These paintings in oils owe their origin to Feininger's earlier watercolors. The *Ship of Stars II* is closely related to the many fantastic "children's drawings," as he called them himself, of the years 1918 and 1919. The other painting derives from the rigid style of his watercolors developed since 1933. The *Ship of Stars* links Feininger's magic fantasy of his early years with his late works. One might, in the *Ship of Stars*, see a forerunner of Feininger's late style or one might think of it as the link that connects the young painter with his later self. A truly magic quality will appear in paintings much later in his life. The *Ship of Stars* still stands alone. If the purely formal pictures served no purpose other than to free the artist from a preoccupation with the object removed from its context, then they were a necessary part of his development.

From the same period, 1932 to 1937, we have paintings that owe their form to the experience of past achievements. The *Mill in Autumn* (page 214) and *Afternoon Light II* (cat. 350), both of 1932, are still pictures of space organized by light. The paint surface itself begins to become more opaque; this process will continue and lead to a different form of painting. Both paintings are desolate and lonely. In *Afternoon Light II* one can observe the new use of patches of color, which no more define the forms but loosen them. This development, as well as the mood of this painting, will reappear in his pictures.

The *Bathers* (page 215) of 1933 is a very somber picture, derived from the earlier *Bathers I* (cat. 109), which Feininger had described as "netherworldly." This figure composition has only one forerunner in the artist's work, the *Portrait of a Tragic Being* (page 93). Here, too, every outline is blurred, and form is achieved by color alone. The paintings are of equal directness and, at the same time, remote and removed, in spite of their Expressionist intensity.

In all the paintings of those years, a tragic isolation can be sensed. In his defense against the world around him, from which he was estranged, Feininger found a resource in his own peculiar form of wit and humor. There is more than a trace of sarcasm and of "Galgenhumor" in *The Red Fiddler* of 1934 (page 133). Here stands the masked magician (thinly disguised as Lyonel Feininger), fiddling on his blue violin while Rome burns, and life goes on its way — the young woman in the front toward seduction, the old man to his grave — and the witch waits for the hunter or the hunted. Feininger's architecture retreats to the wings. Before the backdrop of a stage a play is played, and the diabolic fiddler takes the foreground. This picture is Feininger's answer to the world around him. One may regret that there are so few monumental figure compositions in Feininger's work. His relation to the human figure had always been ambiguous: a great insight and a fear almost of too great an insight, a shy reluctance to probe into the nature of human beings and the caricaturist's knowledge that he knows them too well already.

During the spring and summer of 1934 he returned once more to Deep, and in the autumn took an apartment in Siemensstadt (Berlin), with Julia. In Deep he painted *The Red Fiddler*, contrary to his habit of not painting during the summer months. He spent a few weeks at Kuhtz, at the house of Jutta Schlieffen.

132

18 The Red Fiddler, 1934 (359)

133

It had become nearly impossible to organize exhibitions and sales of modern art. The livelihood of the artists was undermined, and economic distress was added to the spiritual isolation in which they lived. Feininger was more fortunate than many because the deferred payments from Halle still arrived. At the end of December he wrote to his son Lux, "It is a very ... modest little life we are leading. I can make a bed now very decently. ... It's a good thing, sez I, to *have* a bed to make!"[1] It is not uninteresting to note that Feininger from now on will write nearly all his letters in English, whereas before, in Germany, with very few exceptions he wrote in German. Quite unconsciously the feeling of alienation expresses itself in abandoning the German language, revealing that he, as an American, takes no part in the world and the happenings around him.

The year 1935 was not very different from the preceding year. In March, he learned from Schmidt-Rottluff that their pictures were to be judged that day (March 24, 1935) by a Committee. Schmidt-Rottluff thought their chances very slight. The Committee, of course, was a Nazi organization set up to judge "degenerate art." "About my work, except that I am working, I still think best to preserve silence! I will only say that I am hopeful ('hopeful'! in a hopeless period of cultural history, in a land where all cultural elements are systematically persecuted) — one is only hopeful for one's own endeavors."[2]

For the summer he returned once more to the Baltic, for the last time in his life. "I see that without joy, without future I can not work ... all impulse, all breath of life is lacking."[3] He had come to the end of a road.

Then a new road was opened to him. Alfred Neumeyer of Mills College, Oakland, California, invited him to teach at a six-week summer-course session there in 1936. This was the first call the painter had received from America. He was now sixty-five. His work, his life, and his reputation had been built in the context of art in Germany. His name was hardly known in the United States. He had none of the illusions that so many Europeans had. He was an American himself, and he knew how hard the life of an unknown painter would be. This invitation meant a possibility to explore. Some months in America could help him make his decision, and he accepted.

His road now turned back to New York. From Berlin he went to Hamburg, where he had first landed in 1887. Their last meal he and Julia took in a restaurant opposite the old Gewerbeschule where he once had taken his first drawing lessons; on May 6 they embarked on the *Manhattan* for New York.

When they arrived, the friends of Feininger's young days, Kortheuer and Strothmann, met the boat. After a short stay with friends, during which he renewed old acquaintances and met some of the collectors and dealers, among them Marian Willard and I. B. Neumann, they embarked for California on the *Pennsylvania*, traveling through the Panama Canal and landing at San Pedro in California. This first excursion into the tropics, with new colors and different skies, made a deep impression on Feininger, but did not find expression in any of his paintings. In San Pedro the Feiningers were met by Galka Scheyer, who had over many years been active on the West Coast, promoting the interests of her chosen artists: Feininger, Klee, Kandinsky, Jawlensky. The Feiningers stayed with her for a week and she

134

introduced them to new acquaintances and made them welcome. In San Diego he was met by the director of the museum, Mr. Poland, and made other new friends. On June 19, they reached Mills College. At the college he arranged a small exhibition of his works, with paintings lent by Nierendorf, the art dealer. The Pro Arte Quartet was in residence, and the atmosphere of youthful scholarship and interest in the arts brought Feininger hope for a possible future in America. Excursions to San Francisco resulted later in some drawings and watercolors. The scenery of Nevada and the Yosemite National Park, however, proved too new and strange to form itself into pictures for him.

During his visits he met Miss Grace McCann Morley of the San Francisco Museum, Dr. Heil, director of the De Young Museum, and a large number of people interested in his art. Some collectors bought watercolors or drawings, and, although all this may not seem worth recording, these small gestures and new friendships were important; through them Feininger realized that there was hope and a possible livelihood for him in his own country. Ruth Lawrence acquired then the painting *Dröbsdorf I* (cat. 301) for the University Galleries in Minneapolis.

He returned to New York by train, and from New York he revisited New England and the places of his boyhood. At Sharon, Connecticut, the old house where he spent his early life still stood unchanged over the years. "I could scarce credit my eyes; I had thought of it as having long ago disappeared, for it was old and shaky in 1876 already; but no, it stood exactly as I remembered it, only spick and span in a new coat of white paint. On the porch facing the road sat an old, old man in a rocking chair. When I got out of the car and walked in a daze through the gate and up the path leading to the front door ... I spoke to him but he was almost as deaf as a stone. ... The old man thawed somewhat, and asked my name. No sooner had I told him than he shouted out as though electrified: '*Carl* Feininger' ... 'that was a great fiddler! he played at a church concert and took off all the strings of his fiddle but one, and played a tune to bring the roof down!' (the 'tune' was Paganini's *Fantasy on the G-string*). I remembered the young fellow who had been so enthusiastic about my father's playing that my parents spoke of it after the concert. That likely young fellow was this old man, stone deaf.... But after 60 years he still remembered that concert ... it was to me the most unexpected, incredible meeting of my whole life."[4] Later: "My friends took us to the cemetery on the hillside facing Mudge Pond and Indian Mountain; and there, on headstones of graves I read, together with my wife and our friends accompanying us, the names of the folks of my early childhood. That was a part of my 'coming home.'"[5]

In the fall the Feiningers went via Hamburg to Sweden, where their eldest son Andreas lived. At the end of 1936, Laurence had gone to Italy and Theodore Lux was to go to America. Feininger returned to Berlin for his last winter in Germany, now fully determined to leave the country in the following year. His sons were safe, and he saw a future for himself.

The remaining paintings of Feininger's last German period were all painted in the winter of 1936–37. In *Yellow Village Church III* (cat. 382) one can see a beginning of a new striving for monumentality. The planes are fewer, the shapes simpler, the colors stronger. The prismatic interpenetration of space can now be achieved differently by the painter. Color takes the place of line or plane; a super-imposition of color now does the duty that formerly was done by imposition of a plane. There are no less movement and depth, but they are achieved by the means available to an older artist, who has no need to explore the forms but has them in his grasp. The statement becomes simpler and more summary. The color plays a twofold role — it makes the shapes, and it also extends them. Paint is used more thickly, so that a layer of one color on top of another, usually a wildly unexpected combination, can play an independent part.

Black begins to make an appearance. In a manner characteristic of Feininger's contradictory nature, he used black for a light as well as a dark color. Here it is used as the color of something that is dark, but frequently the brightest light, the sun, will be given in black.

Viaduct II (cat. 384) is a recollection of Thuringia, the viaduct over the Ilm. The striving for monumentality is again evident. Though the paint is opaque, the color is brilliant and luminous. There are contrasts of warm and cold harmonies, an interplay of color, rich and paradoxical at the same time. The colors of nature are modified toward the unreal; the whole picture becomes poetic in its association with a reflected reality.

Spring, Vollersroda of 1936 (page 137) is equally poetic. The stillness of a long-forgotten Thuringian village appears as a recollection of the happier days at Wei-mar. He expresses for the last time the lyricism that he had found. He knows that he will not see Germany again. Through the terrible happenings of the day, Fei-ninger sees and remembers what he had come to love — the sky, the peace, and the poetry that the country had once given to him and for which he had expressed his gratitude in his work.

During that last winter Feininger painted his last *Gelmeroda*, No. *XIII* (now at the Metropolitan Museum, New York; page 219). The church at Gelmeroda, which had occupied Feininger's mind for thirty years, since he first saw it in 1906, found in this last picture its final glorification. Through all the processes of thought and exploration of forms, this last version reverts most closely to the first drawings. Superficially, it appears to be nearest to nature, but it is in fact the furthest removed of them all. Here the process of spiritualization has gone so far that it can contain and transcend natural reality without being held down by it. The picture recreates reality on a higher spiritual plane. With this Gelmeroda, Feininger takes leave of Germany, the country of his memories, where he had become the painter he was, the country that had given him fame, the country that was no more. He wrote to Lux, "It is a remarkable state of transition in my work and I feel about twenty-five years younger since I know I am going to get to a country where Fantasy is still appreciated in Art, and Abstraction not an absolute crime, as over here. . . . Of at least 30 paintings I commenced since the Fall last year, only 6 or 8 come to com-pletion. I've wiped all the others away."[6] These are his last recorded sentences from Germany.

While Feininger was preparing for his departure, the Nazi government staged a display that shook the civilized world. Under the title "Degenerate Art" an ex-hibition was assembled in Munich. Paintings that had been appropriated from public

136

19 Spring, Vollersroda, 1936 (374)

and private collections were shown with derogatory and insulting inscriptions to a gaping public. The exhibition's aim was to prove that modern art was the outcome of mental derangement and Bolshevism. It linked with this a crude appeal for the elimination of the mentally sick and, by implication, of modern artists. The exhibition was an incitement to murder.

Feininger's work was included in the exhibition, together with that of all the major artists who had shaped the course of modern painting. His *Teltow II* (National Gallery, Berlin), *Gelmeroda III* (Dresden Museum), *Street of Barns* (Folkwang Museum, Essen), *Vollersroda III*, and two of the *Church of St. Mary* paintings (from the Moritzburg Museum, Halle), as well as watercolors and graphic works, were shown at that time. Rave, in his book *Kunstdiktatur im Dritten Reich*, notes that, again and for the last time, Feininger's work hung next to Franz Marc's *Tower of the Blue Horses* — as the work of the two artists had once hung in the Kronprinzen-Palais when the new art was first officially recognized. With that macabre touch of irony, history marked the end of a civilized period that had harbored the makers of modern art — Germans, Russians, Swiss, and Americans, united in the Blaue Reiter, the Sturm, the Brücke, and the Bauhaus.

Under the Nazi regime, 348 works by Feininger, including graphics, drawings, watercolors, and paintings, were removed from public collections. Some have been rescued or found again; others must be considered lost forever.

When Feininger left, he knew what he owed to Germany, but his Germany was no more — and his America was still a free country. He could not have become the artist he was if he had returned to America early in his life, but he could now return as the artist he had become, and become in the process an American artist. His equipment was his past, and his past included an American childhood.

RETURN TO AMERICA

1937–1941, New York, California

Feininger left Germany in 1937 in the dual role of a refugee and a prodigal son. On June 11, 1937, he left Europe on the *Europa*. He returned to the United States of America richer by fifty years' experience. He wrote one sentence in a letter that he himself hoped would be recorded by history. We do so here: "Well, some day it may be related of myself that at the age of 65 years I entered the Port of New York with $2.00 for all money, (like some of the immensely successful millionaires when they started work with jobs as shoe cleaners) and had to begin life all over. (But a millionaire I shall never be!)"[1] Feininger had returned to the American reality. He had no need of the American myth.

From New York Feininger went without delay to Mills College, where he had again been invited to teach the summer course. Kokoschka, who had been expected as resident painter for the year, had canceled his engagement. The invitation from Mills had reached Feininger earlier in the year and had sped his departure. It made his first few months in America easier than they would otherwise have been.

When Feininger arrived at Mills College, he once more arranged an exhibition, this time on a much larger scale (nearly forty paintings and over sixty drawings could be shown). He had been enabled to bring a large number of his paintings to America, mainly through the help of Curt Valentin. An important group of paintings, particularly pictures of his early period, had to be left in Germany with a personal friend. These pictures have not become accessible to this day, though they are duly recorded in the *œuvre* catalogue. The exhibition was arranged in the way Feininger had arranged his first show at the Bauhaus, as an introduction of his work to his students. Convinced that art is not "teachable," Feininger wanted to impress upon the students that each individual has to find his own development and progress at his own pace, from observation to his own form of expression. Feininger never developed a pedagogic theory, except that he held to his belief in not having a theory with the tenacity of a dogmatic theorist.

The summer in Mills College was followed by a three weeks' visit to San Francisco, where his exhibition from Mills had traveled, to be opened on September 1 together with a Cézanne exhibition; this enabled him to see his own works next to Cézanne's. Feininger wrote in a letter to Schardt, "If some of my nature notes had been hung, as one could study there a number by Cézanne, then the close kinship that exists between us in the observation of nature, would have become clearly visible."[2]

San Francisco impressed him greatly. The Seal Rocks, Point Lobos, the Golden Gate, and the submerged wrecks in the water, the fantastic volcanic coast, awakened in his mind visionary coasts he had dreamed of but never seen. He made some drawings and watercolors from his impressions of the coast and the city. He loved the West Coast, the vastness of the sky and the Pacific; this might well have been a place for him to settle. But he had no real choice. New York was his old home and the center of artistic activity. The museums and the dealers were there. Feininger had to start his life again. He could not afford a creative retirement.

The Feiningers left California on September 3, traveling by rail over the Santa Fe, and took rooms at the Hotel Earle in Greenwich Village. Some later paintings were based on drawings from that site.

He wrote to Theodore Spicer-Simson, "I am in a very unusual frame of mind, at present. Imagine the almost unprecedented home-coming of an American, after nearly 50 years entire absence (with not one visit in the intervening years!), to his native city. The changes that have taken place in that period of time are astonishing enough; but, on the other hand, so much still remains in parts of the city, unchanged, just as it was in the 80s, that it calls up all my fondest boyhood memories. I find myself in a state of continual wonderment, discovering sentiments I certainly never had when I was a boy, but which make me a never-tiring spectator of even the most minute details of the city and its life and goings-on. There is nothing that does not affect me in some way; every step I take . . . is a source of pure delight."[3]

Feininger was back in his old New York. He lived in two worlds – the world of his memories, which had always been the source of his art, and the world of the day, which had to pass before it could enter the world of memories and form itself into paintings. He could not even think of painting, and two years elapsed before his first American pictures were begun. For the present he had to adjust himself to the new world and make it his own. He had to begin a new life and deal with all the practical necessities: finding an apartment that he could afford, gathering a circle of friends, becoming part of the city.

The first years in New York were very hard for him and Julia. They were poorer and thirty years older than they had been when they first set out together to build a new life. In 1938 they settled in a small apartment downtown, not far from where Feininger was born, near Gramercy Park at 235 East 22nd Street, overlooking the East River. In a letter to his friend Theodore Spicer-Simson[4] he wrote, "For us, worry may also put in an appearance, soon; but we are hoping for the best. I find my work very well received here and am astonished to find myself so internationally known and my work appreciated. Only, times are no longer good for the Arts, I fear. Between 'a new car' and a 'painting' you'll find the car takes the premier importance."

Marian Willard arranged his first exhibition of drawings and watercolors at the East River Gallery, but there were few sales. Professor Valentiner, an old member of the Novembergruppe, was in charge of the Masterpieces of Art Building for the New York World's Fair, and he came to the rescue. He commissioned from Feininger large murals for the forecourt of the pavilion. Another commission, for the Marine Transportation Building, was given to Feininger by two young architects. These murals were executed after many preliminary drawings had been submitted. This unusual work occupied Feininger for a year. For the Masterpieces of Art Building he designed the murals for the three walls of the forecourt. The actual painting of the murals, based on Feininger's careful designs and instructions, was undertaken by a young Swedish painter, Olms. The World's Fair murals do not exist any more. They were of great simplicity and perfectly conceived for the architectural setting.

140

Manhattan, from the Earle
pencil sketch, 1937

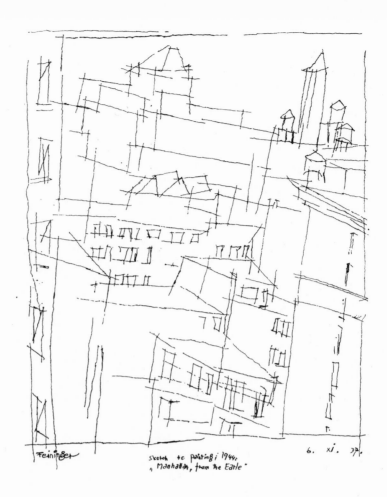

The Marine subject was very much to Feininger's liking, the design nearer in style to his spacious watercolors than to his paintings. These commissions kept Feininger alive; they added nothing to the development of his style.

During this year Mrs. Nelson D. Rockefeller acquired a watercolor for the Museum of Modern Art, and the Yale University library commissioned the bookplate for its collection of Thomas Mann manuscripts. These facts are noted merely to illustrate briefly how his life resembled that of a young and unknown painter. A watercolor sold, a small graphic work commissioned, and four large murals to keep body and soul together — this may be called hopeful for a young painter, but hard for a man of Feininger's age and standing. In a German publication, *Die deutsche Malerei unserer Zeit*, we read that "on his return to the United States Feininger was given important public commissions."[5] Although true, this is only part of the truth, because reality is much harder than history.

His old friend Alfred H. Barr, Jr., and new friends, among them James J. Sweeney, Paul Sachs, Alexander Dorner, Grace McCann Morley, and Marian Willard, all tried to help and make his work and existence known to collectors and the public. The first large exhibition of Feininger's work in New York was arranged by Nierendorf and Mrs. Cornelius Sullivan in their gallery at 57th Street and Park Avenue. One June 4, the Masterpieces of Art Building was opened.

Very slowly Feininger and the circle of artists to which he belonged became better known in America. In 1939 there was a big Klee exhibition. Early in 1939 the Museum of Modern Art arranged a Bauhaus exhibition.

With the expulsion of modern art and modern artists from Germany, other countries began to reap the benefit. America, Switzerland, England — all helped to save the works of these artists, and their fame, formerly confined to Germany, spread over the whole civilized world.

The Feiningers had found a cottage in Falls Village, Connecticut, where he spent the summer months of 1938 and again of 1939, recovering from an illness in the winter. In Falls Village he found rest and peace and until 1944 Falls Village was to take the place of Deep on the Baltic. There Feininger spent his summers, and there contact with nature and quiet recollection helped him to feel his way back into his art. In 1938, he had written from Falls Village to Jawlensky in Germany, "Until now I have not painted here. The break was too great to heal quickly. But it is a beautiful country, offering more than an inward-living painter can use without having to readjust himself completely! Over there: a graveyard of cherished memories; here: impressions that cannot be transformed without a resolute grip and patient struggle."[6] Since then a year had passed, and Feininger was beginning to take roots in his country. He had not yet painted a picture in America.

By the end of 1939 the war in Europe had begun. His son Laurence had come for a brief visit from Italy during the summer. Andreas was in Sweden with his wife, a former Bauhaus student; they decided to come to America and arrived in December. His youngest son Lux had been in the United States for some years now. The threads of Feininger's life were connected again. The European past removed itself, and the American scene took the shape of reality.

In New York he relived his childhood consciously and happily. He went back to Central Park, where he had been as a boy with his admired sea captains and where he now sailed model yachts with his grandson, Thomas. His art owed everything to Europe; he himself owed everything to America. In him, the two traditions became one.

In New York, after his return from Falls Village, he began to paint. On November 19, 1939, there is an entry in Julia's diary, "Leo paints," the first such entry after more than two years. With Feininger, as we know, "memories of things past" had become pictures. Such recollections were often based quite directly on studies after nature, but in every case it was the heightened vision of a later time that formed these notes into pictures, which belonged truly to the moment they were painted. In his first American period we have to modify this conception. Now there are some pictures that were painted from compositions formerly *executed*. It is as if the formative powers had, for a time, deserted him, as if in the new life he had to grasp at some solid achievement from his own past to establish the continuity of his existence as a painter firmly in his mind.

Feininger was nearly seventy. His powers of vision were still strong. His powers of forcing his vision into form he had to reconquer, slowly, painfully. The miracle is not that he had lost it but that he regained it and that among his late works there are many that surpass in depth and vision anything he did in the best days

Manhattan
crayon sketch, 1937

of his life. At this early stage of his American period, in the early 1940s, there were paintings that were echoes and reminiscences of his past art. Feininger went on painting, as a man goes on living, to prove himself — his continuity, his existence, his identity. His search into the recollections of his memory was no different from his search into the collection of his own drawings, which he transformed into new pictures. He had, throughout life, a precarious hold on himself and his art; now he felt it escaping from his grasp. In him all stages of his life were alive together; if they fell apart, his existence would fall apart. His many works were not only the creation of his art but the creation and re-creation of himself.

Three paintings only exist from 1939, all three recollections of the Baltic Sea. *Dunes and Breakwater* (page 221) was bought at the time by John Nicholas Brown. This is a painting of great simplicity of form and vast spatial organization. Such simplicity Feininger had previously found only in his watercolors and drawings. *Storm Brewing* (cat. 389) has a simplicity of a different order: the shape of a three-masted boat is silhouetted across the sun's light, cutting a silhouette in the sea. This picture of simple forms points to the future concern of the artist with shapes and their mystic connections. *Brigantine off the Coast* (cat. 388) returns to a Futurist velocity. In these three pictures, Feininger links his past experience with a tentative step in a new direction.

There are several ways of coming to terms with reality. One is to take its possibilities

143

seriously; another, to let one's mind play over its impossibilities. Both are subjects that modern artists have made into paintings. Side by side with Feininger's pictures of the possibilities of reality, his "Manhattan series," there are other pictures in which his mind has wandered over the fantasies of his youth – still the fantasies of his old age. The crazy trains and boats, the lonely and lost people against the seashore, the frosty fantasy of Thuringian forests – objects and people lost in a world of spook – come to life again in his mind. The subjects are from his own woodcuts and watercolors, but the pictures are not repetitions of pictures once done before in a different medium; these figures and objects are his constant companions, which have lived with him throughout life, and to which he owes a duty as their begetter. They too want to see the light of day; they have come along with him to a new country; and they ask to take shape again. In a playful mood he paints them to please them and to please himself, as an act of loyalty and companionship.

Some such paintings of 1940, like *The Anglers, Panel II* (cat. 393), are based on his own woodcuts. *Spook I* (cat. 395) is a reissue of a watercolor of the twenties. *Spook II* of 1941 (cat. 408; burned in a warehouse fire in Montana) and the *Railroad Train* (cat. 407) of the same year are also examples of this mood in which the painter remains in communication with his imaginary world.

These paintings are not the greatest nor the most important ones, but they contain much of Feininger's mind and life. In many of his great formal compositions the same love of spook and mystery, of wit and sarcasm, has found expression in a way that has passed the obvious and recognizable but prevails as a tone and a mood. The longing for a world between the here and the there, the now and the never, the past and the future, is the impulse of his work.

Last Voyage (cat. 391) is a very sad and lonely picture, symbolic of the mood of those days. In the painting *Ladies at the Seaside* of 1941 (cat. 410), we find ourselves once more on the edge of nowhere. The feeling here of hovering on the edge, of seeing life and dreams float by in the unapproachable distance of a ship on the horizon, is a recurrent theme in Feininger's work. In those sad and wistful pictures he lets the apparitions pass; he has neither the will nor the power to hold them.

The impressions of America found form in a series of Manhattan pictures. *Manhattan I* (page 145) is seen with the wondering eyes of the child and the unbelief of the old man. It is as if Feininger's mind was wide open and the light and the shape of a Manhattan fairy tale was filtering in to be painted, unformed as it came through the mind. He had made a sketch for the picture on an envelope while riding on a bus (page 143).

In *Manhattan II* (page 222), the painter takes hold of himself and tries to wrest a "Feininger" from Manhattan – all the more difficult because Manhattan in Feininger's fifty years' absence had decided to grow rather like his pictures. Just because the new Manhattan came so close to his ideas of space, the transformation from fact to picture was impossibly difficult to achieve. In *Manhattan II*, one can almost hear the painter say, "Have it your way."

Manhattan, Night (page 223) is a disciplined work; the will of the artist and the will of the subject have reached a meeting point between reality and fairy tale. The objective and the subjective have agreed to live together and make a picture.

144

20 Manhattan I, 1940 (398)

Adventure II (page 224), though a Paris recollection, belongs clearly to the now developing Manhattan style. It, too, has the quality of a fairy tale and a dream, the superimposition of his present on his past.

With these four paintings of 1940, Feininger had come to terms with his work. He had regained control and formative powers, and he was well on the way toward the development of a new pictorial conception. By the end of 1940 he could contemplate his development with more hope. "Each year something different than in all the years before finds completion.... I am beginning to surprise myself by this ability for renewal.... Some charcoal compositions for later paintings are important for the work of this winter. They are spatial representations of Manhattan architecture, where I shall try to achieve ... *without* 'symbolism' but through structure and penetration an abstract dematerialization."[7]

Though he was coming to terms with the city and the country, he found it difficult to come to terms with the prevailing attitude toward his art. "I myself am often distressed at the emotional or even sentimental approach of some admirers to my work; and taking it all in all, I am suspicious of the capacity for just appraisal of some of the best of these folks. Just what my work contains of the Remote, is quite past all Americans; in fact, it constitutes a grave hindrance to success here. 'Exhibitionism' in art is the great vogue now. I am at pains to retire behind my work, and there lies the difficulty."[8] This was not only personal shyness, the desire for anonymity that we have met before; it was the expression of a serious doubt about whether the artist can work at all in a competitive world where there is no time left for the slow maturing process of creative art. "Not for nothing have I, for many years, felt anxiety about the conditions for the creative work of artists in this country," he wrote to Schardt, who had now also arrived in the United States. "How often have we watched from Europe the sad spectacle of important European artists settling in the States and losing their rank and their integrity. To think that I could thus diminish (instead of growing in my work) gives me a paralyzing feeling of horror."[9] But Feininger was in a stronger position than many other artists. He had found his own way before through the maze and puzzle of modern stylistic developments and had never deviated from his own vision. And he was, after all, at home, and did not have to play the game of being more advanced than the Americans.

While Feininger was working on his American pictures, the paintings of his past were following him to America, driven there by the forces of history. Curt Valentin, whose efforts on behalf of the still unknown artists of the Brücke and the Blaue Reiter, as well as the Bauhaus painters, had paved the way for a broader understanding of the German contribution to modern art, helped Feininger considerably. Valentin was able to rescue paintings that had been expelled from Germany and thus, apart from helping the living painter, was instrumental in preserving much of his *œuvre*. He could show six of Feininger's most important works formerly in German museums: *Glorious Victory of the Sloop "Maria," Regler Church, Church of the Minorites II, Gelmeroda VIII, X 54,* and *Gables III*.

The political events and the personal insecurity of the year 1940 tore at Feininger's nerves. One of his sons was in Europe; Nazi troops were still marching unhindered over the continent; letters from old friends brought disastrous news. The political

146

as well as the artistic orientation of America, and particularly of New York, was undergoing a transformation. A greater awareness of the implications of the international drama on the national scene foreshadowed the approaching entry of the United States into the war. A large influx of exiles into the United States, many of whom had shaped the course of modern art on the continent of Europe, gave Feininger links with his former existence.

Gropius and Albers of the Bauhaus days, Alexander Archipenko, Curt Valentin, and American sponsors of modern art — Alfred Barr, James J. Sweeney, Katherine Kuh, W. R. Valentiner, Homer St. Gaudens, Talbot Hamlin — were among the European and American friends of those days. He had not come to America alone. A tradition had come with him. He could now write, "This winter I have painted a good deal. More has been destroyed than preserved. Since November I have not missed a day's painting, and am at long last through the difficult period of acclimatization."[10] This was four years after his return to the States. At the end of the year 1941 the Museum of Modern Art acquired Feininger's *Steamer "Odin" II* (page 206), and at the same time it was proposed to arrange a large exhibition. "So we seem to be headed towards better days," he wrote to Lux,[11] giving him this information. The exhibition, however, had to be postponed several times, and did not take place until 1944. Only from the year 1942 on could Feininger look more hopefully toward the future and could a new phase of his art begin to develop. His existence was still very precarious while he was establishing his new mode of painting. He still had to struggle hard for a living. It would be a long and sad story to record — all the hopes and disappointments, the unsold pictures returned from exhibitions, cut prices, and empty promises. To be set against this tale of misery is the genuine help received from his friends. It was still his own past that kept him sustained and alive, morally and actually.

"Last Sunday," he wrote to Schardt, "Julia and I were invited to a supper at the New School for Social Research in honor of the architect Erich Mendelsohn, whom we have known for about 25 years. ... We found the atmosphere most congenial. ... More than half the guests present were from many countries of Europe, and it was a great pleasure to find many people who knew me well for my former work in Germany; in this sort of recognition lies much sustaining power; one is not an object of mere sensational interest for a short moment, but has one's place in the cultural order, and that place is secure and lasting."[12]

MANHATTAN

1942–1949, New York, Falls Village

In Feininger's American paintings we find the logical conclusion of the road he explored throughout his life. His solutions of the problems of space, light, and atmosphere take on greater clarity; they become more abstract in the sense of essential. In his late works one can comprehend what one had to deduce in his earlier work. The uncompromising logic of his thought is admirable. Feininger's approach to his paintings had, from his beginning, been that of a draftsman. The lines enclosing the planes carried the structure of the picture. Color interpreted the form created by the line. Feininger could use a ruler without impeding the individual expressiveness of his line. By varying pressure, by interruption, a nervous personal line was carried along the ruler — or, if occasion demanded, subordinated to the straightedge. Linear composition underlies all his work.

After 1941, his paintings entered a phase that can be described as his "graphic" period, because line alone carries the structure of the picture. This development can be seen in *City at Night* (page 225), a picture of 1941 that belongs to the Manhattan series. Color is no longer confined within limits; it does not support the shape but affects it decisively by being independent of the graphic structure.

In the pictures in the graphic style, color has been freed from its obligation to build space. Freedom from necessity has made it independent. Feininger wrote about his aims at the time: "I am busy at work on a collection of architectural 'visions' . . . New York as a subject for translation into symbol of Space and Atmosphere. . . . New York is the most amazing city in its atmosphere, color, and contrasts in the whole world. . . . Some of it [my work] is in a definitely new application of oil technique, using some graphical elements of line in fields of vigorous color. It was necessary for me to come to the U.S., in order to be able to release myself from the hard compulsion of straight and rigid line . . . it is indeed nothing new or strange to me to now again employ free color and line at times. Only that I have in those many years learned much and can now succeed in cases where I once hesitated."[1] The new development of the graphic style is seen by Feininger as a necessity for breaking the rigidity of form, which he has had to break once before in his life using different means. The monumental solidity of his paintings between 1913 and 1917 was broken by the inner illumination of the planes. Light was then used to break the rigidity of form, and the transparent pictures were the outcome. In his American phase, the free use of color interacts with the free graphic lines of the structure. Color creates the emotional field of action in which the drawing gains its meaning.

"Julia was the first to point out to me the necessity and even the logic of this return to freer form. I have come to believe, myself, that my sense of duty stood in my way for years; for having proceeded so far (in my formal painting), it appeared to me something of a deserting of my course to give up until I had succeeded further

21 Manhattan, Dawn, 1944 (444)

still. It is difficult to give up the attitude of uncompromising steadfastness, even though it ceases to bear new fruit."[2]

We must ask: what prevented Feininger from "succeeding further still" on his previous path? The answer is that the end of that road would lead to pure abstraction, and that was a step that Feininger refused to take. Whenever his development of pictorial form had reached the point where the next step had to lead to nonobjective painting, he did not take the step. At every stage of his art he had more to express than abstract shapes could convey; his visions were of a kind which could be communicated and which he intended to communicate. Whenever he stood at the edge of the abyss he always turned back and began anew on a different road until he reached another end of his development. In this process of advance and return he discovered many forms of pictorial expression, and all of them retained a part of him and a part of reality. The graphic style was Feininger's new answer for the expression of his thought; it was based on the achievements of his own art, which found a new enlargement in its application.

September Clouds and *In the Channel* (cat. 417, 412) may seem like large drawings, and certainly this style has developed from his drawings, but the transformation of a graphic conception succeeds because the lines contain the form almost without color. From his own pictures Feininger has abstracted the lines that still carry the volume they once enclosed. On a solid ground of opaque paint, the fields of color receive the graphic elements; a recollection of space confined by lines is transposed into fields of "unreal" color. Two different forms of nonreality create a new reality.

The paintings of the year 1942 continue the graphic style. But they have more in common than a style; they are linked by a consistent mood of nostalgia, and a strange otherworldliness in their themes. Among them are *Voyage by Moonlight* (cat. 423), *Enchanted Night* (cat. 428), and the *Coast of Nevermore I* (cat. 429). A sea is bordered by a land of icebergs; an unreal ship proceeds on a voyage along the Coast of Nevermore; a dark reflection in the water might be read as the reflection of an invisible sun. The ship in white outline on a dark ground will reappear in *Mirage II* (*Coast of Nevermore;* page 226), and the significance of the white line will then become apparent.

In *Alarm* (cat. 426) the uncertainty of the color and the tentativeness of the line create a world of instability. The mood of the picture is only confirmed, not induced, by the panic of the picture's inhabitants. *Blind Musician at the Beach* (page 151), based on a watercolor drawing of 1915, is a strange picture, but not unexpected if we have understood the artist correctly. A red musician treads on a ground the same color as himself; he becomes visible only by virtue of an area of a near-white parchment color, which silhouettes his existence; without it, he would not even be. He walks precariously on the edge of nothing; his blind man's stick and his lute point into a colorless void. Two sailing ships stand in a world of nowhere. Two beings, neither ghosts nor children, follow the musician. They are not connected; yet they belong. A world of utter loneliness opens before our eyes. Once more a figure passes across the life of the painter. *The White Man,* the *Lady*

22 Blind Musician at the Beach, 1942 (422)

in Mauve, The Red Fiddler, and now the *Blind Musician* — together they give the Ages of Man.

At the end of the year (1942), Feininger had a wonderful surprise which is best told in his own words: "Yesterday I went to the 'Varnishing' (as they persist in calling it) of the new exposition of American painting at the Metropolitan Museum, having one of my paintings included. . . . It is a show to demonstrate the Victory of the American Artist, and when pictures (3000 of them) have gone through the process of being juried, and 300 chosen, . . . there is a second jury to decide which paintings seem worthy of acquisition by the Metropolitan . . . well, there we now have a painting in the pool and a one-in-ten-thousand chance that it might be 'acquired' . . . gosh, was I discouraged when . . . I caught a glimpse of all the folks milling around. . . . But I did discover my 'Gelmeroda' (now modestly designated under the caption: 'Church'), hung very nicely. . . . Probably I am all wrong, but it looked to me to be still a pretty good painting; but, as far as the frame was concerned, it lacked that impressiveness, being but a silver, wedge-shaped, delicate profile of my own designing, some twenty years ago. . . . Still, nobody seemed to object, for no one even glanced at the picture except (for a period of three seconds during which I held my breath) a stout, unstylish-looking leddy in a red hat. . . . To return for a moment to the misleading term: 'Varnishing day' . . . let smile who will at my innocence, I, before leaving the apartment to proceed to the ordeal . . . took care to wrap up a bottle of varnish in a clean white piece of linen bedsheet and conceal a brush in the depths of the pocket of my winter coat, just not to take any chances."[3] On the next day, December 7, he wrote to Lux, "It has been a hectic day. At 9:30 a.m. I was painting and, while so occupied, my thoughts dwelt gloomily on 'Pearl Harbor' and what this day meant in America's and the world's history when suddenly the doorbell rang. . . . I went to the door, opened same, and without stood a letter carrier extending a registered letter. So I signed the receipt and looked at the sender of the missive: Metropolitan Museum of Art, New York, N. Y. — H'm, thinks I — I held the letter playfully out to Mami's sight and gave her 'three guesses.' First she guessed 'Lux,' then 'Andreas,' then she gave up guessing. So I told her from whom the letter was. I then proceeded to open it. . . . A check for $ 2,500.00 lay in my hand, tout comme ça. . . . At 11, I had regained my accustomed imperturbability and was painting as usual (using a ruler) when for the 'steenth time the telephone rang, and this time the call was for me, from the Metropolitan. I received the nicest invitation to an informal luncheon with the Director and others. The time indicated was 1:30. J'ai accepté avec empressement. And now, after three-and-a-half hours of the most hectic, me voilà enfin. — The luncheon was given in the secret recesses of the Museum sousterrain, in a very cosy room; and there may have been some 100 people present. . . . Many acquaintances congratulated me, colleagues, art dealers, I was honestly touched by such evidence of liking and good-feeling. And if I wrote yesterday that no one (except the lady in the red hat) even cast a glance at my poor painting, today it was something quite different! There was a big brass shield fastened on the frame of each prize-winner, and all the nice people were looking out hungrily for those brass shields and where they saw such a one, they just stood in crowds to read the name of the artist and the amount of . . . the prize. And by degrees, some even came to look at the picture itself.... Gosh, dear old son, it was a happy day today." Julia shortly thereafter entered in her diary, "All bills paid, no more debts." That, too, is a turning point in the life of an artist.

Among the paintings of 1943 are restatements of old themes. Two are woodcut pictures, *Chapel in the Woods* (cat. 434) and *Town Gate* (cat. 432); the latter is almost pure black and white, with a touch of independent color roaming freely, playing a game of hide-and-seek in a world where it knows it does not belong. In *Fishermen* (cat. 438) the graphic conception allows color to play a part divorced from the picture, thus creating a new relation between the spectator and the painting. It is as if color had become a free agent, belonging as much to the spectator as to the composition. In *Gables V* (cat. 439) the forms are nearly abstract, linked to remembered reality by the thin lines of a few gables and windows. Pure abstraction, by which is meant shapes owing nothing to their origin in reality, was not Feininger's aim. His abstraction went as far as the mind could reach without snapping the thin thread that links the mind through memory with reality. In *Mirage II* (*Coast of Nevermore*; page 226) we see the reappearance of a ship in white outline. This white line — the line of unreality as opposed to the dark line, the line of reality — will become the carrier of Feininger's last and greatest intentions, communicating his inmost thoughts. The line has always been the carrier of his formative will; it was Feininger's *ultima ratio*.

The paintings of 1944 show the merging of some older conceptions with his new style. This is seen most strongly in *Dunes, Ray of Light II* (page 227), in which a luminosity reminiscent of his work of 1927 is created by new means of color. The vastness of the conception had first been developed in his watercolors, where endless space is held within comprehension by a few lines. *Dunes, Ray of Light II* is a recollection, combining his old vision and his new means.

Dunes, Hazy Evening (cat. 449) begins another development, which will bring forth paintings of a world purified from all worldly recollections. In this painting there is still a foreground of earthly contours and a real moon, but the lines of the sky not only shape space but go into the beyond. The black line of reality and the white line of unreality are more than a graphic device of opposition and contrast.

The series of Manhattan pictures was continued in *Manhattan, the Tower* (cat. 445), *Manhattan, Dawn* (page 149), and *Manhattan, from the Earle* (cat. 446), all of 1944. What appears as an absolute difficulty in the Manhattan problem is that it is hardly possible to extract anything from an abstraction. Though New York skyscrapers are very real, they are already conceived as abstract designs. It is thus an odd meeting when modern architecture and modern painting encounter each other in the same picture, and neither side knows which owes more to the Bauhaus tradition. It is left to the painter only to instill a mood by seeing it in his own light, and for that the little color employed is just sufficient. The problem of how to paint New York had been considered by the artist ever since he had come back to the city. The answer he found was to "resolve them [skyscrapers] in atmospheric space. . . . That seems to be, so far, a possible solution where my own vision is concerned. It is only a question whether I love the city sufficiently more than a thousand other scenes and memories, to make the attempt."[4] In fact, he did

153

both. He painted Manhattan but the "thousand other scenes and memories" return in his paintings.

The beginning of the year 1944 was taken up with preparations for the large exhibition at the Museum of Modern Art. This exhibition became one of the three important events in the artist's public life. The first, the exhibition at the Sturm in 1917, established Feininger as an independent figure of the modern movement in Europe. The second event, the retrospective exhibition at the Berlin National Gallery (Kronprinzen-Palais) in 1931, brought together all the paintings on which the artist's continental fame had been built. The New York exhibition did for America what the two earlier exhibitions had done for Europe. This exhibition established Feininger's name in the United States.

The exhibition was devoted to two artists – Marsden Hartley and Lyonel Feininger. Feininger's section contained over seventy paintings, ranging in date from 1908 to 1944. So many of his most important works had found their way to America that it was possible to make the exhibition almost as representative as the large retrospective exhibition in Berlin had been. Among the forty-nine paintings from his European period that were on view, several had formerly belonged to public collections in Germany, and a large number now came from public collections in the States. The American period was represented by over twenty works, dating from the last five years, 1939 to 1944. Thus it was the first time that the two phases of the artist's life were joined together in a representative collection.

In 1929, when Alfred Barr had first tried to acquaint the American public with Feininger as an American artist, he received, as he recalled in the foreword to the catalogue of this exhibition, no thanks for his effort. Now he succeeded in establish-

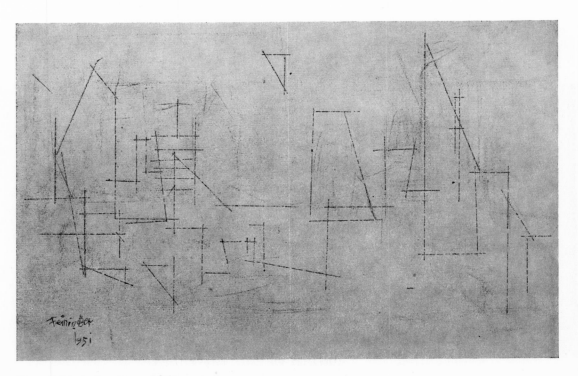

Pen-and-ink drawing, 1951

154

Pen-and-ink drawing, 1948

ing Feininger as an American artist in America. This was the last battle that had
to be won. From then on Feininger's third period as a "struggling" artist was over.
Unlike other painters, Feininger had three such phases in his life: one at the start
of his career as an illustrator, a second at the beginning of his career as a painter,
and, late in life, a third as a painter who had arrived ahead of his fame. But after
the Museum of Modern Art exhibition he could write about the many sales of his
pictures: "a regular landslide of 'success.'"[5]
It would be quite wrong to picture Lyonel Feininger living as a recluse on the
eleventh floor of an apartment house in downtown New York. Actually, he saw
many people, visited all the exhibitions in museums and private galleries, wrote
articles with Julia about artists that he had known, and remained interested in all
that went on around him. He lived not only in his past but very much in the
present.
During the year, he met Léger and Ozenfant. He also formed a new friendship with
Mark Tobey, with whom he had spiritually much in common; each artist understood the other's work. Both were working in a graphic style, and, although they
were too mature to "influence" each other, there is no doubt that their sympathy
and common view mutually strengthened their purposes. Tobey has written some of
the most beautiful lines on Feininger's art.[6] Mark Tobey had invented a calligraphic
style, which he described as "white writing." Feininger, as early as in some of the
Halle pictures, had used a white line in a dark field of color, but this had never been
developed, although the inversion of values interested him. The white line which
now began to appear in his work may owe some stimulus to his understanding of
Tobey's paintings.

155

During 1945 he accepted an invitation from Albers, formerly of the Bauhaus, to teach the summer course at Black Mountain College in North Carolina. Here he met Gropius again and found happiness with old friends in new surroundings. The presence of many musicians and their performances made Feininger very happy. He met Alfred Einstein, the musicologist, with whom he formed a lasting friendship. His joy in the observation of nature was as strong as ever. "The surrounding mountains are pure magic in the blues and greys of recessional distance. . . . There are ridges of overlapping mountains, receding at times into nothing but atmospheric dissolution of pure light."[7] No paintings were based on these observations. Feininger had never formed mountains in his paintings. Earlier, in the Harz mountains in Germany, he had made notes of trees and rock formations, but the mountains as such were too solid to be dissolved and re-created in his paintings.

Mountains presented a problem similar to that posed by the monumental density of Manhattan. Feininger recognized the beauty and immensity of the subject, but it was almost too immense to be transformed, too vast to be penetrated by the mind. In a letter to Gerhard Marcks he wrote, "You may be interested that I paint pictures of the Baltic [Ostseebilder] almost exclusively and have attempted only a few times to form 'New York' in a picture. The city is really too monstrous [ungeheuerlich] and I am not inclined to represent such, in themselves, gigantic things."[8]

This problem is really a fundamental question of painting, and does not concern Feininger alone. The greater the object, its own mass and impact, the greater its own order, the less possible it is for the artist to make something new out of it. To instill monumentality into a monument is not necessary.

A small Thuringian church or a sailing boat on the wide sea, Feininger transformed into monumental conceptions. Faced with the skyscrapers, he could not enlarge their monumentality. He could, as he said, divest them "of all episodical by-work," and "resolve them in atmospheric space."[9]

In 1945, the series of Manhattan subjects was continued with *City Moon* (page 228), a firm graphic composition, where space is created by linear pattern alone. In *Moonwake* (page 230) color lives its own life and fills the picture with its mood. Long after the picture was finished he added the figure "in the wake of the moon" that he had noted one night at the corner of Lexington Avenue and 22nd Street.

One painting of the year 1945 borders on the miraculous. In *Beach Under Gloom* (page 229) the white line has achieved its domination; it is the bare skeleton of all the thought that has been underlying Feininger's compositions throughout his life – here appearing as majestic law. This is a picture of pure thought, the mystery of space in all its magnitude revealed to two small figures.

The fundamental problem of every painting by Feininger is the problem of space and atmosphere. In a letter to Lux he summarized all that moved him toward a deeper understanding of space. "Turner, consciously or unconsciously, has ever since had a part in forming my appreciation for light and shade, magic space, reflections in water and atmosphere. . . . I had discovered 'space' in my caricature work; and that, together with musical space – counterpoint in Bach – formed my firm basis for the upbuilding of atmospheric space, quite apart from Turner's form; distinctly breaking with school perspective so-called. I even as a caricaturist *inverted*

23 Vita Nova, 1947 (471)

157

perspective form. . . . Light and shade and all the atmosphere . . . will still not solve the ultimate problem of painting, which is based upon *spatial interrelationships.*"[10]

The *Altersstil,* or late period of a master, is usually remarkable for looseness of treatment and increased freedom. As the physical powers decline, the visionary powers increase. In the late period of Feininger's work one can observe this loosening of texture, the more summary statements, the visionary moments. As this process continued, the determination of the artist to hold the fleeting shapes in firm bounds increased. The true late period in Feininger's art has no exact beginning. One may place it as late as 1950; yet the appearance of the late style can be placed at the beginning of the 1940s. Some traces can be found in his work of 1945 and will again be counterbalanced by rigorous discipline. The emergence of a new period is heralded by individual pictures, which predate their time of origin. This has happened before in his work, just as there are pictures that "postdate" their time of origin. Feininger ranges backward and forward in his work, and there is never a clear division. There are phases merging into one another; it is possible to extract only the dominant trend at each period.

At the age of seventy-five, Feininger, in a letter to Schardt, describes how he sees his late work. "Economy of means, employment of line with mere accentuation through color to sustain mood and expressive space. . . . I see one marked difference between early and later work: I now 'think' less, and work at times in utter unconsciousness of what may be the final achievement; when the work stands suddenly finished before me on the easel, I experience surprise at times approaching a feeling of terror, that this thing has come to life."[11]

The graphic paintings of the years 1945 to 1947 are more mysterious and removed from reality than those of the preceding years. The *Tower* (cat. 459) is the only Manhattan subject. Three pictures of 1946 go back to earlier motifs — the *Church at Morning* (page 231), the *Church on the Hill* (cat. 466), and *Dusk* (cat. 463). Here the linear treatment can be compared to the paintings of churches of the 1920s. In spite of all difference in method, the essential aims of the artist have undergone no change. The buildings create and carry the space in which they stand; the principles of inversion are at work; and, if color is now applied lightly, it carries its emotional overtones as before. Monumentality has been achieved with new and simpler means.

Vita Nova of 1947 (page 157) is a space construction of fine lines. The picture has a structural transparency; the thin lines are as strong as formerly the shafts of light were. Although less physical energy has been expended, this picture is held together by a greater mental force than before. Equilibrium is firmly stabilized; the lines of cohesion and tension are themselves the active forces that reveal the space.

The aims of Feininger's art were unaltered and followed the same laws that had been the basis of his work; only the expressive means were new in their application and refinement. Now that all else has been removed, the lines have been laid bare and become visible. One cannot go much further than that; and it is not surprising that, in paintings to come, planes will again appear as the formative agents of space.

In *Three Windows* of 1947 (cat. 478) and in *The Baltic (V-Cloud)* (page 232) of

158

1946–47, the pure line has been made invisible and the planes reintroduced as signs for spatial relations.

In 1948 Feininger had to undergo a serious operation during March, at the age of seventy-seven. His constitution was found to be strong and vigorous, and he recovered completely, but only three pictures were executed during the year.

In *Houses by the River I* (page 233) the space is constructed by planes held by graphic lines. It shows the emergence of the combined style of linear definition of colored planes, first developed in his watercolors. The transparency of the planes is achieved not by translucency of color but by direction-giving lines that penetrate the planes invisibly and carry one's thoughts along their directions.

The Hidden Village (page 234) is a graphic picture in which the lines alone hold the structure. The spaciousness of the composition is as monumental in a new way as Feininger's work in his first space constructions of 1914 to 1917. Though the lines have been left bare, they hold as great a mass as Feininger ever concentrated in a picture. The color used is almost noncolor — a parchment tone with some quite realistic touches of red on the roofs and blue in the sky, heightening the effect of unreality by the opposition of true color and noncolor.

Of the pictures of 1949, *Courtyard III* (page 235) is the highest achievement of the purely graphic style, a linear composition of outward simplicity and inner complexity, an abstraction of meaning. It is an example of how the painter can develop his own language without remaining uncommunicative. He abstracts the idea from material reality without thereby denying the reality from which the idea arose. The line is used evocatively; the picture is not invented but distilled. It is the essence of an experience.

The Cutting (page 237) is a painting in which geometry takes hold of nature — or nature reveals its geometry. Fundamentally a composition of three triangles, it contains the laws of the triangle, and the summary of a visible truth.

The development of Feininger's painting in his late years is the outcome of an unchanging attitude to the meaning of nature. "It is one of my inalterable concepts of what art must be in order to remain vital, that, ultimately [letzten Endes], there is no might to be compared with that inherent in Nature, and Abstraction *alone* does not lead to the true solution; it must be born of experience and humility before Nature in all her limitless diversity."[12] Such faith was justified whenever he found his visionary inventions confirmed by nature. "Fog over the waste of water and mottling the moonlit evening sky, looking exactly like one of my own watercolors in ivory black and charcoal gray, with dark patches concealing the outlines."[13] "The sky presented a spectacle of being diagonally crossed from upper right to lower left by a solid grey 'weather front' from the North. If ever I have felt timid in designing my 'Feininger' skies, the spectacle of this ruler-straight division allayed all doubts . . . it's bound, some time or other, to show up in nature."[14] The relation between art and nature in Feininger is one of mutual truth.

THE LAST YEARS

1950–1956, New York, New England

In 1951, a few days before his birthday, Feininger wrote, "You know, I'm just beginning to savour the importance of approaching '80,' although it seems to be a rather over-estimated decade, ... feeling ... full of ideas, and not so old as I had always expected I should. . . . At all events, I expect to 'carry on' as usual for quite some time to come."[1] In New York Feininger went occasionally to the Historical Society to read the history of nineteenth-century New York and to see the collection of models of old ships. He watched the Second Avenue Elevated being dismantled, as he had watched its construction. "I identify myself now to quite an extent with New York, it really is 'old New York,' the one of the Valentine's Manuals I actually can be at home in."[2]

The summer months the Feiningers spent in the country. After their summers in the cottage in Falls Village they had gone to Stockbridge or to Cambridge. In 1951 they stayed in Gropius' house in Lincoln, Massachusetts, where Feininger celebrated his eightieth birthday. They spent the summer of 1953 in Albers' house in New Haven, where Feininger found "windows facing east, south and west, simply ideal, what I always am longing for, light from opposite sources."[3] A month each fall he liked to spend in Plymouth.

Feininger loved the American landscape but never formed it in pictures; yet he absorbed impressions that colored his American work, and such impressions need not be found in the subject matter. He wrote from Plymouth, "I chiefly enjoyed those yellow hydrants ... with red tops and black outlets. This at any rate is pure color. What I really miss is drawing after nature, making notes [Notizen] as at the Baltic, in *Deep*, or in the villages in the vicinity of *Weimar*. Somehow I have no satisfaction from the subjects hereabouts; they form too little of my *inner* preference and only result in naturalistic efforts."[4] But a few weeks later he wrote, "A painting I made on chrome yellow ground two weeks ago is traceable to the gaudy Plymouth hydrants. . . . On a yellow ground tone, the village of *Gaberndorf* with the church steeple in the background. . . ."[5]

The subject of the picture goes back to Thuringia, but the mood of the painter was induced by recent impressions. He was quite conscious that the American scene influenced his work. "Outside the Metropolitan Museum a few grand trees in the late sunlight cast rich shadows over the façade — just delightful. It seems almost queer that I so stress these impressions of trees, and sun, when I do nothing at all about them in my painting. But their *essence* is what enters into my happy mood, and doubtless helps somewhat to modify my customary severities of style."[6]

In Feininger's painting, the human figure had been more and more excluded and, in his last American paintings, rarely appeared. This should not lead to the conclusion that the human figure disappeared from Feininger's art. His late paintings of cosmic events excluded every personification. Only the spirit of the artist inhabits

160

24 Phoenix, 1954 (533)

his late pictures. But the human figure escaped and made itself independent. In a large series of small drawings and watercolors, quite unknown because they were never exhibited or sold and were only given as presents to his family and friends, a whole world of figures came to life in the last years of Feininger's work. "Manikins," he called them, and also "ghosties," "spooks," "little people," "grotesques," "demons," "pixies," "Mysterious Petes," and other names. Drawn in outline, either straight with a ruler or freely and nervously in pen and ink, a fantastic world of mysterious types appears (a rare appearance in his paintings is found in the two beings following the *Blind Musician*). These fantastic figures summarize Feininger's lifetime of silent observation — Jesuits, small children, workmen, teachers, haughty ladies, crumpled ghosts, gentlemen in high hats, and street urchins — each carries its linear outline and characteristic color. How American these grotesques are can be understood if one compares them with the mysticism of Klee's figures on the one hand and of Thurber's on the other. True nonsense, without mystic overtones, these sprites are entirely irresponsible and harmless. They are alive in the way that any creation is alive; they move when we are not looking; and they are as good-natured as their maker.

His watercolors gain new importance in his *œuvre;* they become even greater and more spacious — of such beauty and wisdom as only old age can hold. In the calm of the large planes he surpasses the Japanese woodcut, but a similar feeling for absolute space, for the value of line, for gradations and intervals seems to emanate from his spirit.

Feininger's late drawings must be considered as the essential expression of his art. Reality assembles itself in the meeting of the lines (pages 154, 155). With an extreme ascetic economy of means, shapes and perspectives define themselves. In concentration and precision of the imagination, each drawing appears a statement of finality. In his late drawings, Feininger drew the last consequences of his thought. The laws of this world are made visible, and they conform to Goethe's definition of harmony in the classical order: the balance of the unequal, the contrast of similarities, the harmony of dissimilarity, unity through polarity, rest through tension.[7] That was Feininger's ultimate knowledge, revealed in his drawings. Reason demands a classical expression. The laws are those of the unity of opposites. Feininger's dialectical thinking finds the formal relations in space. There is something miraculous in his late work, a mystery different from that of any other artist of his generation. It is as if he discovered an innate truth; not as if he forced a form or structure on the world, but as if he revealed what had always been there but had remained hidden until he discovered it. He did not abandon the quest for "truth" and "beauty." If he broke, as did other modern painters, the formal perspective framework of the Renaissance painters, if he went parallel to the modern discoveries of new conceptions of time and space, if he was not afraid of fantasy and experiment in the hope of discovery, he aimed at the discovery of a truth. In that search he found also a new beauty. He has proved, what should be common knowledge, that the new is only part of a tradition. Like Cézanne he has given firm form to the world. He has made of his impressions something that has duration. Feininger's work can be understood by the senses and by the ordering mind. It will never lend itself to violent debate;

162

25 Yachts, 1950 (501)

as he himself stood aloof from the battles of the day and won his own victory, so his pictures will remain as silent monuments of his vision and his greatness.

At a great age, if the mind is still alive and receptive, a new phase opens. What is commonly called wisdom has always been considered the prerogative of the old. Such wisdom in a painter, who has gone through a long life of visual impressions, summarizes experiences and hardly perceives the material details. More and more the imponderable external aspects of reality disappear, and the essence of things and places is perceived in a mood of receptive forgetfulness. The artist closes his eyes, which have already seen so much, and contemplates the totality of his life and his world. He wrote to his son, "This summer has shown me that there are such times in one's elder life when one retires deeply into the néant of emotion, into a dreamland which is soothing indeed."[8] A new vision is induced that receives more of the hidden overtones of a reality fuller of events than the youthful searching eye can perceive.

It is not essential to accept the visionary gift of old age as an awareness of a truth beyond the grave or the realization of a different world of a different order. The awareness of the visionary artist goes as deeply into reality as reality allows, no further. Beyond that barrier lies mysticism, if anything lies there at all. What man can perceive becomes by that very fact part of reality. An extension of the senses is possible, but the breaking point comes when the mind loses touch with this world. Art is the spirit made visible or vision made material. Were it not for the material existence of what is usually described as spiritual (thus placing it in a false antagonism to itself), no art could ever have existed. Art is proof that the spiritual and the material are one and the same, but different in state. The artist has faith in the truth of his vision. His work gropes for the final form that the realization of his vision demands. A picture is not an ideal creation; a picture is a material fact, wrung in hard labor from the reality of the mind — to be brought into this world, to become a reality for all men.

We place the beginning of the last phase of Feininger's work in the year 1950, though there are traces of his last style running through pictures of earlier periods. The high point of his graphic style had been reached in *Courtyard III*; his later achievements are foreshadowed in earlier pictures, such as *Beach Under Gloom*.

In the years 1950 and 1951, the past, the present, and the future of all Feininger's art merged in a number of great pictures. In *Yachts* (page 163), his love and understanding of boats and the sea are manifested in one great composition. This is built of three triangles — of sea, of sky, and of light — counterpointed by the triangles of the yachts. It keeps this triplicity in color, which is essentially divided into three ranges — the near-black sea, the white sails, and the bluish-green sky. The rhythm of three sweeps the whole picture. The boats, material and ethereal at the same time, are composed of three sails. The forces are counterpointed, the direction of the boats against the direction of the light. The tension within the balance is enormous and calculated to the finest point of the bearable.

As in his earliest pictures, light is used as force penetrating space and revealing it in the process. The luminosity and transparency of the planes are retained, but

26 Sunset Fires, 1953 (530)

are produced with different means. The emotional content of the picture is his old longing for the sea and the infinity of space.

Spell of 1951 (page 238) could only have been painted from the height reached by *Courtyard III*. In *Courtyard III* the picture has almost been emptied of emotional content to the point where pure thought rules supreme. In *Spell* the structure of rational clarity is pervaded by two unreal colors – a pinkish mauve, and a blue with pink echoes. It is pure poetical apparition of space in colored light.

The human spirit reaches far enough to include in its apprehension the unity of events, the interacting relations between man and nature.

In *Lunar Web* (page 167) the development that began with the two versions of *Coast of Nevermore* and was continued in *Beach Under Gloom* reaches a point where the picture has been freed from all remnants of association with reality. The white line of unreality creates an image of space on a ground of brown and olive green, astonishingly luminous for such somber colors. The white line creates its own light and, when the negative line appears in blue, it has added to itself a quality of heightened unreality. It has the power of nonexistence. Each plane created by the lines holds its own mystery transcending the boundaries of its shape. The sharpness of the dynamic clashes of direction is held by the superior power of the moon; the web of destiny that the lines reveal is a cosmic event. The mystery of creation becomes comprehensible in the creation of the human order, in the refusal to recognize chaos as anything but lack of poetry. To achieve it, all Feininger's thought and experience had to come together in one great moment of power, to crystallize into an image of cosmic awareness, which will last forever.

As a counterpart to such concentration of vision a work appears, *The Vanishing Hour* (cat. 514), in which one can see either a crumbling of all form and a complete loss of power by the artist, or, more truly, an awareness of the other side of reality, a picture that does not obey the laws of man. To Feininger this experience, which comes to painters in their very late years, was not new. In his earliest work there was an awareness of hidden powers and hidden mysteries which peer occasionally through the recesses of humanized reality; then they were controlled and seen as the comic side of unreality. In his late years, the awareness that unreality and death are realities took hold of his mind. Pictures like *The Vanishing Hour* and, a few years later, *Shadow of Dissolution* (page 169) reveal the trembling moment when man becomes aware that his world of thought and form lives and dies with him.

Feininger knew that art is form and that form is life, that the inexpressible is formless and that formlessness is death. To keep hold on form is to keep hold on life. He wrote to Lux, "I am nearing the stage where I am even commencing to annihilate precise forms, in the interest – as it appears to me – of unity. This is a precarious stage to enter into, and I occasionally am brought up short and revert to something contradictional as a corrective."[9] Never has the eternal struggle for form against formlessness been more clearly expressed. The classic fights for life and the retention of form; the romantic longs for formlessness and death.

During the remaining years of Feininger's life, his creative power did not weaken, though it cost him increasing efforts of will and strength to achieve the tasks he set

166

27 Lunar Web, 1951 (513)

himself. "Painting for me, is harder today than formerly, the strain not so easy to take ... but on the other hand, if I may say so, the paintings are in some respects *deeper*," he wrote on March 18, 1954, and in the same letter said that he wished to "use the last years well. 'The end crowns the work,' as it was never the individual work which counted for me but the whole work."[10] Every painting is a part of himself and his thought; together, all form his life and his art.

Crépuscule of 1952–53 (page 240) is related to *Spell*; it is a Manhattan subject of transparent beauty and mystery. Form is firmly held, not as volume but rather as an extended shadow of reality. The colors are improbable in their cold unreality. These paintings are very closely related to Feininger's earliest work. The weightlessness of the figures is here echoed by the weightlessness of the pictorial shadows. Unlike the man who has lost his shadow in Feininger's early caricatures, in these paintings it is the shadow that has lost its body and lives a life of emanation.

Phoenix of 1954 (page 161) belongs to the same development. The shadow and the reality are not separated; they give an insight into their interdependence. The skyscrapers, as once did Gelmeroda, create their own space of vibrating color.

Barque at Sea (cat. 522) is the equivalent of *The Vanishing Hour*. Here boat and sea take leave of their creator, as, in *The Vanishing Hour*, the city appeared to him in its "other" aspects, no more of this world. It is a sad picture, of black, white, and blue, with a ship sailing out of the life of the artist.

Crest and Image of 1952 (page 242) is the final restatement of the sea without ships or man — only the moon, the heavens, and the dark sea below, with two lines of a beam opening to eternity.

In *Fenris Wolf* (page 243), the "other side" of the world appears in linear order. The cloud, which swallows the moon, is a cosmic tragedy. The painter's geometry returns to the magic origin of harmony and mathematics, where the harmony of the whole world reveals itself in the magic of proportions.

Sunset Fires (page 165) is a vision of the end or the beginning of the world, chaos taking form, the artist creating order. Where there was only untamed force, here man, as the only principle of order, asserts himself.

In *Shadow of Dissolution* (page 169) the painter sees the end of his world. Form escapes, reality returns to shadow, and the ball of life rolls to the dark side of the world, where light does not enter, where vision is no more, where the mind has lost the power of recognition, and where even the creator is powerless. The artist as seer anticipates such vision, and the nearness of the end of life casts the shadow of dissolution before.

Feininger had two more years to live and work, but only one of the pictures of 1955 was completed and signed; his signature we must respect as his own final verdict of completion. In *Evening Haze* of 1955 (page 244) shapes are emerging from a blue haze, intersected by the white line of unreality; it is a visionary painting. There exist several similar paintings, which, if acknowledged by the artist, could be included here. Four versions of Brooklyn Bridge remained unfinished; other paintings, which were destroyed by the artist, exist only as colored shadows on photographic slides.

Arranging the material for a large retrospective exhibition in Europe, he wrote,

28 Shadow of Dissolution, 1953 (532)

"I am most awfully happy that the show will come off — it is a 'Rechtfertigung' of a sort and really a 'Danksagung' toward many friends over there. . . . A good 'last effort' I think."[11] Feininger felt that his road was coming to an end; he was unchanged — cheerful and hopeful. He wrote about his eighty-fourth birthday, "But we were all happy and I felt grown up at last."[12]

Nearly fifty years after he had begun to paint, Feininger was as courageous in experimenting as in the days when he was accused by a critic of "juggling with possibilities." "For me this is like a 'last lap' on the track, the 'Home Run,' speaking in terms of sporting. I am almost scared of what I did yesterday; it is, in a way, outrageous; but I think I must 'get ahead' of my own courage if there is to be anything decisive attained. So let me be 'scared' . . . why should one stop *exploration?* . . . even if it seems a bit foolhardy? Later on it may appear quite all one hoped for."[13]

During the last years of his life, periods of tiredness, from which it took longer than before to recover, alternated with periods of well-being. On November 19, 1955, he wrote to Lux, "The doctor gave me yesterday the green light, but under express warning that I am still to be very careful and that I avoid overexertion. This doesn't look too good to me at this moment, for there is little one can achieve without exertion." In his last recorded letter, January 3, 1956, he wrote, "During the summer I have consciously confined myself to new experiments and prepared for fresh . . . activity in painting [Mal-Tätigkeit]. . . . I won't let myself be told that the time has come to be satisfied with dilutions [Abschwächungen]."[14] In this spirit he approached the end of his life. As long as he lived, he fought the battle that he had joined, for the renewal of his own art and the art of his time.

On January 13, 1956, Lyonel Feininger died. His hopes had been fulfilled. He had accomplished his work and "given to mankind a new perspective of the world."

170

PLATES

1 The White Man, 1907 (23)

2 Street in Paris (Pink Sky), 1909 (43)

174

3 Emeute, 1910 (52)

4 Bicycle Race, 1912 (94)

176

5 Gelmeroda I, 1913 (98)

6 High Houses II, 1913 (99)

178

7 Bridge I, 1913 (100)

8 Gelmeroda II, 1913 (101)

180

9 Benz VI, 1914 (124)

10 Girl with green Stockings, 1915 (140)

11 Jesuits III, 1915 (135)

12 Gelmeroda IV, 1915 (146)

184

13 Groß-Kromsdorf I, 1915 (151)

14 Head in Architecture, 1917 (169)

15 Woman's Head (Julia), 1916 (161)

16 Gelmeroda VII, 1917 (170)

188

17 Behind the Church, second version, 1917 (182)

189

18 Bridge III, 1917 (174)

190

19 Teltow II, 1918 (185)

20 Zirchow VII, 1918 (189)

192

21 Gothen, 1919 (194)

22 Church of Niedergrunstedt, 1919 (199)

23 The Cathedral, 1920 (209)

24 Hopfgarten, 1920 (215)

25 Viaduct, 1920 (210)

26 Ober-Weimar, 1921 (220)

27 Gaberndorf I, 1921 (218)

28a Clouds above the Sea II, 1923 (255)   28b Blue Marine, 1924 (242)

29 Gaberndorf II, 1924 (249)

30 Blue Cloud, 1925 (256)

31 Yellow Cloud, 1925 (260)

32 Gables I, Lüneburg, 1925 (257)

53 Church of the Minorites II, 1926 (264)

34 Steamer »Odin« II, 1927 (273)

35 Architecture with Stars, 1927 (276)

36 a Moonlight on the Beach, also: Evening on the Shore, 1927 (274)

36 b Sunset on the Sea, 1927 (289)

208

57 Gelmeroda XII, 1929 (311)

38 Gables III, 1929 (313)

39 Church of St. Mary I, 1929 (316)

40 Church of St. Mary with the Arrow, 1930 (333)

41 The Towers above the City, 1931 (341)

42 Mill in Autumn, 1932 (347)

214

43 Bathers, 1933 (353)

44 Stars above the Town, 1952 (351)

216

45 Mill in Spring, 1935 (371)

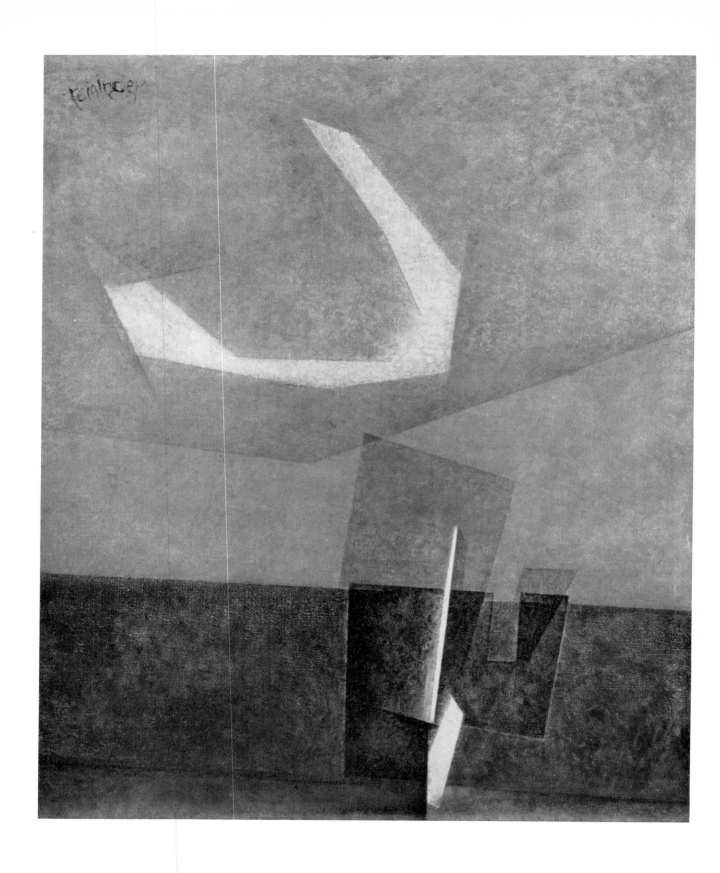

46 Cloud, 1936 (373)

218

47 Gelmeroda XIII, 1936 (375)

48 Four-Masted Barque, 1937 (383)

49 Dunes and Breakwaters, 1939 (390)

50 Manhattan II, 1940 (399)   Right: 51 Manhattan, Night, 1940 (396)

223

52 Adventure II, 1940 (402)   Right: 53 City at Night, 1941 (405)

54 Mirage II (Coast of Nevermore), 1943 (433)

55 Dunes, Ray of Light II, 1944 (447)

228

Left: 56 City Moon, 1945 (455)

Above: 57 Beach under Gloom, 1945 (458)

58 Moonwake, 1945 (460)

59 Church at Morning, 1946 (465)

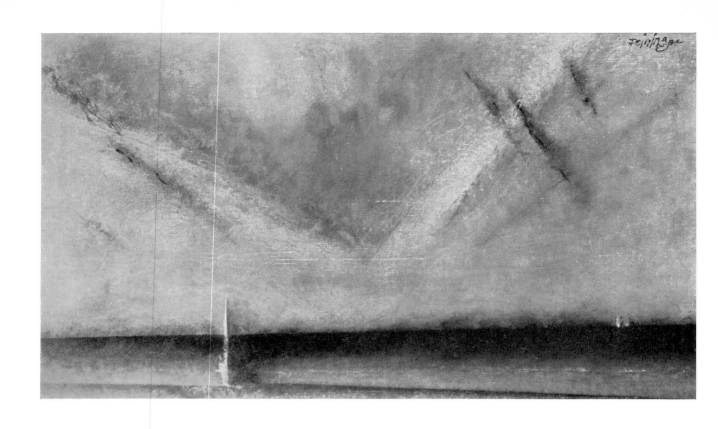

60 The Baltic (V-Cloud), 1947 (472)

61 Houses by the River I, 1948/49 (482)

62 The Hidden Village, 1948 (481)

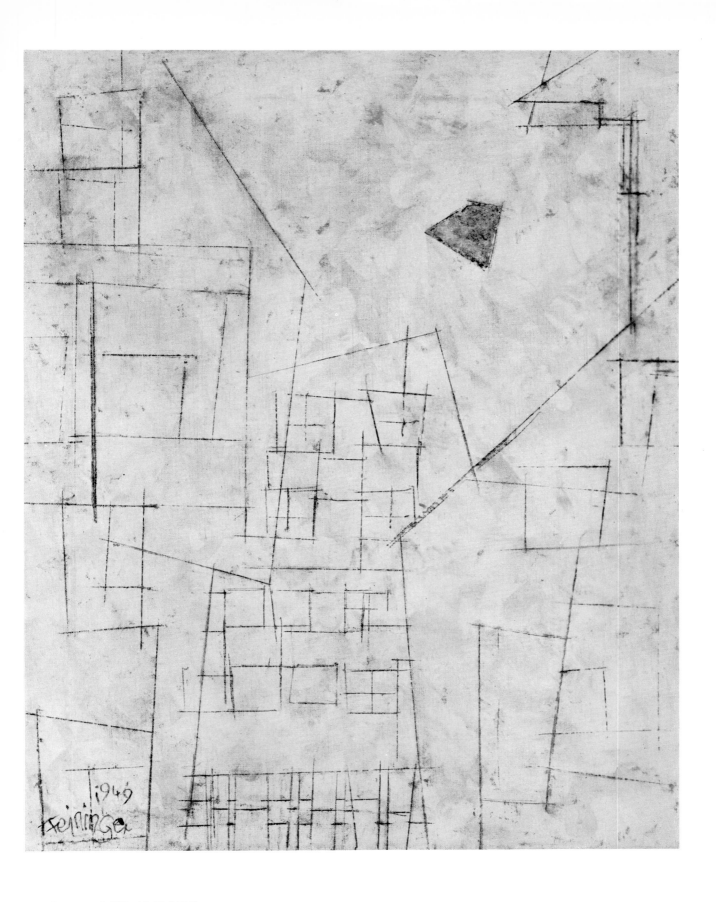

63 Courtyard III, 1949 (494)

235

64 The Factory, also: Factory Windows in Manhattan, 1949 (490)

65 The Cutting, 1949 (491)

66 The Spell, 1951 (509)

Right: 67 Manna-Hata, 1952 (517)

68 Crépuscule, 1952/53 (521)

240

69 Edged Spaces, 1954 (537)

70 Crest and Image, 1952 (515)

71 Fenris Wolf, 1954 (535)

72 Evening Haze, 1955 (539)

OEUVRE CATALOGUE

compiled by Julia Feininger

FOREWORD

This catalogue records every oil painting by the artist known to me. All titles given in this English edition are valid as supported by Lyonel Feininger. All references to titles or other remarks in his own writing on the backs of stretchers or canvases are mentioned without exception.

In the middle of the 1920s Lyonel Feininger and I started to assemble a record of his oils painted until that period. We made use of exhibition catalogues, our own notes, and, as a great help, the answers supplied by owners of his works to our carefully prepared questionnaire sheets. From about 1926 until Mr. Feininger's death in 1956 we kept a record of every finished oil painting. The German listing ends in 1957. The German titles were changed into English by Mr. Feininger himself after returning to America; after 1939 all titles are in English.

As a result of recent events, especially in Germany following the second World War, changes have taken place both in location and ownership of his works. Former museum property has found its way into private collections, and vice versa; and paintings thought to have been lost, or even destroyed, have unexpectedly reappeared. A new distribution of Feininger's work has taken place, not only within Europe but between Europe and America.

This first catalogue of oil paintings records all changes of ownership that could be traced; only in a few instances has it been necessary to state "Whereabouts unknown." All names known from the first listings as first owners are given. Successive owners are mentioned under full name and city, or as "Private collection," where such citation has been requested. Museums are acknowledged as they are publicly known. Because of the present complicated situation in Germany a number of paintings, especially from the early period, have, for a variety of reasons, been listed as "Inaccessible."

I wish to express my deep appreciation to all those owners and friends, too numerous to be mentioned singly, who have co-operated by supplying detailed information and, in many instances, equally valuable photographs. Profound thanks are due to many collaborators, who have found the interest and time to provide addresses and data about works vital to the preparation of this first œuvre catalogue of Lyonel Feininger.

Specific mention must be made, as a token of my gratitude, to those who have been instrumental in a particular way, namely: Mrs. Lillie Hess, York, England, for her never-failing help in assisting with the preparation of this catalogue for the German edition; Mr. Karl Heinz Janda of the National Gallery, Berlin, for his untiring and courageous assistance in finding and following up clues in places inaccessible to me; Mr. Bernard Karpel of the Museum of Modern Art, New York, for scholarly advice and for his interest and help in building up a record of Feininger's oil paintings in photo copy; and Mr. Alex Vömel, of the Vömel Art Gallery in Düsseldorf, who has been able, in an almost miraculous way, to trace works that have gone through many hands finally to turn up in unexpected places.

Also to those whose special contribution has been useful to the completion of this project: Dr. A. Blum, Blaricum, Holland; Professor Richard Dröcker, Stuttgart; Mr. Myrtil Frank, The Hague; Mr. Roman Norbert Ketterer, Stuttgart; Miss E. Louise Lucas, of the Fogg Art Museum, Harvard University, Cambridge, Massachusetts; Mrs. Lucie Mitton, New York; Professor Ernst Scheyer, Wayne State University, Detroit; Dr. Max Stern, Dominion Art Gallery, Montreal; Professor Fritz Strich, Bern; the late Dr. W. R. Valentiner; Miss Jane Wade, New York; the late Mr. Tom van Waveren; Mrs. Marian Willard Johnson, New York; and Dr. Hans Maria Wingler, Frankfurt.

New York, 1961   Julia Feininger

1907

1 [STILL LIFE]
oil on board, 16½ × 14½″
unsigned
dated at lower right: 21. Apr. 07
(painted in Paris,
first attempt in oil)
Inaccessible

2 [STILL LIFE]
oil on board, 20 × 15″
unsigned
at lower right: Apr. 22. 07
(painted in Paris)
Inaccessible

3 [STILL LIFE]

oil on board, 7 × 5½″
unsigned
(painted in Paris, spring 1907)
Alois W. Schardt, U.S.A.

4 [STUDY AFTER NATURE (The
Towers of Notre-Dame from Across
the River)]

oil on board, 7 × 5½″
unsigned
(painted in Paris, spring 1907)
Alois W. Schardt, U.S.A.

5 [BRIDGE, HOUSES]
(unfinished)

oil on board, 7 × 5½″
unsigned
(painted in Paris, spring 1907)
Alois W. Schardt, U.S.A.

6 [HOUSE IN GARDEN]

oil on board, 5½ × 7″
unsigned
on back: painting no. 7
(painted in Paris, spring 1907)
Alois W. Schardt, U.S.A.

7 [ALLEY WITH CARRIAGE]

oil on board, 5½ × 7″
unsigned
on back of painting no. 6
(painted in Paris, spring 1907)
Alois W. Schardt, U.S.A.

8 [VILLA BY THE SEINE I]
oil on board, 19¾ × 13⅓″
unsigned
(painted in Paris)
Inaccessible

9 [VILLA BY THE SEINE II]
oil on board, 13¾ × 19½″
upper right: Feininger 07
(painted in Paris)
Inaccessible

10 THE PROPOSAL
(Die Werbung)
oil on canvas, 26¾ × 21″
unsigned
(painted in Paris)
Inaccessible

11 [CHURCH]

oil on board, 5½ × 7″
unsigned
on back: *Juli 1907*
Güntherstal b. Freiburg
Alois W. Schardt, U.S.A.

12 HOUSES ON THE HILLSIDE
(Häuser am Berghang)
oil on board, 7¾ × 12¾″
unsigned
(painted in Güntherstal near Freiburg, Breisgau, Germany,
summer 1907)
Inaccessible

13 STEEPLE BEHIND TREES
(Kirchturm hinter Bäumen)
oil on board, 13½ × 10¼″
unsigned
(painted in Güntherstal near Freiburg, Breisgau, Germany,
summer 1907)
Inaccessible

14 FARMHOUSE IN ORCHARD
(Bauernhaus mit Obstbäumen)

oil on board, 14³/₄×24¹/₄″
lower right: Feininger 07
(painted on the isle of Rügen,
Baltic, late summer 1907)
Inaccessible

15 EDGE OF THE WOOD, LOBBE
(Waldrand bei Lobbe)

oil on board, 24¹/₄×24³/₄″
upper right: Feininger 1907
(painted in Lobbe on the isle of
Rügen, Baltic, late summer 1907)
Inaccessible

16 DUNE, BEACH, SEA
oil on board, 14³/₄×19³/₄″
unsigned
(painted in Lobbe on the isle of
Rügen, Baltic, late summer 1907)
Inaccessible

17 HAYSTACKS
oil on board, 13³/₄×19³/₄″
unsigned
(painted in Lobbe on the isle of
Rügen, Baltic, late summer 1907)
Inaccessible

18 FARMHOUSE IN BRIGHT
SUNLIGHT
oil on board, 15¹/₄×19¹/₂″
unsigned
(painted in Lobbe on the isle of
Rügen, Baltic, late summer 1907)
Inaccessible

19 FARMHOUSE (GRAY MOOD)
oil on board, 14³/₄×19¹/₄″
unsigned
(painted in Lobbe on the isle of
Rügen, Baltic, late summer 1907)
Inaccessible

20 ROAD, AUTUMN WIND
oil on board, 15×20″
unsigned
(painted in Lobbe on the isle of
Rügen, Baltic, late summer 1907)
Inaccessible

21 HAYSTACKS
(Heuhaufen)
oil on board, 15¹/₄×19¹/₂″
unsigned
(painted in Lobbe on the isle of
Rügen, Baltic, late summer 1907)
1. Arthur Berson, Berlin
Whereabouts unknown

22 FARMHOUSE IN LOBBE
(Bauernhaus in Lobbe)
oil on board, 14¹/₄×20″
unsigned
(painted in Lobbe on the isle of
Rügen, Baltic, late summer 1907)
1. Arthur Berson, Berlin
Whereabouts unknown

23 THE WHITE MAN
oil on canvas, 26³/₄×21″
unsigned
(painted after return to Paris,
fall 1907)
on back of earliest existing photo
in Feininger's own hand:
*2nd painting, Lyonel Feininger,
Paris 1907 The White Man*
(Feininger probably meant the
second painting on canvas. – J. F.)
Estate of the artist
Plate 1

24 ARCUEIL I

oil on canvas, 26¹/₂×21¹/₂″
unsigned
(painted in Paris, fall 1907)
Inaccessible

1908

25 LOCOMOTIVE

oil on canvas, 17¹/₄×32″
lower right: Feininger 08
(painted in Paris)
Andreas Feininger, New York

26 STILL LIFE
oil on canvas, 13³/₄×19³/₄″
unsigned
Inaccessible

27 JESUITS I
oil on canvas, 23³/₄×21¹/₄″
lower left: Feininger
Inaccessible

28 CARNIVAL IN GELMERODA II
oil on canvas, 28³/₄×26³/₄″
lower left: Feininger 08
Inaccessible

29 PEDESTRIANS

oil on canvas, 15¹/₂ × 11¹/₂″
unsigned
Inaccessible

30 CARNIVAL

oil on canvas, 27 × 21¹/₄″
signature: ?
Inaccessible

31 THE MANHOLE I
(Das Kanalisationsloch I)

oil on canvas, 31³/₄ × 25³/₄″
lower right: Feininger 08
(painted in Paris)
Estate of the artist
Colorplate 1

32 ON THE QUAY
(Am Quai)

oil on canvas, 27³/₄ × 31¹/₂″
lower right: Feininger
on back of stretcher, top at right
of center written in blue pencil:
Am Quai, 1908
at left, very faint, also in pencil:
Finished December 22nd 08
Estate of the artist

33 WEDDING TRIP

oil on canvas, measurements: ?
signature: ?
1. Sold in 1920 in the Kunstverein,
Heidelberg

Whereabouts unknown

34 NEWSPAPER READERS I

oil on canvas, 28³/₄ × 26³/₄″
lower right: Feininger

34

1. Jacques Casper, Berlin
2. Direktor Katzenstein,
   Düsseldorf
Painting disappeared in Paris
during Nazi occupation

35 THE RED CLOWN I

oil on canvas, measurements: ?
signature: ?
1. Sold in 1919 at J. B. Neumann,
   Berlin, at Feininger one-man
   show

Whereabouts unknown

1909

36 VILLAGE, DUSK
(Dämmerdorf)

oil on canvas, 31¹/₂ × 39¹/₂″
lower left: Feininger
Inaccessible

37 DIABOLO PLAYERS

oil on canvas, 15¹/₂ × 26″
signature dim, but discernible,
lower right: Feininger
(signature made out on photo)
Inaccessible

37

38 STILL LIFE (WITH ORANGES)

oil on canvas, 31¹/₂ × 39¹/₂″
upper right: Feininger 09
(painted on April 5, 1909)
Inaccessible

**39 GIRL IN PINK AND LITTLE
MEN**

oil on canvas, 17¹/₂ × 14″
signature: ?
Inaccessible

40 FIGURES, DUSK

oil on canvas, 16¹/₄ × 14¹/₄″
lower left: Feininger 09
on back of stretcher, upper left:
L. Feininger
in blue pencil: *April 6th + 7th 1909*

Moritz Noack, Munich

41 SMALL BLUE LOCOMOTIVE
oil on canvas, 15³/₄×17¹/₄″
signature: ?
Inaccessible

42 NEWSPAPER READERS
(Zeitungsleser)
oil on canvas, 20×25″
upper right: Feininger 09
Inaccessible

43 STREET IN PARIS (PINK SKY)
oil on canvas, 39¹/₂×32″
lower left: Feininger
on back of stretcher written in soft
pencil:
Sund. May 23 09
Sund. June 6 09
Owen and Leona Elliot Trust,
Cedar Rapids, Iowa
Plate 2

44 GREEN BRIDGE

oil on canvas, 39×31³/₄″
lower left: Feininger
on back of stretcher, top, written
in pencil: *First exhibited 1911 at
the Salon des Indépendants in Paris*
on bottom piece of stretcher, also
in pencil: *finished Thursday May
6th 1909*
Estate of the artist

45 SMALL-TOWN MOTIVE
(OLD WEIMAR)
oil on canvas, 23³/₄×28¹/₂″
lower left: Feininger
on back of stretcher: *Old Weimar (Small Town Motive)*

1. Maria Zuntz, Germany
2. Private Collection, Frankfurt/M.

45

46 WOMAN IN PINK
oil on canvas, 25×20″
signature: ?
1. Francis Christophe, Berlin
Whereabouts unknown

47 SUNRISE
(Häuser und Menschen)

oil on canvas, 21¹/₂×18″
lower right: Feininger
1. Max Haar, Weimar
2. Private Collection, Krefeld

48 LONGUEIL, NORMANDY

oil on canvas, 31¹/₂×39³/₄″
lower right: Feininger
1. Eugen Buchthal, Berlin
2. Miss Clara Hoover, New York

49 YELLOW STREET I
oil on canvas, 23³/₄×21¹/₄″
lower right: Feininger 09

1. Mrs. Helene Goldschmidt,
   Berlin

Whereabouts unknown

1910

50 VELOCIPEDISTS
(Draisinenfahrer)

oil on canvas, 37¹/₂×33¹/₂″
lower right: Feininger 10
Inaccessible

51 FIN DE SÉANCE

oil on canvas, 37¹/₂×33³/₄″
upper left: Feininger 10
Inaccessible

52 ÉMEUTE
oil on canvas, 41×37¹/₂″
upper right: Feininger 10

Estate of the artist
Plate 3

53 OLD AMERICAN
    LOCOMOTIVE

oil on canvas, 19³/₄ × 39¹/₂″
upper right: Feininger 1910
on back of stretcher: *Sunday
July 3rd 1910*
Estate of the artist

54 SMALL AMERICAN
    LOCOMOTIVE
oil on canvas, 19³/₄ × 25³/₄″
signature: ?
Private Collection, Germany

55 SELF-PORTRAIT WITH
    CLAY PIPE

oil on canvas, 24 × 19³/₄″
signature: ?
Private Collection, Germany

56 LOCOMOTIVE WITH THE BIG
    WHEEL I
oil on canvas, 21³/₄ × 39¹/₂″
lower right: Feininger
Inaccessible

57 RAILROADMEN
oil on canvas, 22¹/₄ × 35¹/₄″
upper left: Feininger
Inaccessible

58 TOWN
oil on canvas, 14¹/₄ × 15″
upper right: Feininger 10

1. Dr. Wittgensteiner, Berlin
Whereabouts unknown

59 ROAD IN RAIN, NEPPERMIN
oil on canvas, 15¹/₂ × 24″
lower right: Feininger 10
1. Dr. August Bonnin, Berlin
Whereabouts unknown

60 STREET IN DUSK
    (Straße im Dämmern)

oil on canvas, 31¹/₂ × 39¹/₂″
lower left: Feininger 10
on back, on the canvas folded
around the stretcher at lower left
corner in Feininger's own handwriting: *Straße im Dämmern* 1910
1. Private Collection, Germany
2. Landesgalerie, Hanover

61 MOONRISE IN NEPPERMIN

oil on canvas, 15¹/₄ × 25″
unsigned
on back of canvas: at the request
of the owner in 1948 authorship
was confirmed, and a piece of paper
glued to the canvas bears the
signature *Lyonel Feininger*
Dr. Walter Kaesbach,
Hemmenhofen ü. Radolfzell,
Germany

1911

62 STILL LIFE ON BLUE TABLE
oil on canvas, 22¹/₂ × 28″
signed in white area below to left
of center: Feininger

62

on back of stretcher, written in
thick pencil: *January 1911*
Private Collection, London

63 CARNIVAL IN ARCUEIL

oil on canvas, 41 × 37¹/₂″
upper left: Feininger 1911
Inaccessible

64 BELGIAN RAILWAY
oil on canvas, 29¹/₂ × 37¹/₂″
lower right: Feininger
Inaccessible

65 STILL LIFE WITH LEMONS

oil on canvas, 13³/₄ × 15³/₄″
upper right: Feininger 1911
on back of stretcher: *Lyonel Feininger 1911, Erinnerung an den
heißen Sommer*
Estate of the artist

253

66 DIABOLO PLAYERS II
(unfinished)
oil on canvas, 22×17³/₄″
signature: ?
Inaccessible

1912

67 ANGLER WITH BLUE FISH I
oil on canvas, 22×28³/₄″
lower right: Feininger 12
Inaccessible

68 ANGLER WITH BLUE FISH II

oil on canvas, 22¹/₄×29¹/₄″
lower right: Feininger
Inaccessible

69 SAILBOAT
oil on canvas, 16×19″
lower right: Feininger 12

Andreas Feininger, New York

70 TOWN HALL, SWINEMÜNDE
(Rathaus von Swinemünde)

oil on canvas, 27¹/₂×23¹/₂″
upper left: Feininger

254

on back of stretcher, written in
pencil: *Tues. March 26, 1912*
written in crayon: *Rathaus von
Swinemünde*

Estate of the artist

71 BATHERS ON THE BEACH I

oil on canvas, 19¹/₄×25″
lower left: Feininger 1912
on back of stretcher: *April 1912
Bathers*
1. F. R. Schon, Toronto
2. Busch-Reisinger Museum,
   Harvard University,
   Cambridge, Massachusetts

72 [PEDESTRIANS]
(Spaziergänger)

oil on canvas, measurements: ?
unsigned
Identification only from existing
photo. In Professor Alois J.
Schardt's handwriting on back
of photo: *Spaziergänger,
Frühjahr 1912*
Whereabouts unknown

73 BLUE BARQUE IN RED
WATERS
oil on canvas, 15³/₄×19″
upper right: Feininger 1912
Inaccessible

74 ON THE QUAY
(Am Quai)

oil on canvas, 15³/₄×19″
upper left: Feininger 1912
inscription on back of stretcher,
written in ink: *Lyonel Feininger
1912 Am Quai s.l. alten Freun-
den Familie Otto Löwenstein ge-
widmet Weihnachten 1932*
1. Otto Löwenstein, Germany
2. Karl Loewenstein, Amherst,
   Massachusetts

75 BRIDGE O

oil on canvas, 35¹/₄×45″
signature: ?
Inaccessible

76 VOLLERSRODA I
oil on canvas, 31¹/₂×39³/₄″
lower left: Feininger
Private Collection, Germany

77 [AT THE SEINE, PARIS, 1912]
(An der Seine, Paris, 1912)
oil on canvas, measurements: ?
signature: ?
Comment on title in Feininger's
own hand on back of a photo:
*Lyonel Feininger, 1912
An der Seine, Paris
(Bild vernichtet)*
Destroyed by the artist

78 TRUMPETERS

oil on canvas, 37×31½″
lower left: Feininger
Inaccessible

79 STILL LIFE

oil on canvas, 21³/4×29³/4″
unsigned
Inaccessible

80 MAN WITH UMBRELLA
oil on canvas, 19×16″
lower right: Feininger 12
1. Otto Ralfs, Brunswick, Germany
Destroyed in bombing raid

81 THE MESSENGER
(Der Bote)

oil on canvas, 19×15³/4″
lower right: Feininger

on back of stretcher written
in black pencil: *July 1912*
in blue pencil: *Der Bote*
Erich Scheyer, Maryport,
Cumberland, England

82 STUDY, ON THE CLIFFS
(EARLY ATTEMPT AT CUBIST
FORM)

oil on canvas, 17³/4×23³/4″
lower left: Feininger 1912
1. Mrs. Anne Klestadt, Düsseldorf
2. Mr. and Mrs. Gerald Jonas,
   Cincinnati

83 ZIRCHOW I
oil on canvas, 27¼×39″
upper left: Feininger
1. Dr. Walter Kaesbach Foundation
   Mönchen-Gladbach, Germany
Seized by the Nazis

84 MAN IN RED AND FIGURES
BY THE SHORE

oil on canvas, 17½×27¼″
unsigned
picture has been relined
1. Alois J. Schardt, Berlin
2. Alois W. Schardt, U.S.A.

85 HIGH HOUSES I
oil on canvas, 39½×31½″
upper left: Feininger
1. Bernhard Köhler, Berlin
Destroyed in bombing raid

85

86 TELTOW I

oil on canvas, 31½×39½″
unsigned
1. Paul Poiret, Paris
Whereabouts unknown

87 FISHERFLEET IN SWELL

oil on canvas, measurements: ?
signature: ?
1. Sold in 1919 at J. B. Neumann,
   Berlin, at Feininger one-man
   show
2. Private Collection

88 THE WAVE
oil on canvas, measurements: ?
signature: ?
1. Sold in 1919 at J. B. Neumann,
   Berlin, at Feininger one-man
   show
Whereabouts unknown

255

89 VILLAGE, ALT-SALLENTHIN
oil on canvas, measurements: ?
signature: ?
1. Sold in 1919 at J. B. Neumann, Berlin, at Feininger one-man show
Whereabouts unknown

90 BENZ

oil on canvas, 15³/₄×19″
upper right: Feininger 12
Inaccessible

91 BALLOON CARNIVAL
oil on canvas, 27¹/₂×22″
upper right: Feininger
Destroyed by the artist, May 13, 1950

92 THE ENCOUNTER
oil on canvas, 21¹/₂×18¹/₂″
lower right: Feininger
1. Gustav Jung, Hagen, Germany
Whereabouts unknown

93 PIER
(Landungsbrücke)

oil on canvas, 28¹/₂×32¹/₂″
lower right: Feininger 12
1. F. R. Schon, Toronto
2. Frederick Mendel, Saskatoon, Canada

94 BICYCLE RACE
(Die Radfahrer)
oil on canvas, 31¹/₂×39¹/₂″
lower left: Feininger 1912
on back of stretcher: *Lyonel Feininger 1912 (Die Radfahrer)*
on back of canvas in oil: *Feininger 1912*
Maria Möller-Garny, Cologne
Plate 4

95 SIDE-WHEEL STEAMER AT THE LANDING

oil on canvas, 15³/₄×19″
upper left: Feininger
1. Hugo Simon, Berlin
2. Private Collection, New York

96 PIER

oil on canvas, 18×23¹/₂″
lower left: Feininger 12
1. Alfred Hess, Erfurt, Germany
2. Mrs. Tekla Hess, York, England

1913

97 VILLAGE, ALT-SALLENTHIN
(Dorfstraße)

oil on canvas, 31³/₄×39¹/₂″
unsigned
1. Mrs. Sophie Gerhard, Bonn
2. Museum Folkwang, Essen, Germany

97

98 GELMERODA I
oil on canvas, 39¹/₂×31¹/₂″
upper left: Feininger
on back of stretcher, written in pencil: *Feininger Gelmeroda 1*
Stefan Pauson, Giffnock, Glasgow
Plate 5

99 HIGH HOUSES II
oil on canvas, 39¹/₂×31¹/₂″
upper left: Feininger 13
1. Mrs. Helene Goldschmidt, Berlin
2. Mr. and Mrs. Roy R. Neuberger, New York
Plate 6

100 BRIDGE I *
oil on canvas, 31¹/₂×39¹/₂″
upper left: Feininger 13
on back of canvas: *Feininger 1913*
(* First attempt at this version of *Bridge*, painted in Weimar, 1913, discarded; given to a friend, Hans Adolph Heiman, at his request. Nothing known, and no information has been obtainable about Mr. Heiman; he died a few years ago in Manila. – J. F.)
1. Dr. W. Mayer, Tübingen, Germany
2. Städtische Galerie, Hanover
3. Washington University, St. Louis
Plate 7

101 GELMERODA II
oil on canvas, 39¹/₂×31⁵/₈″
lower left: Feininger
on back of stretcher, written in ink: *Lyonel Feininger 1913 Zehlendorf-Mitte b. Berlin Königstr. 32*
also in Feininger's own handwriting: *Gelmeroda III*
(This is at variance with the number under which the painting has been listed. – J. F.)
Private Collection, New York
Plate 8

102 GELMERODA III

oil on canvas, 39½×31½″
upper right: Feininger
(Mentioned in letters to Julia 1913;
on back of a photo the years
1914–15 are mentioned; last
touches 1917. – J. F.)

1. Stadtmuseum Dresden
   Seized in action "Degenerate
   Art" in 1937
2. Adolphe J. Warner, New York

103 THE MANHOLE II

oil on canvas, 39½×31½″
upper left: Feininger

1. Alfred Hess, Erfurt, Germany
2. Denys Sutton, London

104 MAN STANDING BEFORE
CLIFFS

oil on canvas, 17¼×14¼″
lower right: Feininger 13

1. Moritz Noack, Munich
2. Brigitte Röseler, Hamburg
3. Manfred and Lilo Behr,
   Stuttgart

105 [SIDE WHEELER I
(MAIL STEAMER)]
(Der Raddampfer I)

oil on canvas, 31¾×39¾″
upper left: Feininger 1913
on back of stretcher: *Lyonel Feininger 1913 Der Raddampfer*

Maria Möller-Garny, Cologne

106 PORTRAIT STUDY OF JULIA

oil on canvas, 19×15¾″
unsigned
Inaccessible

107 BENZ
oil on canvas, 19×24½″
signature: ?
Inaccessible

108 PIRATE SCHOONER (sketch)
oil on canvas, 15¾×24½″
upper right: Feininger 13
Inaccessible

109 BATHERS I
(Badende I)

oil on canvas, 31½×39½″
lower right: Feininger
(German title in Feininger's own
handwriting on back of photo. –
J. F.)

1. Collection Sinclair, Kassel
Sold in auction at Kunstverein,
Kassel
Whereabouts unknown

110 ZIRCHOW II

oil on canvas, 31½×39½″
lower right: Feininger 13
(Painting has been relined;
photograph taken of back before
relining bears only signature of
artist and date. – J. F.)

1. Collection Ettlinger, Vienna
2. Mrs. Edith Gregor Halpert,
   New York

111 ON THE BRIDGE

oil on canvas, 23³/₄ × 24³/₄″
lower left: Feininger 1913
painting mounted on new stretcher

1. Dr. W. Fulda, Germany
2. Mr. Wigbert Langgut, Lohhof
   near Munich

112 SLEEPING WOMAN (JULIA)
(Die Schläferin – Julia)

oil on canvas, 31¹/₂ × 39¹/₂″
lower left: Feininger
on back of stretcher, top
horizontal, written in India ink:
Lyonel Feininger
on cross piece, horizontal, in India
ink applied with brush: *1913
Die Schläferin Sleeping Woman –
Julia*
Estate of the artist

113 HARBOR MOLE
(Hafenmole)
oil on canvas, 31³/₄ × 39³/₄″
lower right: Feininger
1. F. R. Schon, Toronto
2. Mr. and Mrs. John Drew,
   Pittsburgh
Colorplate 2

114 JESUITS II

oil on canvas, 28¹/₂ × 24″
lower left: Feininger 13
1. Buller Collection, Düsseldorf
2. Morton D. May, St. Louis

115 ON THE BEACH
(Am Strand)

oil on canvas, 15³/₄ × 19¹/₄″
lower left: Feininger
on back of stretcher (top), in blue
crayon: *Feininger 1913
Am Strand 1913*
before restoring of paint surface
at lower left the old signature:
Feininger 13; faint but perfectly
readable on an old photo
1. Willy Hahn, Berlin-Charlottenburg
2. Mr. and Mrs. L. F. Gittler,
   New York
3. Peter Nathan, Zurich

116 THE BEACON
(Leuchtbake)

oil on canvas, 39¹/₂ × 31¹/₂″
upper left: Feininger
1. Ferdinand Möller, Berlin
2. Museum Folkwang, Essen,
   Germany

117 THE SIDE-WHEELER II
(Raddampfer II)
oil on canvas, 31¹/₂ × 35³/₄″
lower right: Feininger 13
on back of stretcher written in ink:
1913-14 Raddampfer II
The Detroit Institute of Arts

117

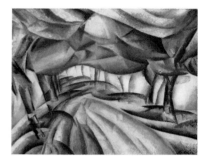

1914

118 COUNTRY ROAD TO NIEDER-
GRUNSTEDT
(Landweg nach Nieder-Grunstedt)

oil on canvas, 31¹/₂ × 39¹/₂″
lower right: Feininger
on back of canvas in oil:
Feininger 1914
on back of stretcher, top, written
in India ink: *Landweg nach Nieder-
Grunstedt*
Estate of the artist

119 UMPFERSTEDT I

oil on canvas, 31¹/₄ × 39¹/₂″
lower right: Feininger 1914
on back of stretcher written in
crayon: *1914 Umpferstedt I*
Andreas Feininger, New York

120 UMPFERSTEDT II

oil on canvas, 39¹/₂×31¹/₂″
upper left: Feininger
on back of stretcher in black ink:
Umpferstedt II

1. Dr. Walter Arensberg,
   Los Angeles
2. The Louise and Walter Arensberg Collection, Philadelphia
   Museum of Art

Colorplate 3

121 MARINE

oil on canvas, 31¹/₂×39¹/₂″
signature: ?

1. Herwarth Walden, Berlin
   Burned during World War II in
   Berlin

122 NIEDER-GRUNSTEDT IV

oil on canvas, 31¹/₂×39¹/₂″
lower right: Feininger

1. Max Würzburger, Berlin
2. Charles Bewley, Eire
   Whereabouts unknown

123 NIEDER-GRUNSTEDT VI

oil on canvas, 31¹/₂×39³/₈″
lower left: Feininger

1. S. Stiebel, Frankfurt/M.
   Seized by the Nazis

124 BENZ VI

oil on canvas, 40×49¹/₄″
lower left: Feininger 14

1. Museum, Stettin, Germany
2. Mr. and Mrs. John B. Holt,
   Georgetown, Maine

Plate 9

125 STREET OF BARNS
(Scheunenstrasse)

oil on canvas, 49¹/₄×39¹/₂″
lower right: Feininger

1. Museum Folkwang, Essen,
   Germany
   Seized in action "Degenerate Art"
   1937

**126 CHURCH OF GROSS-KROMS-
DORF**

oil on canvas, 35¹/₂×39¹/₂″
upper left: Feininger 1914

1. Dr. Stange, Bonn
2. Dr. Schürer, Mühlheim/Ruhr

127 BRIDGE II
(Brücke II)

oil on canvas, 32×39³/₄″
lower right: Feininger

on left side of stretcher, on canvas
folded over, written in India ink:
Brücke II Winter 1914–15
Estate of the artist

128 ZIRCHOW III

oil on canvas, 31¹/₂×39¹/₂″
upper right: Feininger
on back of canvas, in black color:
Feininger

1. H. von Garvens, Hanover
   Whereabouts unknown

129 BATHERS ON THE BEACH
(Badende am Strande)

oil on canvas, 15³/₄×27¹/₄″
upper right: Feininger 14
on back of stretcher in blue pencil:
1914 Badende am Strande
on back of canvas, in India ink:
Mai, 1914
Estate of the artist

130 RAINY DAY BY THE SEA

oil on canvas, 17³/₄×27¹/₂″
lower right: Feininger 14
Stefan Pauson, Giffnock, Glasgow

151 GAS TANKS, SCHÖNEBERG
(Gasanstalt, Schöneberg)
oil on canvas, 27¹/₄×36³/₄″
signature: ?
Inaccessible

1914–15

152 BATHERS ON THE BEACH

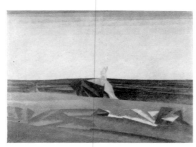

oil on canvas, 21¹/₄×30¹/₄″
lower left: Feininger
painted in 1914; on back of
stretcher: *January 1915* (signed)
1. F. R. Schon, Toronto
2. G. David Thompson, Pittsburgh
3. Private Collection, New York
4. Peter Nathan, Zurich

1915

133 ALLÉE

oil on canvas, 31³/₄×39¹/₂″
lower right: Feininger
on back of stretcher written in
India ink: *Lyonel Feininger 1915
Allée 1915*
Estate of the artist

134 HARBOR OF SWINEMÜNDE
oil on canvas, measurements: ?
signature: ?
1. Hugo Simon, Berlin
Disappeared in Paris during Nazi
occupation

135 JESUITS III
oil on canvas, 29¹/₂×23¹/₂″
lower left: Feininger
Estate of the artist
Plate 11

136 WOMAN'S HEAD WITH
GREEN EYES
(Frauenkopf mit grünen Augen)

oil on canvas, 27¹/₂×24¹/₂″
upper left: Feininger 15
on back of stretcher written in
crayon: *19. April 1913*
(signature on painting: 1915)
Estate of the artist

137 SELF-PORTRAIT
(Selbstbildnis)
oil on canvas, 39¹/₂×31¹/₂″
upper left: Feininger 15
on back of stretcher:
*Lyonel Feininger Selfportrait 1915
Selbstbildnis 1915*
Estate of the artist
Colorplate 4

138 LOCOMOTIVE WITH THE BIG
WHEEL
(Die Lokomotive mit dem grossen
Rad)

oil on canvas, 22×47¹/₂″
signed at right in light area:
Feininger 15

on back of stretcher written in
crayon: *1915 Die Locomotive mit
dem grossen Rad*
Estate of the artist

139 BATHERS
(Badende am Strande)

oil on canvas, 17¹/₄×30³/₄″
lower left: Feininger 15
on back of stretcher written in ink:
*Lyonel Feininger July 1915
Badende am Strande*
1. Dr. Walter Kaesbach, Hemmenhofen, Bodensee, Germany
2. A. F., Düsseldorf

140 GIRL WITH GREEN
STOCKINGS
oil on canvas, 35¹/₂×31¹/₂″
upper left: Feininger 15
on back of stretcher in oil:
*Feininger 1915 Girl with Green
Stockings*
Estate of the artist
Plate 10

141 SAILBOATS WITH BLACK
SAILS

oil on canvas, 17³/₄×25³/₄″
lower left: Feininger 15
on back of stretcher written in
India ink: *Lyonel Feininger 1915
Sailboats with Black Sails*
Estate of the artist

142 HARBOR OF NEPPERMIN
(Hafen von Neppermin)

oil on canvas, 31³/₄ × 39¹/₂"
lower right: Feininger 15
on back of stretcher: *Hafen von
Neppermin 1915*
on back of canvas: *Feininger 15*
   F
   I

1. Museum, Krefeld, Germany
2. Joseph H. Hirshhorn, New York

143 RAINY DAY

oil on canvas, 39¹/₂ × 31¹/₂"
upper right: Feininger 15
Estate of the artist

144 PROMENADE (ARCUEIL II)

oil on canvas, 35¹/₂ × 28¹/₂"
upper left: Feininger 15
Estate of the artist

145 THE CHURCH TOWER,
MELLINGEN
(Mellingen II)

oil on canvas, 39¹/₂ × 31"
lower right: Feininger 15
on back of stretcher written in ink:
*Lyonel Feininger 1915
Mellingen II*

1. Miss von Dulong
2. Prof. Otto F. Salvisberg, Zurich
3. Private Collection, Switzerland

146 GELMERODA IV

oil on canvas, 39¹/₂ × 31¹/₂"
lower right: Feininger 15
on back of canvas in oil:
1: GELMERODA
b: Gelmeroda

1. Eric Mendelsohn, San Francisco
2. The Solomon R. Guggenheim
   Museum, New York

Plate 12

147 TRUMPETER IN THE VILLAGE

oil on canvas, 23³/₄ × 29¹/₂"
lower right: Feininger 15
on back of canvas written in India
ink: *Sept. 1915*

Estate of the artist

148 [BLIND ALLEY]
(Schlossgasse)

oil on canvas, 39¹/₂ × 31³/₄"
lower left: Feininger 15
on top edge of folded-over canvas
in ink: *Schlossgasse Oct. 1915*
on top of stretcher, in blue crayon:
Feininger Schlossgasse

1. Meyer-Brodnitz, Berlin
2. Ludwig Fischer, Frankfurt/M.
3. Dr. Max Fischer, Frankfurt/M.
4. William H. Lane Foundation,
   Leominster, Massachusetts

149 MARINE

oil on canvas, 23³/₄ × 29¹/₂"
lower right: Feininger
Prof. Hans Scharoun, Berlin

150 STREET: AM PALAIS

261

oil on canvas, 40×32″
upper left: Feininger
on back of stretcher: *Jan. 15*

1. Collection Falk, Mannheim
2. Dr. Rosenhain, Hanover
3. Mrs. Gertrud Rosenhain,
   Jackson Heights, New York

151 GROSS-KROMSDORF I
oil on canvas, 39¹/₂×31¹/₂″
lower right: Feininger
on crosspiece of stretcher
written in pencil: *L. Feininger,
Zehlendorf-Mitte, Königstraße*
Private Collection, Minneapolis
Plate 13

152 STILL LIFE WITH BRUSHES
(Stilleben mit Pinseln)

oil on canvas, 18×32″
lower left: Feininger 15
Inaccessible

1916

153 ZIRCHOW V
oil on canvas, 31⁷/₈×39⁵/₈″
lower right: Feininger 1916
The Brooklyn Museum (Gift of
Otto J. and Eloise A. Spaeth Foundation and J. B. Woodward Fund)
Colorplate 5

154 THE BLUE CLOWN

oil on canvas, 19×16″
upper right: Feininger 1916
Estate of the artist

155 BEHIND THE CHURCH
(THE SQUARE)
(Hinter der Stadtkirche)

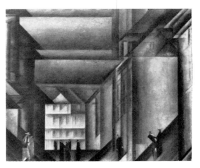

oil on canvas, 29×35¹/₂″
lower left: Feininger 1916
on back of stretcher in pencil:
March 1916

1. Georg Kaiser, Germany
2. Alfred Hess, Erfurt, Germany
3. Leicester Museum and Art
   Gallery, England

156 STILL LIFE WITH SAMOVAR
(Stilleben mit Krügen)

oil on canvas, 31¹/₂×39¹/₂″
upper right: Feininger 16
on back of stretcher: *Stilleben
mit Krügen*

1. Fritz Beindorff, Hanover
2. Kunstmuseum der Stadt
   Düsseldorf

157 THE DESERTED CHILD
(Das verlassene Kind)
oil on canvas, 29¹/₂×24″
upper right: Feininger 16
on back of old photo, in Feininger's
own handwriting the following
comment:
*was in Walter Rathenau's collec-
tion ... the painting I now posess,
having exchanged another for it
from it's later posessor*
(Later owner not known. J. F.)

1. Walther Rathenau, Berlin
2. Estate of the artist

157

158 ZOTTELSTEDT I

oil on canvas, 31³/₄×39¹/₂″
upper left: Feininger 1916
Inaccessible

159 THE STARGAZERS
(Menschen, Mond, Sterne)

oil on canvas, 19×16″
upper left: Feininger
Private Collection, London

160 STREETCLEANERS
oil on canvas, 47×59″
lower right: Feininger 16
Estate of the artist

160

161 WOMAN'S HEAD (JULIA)

oil on canvas, 19×16″
lower right: Feininger 16
on an existing photo, in Feininger's
own handwriting:
Lyonel Feininger, 1916
Head of a Woman
(Tête de femme)

1. Eric Mendelsohn,
   San Francisco
2. Mrs. Madeleine H. Russell,
   San Francisco

Plate 15

162 ZIRCHOW VI

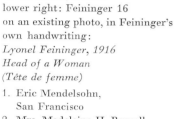

oil on canvas, 31¹/₈×39¹/₂″
upper right: Feininger

1. Museum Moritzburg, Halle
2. Karl Nierendorf, New York
Disappeared from the Nierendorf
Estate
Whereabouts unknown

163 THE GREEN BRIDGE II
(Grüne Brücke II)

oil on canvas, 49¹/₂×39¹/₂″
lower left: Feininger
on back of stretcher written in
crayon: *Grüne Brücke II 1916*

1. Major Hülsmann, Berlin
2. The North Carolina Museum of
   Art, Raleigh (Gift of Mrs.
   Ferdinand Möller, Cologne)

163

164 VOLLERSRODA III

oil on canvas, 31¹/₂×39¹/₂″
upper right: Feininger 16

1. Nationalgalerie, Berlin
2. Museum Moritzburg, Halle
3. Frank Loesser, New York

165 [NEWSPAPER READERS II]
(Zeitungsleser II)

oil on canvas, measurements: ?
signature: ?
(Title on existing photo in Feininger's own handwriting. – J. F.)

1. Major Hülsmann, Berlin
Whereabouts unknown

166 TOWN IN MOONLIGHT
(Stadt in Mondlicht)

oil on canvas, 33³/₄×30″
lower right: Feininger 16
Inaccessible

167 THE LOVERS

oil on canvas, 17¹/₄×15³/₄″
lower left: Feininger 16

1. Wassily Kandinsky, Paris
Whereabouts unknown

1917

168 MARKWIPPACH

oil on canvas, 31³/₄×39³/₄″
upper left: Feininger 17
on back of stretcher written in
crayon: *Markwippach 1917*
The Cleveland Museum of Art
Colorplate 7

169 HEAD IN ARCHITECTURE
(Kopf in Architektur)

oil on canvas, 38×31¹/₂″
lower right: Feininger 17
on back of stretcher:
Kopf in Architektur
Head in Architecture
on back of canvas: *Feininger 1917*
Estate of the artist
Plate 14

170 GELMERODA VII

oil on canvas, 39¹/₂×32″
upper right: Feininger 17
on back of stretcher, written in
ink: *Lyonel Feininger 1917*
Gelmeroda VII

1. Hermann Lange, Krefeld,
   Germany
2. Private Collection, Krefeld,
   Germany

Plate 16

263

171 LEHNSTEDT

oil on canvas, 31×39½"
lower right: Feininger
1. F. R. Schon, Toronto
2. Private Collection, New York
3. Stephen M. Kellen, New York

172 HIGH HOUSES III

oil on canvas, 39½×31"
upper right: Feininger
1. F. R. Schon, Toronto
2. Miss Isabel McLaughlin,
   Toronto

173 DENSTEDT

oil on canvas, 34¼×46½"
upper left: Feininger 17
on back of stretcher written in
light-brown oil paint: *Lyonel
Feininger 1917 Denstedt*
Estate of the artist

174 BRIDGE III
oil on canvas, 31½×39½"
lower left: Feininger 17
1. Walter Kaesbach, Hemmenhofen, Bodensee, Germany
2. Wallraf-Richartz Museum,
   Cologne (Sammlung Haubrich)
Plate 18

175 STREET IN KROMSDORF
(Straße in Kl. Kromsdorf)

oil on canvas, 29½×39½"
lower left: Feininger
in Feininger's own handwriting
on back of existing photo:
*Lyonel Feininger Straße in
Kl. Kromsdorf*
Collection Harry Fuld, Berlin
Burned

176 STEAMER "ODIN" I
(LEVIATHAN)

oil on canvas, 32×39½"
lower right: Feininger
on back of stretcher in India ink
applied with brush: *1917
Leviathan*
Pat and Lux Feininger,
Cambridge, Massachusetts

177 STILL LIFE WITH PITCHER
oil on canvas, 15¾×19"
upper right: Feininger 17
on back of stretcher written in
India ink: *Feininger 1917
Stillife* [sic] *(with Pitcher)*
Estate of the artist

177

178 STILL LIFE WITH COLORED
PLATE

oil on canvas, 28×22½"
upper left: Feininger
upper right: Feininger 17
on back of stretcher in
pencil: *59×73 cm*
Dr. R. C. Schon, Toronto

179 THE HOLLOW LANE
(Die Hohle Gasse [Hohlweg])

oil on canvas, 39½×31½"
upper right: Feininger
1. Bernhard Köhler, Berlin
   Burned in bombing raid

264

180 SHIPS

oil on canvas, 27¹/₂×33″
upper left: Feininger 17

1. Gustav Jung, Hagen/Westfalen,
Germany
Whereabouts unknown

181 BATHERS II
(Badende II)

oil on canvas, 33³/₄×40″
lower left: Feininger 17
on back of stretcher: *Badende*

1. Harry Fuld, Berlin
2. Harry Fuld, Jr., London
Colorplate 6

182 BEHIND THE CHURCH II
(Hinter der Kirche II)

oil on canvas, 39³/₄×49¹/₂″
lower right: Feininger 17
on back of stretcher: *Hinter
der Kirche II, Erfurt* (a mistake,
it is the church in Weimar – J. F.)
Estate of the artist
Plate 17

183 EHRINGSDORF

oil on canvas, 23³/₄×29¹/₂″
lower right: Feininger

1. Bernhard Köhler, Berlin
Burned in bombing raid

184 LEGEFELD

oil on canvas, measurements: ?
signature: ?
Painting mentioned in letter
(to Julia) of August 17, 1917
Exhibited in Sturm show, 1917,
no. 46 in Sturm catalogue
Whereabouts unknown

1918

185 TELTOW II

oil on canvas, 39¹/₂×49¹/₂″
upper left: Feininger 18
on back of stretcher written in
crayon: *Teltow*

Nationalgalerie, Berlin
acquired in 1919
removed after 1933
back in Nationalgalerie, Berlin,
Plate 19

186 YELLOW STREET II

oil on canvas, 37×34″
lower right: Feininger

F. R. Schon, Toronto

187 MELLINGEN V

oil on canvas, 31³/₄×39¹/₂″
upper right: Feininger
on back of stretcher in ink:
Mellingen V

1. Dr. Alois J. Schardt, Berlin
2. Alois W. Schardt, U.S.A.

188 THE MILL

oil on canvas, 39¹/₂×49¹/₂″
lower right: Feininger 18

1. Wilhelm Schön, Sosnowiec,
Poland
Whereabouts unknown

189 ZIRCHOW VII

oil on canvas, 31¹/₂×39¹/₂″
lower left: Feininger 18
on back of stretcher in black India
ink: *Lyonel Feininger 1918
Zirchow VII*

Julia Feininger, New York

Plate 20

190 NORMAN VILLAGE I

oil on canvas, 31¹/₂×39¹/₂″
lower right: Feininger 18

1. Dr. F. Kantorowicz, Berlin
2. Dr. Blum, Blaricum, Holland

191 BRIDGE IV
(Brücke in Weimar)

oil on canvas, 25×35″
lower left: Feininger 18
on back of stretcher: *Lyonel
Feininger 1918 Brücke in
Weimar*

1. Major Hülsmann, Berlin
2. Maria Möller-Garny, Cologne

192 NIEDER-GRUNSTEDT

oil on canvas, 31¹/₂×39¹/₂″
upper right: Feininger 1918

Destroyed by the artist about 1950

1919

193 BRIDGE V
(Brücke V)

oil on canvas, 31½×39¾″
lower right: Feininger 1919
on back of stretcher in blue crayon:
Brücke V 1919

Philadelphia Museum of Art

194 GOTHEN

oil on canvas, 31½×39½″
lower left: Feininger 1919
on back of stretcher: *Lyonel
Feininger Gothen*

Andreas Feininger, New York

Plate 21

195 VILLAGE NEPPERMIN

oil on canvas, 31½×39½″
upper left: Feininger 19
on back of stretcher: *Lyonel Feininger 1919 Village Neppermin*
on back of photo, in Feininger's
own handwriting: *le Village de
Neppermin, 1919*

Pat and Lux Feininger, Cambridge,
Massachusetts

196 MARINE

oil on canvas, 24½×30″
lower left: Feininger

1. Dr. Walter Kaesbach, Hemmenhofen, Bodensee, Germany
2. Mrs. Scheufelen, Oberlennin-
   gen, Württemberg, Germany

197 THE RED CLOWN

oil on canvas, 28½×24½″
lower left: Feininger 1919
on back of stretcher in crayon:
1919 The Red Clown

Rev. Dr. Laurence Feininger,
Trento, Italy

198 HIGH HOUSES IV

oil on canvas, 39⅞×31½″
lower left: Feininger 19

1. Alfred Hess, Erfurt, Germany
2. E. L. T. Mesens, London
3. Eric Estoric, London

199 CHURCH OF NIEDER-
GRUNSTEDT

oil on canvas, 39¾×49½″
lower left: Feininger 1919
on back of stretcher: *Feininger
1919*

1. Mayer-Freudenberg, Berlin
2. Maria Daus, Berlin-Nicholassee
3. Galerie des 20. Jahrhunderts,
   Berlin

Plate 22

200 THE STUDIO WINDOW
(Das Atelierfenster)

oil on canvas, 39½×31½″
lower right: Feininger 1919
on back of stretcher: *Lyonel Feininger 1919 Atelierfenster*

1. A. Fischer, Essen, Germany
2. Städtisches Kunstmuseum,
   Duisburg, Germany

201 UMPFERSTEDT III

oil on canvas, 39½×31½″
upper left: Feininger 19

1. Dr. Victor Wallerstein, Berlin
Whereabouts unknown

1920

201 a PIER
oil on canvas, 33¹/₂×39¹/₂″
lower right: Feininger 20
Unfinished
Inaccessible

202 NORMAN VILLAGE II

oil on canvas, 30³/₄×38⁵/₈″
lower right: Feininger 20
Hans Scharoun, Berlin
(on loan to Staatsgalerie, Stuttgart,
where it is called *Häuser*)

203 THE RED STREET SWEEPER
oil on canvas, 15³/₄×19″
lower right: Feininger 1920
Burned 1946 in a warehouse fire
in Montana

204 HUNTER'S LODGE
(Die kleine Försterei)

oil on canvas, 16×16″
upper left: Feininger 20
on back of stretcher: *14. Juni 1920
Die kleine Försterei*
Estate of the artist

205 ANGLER AND CANAL BOAT
oil on canvas, 16¹/₄×18¹/₂″
lower right: Feininger 20
1. Gerhard Marcks, Cologne
   Destroyed in bombing raid

206 CHURCH OF VOLLERSRODA

oil on canvas, 15³/₄×18¹/₄″
upper right: Feininger 20
1. Wilhelm Schön, Sosnowiec,
   Poland
Whereabouts unknown

207 COAST, WINDMILL, SHIP
oil on canvas, measurements: ?
signature: ?
1. Private Collection, Germany
Whereabouts unknown

208 EICHELBORN

oil on canvas, 31¹/₂×40¹/₂″
upper right: Feininger
1. Dr. William R. Valentiner,
   Raleigh, North Carolina
2. Estate of Dr. Valentiner

209 CATHEDRAL
(Dom)
oil on canvas, 35¹/₂×45″
lower right: Feininger 20
on back of canvas (probably in oil):
Lyonel Feininger '20 Dom
1. Mrs. K. Bernhard-Robinson,
   Berlin
2. Mrs. Barton H. Lippincott,
   Fort Washington, Pennsylvania
Plate 23

210 VIADUCT
oil on canvas, 39³/₄×33³/₄″
lower right: Feininger 1920
on back of stretcher written in
crayon: *Feininger 1920 Viadukt*
The Museum of Modern Art,
New York (Acquired through the
Lillie P. Bliss Bequest)
Plate 25

211 BEACHCOMBERS
(Lastträger am Meeresstrand)

oil on canvas, 23³/₄×29¹/₂″
upper left: Feininger 1920
on back of stretcher: *1920 Lastträger am Meeresstrand*
Estate of the artist

212 PORTRAIT OF A TRAGIC
BEING
oil on canvas, 33¹/₂×31¹/₂″
lower right: Feininger 20
on back of stretcher: *Lyonel
Feininger October 1920
Portrait of a Tragic Being*
Estate of the artist
Colorplate 8

213 BATTLE FLEET

oil on canvas, 16×19″
upper left: Feininger 1920
1. Wilhelm Schön, Sosnowiec,
   Poland
Whereabouts unknown

214 CHURCH (OF MELLINGEN)
(Kirche)

oil on canvas, 23³/₄ × 29³/₄″
lower left: Feininger 20
on back of stretcher: *Kirche*
Kunst- und Museumsverein,
Wuppertal, Germany

215 HOPFGARTEN
oil on canvas, 25 × 32¹/₂″
lower right: Feininger 20
1. Museum der Bildenden Künste,
   Leipzig
2. Minneapolis Institute of Arts
Plate 24

216 THE PRIVATEERS
(Die Rheeder)

oil on canvas, 14³/₄ × 17¹/₂″
lower right: Feininger 1920
on back of stretcher written in
crayon: *Feininger 1920
Die Rheeder*
Maria Möller-Garny, Cologne

1921

217 GELMERODA VIII
oil on canvas, 39¹/₂ × 31¹/₂″
lower left: Feininger 1921
on back of stretcher written in blue
pencil: *Gelmeroda VIII
1920–1921*

217

1. Landesmuseum, Weimar
2. Whitney Museum of American
   Art, New York

218 GABERNDORF I
oil on canvas, 31¹/₂ × 39¹/₂″
lower right: Feininger 1921
on back of stretcher written in ink:
Lyonel Feininger Gaberndorf
on back of canvas (not known
whether written by the artist):
Gaberndorf 243
1. Collection Gabrielson, Göteborg,
   Sweden
2. Mrs. Stina Gretzer, Copenhagen
Plate 27

219 GROSS-KROMSDORF III

oil on canvas, 39¹/₂ × 31¹/₂″
upper left: Feininger 1921
Estate of the artist

220 OBER WEIMAR
oil on canvas, 31¹/₂ × 39¹/₂″
lower right: Feininger 1921
1. M. Tak van Poortvliet, Holland,
   bequeathed 1936 to:
2. Museum Boymans, Rotterdam
Plate 26

221 ARCHITECTURE II (THE MAN
FROM POTIN)
(Architektur II)

oil on canvas, 39¹/₂ × 51″
lower right: Feininger 1921
on back of stretcher in India ink
applied with brush: *Lyonel Feininger Architecture II*
Pat and Lux Feininger,
Cambridge, Massachusetts

222 NIGHTHAWKS
(Nachtvögel)

oil on canvas, 23¹/₂ × 19³/₄″
upper right: Feininger
Inaccessible

1922

223 CHURCH OF HEILIGENHAFEN
(Kirche am Wasser)

oil on canvas, 15³/₄×23³/₄″
lower right: Feininger 1922
on back of stretcher written in
crayon or charcoal: *L. Feininger
1922*
Kirche am Wasser 1922

1. Max Würzburger, Berlin
2. Mr. Charles H. Babcock,
   Winston-Salem, North Carolina

226

224 FISHING FLEET
(Fischerflotte)

oil on canvas, 15³/₄×19″
upper left: Feininger 22

1. Collection Fahrenholz, Magdeburg, Germany
   Burned in World War II

225 MELLINGEN VI

oil on canvas, 31¹/₂×39¹/₂″
lower right: Feininger 22

1. A. Sommerfeld, Berlin
2. George F. J. Bergman,
   Randwick-Sidney, New South
   Wales
3. Mr. and Mrs. Romie Shapiro,
   New York

226 WINDMILL IN WERDER
(Windmühle in Werder)
oil on canvas, 19×15³/₄″
lower right: Feininger 22
(title on frame in blue crayon)
Carter C. Higgins, North Brook-
field, Massachusetts

227 LADY IN MAUVE
oil on canvas, 39¹/₂×31¹/₂″
lower left: Feininger 22

Pat and Lux Feininger,
Cambridge, Massachusetts

Colorplate 9

228 SMALL HARBOR
(Kleine Hafenstadt [Hafenstädt-
chen])

oil on canvas, 15³/₄×21¹/₄″
upper left: Feininger 1922
on back of stretcher written in ink:
Kleine Hafenstadt
and *Hafenstädtchen*

1. Mrs. K. Bernhard-Robinson,
   Berlin
2. Private Collection, New York

1923

229 HULKS
oil on canvas, 15¹/₄×21″
upper left: Feininger
on back of stretcher in India ink:
Feininger 1923 Hulks

Estate of the artist

229

230 CLOUD I
(Wolke mit rotem Segelboot)

oil on canvas, 15¹/₂×26¹/₂″
upper right: Feininger 1923
on back of stretcher written in ink:
1923 Wolke mit rotem Segelboot, I

Stefan Pauson, Giffnock, Glasgow

231 POND IN GELMERODA
(Dorfteich von Gelmeroda)

oil on canvas, 34×44″
lower right: Feininger
on back of stretcher: *Dorfteich
von Gelmeroda*

1. Harry Fuld, Berlin
2. Peter H. Fuld, London

232 SÜSSENBORN
oil on canvas, 17³/₄×22″
lower left: Feininger

1. Mr. Terstappen, Mönchen-
   Gladbach, Germany
2. Myrtil Frank, The Hague

232

233 CLOUDS ABOVE THE SEA I
(Wolken am Meer I)

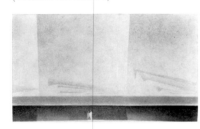

oil on canvas, 14¼×23¾″
lower left: Feininger 23
on back of stretcher in black ink:
Wolken am Meer 1. Fassung
1. Moritz Noack, Obersdorf,
   Germany
2. Private Collection, New York

234 THE BAY
(Die Bucht [Das hohe Ufer])

oil on canvas, 20½×30½″
lower right: Feininger 23
on back of stretcher: *Lyonel Feininger 1923 Das hohe Ufer*
1. Mr. Pariser, London
Sold at 1956 auction, Ketterer,
Stuttgart:
2. Wilhelm Grosshennig
3. Kurt Forberg, Düsseldorf,
   Germany

235 CLOUDS ABOVE THE SEA II
(Wolken am Meer II)
oil on canvas, 14¼×24″
upper left: Feininger
on back of stretcher: *1923
Wolken am Meer II. Fassung*

270

Pat and Lux Feininger,
Cambridge, Massachusetts
Plate 28 a

236 TROISTEDT

oil on canvas, 31½×39½″
upper right: Feininger 1923
on back of stretcher in ink:
Lyonel Feininger 1923 Troistedt
1. Städtische Kunstsammlung,
   Wiesbaden
2. Hermann Lange, Krefeld,
   Germany
3. Private Collection, Krefeld

237 THE ISLAND
(Die Insel)

oil on canvas, 18¼×29¼″
lower left: Feininger 1923
Private Collection, Munich

1924

238 BENZ

oil on canvas, 15×18¾″
lower right: Feininger 24
on back of stretcher: *Lyonel
Feininger 1924 Benz*
Estate of the artist

239 YELLOW BARNS
(Dorf)

oil on canvas, 19½×30½″
upper left: Feininger 1924
on back of stretcher: *1924 Dorf*
Owen and Leona Elliot Trust,
Cedar Rapids, Iowa

240 STRANDED BRIG
(Das gestrandete Schiff)

oil on canvas, 11¾×18¾″
upper left: Feininger
on back of stretcher: *1924
Das gestrandete Schiff
März 1924*
Pat and Lux Feininger, Cambridge,
Massachusetts

241 ALT-SALLENTHIN

oil on canvas, 17¾×28½″
upper left: Feininger 24
on back of stretcher: *Lyonel
Feininger 1924*
Estate of the artist

242 BLUE MARINE
(Blaue Marine)
oil on canvas, 18¾×33″
lower right: Feininger 24
on back of stretcher in ink:
*Lyonel Feininger 1924 (Blaue
Marine)*
Munson-Williams-Proctor Insti-
tute, Utica, New York
Plate 28 b

243 VILLAGE CHURCH (NIEDER-REISSEN) *

oil on canvas, 19¹/₄×30″
upper right: Feininger 24
on back of stretcher written in
India ink: *Lyonel Feininger
Nieder-Reissen* (crossed out –
underneath written): *Village
Church*
* (Actually Ober-Reissen. – J. F.)
1. Julia Feininger, New York
2. Rev. Dr. Laurence Feininger,
   Trento, Italy

244 SHIPS AND RED SUN
(Schiffe und rote Sonne)

oil on canvas, 10¹/₄×15³/₄″
lower left: Feininger 24
on back of stretcher written in ink:
*Pulu's Ostereichen 1924
(20. Apr. 1924)*
Julia Feininger, New York

245 BUTTELSTEDT

oil on canvas, 16³/₄×19¹/₄″
upper right: Feininger
on back of stretcher written in
India ink: *1924 Buttelstedt*
Estate of the artist

246 OLD AMERICAN LOCOMOTIVE
(1914–1924)

oil on canvas, 22¹/₂×47¹/₄″
upper left: Feininger
Estate of the artist

247 LÜNEBURG

oil on canvas, 18¹/₂×24¹/₄″
lower right: Feininger 24
1. Peter Harlan, Burg Sternberg
   (Lippe), Germany
2. Myrtil Frank, The Hague

248 CHURCH OF THE
MINORITES I
(Barfüßerkirche I)

oil on canvas, 39¹/₄×31¹/₄″
upper right: Feininger 24
on back of stretcher:
*Lyonel Feininger 1924
Die Barfüßerkirche in Erfurt*
1. Collection Alfred Hess, Erfurt,
   Germany
2. Dr. Ferdinand Ziersch,
   Wuppertal-Barmen, Germany

249 GABERNDORF II

oil on canvas, 39¹/₈×50¹/₂″
upper right: Feininger 24
on back of stretcher in script, ink:
Feininger; in letters: *Gaberndorf II*
(Canvas has been mounted on panel,
the back of which is covered with
canvas so that the rear of the
original canvas cannot be seen.)
Nelson Gallery – Atkins Museum,
Kansas City, Missouri (Friends of
Art Collection)
Plate 29

250 SILVER STARS

oil on canvas, 20³/₄×16″
upper right: Feininger
Inaccessible

251 BALTIC KETCH
(Ostsee-Schoner)

oil on canvas, 16¹/₂×28″
lower left: Feininger 24
on back of stretcher written in
black ink: *Lyonel Feininger 1924
Ostsee-Schoner*
1. Dr. h. c. Richard Doetsch-
   Benziger, Basel
2. Estate Dr. h. c. R. Doetsch-
   Benziger, Basel

271

252 PANEL "MARINE"

oil on canvas, 15³/₄ × 16¹/₂″
lower right: Feininger 24

1. Wassily Kandinsky, Paris
Whereabouts unknown

1925

253 TOWN GATE-TOWER II
(Torturm II)
oil on canvas, 39¹/₂ × 31¹/₂″
lower left: Feininger 25
on back of stretcher written in
India ink: *Lyonel Feininger
Torturm II*
Andreas Feininger, New York
Colorplate 10

254 NERMSDORF I

oil on canvas, 15³/₄ × 26³/₄″
upper right: Feininger 25
on back of stretcher: *Lyonel
Feininger 1925 Nermsdorf 1*
on back of canvas in oil:
Feininger 25

1. Dr. Herrmannsdorfer, Berlin
2. Dr. Franz Gluch, Cologne

255 PINK CLOUD I
(Rosa Wolke)
oil on canvas, 17¹/₂ × 30¹/₂″
lower left: Feininger 25
on back of stretcher: *Lyonel
Feininger (Rosa Wolke)*

1. Ernst Henke, Essen, Germany
2. Private Collection, Germany

255

256 BLUE CLOUD
oil on canvas, 19 × 26¹/₂″
lower left: Feininger 25
on back of stretcher in India ink:
Feininger 1925 Blue Cloud

Estate of the artist

Plate 30

257 GABLES I, LÜNEBURG
oil on canvas, 37³/₄ × 28¹/₂″
upper right: Feininger 25

Mr. and Mrs. Charles B. Meech,
Minneapolis

Plate 32

258 RAINBOW

oil on canvas, 17¹/₂ × 30¹/₂″
lower right: Feininger
on back of canvas written in ink:
Lyonel Feininger 1924 Rainbow
(Finished and signed in 1925. – J.F.)

1. Mr. and Mrs. David F. Seifer-
held, New York
2. Mr. and Mrs. Paul M. Hirsch-
land, Great Neck, Long Island

259 YACHT RACE
(Yachtrennen)

oil on canvas, 17¹/₂ × 30¹/₂″
lower left: Feininger 25
on back of stretcher written in ink:
*Lyo. Feininger 1925
Yachtrennen*

1. Dr. Eiermann, Dresden
2. Dr. E. Schmidt-Ott, Wuppertal-
Elberfeld, Germany

260 YELLOW CLOUD
(Wolke II)
oil on canvas, 16¹/₄ × 26³/₄″
upper right: Feininger 25
on back of stretcher written in ink:
Lyonel Feininger 1925 Wolke II

1. Dr. Rudolph, Germany
2. Mr. and Mrs. Martin Erlanger,
Rye, New York

Plate 31

261 HAMMERSTEDT
oil on canvas, 31¹/₂ × 39¹/₂″
lower right: Feininger

Destroyed by the artist

1926

262 TOWN GATE-TOWER I
(Torturm I)

oil on canvas, 24¹/₂ × 18¹/₂″
lower right: Feininger
on back of stretcher written in
black ink: *Lyonel Feininger 1925
Torturm I angefangen 1924
vollendet 1926*

1. Dr. h. c. Richard Doetsch-
Benziger, Basel
2. Estate Dr. h. c. R. Doetsch-
Benziger, Basel

263 GELMERODA IX

oil on canvas, 39¹/₂×31⁷/₈″
upper left: Feininger 1926
on back of stretcher written in
India ink: *Feininger*
Gelmeroda IX
1. Collection Bienert, Dresden
2. Museum Folkwang, Essen,
   Germany
Colorplate 16

264 CHURCH OF THE
MINORITES II
(Barfüßerkirche II)

oil on canvas, 47×45″
upper left: Feininger 1926
on back of stretcher written in
(what appears to be) ink:
L. Feininger 1926
Barfüßerkirche II
1. Museum am Anger, Erfurt,
   Germany
2. Walker Art Center, Minneapolis
Plate 33

265 GLORIOUS VICTORY OF THE
SLOOP "MARIA"
oil on canvas, 21¹/₂×33¹/₂″
lower right: Feininger 1926
on back of stretcher: *Lyonel*
Feininger 1926
1. Staatsgalerie, Dresden
2. City Art Museum of St. Louis
Colorplate 12

266 BRIGANTINE AND STEAMER

oil on canvas, 13¹/₂×17¹/₄″
upper left: *Papileo s.l. Lux*
11. Juni 26
Pat and Lux Feininger, Cambridge,
Massachusetts

267 CALM DAY AT SEA I
(Segelschiffe am Abend)

oil on canvas, 16¹/₂×29″
upper left: Feininger 1926
on back of stretcher in oil:
Feininger 1926 Segelschiffe
am Abend
Alfred Vogel, Mönchen-Gladbach,
Germany

268 THE BIRD CLOUD
(Vogelwolke [Wolke nach dem
Sturm])
oil on canvas, 16³/₄×27³/₄″
lower right: Feininger 1926
on back of stretcher:
L. Feininger Bird Cloud, 1926
Busch-Reisinger Museum,
Harvard University, Cambridge,
Massachusetts
Colorplate 11

269 SMALL MASK
(Maske)

oil on canvas, 19×15³/₄″
lower left: Feininger
on back of stretcher: *Maske*
1923–26
Marianne Noack, Munich

1927

270 CALM AT SEA II

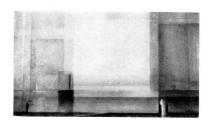

oil on canvas, 17×30″
upper right: Feininger
1. Private Collection, Germany
Whereabouts unknown

271 SAILING-YACHTS

oil on canvas, 18¹/₄×30″
lower right: Feininger
1. Private Collection, Germany
Burned

272 ARCHITECTURE III
(GABLES II)
oil on canvas, 17³/₄×28″
upper right: Feininger 27
Julia Feininger, New York
indefinite loan to:
Busch-Reisinger Museum,
Harvard University, Cambridge,
Massachusetts
Colorplate 14

273 STEAMER "ODIN" II
oil on canvas, 26¹/₂×39¹/₂″
lower left: Feininger
on back of stretcher written in
pencil: *Lyonel Feininger 1927*
Steamer Odin
The Museum of Modern Art,
New York (Acquired through the
Lillie P. Bliss Bequest)
Plate 34

274 MOONLIGHT ON THE BEACH
(Abend am Meere)
oil on canvas, 17³/₄×30¹/₄″
lower left: Feininger
on back of stretcher written in
black crayon: *Feininger 1927
Abend am Meere;* (also *Evening
on the Shore*)
Private Collection, U.S.A.
Plate 36 a

275 TOWN HALL II, ZOTTELSTEDT

oil on canvas, 31¹/₂×39¹/₂″
lower left: Feininger 27
Mrs. Irving Rabinowitz, South
Miami, Florida

276 ARCHITECTURE WITH STARS
oil on canvas, 15³/₄×20″
lower right: Feininger 27
on back of stretcher: *Lyonel
Feininger 1927 Architecture with
Stars*
Rev. Dr. Laurence Feininger,
Trento, Italy
Plate 35

277 CATHEDRAL OF CAMMIN
(Camminer Dom)

oil on canvas, 17¹/₂×28³/₄″
lower right: Feininger 27
1. Frau Schuster von Wijlerberg,
   Wijlerberg/Rhine, Germany
   Burned in World War II

278 MARINE (1927)
oil on canvas, 21³/₄×35¹/₂″
lower right: Feininger
Estate of the artist
Colorplate 13

279 WINDMILL, USEDOM

oil on canvas, 16³/₄×24³/₄″
lower right: Feininger
1. Otto Ralfs, Brunswick, Germany
2. Herbert Frank, New York

280 BROKEN GLASS
(Glasscherbenbild)
oil on canvas, 28¹/₂×27³/₄″
upper right: Feininger
Robert E. Gross, Burbank,
California
Colorplate 15

281 YELLOW VILLAGE CHURCH I
(Gelbe Dorfkirche I)

oil on canvas: 31³/₄×39″
upper right: Feininger
1. Museum Reina, Dessau,
   Germany
2. Karl Nathan, New York

282 VILLAGE MARKWIPPACH
(Dorf)

oil on canvas, 16¹/₂×28¹/₂″
lower right: Feininger
on back of stretcher written in ink:
Feininger Dorf
Phillips Collection,
Washington, D.C.

283 MOUTH OF THE REGA I
(Regamündung I)

oil on canvas, 12¹/₄×21³/₄″
upper right: Feininger 27
1. Sold through Buchholz Gallery,
   New York, to Boston Art Gallery
   Whereabouts unknown

284 MOUTH OF THE REGA II
(Regamündung II)

oil on canvas, 16¹/₂×28¹/₂″
lower right: Feininger 27
on back of stretcher written in pen
and ink: *Regamündung II, 1927*
Erich Scheyer, Maryport, Cumberland, England

285 THE POWDERTOWER I
(Der Pulverturm I)

oil on canvas, 19×55″
lower right: Feininger 27
on back of stretcher in ink:
Pulverturm
1. L. Zeuner, Kaiserslautern,
   Germany
2. Mr. and Mrs. Kurt H. Grune-
   baum, Harrison, New York

286 CHURCH OF THE ST. CLARA
NUNS
(Klarissenkirche)

oil on canvas, 39¹/₂ × 31¹/₂″
upper right: Feininger

1. Städtische Gemäldegalerie,
   Kassel
2. Bill Bomar, Fort Worth, Texas

287 HOUSES BY THE RIVER
(Häuser am Fluß)

oil on canvas, 18¹/₄ × 30″
lower right: Feininger

1. Deutsche Kunstgemeinschaft,
   Berlin
Whereabouts unknown

288 BEFORE THE RAIN
(Regenklarheit)

oil on canvas, 17 × 31¹/₄″
upper left: Feininger 1927

1. Alfred Hess, Erfurt, Germany
2. Museum am Anger, Erfurt
3. Seized by the Nazis
4. Drs. Fritz and Peter Nathan,
   Zurich

289 SUNSET ON THE SEA I
(Sonnenuntergang am Meere I)
oil on canvas, 16¹/₂ × 33¹/₄″
lower right: Feininger 1927

on back of stretcher: *Sonnenunter-*
gang am Meere, I Feininger 1927

1. Alfred Rose, New York
2. The Solomon R. Guggenheim
   Museum, New York
   (Acquired in 1948 from the
   Estate of Karl Nierendorf)
Plate 36 b

290 CHURCH ABOVE THE TOWN
(Kirche über Stadt)

oil on canvas, 31¹/₂ × 39¹/₂″
lower right: Feininger 27
on back of stretcher written in
India ink, then planed away, some
still readable: *Ki . . . . Stadt 1927*
Estate of the artist

291 DUNES AT EVENING

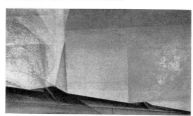

oil on canvas, 15³/₄ × 28″
upper left: Feininger 27

1. Mrs. R. Maitland, Los Angeles
2. Dr. and Mrs. John Gilbert
   Dean, Wilton, Connecticut

292 WOMAN WITH RED HAIR

oil on canvas, 27¹/₂ × 23³/₄″
lower right: Feininger
Estate of the artist

293 WOMAN WITH BLUE HAIR

oil on canvas, 31 × 26¹/₂″
unsigned
Estate of the artist

294 DRÖBSDORF

oil on canvas, 39¹/₂ × 49¹/₂″
unsigned
Measurements on stretcher in
Feininger's handwriting:
100 × 125 cm
(Probably first version. – J. F.)
Estate of the artist

1928

295 GELMERODA XI

oil on canvas, 39¹/₂ × 31¹/₂″
lower left: Feininger 1928
Rev. Dr. Laurence Feininger,
Trento, Italy
Painting inaccessible

296 SIDE-WHEELER III

oil on canvas, 39¹/₂ × 49¹/₂″
lower right: Feininger

Estate of the artist

297 CLOUDS ABOVE THE SEA III

oil on canvas, 21 × 37″
upper right: Feininger 1928

1. Otto Ralfs, Brunswick, Germany
   Painting burned in bombing raid

298 CHURCH IN THE WOODS

oil on canvas, 18¹/₂ × 15¹/₂″
upper right: Feininger 28

1. Fernando Puma, U.S.A.
2. Charles A. Wyman,
   New York

299 PINK CLOUD II

oil on canvas, 17¹/₄ × 30³/₄″
upper right: Feininger 28

Private Collection, Germany

300 BOATS IN FOG
(Segelboote im Nebel)

oil on canvas, 13¹/₄ × 22¹/₄″
lower right: Feininger 1928
on back of stretcher written in ink:
Lyonel Feininger 1928
Segelboote im Nebel

1. Alfred Hess, Erfurt, Germany
2. A. Ortweiler, Örebro, Sweden

301 DRÖBSDORF I

oil on canvas, 32¹/₈ × 39³/₄″
lower left: Feininger
on stretcher, back, upper left,
written in black ink: *Feininger –*
1928 Dröbsdorf

Collection of the University
Gallery, University of Minnesota,
Minneapolis

302 THE GRÜTZTURM
(Der Grützturm)

oil on canvas, 39⁷/₈ × 31⁷/₈″
upper right: Feininger 28

on back of stretcher written in
black color: *1928 Der Grützturm*

1. Schlesisches Museum, Breslau
2. Hessisches Landesmuseum,
   Darmstadt

303 RAINBOW II
(Regenbogen II)

oil on canvas, 11¹/₂ × 23″
lower right: Feininger
on back of stretcher written in ink:
Lyonel Feininger 1928
Regenbogen II

1. John Becker, New York
2. Charles H. Babcock,
   Winston-Salem, North Carolina

304 EDGE OF THE WOODS
(PINE WOODS)

oil on canvas, 23³/₄ × 29¹/₂″
lower right: Feininger
on back of stretcher in India ink:
Lyonel Feininger Pine Woods
Estate of the artist

1929

305 THE BIG CUTTERS
(Die grosse Kutterklasse)

oil on canvas, 14¹/₂×27¹/₂″
upper left: Feininger 29
on back of stretcher in oil:
Feininger 29
Die große Kutterklasse
on back of canvas:
Lyonel Feininger 1929
Die große Kutterklasse
Professor Dipl. Ing. Ludwig
Lemmer, Berlin-Grunewald and
Remscheid (Rhineland), Germany

306 X 54

oil on canvas, 17×28¹/₂″
upper right: Feininger 29
on back of stretcher written in ink:
X 54 1929
1. Verein Freunde der National
   Galerie, Berlin
2. Private Collection, U.S.A.

307 YACHTS
(Yachten)

oil on canvas, 18¹/₄×28¹/₂″
upper right: Feininger 1929
on back of stretcher in ink:
L. Feininger Yachten
1. Collection Dr. h. c. Richard
   Doetsch-Benziger, Basel
2. Private Collection, Switzerland

308 CALM AT SEA III
(Stiller Tag am Meer III)
oil on canvas, 19¹/₄×14¹/₄″
upper right: Feininger 29
Alois W. Schardt, U.S.A.
Colorplate 17

309 POSSENDORF I (VILLAGE
CHURCH IN POSSENDORF)

oil on canvas, 31¹/₂×39¹/₂″
lower right: Feininger 29
on back of stretcher written in
crayon: *Lyonel Feininger 1929*
Village Church in Possendorf
The Pennsylvania Academy of Fine
Arts, Philadelphia

310 GABERNDORF III
oil on canvas, 39¹/₂×51³/₄″
upper right: Feininger 29
1. Charles Bewley, Eire
Whereabouts unknown

311 GELMERODA XII

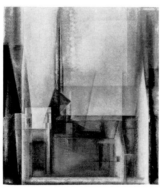

oil on canvas, 39¹/₂×51³/₄″
upper right: Feininger 29
Museum of Art, Rhode Island
School of Design, Providence
Plate 37

312 VILLAGE STREET
(Dorfstraße)

oil on canvas, 31¹/₂×39¹/₂″
upper right: Feininger
on back of stretcher in reddish
brown oil, brushed on:
Dorfstraße 1927–29
The Art Institute of Chicago
(Gift of Mr. and Mrs. Sigmund
Kunstadter)

313 GABLES III (LÜNEBURG II)
oil on canvas, 42¹/₂×54³/₄″
upper left: Feininger 29
1. Staatsgalerie, Dresden
2. Mr. and Mrs. Stanley R. Resor,
   Greenwich, Connecticut
3. Mrs. John Sargent Pillsbury,
   Minneapolis
Plate 38

314 LIGHTED WINDOWS I
(Beleuchtete Häuserzeile I) *

oil on canvas, 14¹/₄×22″
lower left: Feininger
on back of stretcher written in ink:
1929 Beleuchtete Häuserzeile 1
* In Dresden Gallery called
Nächtliche Straße
1. Private Collection, Germany
2. Staatliche Kunstsammlungen,
   Gemäldegalerie, Dresden

315 POSSENDORF II

oil on canvas, 16¹/₂×21¹/₂″
lower right: Feininger

on back of stretcher written in
India ink: *Feininger – 1930
Possendorf II*
(Painted in Halle late fall, 1929 –
finished and signed in 1930. – J. F.)
Sold at Lilienfeld Gallery, New
York, to:
1. Mrs. Otto Spaeth, U.S.A.
2. Brooklyn Museum, exchanged,
   and back to artist
Sold at Willard Gallery, New
York, to:
3. Private Collection, New York

316 CHURCH OF ST. MARY I,
HALLE
(Marktkirche in Halle a. d. Saale)
oil on canvas, 39¹/₂ × 32¹/₄″
upper left: Feininger 29
on back of stretcher:
*Lyonel Feininger 1929
Marktkirche in Halle a. d. Saale*
1. Museum Moritzburg, Halle,
   Germany
2. Städtische Kunsthalle,
   Mannheim
Plate 39

317 AM TRÖDEL, HALLE

oil on canvas, 39¹/₂ × 32¹/₄″
lower left: Feininger 29
on back of stretcher in oil:
Feininger 1929
1. Museum Moritzburg, Halle,
   Germany
2. Private Collection, Munich

318 MOUTH OF THE REGA III
(Regamündung III)
oil on canvas, 19 × 30¹/₄″
lower right: Feininger

318

on back of stretcher:
Regamündung III Nov. 1929
1. Dr. K. Krekeler, Cologne
2. Private Collection, Germany

319 MARINE, HARBOR OF
PEPPERMINT
(Hafen von Peppermint)

oil on canvas, 11¹/₄ × 16¹/₂″
lower right: Feininger
on back of stretcher in black India
ink: *Marine (Hafen von Peppermint!) Feininger s. l. Klee z.
18. 12. 29*
1. Paul Klee, Bern
2. Felix Klee, Bern

1930

320 CHURCH, WEIMAR
(Stadtkirche, Weimar)
oil on canvas, measurements: ?
signature: ?
Destroyed by the artist

321 SKERRY-CRUISERS
(Schärenkreuzer)

oil on canvas, 17³/₄ × 30¹/₂″
upper right: Feininger 30

1. Museum, Elberfeld, Germany
2. P. M. Röwde, Oslo
3. Private Collection, New York

322 SUNSET AT DEEP

oil on canvas, 18³/₄ × 30³/₄″
lower right: Feininger 30
on back of stretcher written in ink:
Lyonel Feininger 1930 Sunset
Museum of Fine Arts, Boston

323 TOWN HALL, TREPTOW ON
THE REGA
(Rathaus in Treptow a. Rega)

oil on canvas, 19³/₈ × 30¹¹/₁₆″
upper right: Feininger
on back of stretcher written in ink:
*Lyonel Feininger Rathaus in
Treptow a. Rega 1930*
1. Dr. K. Krekeler
2. Mr. and Mrs. Walter Bareiss,
   Greenwich, Connecticut

324 REGLER CHURCH *
(Regler Kirche, Erfurt)

oil on canvas, 50 × 40¼″
upper left: Feininger

* repeatedly listed in exhibitions
(Buchholz Gallery) as *Village
Church*

1. Magistrate of Dessau, Anhaltisches Landesmuseum, Dessau,
   Germany
2. G. David Thompson, Pittsburgh
   Sold through Beyeler, Basel,
   1957 to:
3. Museum of Fine Arts, Boston

325   BARNS AT NIGHT
(Scheunen bei Nacht)

oil on canvas, 16¼ × 21¼″
lower right: Feininger
on back of stretcher written in
black ink: *Lyonel Feininger 1930
Scheunen bei Nacht*

1. Dr. h. c. Richard Doetsch-
   Benziger, Basel
2. Estate Dr. h. c. R. Doetsch-
   Benziger, Basel

326   X 21 *

oil on canvas, 11½ × 21″
lower left: Feininger
on back of stretcher written in ink:
*Lyonel Feininger 1930
X – 21 – 1930*

* (A copy with slight variations,
not by Feininger, is in circulation. –
J. F.)
1. John Becker, New York
2. Private Collection, U.S.A.

327   CHURCH OF ST. MARY, HALLE
(Marktkirche in Halle)

oil on canvas, 39½ × 33½″
upper right: Feininger 30
on back of stretcher:
*Feininger, Lyonel 1930
Marktkirche in Halle*

1. Museum Moritzburg, Halle
2. Prof. Dr. Anselmino,
   Wuppertal, Germany
3. Bayrische Staatsgemäldesammlungen, Munich

328   PYRAMID OF SAILS
(Segelpyramide)

oil on canvas, 18¼ × 28¾″
upper right: Feininger
on back of stretcher in oil:
*Lyonel Feininger 1930
Segelpyramide*

1. Museum Reina, Dessau, Anhalt,
   Germany
2. Dr. Max Fischer, Stuttgart

329   SMALL YACHT

oil on canvas, 14¼ × 21¾″
lower left: Feininger 30

on back of stretcher:
Lyonel Feininger 1930
1. John Becker, New York
2. Private Collection, U.S.A.

330   RUIN BY THE SEA

oil on canvas, 26¾ × 43½″
upper left: Feininger 1930

1. Sold in 1935 at Galerie Möller,
   Berlin
   Whereabouts unknown

331   THE RED TOWER I, HALLE

oil on canvas, 39¾ × 31½″
lower right: Feininger 1930
1. Museum Moritzburg, Halle
Removed during Nazi regime

332   THE RED TOWER II, HALLE

oil on canvas, 39¾ × 33½″
lower right: Feininger
1. Museum Moritzburg, Halle
2. Mr. and Mrs. Robert T. Markson,
   Beverly Farms, Massachusetts

279

333 CHURCH OF ST. MARY
WITH THE ARROW, HALLE
(Marienkirche mit dem Pfeil
[Marienkirche von Osten (mit
Pfeil)]) *

oil on canvas, 39½×32¾″
upper right: Feininger 1930
* called *Marktkirche* in Moritzburg
Gallery
1. Museum Moritzburg, Halle
Removed by Nazis; in 1957
restituted to:
2. Staatliche Galerie Moritzburg,
   Halle
Plate 40

1931

334 MELLINGEN
oil on canvas, 32×39¾″
upper right: Feininger 31
Destroyed by the artist

335 CATHEDRAL CHOIR, HALLE
(Domchor, Halle)

oil on canvas, 39½×32¼″
upper right: Feininger 31
1. Museum Moritzburg, Halle
2. Prof. Harmsen, Germany
3. Kunsthalle, Hamburg

336 WEST-DEEP
oil on canvas, 17½×32¾″
lower right: Feininger 31
1. August Zuntz, Berlin
Disappeared during Nazi regime

337 THE MOTOR BOAT
oil on canvas, 17¾×30½″
upper left: Feininger 31

337

on back of stretcher:
L. Feininger 1931
1. Julia Feininger, New York
Indefinite Loan to the Cleveland
Museum of Art

338 THE BÖLBERGASSE, HALLE

oil on canvas, 39½×32¾″
upper right: Feininger 31
1. Museum Moritzburg, Halle
   Removed during Nazi regime
   and later burned

339 THE CATHEDRAL, HALLE
(Der Dom)

oil on canvas, 34×49″
upper right: Feininger 31
1. Museum Moritzburg, Halle
1937 confiscated in action
"Degenerate Art"
Reacquired in 1948, since then in:
2. Staatliche Galerie Moritzburg,
   Halle

340 CHURCH OF ST. MARY AT
NIGHT, HALLE
(Marienkirche bei Nacht)

oil on canvas, 39½×32¼″
upper right: Feininger 31
1. Museum Moritzburg, Halle
Whereabouts unknown

341 THE TOWERS ABOVE THE
CITY, HALLE
(Die Türme über der Stadt)

oil on canvas, 34¾×49″
upper left: Feininger
1. Museum Moritzburg, Halle
2. Wallraf-Richartz Museum,
   Cologne (Sammlung Haubrich)
Plate 41

1932

342 MAGIC SEA
(Magisches Meer)

oil on canvas, 15¾×26″
lower left: Feininger
1. Julia Feininger, New York
Burned 1946 in warehouse fire
in Montana

343 WESTERN SEA
(Westliches Meer)

oil on canvas, 23¹/₂×30″
lower left: Feininger 32
on back of stretcher written in ink:
*Lyonel Feininger 1932 Westliches
Meer*

Museum of Fine Arts, Springfield,
Massachusetts

344 MARINE

oil on canvas, 17¹/₄×28¹/₄″
lower right: Feininger 32
on back of stretcher:
Lyonel Feininger 1932

Private Collection A.C., Germany

345 YELLOW LANE
(Gasse I)

oil on canvas, 39¹/₂×31¹/₂″
lower left: Feininger 32
on back of stretcher written in ink:
Lyonel Feininger 1932 Gasse I

Mrs. Harry Jason, New York

346 MARINE WITH ORANGE SKY

oil on canvas, 16¹/₄×29¹/₂″
upper right: Feininger 1932

1. Carl Neumann, Wuppertal-
   Barmen, Germany
   Burned in bombing in 1943

347 MILL IN AUTUMN
(Mühle im Herbst)

oil on canvas, 39¹/₂×31¹/₂″
lower left: Feininger 1932
on back of stretcher written in ink:
Lyonel Feininger 1932
Mühle im Herbst

Lawrence Bloedel, Williamstown,
Massachusetts

Plate 42

348 LANE IN TREPTOW
(Treptow a. Rega I)

oil on canvas, 31¹/₂×39¹/₂″
upper right: Feininger 32
on back of stretcher written in ink:
Feininger 1932
Treptow a. Rega I

Estate of the artist

349 AFTERNOON LIGHT I
(Straße in Treptow)

oil on canvas, 31¹/₂×39¹/₂″
lower right: Feininger 32
Inaccessible

350 AFTERNOON LIGHT II
(Straße in Treptow II)

oil on canvas, 31¹/₂×39¹/₂″
upper right: Feininger 1932

1. Encyclopaedia Britannica,
   Collection of Contemporary
   American Painting, Chicago
   Collection disbanded

Whereabouts unknown

350

351 STARS ABOVE THE TOWN

oil on canvas, 35³/₄×39⁷/₈″
lower right: Feininger 21
(Finished in 1932 though dated *21*
in front of the canvas. – J. F.)

Estate of the artist

Plate 44

352 LIGHTED WINDOWS II
(Beleuchtete Häuserzeile II)

oil on canvas, 17¹/₄×28¹/₂″
lower right: Feininger
on back of stretcher written in
black ink: *Lyonel Feininger 1932*
Beleuchtete Häuserzeile II

1. Dr. h. c. Richard Doetsch-
   Benziger, Basel
2. Estate Dr. h. c. Doetsch-
   Benziger, Basel

1933

353 BATHERS

oil on canvas, 21¹/₂×20³/₄″
lower left: Feininger 1933
Estate of the artist

Plate 43

354 YELLOW VILLAGE CHURCH II

oil on canvas, 15³/₄×19″
lower left: Feininger 33
on back of stretcher in India ink:
Lyonel Feininger
Yellow Village Church II
Estate of the artist

355 MARINE (after woodblock)

oil on canvas, 19¹/₄×20″
upper left: Feininger
on back of stretcher:
Lyonel Feininger 1933
Estate of the artist

356 CARAVELS

oil on canvas, 14¹/₂×17⁵/₈″
upper left: Feininger
on back of stretcher:
Lyonel Feininger 1933 Caravels
Rev. Dr. Laurence Feininger,
Trento, Italy

357 ON THE BEACH
(FIGURES AT THE SEASHORE)

oil on canvas, 16×20¹/₂″
lower left: Feininger
on back of stretcher: *Lyonel*
Feininger 1933 Figures at the
Seashore
Estate of the artist

358 DUNE, RAY OF LIGHT I
(Düne)

oil on canvas, 19×30¹/₄″
upper right: Feininger 33
on back of stretcher in pencil:
Lyonel Feininger 1933
in crayon: *Düne*
on back of canvas: *L. Feininger*
1933
Mr. and Mrs. Herbert Ralston,
New York

1934

359 THE RED FIDDLER
(Der rote Geiger)
oil on canvas, 39¹/₂×31¹/₂″
upper right: Feininger 34
Pat and Lux Feininger, Cambridge,
Massachusetts
Colorplate 18

360 CAMMIN
oil on canvas, 23³/₄×19³/₄″
lower left: Feininger 1934
1. Karl Nierendorf, New York
Whereabouts unknown

361 THE POWDER TOWER II

oil on canvas, 19×28¹/₂″
upper right: Feininger 1934
on back of stretcher written in ink:
Lyonel Feininger 1934

1. Dr. Richard Sterba, Germany
2. Dr. and Mrs. R. O. Fehr,
   Schenectady

362 THE BLUE ISLAND

oil on canvas, 15³/₄×19″
upper left: Feininger
on back of stretcher written in
India ink: *L. Feininger 1934*
Die Blaue Insel (energetically
crossed out. – J. F.)
Lore Feininger, Berlin-Charlottenburg

363 FOUR-MAST BARK AND
SCHOONER *
(Viermast Bark)

oil on canvas, 15³/₄×24⁵/₈″
lower left: Feininger

on back of stretcher written in
pencil: *L. Feininger 1934
Viermast Bark*

* Called: *Fourmasted Schooner*
in Guggenheim Museum

The Solomon R. Guggenheim
Museum, New York

364 TAUBACH

oil on canvas, 15³/₄×19″
upper right: Feininger 34

1. Julia Feininger, New York
   Burned 1946 in warehouse fire
   in Montana

365 DALMATIA
(Dalmatien)

oil on canvas, 15³/₄×19″
upper right: Feininger 1934
on back of stretcher written in
India ink: *L. Feininger 1934
Dalmatien*

Andreas and Wysse Feininger,
New York

1935

366 COAST OF PATAGONIA
(FARAWAY ISLANDS)

oil on canvas, 18¹/₄×28¹/₂″
lower left: Feininger
on back of stretcher written in ink:
*Lyonel Feininger 1935 Faraway
Islands*

Private Collection, Brooklyn,
New York

366

**367 GERMAN FOUR-MAST
BARQUE**

oil on canvas, 15³/₄×19″
upper right: Feininger
on back of stretcher, apparently in
India ink: *L. Feininger 1935
Barque*

Mr. and Mrs. Kenneth Parker,
Janesville, Wisconsin

368 SHIP OF STARS I
(Sternenschiff I)

oil on canvas, 16⁵/₈×28³/₈″
lower right: Feininger
on back of stretcher written in oil:
L. Feininger 1935 Sternenschiff

1. Karl Nierendorf, New York
2. The Solomon R. Guggenheim
   Museum, New York

369 VISION OF A BARK
(Vision einer Bark)

oil on canvas, 16¹/₈×29¹/₂″
lower right: Feininger
on back of stretcher written in ink:
Feininger 1935 Vision einer Bark

Private Collection, Germany

370 STREET IN SUNSHINE

oil on canvas, 19×15³/₄″
upper left: Feininger
on back of stretcher in heavy
brushmarks: *Feininger (?) 1935
Street in Sunshine*

1. Walter Laib, Detroit
2. Mrs. A. L. Spitzer, New York

371 MILL IN SPRING

oil on canvas, 39¹/₂×31¹/₂″
lower right: Feininger
The Currier Gallery of Art,
Manchester, New Hampshire
Plate 45

372 CHURCH OF VOLLERSRODA
(Vollersroda Kirche)

oil on canvas, 31¹/₂×39¹/₂″
upper left: Feininger 35
on back of stretcher written in
India ink: *Lyonel Feininger 1935
(Vollersroda) Kirche*

Rev. Dr. Laurence Feininger,
Trento, Italy

1936

373 CLOUD
(Bild mit heller Form)

oil on canvas, 19×15¾″
upper left: Feininger
on back of stretcher (top) in oil:
Lyonel Feininger 1936 Cloud

1. Karl Nierendorf, New York
2. The Solomon R. Guggenheim
   Museum, New York

Plate 46

374 SPRING, VOLLERSRODA

oil on canvas, 39½×31½″
lower right: Feininger 36
Prof. Dr. Otto Hennig, Augsburg,
Germany

Colorplate 19

375 GELMERODA XIII*

oil on canvas, 39½×31⅝″
lower right: Feininger
on back of stretcher in black paint
or India ink wash: *Lyonel
Feininger 1936*

* Since 1953 this painting has been
called *Church at Gelmeroda*

The Metropolitan Museum of Art,
New York (George A. Hearn Fund)

Plate 47

376 DUNES AT EVENTIDE *

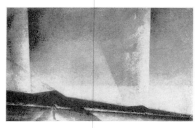

oil on canvas, 19×30½″
lower left: Feininger 36
on back of stretcher in oil:
*Lyonel Feininger, 1936 Dunes at
Eventide*

* Title in Guggenheim Museum:
Dunes, Evening

1. William Dieterle, Hollywood,
   California
Sold through Karl Nierendorf to:
2. The Solomon R. Guggenheim
   Museum, New York

377 MILL (WINDMILL)

oil on canvas, 19×29½″
lower right: Feininger
written on stretcher in India ink,
applied with brush: *Lyonel
Feininger, 1936 Windmill*

Estate of the artist

378 BARQUE AT SEA

oil on canvas, 19×15¾″
lower left: Feininger
on back of stretcher written in ink:
*Lyonel Feininger 1936 Barque at
Sea*

Pat and Lux Feininger, Cambridge,
Massachusetts

1937

379 DUNES AT EVENTIDE II

oil on canvas, 19×30¼″
lower left: Feininger 37

1. Charles Samson, U.S.A.
Whereabouts unknown

380 THE TUG

oil on canvas, 15¾×19″
lower right: Feininger 37

Mrs. Fredrica P. Halley, Tulsa,
Oklahoma

381 DREAM ACROSS THE RIVER

oil on canvas, 14¼×27½″
upper left: Feininger
on back of stretcher written in ink:
Feininger 1937 Magic River

1. Nancy Wilson Ross (Mrs. Stanley Young), Old Westbury,
   Long Island

382 YELLOW VILLAGE
CHURCH III

oil on canvas, 31½×39½″
upper right: Feininger 1937
on back of stretcher written in
ink (?) or crayon (?): *Lyonel Feininger 1937 Village Church*

Mr. and Mrs. Ralph F. Colin, New
York

383 FOUR-MASTED BARK
oil on canvas, 17¹/₂×18¹/₄″
upper right: Feininger 37
on back of stretcher: *Lyonel
Feininger, 1937*
originally signed on back of canvas
in oil: *Feininger 37*
Mr. and Mrs. Sidney F. Brody,
U.S.A.
Plate 48

384 VIADUCT II

oil on canvas, 23³/₄×29¹/₂″
upper left: Feininger 37
(very indistinct)
present signature: upper right:
Feininger
on back of stretcher written in
India ink: *Lyonel Feininger
Viaduct II*
Private Collection, Krefeld,
Germany

385 MID-OCEAN
(Schwarze Welle)

oil on canvas, 19×28¹/₂″
upper right: Feininger
on back of stretcher: *Feininger
1937 Mid-Ocean*
Private Collection, Switzerland

386 SHIP OF STARS II
(Sternenschiff II)
oil on canvas, 19³/₄×28¹/₂″
lower left: Feininger

386

on back of stretcher written in
India ink: *Feininger 1937
Ship of Stars (Sternenschiff II)*

1. Pat and Lux Feininger,
   Cambridge, Massachusetts

387 DUNES WITH NEW MOON
(Dünen mit Mondsichel)

oil on canvas, 16⁷/₈×28¹/₂″
upper right: Feininger 37
on back (not mentioned
where – J. F.): *Lyonel Feininger
Dünen mit Mondsichel*
also: *Lyonel Feininger, | 1937 |
Dunes (with new moon)*

1. Charles Samson, Jr., U.S.A.
2. Kunstmuseum der Stadt
   Düsseldorf

1939

388 BRIGANTINE OFF THE COAST

oil on canvas, 18×30¹/₂″
upper right: Feininger 1939
on back of stretcher written
in crayon: *Feininger 1939*

Mr. and Mrs. Harold E. Grove,
New York

389 STORM BREWING

oil on canvas, 19×30¹/₂″
lower right: Feininger
on back of stretcher written in
ebony pencil: *Lyonel Feininger
1939 Storm Brewing*
Estate of the artist

390 DUNES AND BREAKWATERS
oil on canvas, 21×37¹/₂″
lower right: Feininger
John Nicholas Brown, Newport,
Rhode Island
Plate 49

1940

391 LAST VOYAGE

oil on canvas, 19×30³/₄″
lower left: Feininger
Martha Jackson, New York

392 AT THE SEA SIDE, PANEL I

oil on canvas, 19×19″
upper right: Feininger

on back of stretcher written in crayon: *Lyonel Feininger March 7th 1940 At the Sea Side Panel 1*

Estate of the artist

393 THE ANGLERS, PANEL II

oil on canvas, 15×20″
upper left: Feininger
on back of stretcher: *Lyonel Feininger 1940 The Anglers Panel II*

Estate of the artist

394 Untitled (a sketch)

oil on canvas, 14×29″
unsigned
on back of stretcher written in India ink on paper glued to the stretcher, with underscorings in red crayon: *N.Y. June 11th, 1940* Transcript of dedication: *To my dear* Lux, *on the auspicious occasion of his 30th birthday, this preliminary sketch to what may some day become a full-fledged painting, representing "The Queen of the Hudson": the side-wheeler "Mary Powell," is dedicated with great affection by his old Laddie, yclept* Papileo

Pat and Lux Feininger, Cambridge, Massachusetts

395 SPOOK I

oil on canvas, 21×21″
lower right: Feininger
on back of stretcher written in black pencil: *Lyonel Feininger 1940 Spook I*

Phillips Collection, Washington, D.C.

395

396 MANHATTAN, NIGHT

oil on canvas, 24×17″
lower right: Feininger
on back of stretcher written in pencil: *Night 1940*

Marian Willard Johnson, New York

Plate 51

397 RUIN ON THE CLIFF II

oil on canvas, 19×28¹/₂″
lower right: Feininger
on back of stretcher in crayon: *Lyonel Feininger 1940 Ruin on the Cliff*

Rev. Dr. Laurence Feininger, Trento, Italy

398 MANHATTAN I

oil on canvas, 39¹/₂×31¹/₂″
lower right: Feininger 40

Estate of the artist

Colorplate 20

399 MANHATTAN II

oil on canvas, 38×28¹/₂″
upper left: Feininger
on back of stretcher written in blue crayon: *Manhattan II 1940 Lyonel Feininger*
written in pencil: *Manhattan II*

Fort Worth Art Association, Texas

Plate 50

400 ARCHITECTURAL COMPOSITION I

oil on canvas, 24×36″
lower right: Feininger
on back of stretcher: *Lyonel Feininger 1940 Architectural Composition 1*

Estate of the artist

401 ADVENTURE I

oil on canvas, 19³/₄×16⁵/₈″
upper right: Feininger 1940
on back of stretcher written in crayon: *Feininger 1940 Adventure I*

Estate of the artist

402 ADVENTURE II

oil on canvas, 24×15¹/₂″
lower right: Feininger
on back of stretcher written in crayon: *Lyonel Feininger 1940 1951 Adventure II*
(F. worked over the face of the man at left, probably in 1951. – J. F.)

Estate of the artist

Plate 52

403 NAVVIES, SHOVING FREIGHT CAR

oil on canvas, 23¹/₂×30⁵/₈″
upper left: Feininger
on back of stretcher written in
crayon: *1940 Men moving Freight Car*
Estate of the artist

404 THE WHITE CORNER

oil on canvas, 28¹/₂×21″
lower left: Feininger 1940
indications about size and
signature from Buchholz Catalogue
1941
Destroyed by the artist

1941

405 CITY AT NIGHT

oil on canvas, 36×24″
lower right: Feininger
The Wolf Collection, King's Point,
Long Island
Plate 53

406 GABLES IV

oil on canvas, 24¹/₂×28¹/₂″
upper left: Feininger

on back of stretcher (top) written
in ink: *Lyonel Feininger 1941
Old Gables IV*
Estate of the artist

407 RAILROAD-TRAIN

oil on canvas, 19×28″
lower right: Feininger
on back of stretcher written in
crayon: *Lyonel Feininger 1941
Railroad-Train*
Estate of the artist

408 SPOOK II

oil on canvas, 24×19″
upper left: Feininger
1. Julia Feininger, New York
   Burned 1946 in warehouse fire
   in Montana

409 VIGNETTE (BRIG)

oil on canvas, 20×24″
upper left: Feininger
on back of stretcher: *1941
Vignette (Brig)*
Estate of the artist

410 LADIES AT THE SEA SIDE

oil on canvas, 18×23″
upper left: Feininger
on back of stretcher written in
pencil: *Lyonel Feininger 1941
Ladies at the Sea Side*
Estate of the artist

411 THE NIGHT EXPRESS

oil on canvas, 14×17″
lower left: Feininger
on back of stretcher written in
crayon: *Lyonel Feininger 1941
The Night Express*
Conrad R. Feininger,
Cambridge, Massachusetts

412 IN THE CHANNEL

oil on canvas, 19×30¹/₄″
upper right: Feininger

on back of stretcher in pencil:
Lyonel Feininger
in oil: *1941 In the Channel*
Sweet Briar College, Sweet Briar,
Virginia

413 FISHER OFF THE COAST

oil on canvas, 19 × 36″
lower right: Feininger 41
on back of stretcher: *Lyonel
Feininger 1941
Fisher off the Coast*

1. John S. Newberry, New York
2. The Detroit Institute of Arts
   (Gift in Memory of Dr. W. R.
   Valentiner)

414 REGATTA (THE RAINBOW II)

oil on canvas, 17 × 36″
upper left: Feininger
on back of stretcher in India ink
applied with brush:
1941 Regatta
Estate of the artist

415 PEACEFUL NAVIGATION

oil on canvas, 17 × 17″
upper right: Feininger

on back of stretcher written in ink:
*Lyonel Feininger 1941 Peaceful
Navigation*

Mrs. Margarete Schultz,
Great Neck, Long Island

416 BIG CLOUD

oil on canvas, 18 × 28″
upper left: Feininger
Estate of the artist

417 SEPTEMBER CLOUDS

oil on canvas, 19 × 30³/₈″
upper left: Feininger
Private Collection, U.S.A.

1942

**418 THE ANGLERS
(BLACK BRIDGE)**

oil on canvas, 17 × 23″
lower left: Feininger
on back of stretcher written in
ebony pencil: *Lyonel Feininger
1942 The Anglers*
Estate of the artist

419 CHURCH (GREEN-BLACK)

oil on canvas, 27 × 34″
lower left: Feininger 42
Estate of the artist

**420 PHANTOM SHIP
(THE DARK WAVE II)**

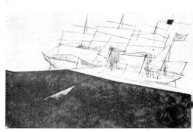

oil on canvas, 18 × 28″
upper left: Feininger
on back of stretcher written in ink:
Feininger Phantom Ship 1942
Estate of the artist

**421 MIRAGE I
(ISLANDS IN THE SKY)**

oil on canvas, 12 × 27″
upper left: Feininger
on back of stretcher written in
crayon: *Lyonel Feininger 1942
Mirage Julia Dear 5th April 1944*

1. Julia Feininger, New York
2. Andreas Feininger, New York

**422 BLIND MUSICIAN AT THE
BEACH**

oil on canvas, 15 × 20″
lower right: Feininger
Mr. and Mrs. Ernst Fabisch,
New York
Colorplate 22

423 VOYAGE BY MOONLIGHT

oil on canvas, 15³/₄×19″
lower left: Feininger
on back of stretcher written in
pencil: *Lyonel Feininger 1942
Voyage by Moonlight*
on back of canvas: *To Karsten and
Elinor, from Leo
17. Dec. 1944*

Collection Karsten and
Eleanor Pelham Stapelfeldt,
New York

424 MARCH DAY

oil on canvas, 22×29″
upper right: Feininger

1. Julia Feininger, New York
   Burned in 1946 in warehouse
   fire, in Montana

425 CATHEDRAL (CAMMIN)

oil on canvas, 19×28″
upper right: Feininger
on back of stretcher from left to
right on top written in black
crayon: *Lyonel Feininger 1942
Cathedral (Cammin)*

The Cleveland Museum of Art
(Gift of Leonard C. Hanna, Jr.)

426 ALARM *

oil on canvas, 36×25″
upper right: Feininger

* Title in Cranbrook Academy:
Church in Winter

Cranbrook Academy of Art,
Bloomfield Hills, Michigan

427 VOLCANO

oil on canvas, 19×20″
upper left: Feininger
on back of stretcher written in
charcoal: *Lyonel Feininger 1942
Volcano*

Estate of the artist

428 ENCHANTED NIGHT

oil on canvas, 16×19″
upper left: Feininger
on back of stretcher written in
crayon: *Lyonel Feininger 1942
Enchanted Night*

1. Julia Feininger, New York
2. Wysse Feininger, New York

429 COAST OF NEVERMORE I

oil on canvas, 20×36″
upper left: Feininger

Mr. and Mrs. John B. Dempsy,
Cleveland

430 CLOUDS ABOVE THE SEA IV

oil on canvas, 23×34″
upper left: Feininger
on back of stretcher written in
pencil: *1942 Clouds above the
Sea IV*

Andreas and Wysse Feininger,
New York

431 POSSENDORF III

oil on canvas, 19³/₄×23³/₄″
upper right: Feininger

on back of stretcher written in soft
pencil: *Lyonel Feininger 1942
Possendorf III*
Estate of the artist

1943

432 TOWN GATE

oil on canvas, 19×20″
upper right: Feininger
on back of stretcher written in
ebony pencil: *Lyonel Feininger
1943 Town Gate*
crossed out: *of Ribnitz*
Estate of the artist

**433 MIRAGE II
(COAST OF NEVERMORE)**
oil on canvas, 19×32″
lower left: Feininger
Private Collection, U.S.A.
Plate 54

434 CHAPEL IN THE WOODS

oil on canvas, 19×15″
lower left: Feininger

on back of stretcher written in
ebony pencil: *Lyonel Feininger
1943 Chapel in the Woods*
Rev. Dr. Laurence Feininger,
Trento, Italy

435 HORIZON (THE SKYLINE)

oil on canvas, 16×29″
upper right: Feininger
on back of stretcher written in
pencil: *Lyonel Feininger 1943
Skyline*
Mr. and Mrs. Arthur E. Motch,
Cincinnati

436 VILLAGE IN THURINGIA
oil on canvas, 16×20″
upper right: Feininger
1. Curt Valentin, New York
Disappeared after his death
Whereabouts unknown

437 RUE ST.-JACQUES, PARIS
oil on canvas, 19×16″
upper left: Feininger
1. Private Collection, New York
2. Mr. and Mrs. Hans Arnhold,
New York

438 FISHERMEN

oil on canvas, 15×23″
lower left: Feininger
on back of stretcher top written in
ink: *Lyonel Feininger 1943
Fishermen*
1. J. W. Alsdorf, Winnetka,
Illinois
2. Willard Gallery, New York

439 GABLES V (OLD GABLES)

oil on canvas, 18×29″
lower left: Feininger
on back of stretcher written in
pencil: *Lyonel Feininger 1943
Old Gables*
1. Philipp Goodwin, New York
2. Yale University Art Gallery,
New Haven

440 OLD STONE BRIDGE

oil on canvas, 21×28″
lower left: Feininger

Sold at Lilienfeld Gallery,
New York, to:
Lucien B. Day (address unknown)

1944

441 GABLES VI

oil on canvas, 17 × 28″
upper right: Feininger
on back of stretcher written in
pencil: *Lyonel Feininger 1944
Old Gables (VI)*

Mr. and Mrs. James Taylor Dunn,
St. Paul, Minnesota

442 DUNES, MOONGLOW

oil on canvas, 24 × 36″
upper right: Feininger

Dr. and Mrs. E. L. Froelicher,
New York

443 BLUE COAST

oil on canvas, 18 × 34″
upper left: Feininger

The Columbus Gallery of Fine Arts

444 MANHATTAN, DAWN
oil on canvas, 35 × 28″
upper right: Feininger

1. Julia Feininger, New York
2. Pat and Lux Feininger,
   Cambridge, Massachusetts
3. Andreas Feininger, New York

Colorplate 21

445 MANHATTAN, THE TOWER

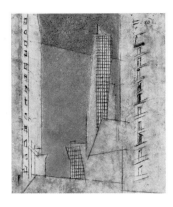

oil on canvas, 39¹/₂ × 31¹/₂″
upper right: Feininger 1944

Mrs. Drew Chidester,
San Francisco

446 MANHATTAN, FROM THE EARLE

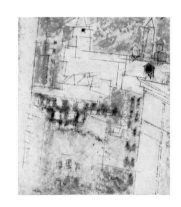

oil on canvas, 35 × 28″
upper right: Feininger
on back of stretcher: *Lyonel Feininger 1944 Manhattan (from
the Earle)*

Estate of the artist

447 DUNES, RAY OF LIGHT II
oil on canvas, 20 × 35″
upper left: Feininger
on back of stretcher written in
pencil: *Lyonel Feininger 1944
Dunes, with Ray of Light II*

Albright Art Gallery, Room of
Contemporary Art Collection,
Buffalo

Plate 55

448 MILL IN SNOW

oil on canvas, 15 × 22″
upper right: Feininger
on back of stretcher written in
pencil: *Lyonel Feininger 1944
III 24 1944
Windmill (in Snow)*
Estate of the artist

449 DUNES, HAZY EVENING

oil on canvas, 24 × 41″
upper left: Feininger
on back of stretcher in black
crayon: *Lyonel Feininger 1944
Dunes, Hazy Evening*
Mrs. Daniel Crena de Jongh,
Wilton, Connecticut

450 MIRAGE III
(COAST OF NEVERMORE)

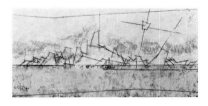

oil on canvas, 15 × 30″
lower left: Feininger
on back of stretcher written in
pencil: *Mirage III
(Coast of Nevermore)
Lyonel Feininger 1944*

Mr. and Mrs. Dan Johnson,
New York

1945

451 DUNES, COAST OF DEEP

oil on canvas, 18×32″
upper left: Feininger 45
on back of stretcher written in
pencil: *Lyonel Feininger 1945*
Philbrook Art Center, Tulsa,
Oklahoma

452 DESERT-SEA

oil on canvas, 14×26″
upper right: Feininger
on back of stretcher written in ink:
Lyonel Feininger
February 9, 1945 Desert-Sea
Mrs. Toni Stolper, New York

453 NEW YORK BUILDINGS I

oil on canvas, 16×23″
upper right: Feininger
on back of stretcher written in
crayon: *Lyonel Feininger*
25. IV 45 N.-Y. Buildings (I)
Estate of the artist

454 AFTERGLOW I
oil on canvas, 19×31″
lower right: Feininger

454

on back of stretcher, apparently in
India ink: *Lyonel Feininger 1945*
Afterglow
Mr. and Mrs. Kenneth Parker,
Janesville, Wisconsin

455 CITY MOON
oil on canvas, 28½×21¼″
upper right: Feininger
on back of stretcher, top, in pencil:
City Moon 1945
bottom stretcher in green pencil:
The White Cor..r
crossed out with lines through it
Nebraska Art Association,
University of Nebraska, Lincoln

Plate 56

456 WEIRD MOON

oil on canvas, 24×36″
upper left: Feininger
on back of stretcher written in
crayon: *Lyonel Feininger 1945*
(on long side and on short side of
stretcher)

Andreas Feininger, New York

457 MANHATTAN, DUSK

oil on canvas, 23×36″
upper right: Feininger
on back of stretcher written in soft
pencil: *Lyonel Feininger 1945*
Manhattan, Dusk

Mr. and Mrs. C. Bagley Wright,
Seattle

458 BEACH UNDER GLOOM
oil on canvas, 17×34″
lower right: Feininger
on back of stretcher written in
crayon: *Lyonel Feininger 1945*
Beach under Gloom

Mr. and Mrs. Werner E. Joston,
New York

Plate 57

459 THE TOWER

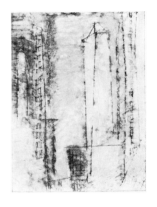

oil on canvas, 23×16″
upper right: Feininger
on back of stretcher written in
pencil: *The Tower 1946* (date of
exhibition at Buchholz Gallery,
New York – J. F.)

Mrs. Walter A. Everitt, New York

460 MOONWAKE
oil on canvas, 30×23″
lower right: Feininger
on back of stretcher written in
crayon: *Lyonel Feininger 1945*
Moonwake 30×23

Estate of the artist

Plate 58

461 ARCHITECTURE WITH
STARS II

oil on canvas, 16×28″
upper left: Feininger
on back of stretcher written in
pencil: *Lyonel Feininger 1945,
Architecture with Stars, II*

Estate of the artist

462 FLAMING CLOUDS

oil on canvas, 19×34″
upper left: Feininger
on back of stretcher: *Feininger
1945*

Dr. Karl Lilienfeld, New York

1946

463 DUSK

oil on canvas, 28×39″
upper left: Feininger
on back of stretcher written in
charcoal: *Lyonel Feininger
Jan. 1946 Dusk*

Rev. Dr. Laurence Feininger,
Trento, Italy

464 MANHATTAN III

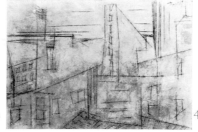

oil on canvas, 17×24″
upper right: Feininger
Acquired by Mr. Samuel Bohn
(address unknown), at Buchholz
Gallery, 1946

465 CHURCH AT MORNING
oil on canvas, 39½×31½″
upper right: Feininger
on back of stretcher written in
crayon: *Lyonel Feininger 1946
Church at Morning*

Blanden Memorial Art Gallery,
Fort Dodge, Iowa
Plate 59

466 CHURCH ON THE HILL

oil on canvas, 39½×31½″
upper left: Feininger
Given from the Collection of
Mr. William E. Scott to the Fort
Worth Art Association, Texas

467 B-B TOWN
oil on canvas, 15½×26″
lower right: Feininger
on back (top) of stretcher: *Lyonel
Feininger 1946 B-B Town*

1. Mrs. Florence May, Atlanta,
   Georgia
2. Robert P. Saidenberg, New York

467

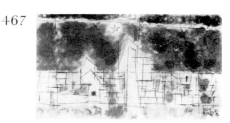

468 DISTANT ISLAND

oil on canvas, 20×35″
upper right: Feininger

1. Sold by Curt Valentin Gallery
   during group show
   in South America
   Whereabouts unknown

469 YACHT RACE,
(RACING SKERRY CRUISERS)

oil on canvas, 13×25″
upper left: Feininger
on back of stretcher:
Lyonel Feininger

J. Fred Seiberling, Akron, Ohio

470 DIVERTISSEMENT (FISHING
SMACKS)

oil on canvas, 17×23″
upper left: Feininger
on back of stretcher written in
pencil: *Lyonel Feininger 1946
Fishing Smacks (Divertissement)*

Estate of the artist

293

1947

471 VITA NOVA
oil on canvas, 31½×39½"
lower right: Feininger
on back of stretcher: *Lyonel
Feininger 1946/47 Vita Nova*
Rev. Dr. Laurence Feininger,
Trento, Italy
Colorplate 23

472 THE BALTIC (V-CLOUD)
oil on canvas, 17×29"
upper right: Feininger
on back of stretcher in crayon:
Lyonel Feininger 1946/47
in India ink, applied with brush:
The Baltic
Estate of the artist
Plate 60

473 SEASCAPE

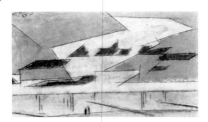

oil on canvas, 15×22"
upper left: Feininger
on back of stretcher written in
pencil: *Lyonel Feininger 1947
Seascape*
Dr. and Mrs. Steven van Riper,
Detroit

474 MOUNTAIN VILLAGE II

oil on canvas, 15×22"
upper right: Feininger
on back of stretcher: *Lyonel Feininger 1947 Mountain Village II*
Estate of the artist

475 QUEEN OF THE HUDSON
oil on canvas, 14×28"
upper left: Feininger

475

on back of stretcher, upper
horizontal stretcher-strip,
in lithographic pencil:
*Lyonel Feininger 1947 The Queen
of the Hudson*
on lower horizontal stretcher-strip
(upside down) in pencil: *Lyonel
Feininger, 1947, Mary Powell*
partly obliterated: *Jan. 7th, 1947
Dream Hill*
Pat and Lux Feininger,
Cambridge, Massachusetts

476 TOWN HALL OF CAMMIN
(sketch)

oil on canvas, 25×20"
lower right: Feininger
on back of stretcher in India ink:
*Lyonel Feininger 1947
Town Hall of Cammin*
Estate of the artist

477 BALTIC, A RECOLLECTION

oil on canvas, 20×35"
upper right: Feininger
on back of stretcher in black oil
paint: *Lyonel Feininger 1947
Baltic: A Recollection*
The Toledo Museum of Art

478 THREE WINDOWS

oil on canvas, 16×28"
lower right: Feininger
on back of stretcher written in
pencil: *Lyonel Feininger 1947
Three Windows*
Mr. and Mrs. Sigmund Kun-
stadter, Highland Park, Illinois

479 RAINBOW OVER THE DUNES

oil on canvas, measurements: ?
upper left: Feininger
information from existing
photograph
1947 (?)
Whereabouts unknown

1948

480 AFTERGLOW II

oil on canvas, 17×24"
lower left: Feininger
on back of stretcher written in
pencil: *Lyonel Feininger May 8,
1948*
Rev. Dr. Laurence Feininger,
Trento, Italy

481 THE HIDDEN VILLAGE

oil on canvas, 20×24″
lower left: Feininger
on back of stretcher written in
pencil: *L. Feininger 1948
The Hidden Village*
Estate of the artist
Plate 62

1948-49

482 HOUSES BY THE RIVER I

oil on canvas, 20×30″
lower right: Feininger
on back of stretcher written in
pencil: *Lyonel Feininger
November 48 – January 49
Houses by the River I*
Mr. and Mrs. Robert F. Windfohr,
Fort Worth, Texas
Plate 61

1949

483 COURTYARD I

oil on canvas, 21×18″
upper left: Feininger
on back of stretcher written in
pencil: *Lyonel Feininger 1949,
March 29th Courtyard I*
Mr. and Mrs. Alfred H. Hetkin,
New York

484 THE TREES

oil on canvas, 23×27″
lower left: Feininger
on back of stretcher: *Lyonel
Feininger April 1949*
on same stretcher (shorter side):
*Lyonel Feininger 1944
Manhattan (sunlit)*
Estate of the artist

484

485 THURINGIAN VILLAGE
(STREET IN MELLINGEN,
THURINGIA)

oil on canvas, 20×25″
lower right: Feininger
on back of stretcher written in
pencil: *. . . .inger, May 26th 1949
Street in Mellingen, Thuringia*
William Suhr, New York

486 IN SNOW

oil on canvas, 18×27″
upper right: Feininger

on back of canvas: a sketch
on back of stretcher written in
pencil: *Feininger 1949*
Private Collection, New York

487 COURTYARD II

oil on canvas, 20×18″
lower left: Feininger

487

on back of stretcher written in
crayon: *Lyonel Feininger 1949
Courtyard II*
Estate of the artist

488 WALLS AND WINDOWS

oil on canvas, 19×15″
upper left: Feininger
on back of stretcher written in
pencil: *Lyonel Feininger 1949
Walls and Windows*

1. Bernard Friedman, New York
Through Saidenberg Gallery to:
2. Mr. and Mrs. Everett N.
Carpenter, Milwaukee

489 STEAMBOAT LANDING

oil on canvas, 19×24″
upper left: Feininger

on back of stretcher written in
pencil: *Lyonel Feininger 1949*
Steamboat Landing
(after a sketch of 1915 – J. F.)

Estate of the artist

490 THE FACTORY (FACTORY
WINDOWS IN MANHATTAN)

oil on canvas, 28×21″
lower right: Feininger 49
on back of stretcher written in
charcoal: *Lyonel Feininger*
written in pencil: *Factory*
Windows in Manhattan

Estate of the artist

Plate 64

491 THE CUTTING

oil on canvas, 17×28″
lower left: Feininger
on back (shorter side of stretcher)
written in pencil: *1949*
The Cutting

Rev. Dr. Laurence Feininger,
Trento, Italy

Plate 65

492 WANDERERS BY THE SEA II

oil on canvas, 15½×21″
lower left: Feininger

on back of stretcher written in ink:
Lyonel Feininger 1949
Wanderers by the Sea

Estate of the artist

493 CHURCH OF OLD TREPTOW

oil on canvas, 14×19″
upper right: Feininger
on back of stretcher: *Lyonel Fei-*
ninger 1949 Church of Old
Treptow

Abbot L. Mills, Washington, D.C.

493
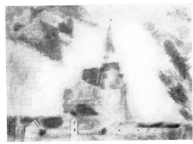

494 COURTYARD III

oil on canvas, 24×19″
lower left: Feininger 1949
on back of stretcher written in
pencil: *Lyonel Feininger*
Courtyard III
written in crayon: *Dec. 10, 1949*
on back of canvas is an unfinished
painting of a cityscape

Miss Adelaide Milton de Groot,
New York

Plate 63

495 CLOUDBANK

oil on canvas, 16×28″
upper left: Feininger

Sold at Curt Valentin Gallery
Whereabouts unknown

496 DUNES

oil on canvas, 18×30″
lower left: Feininger

Private Collection, U.S.A.

497 THE RED STREET SWEEPER II

oil on canvas, 16×20″
upper left: Feininger
written on back of stretcher:
Lyonel Feininger 1920–49
The red Streetsweeper
Feininger's own replica of:
the Red Streetsweeper of 1920
(205), burned 1946 in warehouse
fire in Montana. Copied from a
35-mm photo
Estate of the artist

1950

498 LOFT BUILDING

oil on canvas, 15×28″
upper right: Feininger
on back of stretcher: *Lyonel*
Feininger 1950 The Factory
Loft Building
Dr. and Mrs. David Bloom,
New York

499 HOUSES BY THE RIVER II

oil on canvas, 20×30″
upper left: Feininger
on back of stretcher: *Feininger*
1950 Houses by the River II
Estate of the artist

500 HARBOR OF MEMORY

oil on canvas, 24×36″
upper left: Feininger
on back of stretcher written in
crayon: *L. Feininger 1950*
Harbor of Memory
Estate of the artist

501 YACHTS

oil on canvas, 21×36″
upper left: Feininger
on back of stretcher written in
pencil: *Lyonel Feininger 1950*
Yachts
Mrs. Ernest Frederick Eidlitz,
Riverdale, New York
Colorplate 25

502 Working Panel for Mural in the
First-Class Dining Room of the
SS *Constitution*

oil on canvas, 10×42″
lower left: Feininger
Estate of the artist

1951

503 SUMMER SKYLINE

oil on canvas, 15×24″
upper right: Feininger 51
1. Alfred Jaretzki, Jr.
   As a gift to:
2. Wadsworth Atheneum,
   Hartford, Connecticut

504 DEAD END

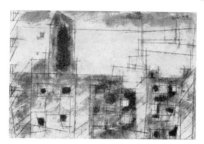

oil on canvas, 16⅞×24″
lower right: Feininger 51
on back of stretcher:
Lyonel Feininger 1951
Mr. and Mrs. Otto Spaeth,
New York

505 MANHATTAN SUBJECT

oil on canvas, 15×22″
upper right: Feininger
on back of stretcher written in
pencil: *Lyonel Feininger 1951*
Manhattan Subject
March 31, 1951
Joseph H. Hirshhorn, New York

506 OLD GABLES

oil in canvas, 16×24″
upper right: Feininger 1951
on back of stretcher written in
lithograph pencil: *Lyonel Feininger*
Old Gables 1951
1. Harry J. Caesar, Salem Center,
   New York
2. W. Mason Smith, Jr.,
   New York

507 GAY PASSAGE

oil on canvas, 18×28″
lower left: Feininger
on back of stretcher written in
pencil: *Lyonel Feininger June 5,*
1951 Gay Passage
James B. Morrison Memorial
Collection, Des Moines Art Center,
Iowa

508 SPRING (BOY MEETS GIRL)

oil on canvas, 13×20″
upper left: Feininger
on back of stretcher written in
pencil: *L. Feininger, 1951*
Mr. and Mrs. Erlo van Waveren,
New York

509 THE SPELL

oil on canvas, 50×24″
lower right: Feininger 1951
on back of stretcher written in
pencil: *Lyonel Feininger 1951*
in ink: *Spell*
Mr. and Mrs. Sigmund Kun-
stadter, Highland Park, Illinois
Plate 66

510 CHIMNEY POTS

oil on canvas, 20×23″
lower right: Feininger

on back of stretcher written in
pencil: *Lyonel Feininger 1951
Chimney Pots*

Andreas Feininger,
New York

511 COMPOSITION: GABLES I

oil on canvas, 15×24″
upper left: Feininger
on back of stretcher written in
pencil: *Lyonel Feininger 1951
Composition Gables I*

Andreas Feininger, New York

512 HOUSES AT NIGHT

oil on canvas, 16×24″
upper left: Feininger

1. M. van Bouren, The Spa,
   Safety Harbor, Florida
2. Mr. and Mrs. Arthur Wiesen-
   berger, New York

513 LUNAR WEB

oil on canvas, 21×36″
lower right: Feininger 1951
on back of stretcher written in
pencil: *Lyonel Feininger 1951
Moonweb in the Connecticut
Hills known as Lunar Web*

Mr. and Mrs. Milton Lowenthal,
New York

Colorplate 27

513a Free replica of *Still Life with
Samovar* (156)

oil on canvas
measurements: ?
upper left: Feininger

Painting destroyed by the artist

1952

514 THE VANISHING HOUR

oil on canvas, 19×32″
lower right: Feininger
on back of stretcher written in
crayon: *Lyonel Feininger 1951-2,
The Vanishing Hour*
Estate of the artist

515 CREST AND IMAGE

oil on canvas, 20×30″
upper right: Feininger
on back of stretcher written in
pencil: *Lyonel Feininger 1952
Crest and Image*
Manufacturers Trust Company,
New York

Plate 70

516 [PULU'S "EASTER EGG"]

oil on canvas, 16×10″
unsigned

on back of stretcher: *1952 Pulu's
Easter Egg 16×10″*
on back of canvas: *Feininger 1952*
Julia Feininger, New York

517 MANNA-HATA

oil on canvas, 28×18″
lower left: Feininger
on back of stretcher written in
crayon: *Lyonel Feininger Manna-
Hata*
Mr. and Mrs. Alan H. Rosenthal,
New York
Plate 67

518 COMPOSITION: CITY HOUSES

oil on canvas, 16×24″
lower left: Feininger
on back of stretcher written in
pencil: *Lyonel Feininger 1952
Composition City Houses*
Mrs. Barbara Wilk, Ridgefield,
Connecticut

519 FACTORY AT NIGHT

oil on canvas, 18×22″
upper left: Feininger 52
on back of stretcher written in
charcoal (perishable):
Lyonel Feininger 1952
Estate of the artist

520 COMPOSITION: GABLES II

oil on canvas, 15×24″
upper left: Feininger
Estate of the artist

520

1952-53

521 CRÉPUSCULE
oil on canvas, 30×23″
lower right: Feininger
on back of stretcher written in
pencil: *Lyonel Feininger 1952–53*
Crépuscule
Wysse Feininger, New York
Plate 68

1953

522 BARQUE AT SEA

oil on canvas, 18×30″
upper left: Feininger 53
on back of stretcher:
Lyonel Feininger 1952–53
Barque at Sea
Pat and Lux Feininger,
Cambridge, Massachusetts

523 RUE ST.-JACQUES, PARIS

oil on canvas, 36×27¾″
upper left: Feininger
on back of stretcher written in
India ink: *Lyonel Feininger 1953*
Rue St.-Jacques, Paris
Estate of the artist

524 COMPOSITION: GABLES III

oil on canvas, 15×24″
upper left: Feininger
on back of stretcher written in
pencil: *Lyonel Feininger 1953,*
Composition Gables III
Estate of the artist

525 COMPOSITION: GABLES IV

oil on canvas, 15×24″
upper left: Feininger
R. S. Field, Long Island City

526 WHITE WALLS

oil on canvas, 24×17″
lower right: Feininger
on back of stretcher written in
pencil: *Feininger 1953 White*
Walls
Mr. and Mrs. Alan H. Temple,
Scarsdale, New York

527 COMPOSITION: GABLES V

oil on canvas, 15×24″
upper right: Feininger
on back of stretcher written in
pencil: *Feininger 1953*
Composition Gables 5
on back of canvas:
Lyonel Feininger 1953
Composition Gables 5

Joseph H. Hirshhorn, New York

528 VILLAGE

oil on canvas, 15×20″
unsigned
on back of stretcher written in
pencil: *Lyonel Feininger 1953*
Village
on back of canvas: *Feininger 1953*
Joseph H. Hirshhorn, New York

529 LITTLE HOUSE IN THE
FOREST

oil on canvas, 19×18″
upper right: Feininger

on back of stretcher written in
ebony pencil: *Lyonel Feininger
1953 Little House in the Forest*
Estate of the artist

530 SUNSET FIRES
oil on canvas, 24×36″
upper left: Feininger
on back of stretcher written in
pencil: *Lyonel Feininger 1953
Sunset Fires*
Andreas Feininger, New York
Colorplate 26

551 GABERNDORF
(GERMAN VILLAGE)

oil on canvas, 15×24″
upper right: Feininger
on back of stretcher:
*Lyonel Feininger Nov. 1953
Gaberndorf
Gaberndorf (German Village)*
Dr. Karl Lilienfeld, New York

552 SHADOW OF DISSOLUTION
oil on canvas, 36×30″
upper right: Feininger
on back of stretcher:
*Lyonel Feininger 1953
Shadow of Dissolution*
Rev. Dr. Laurence Feininger,
Trento, Italy
Colorplate 28

1954

533 PHOENIX
oil on canvas, 33×24″
upper right: Feininger
on back of stretcher written in
pencil: *Lyonel Feininger 1953–54*
Mr. and Mrs. James S. Schramm,
Burlington, Iowa
Colorplate 24

534 COMPOSITION: GABLES VI

oil on canvas, 15×24″
upper right: Feininger
on back of stretcher (top)
written in India ink:
*Lyonel Feininger Composition
Gables VI 1953*
on right-hand side of stretcher:
finished January 2nd 1954
Andreas Feininger,
New York

535 FENRIS WOLF
oil on canvas, 20×30″
upper right: Feininger 1954
on back of stretcher written in
pencil: *Lyonel Feininger 1953–54
Fenris Wolf*
Mr. and Mrs. Robert D. Straus,
Houston, Texas
Plate 71

536 SAILS

oil on canvas, 17×30″
upper right: Feininger
on back of stretcher written in ink:
*Lyonel Feininger 14. Feb. 1954
Sails*
Mrs. Albert List, Byram,
Connecticut

537 EDGED SPACES
oil on canvas, 30×24″
upper left: Feininger
Mr. and Mrs. John S. Schulte,
New York
Plate 69

538 POSSENDORF IV

oil on canvas, 20×25″
upper right: Feininger
on back of stretcher written in
ebony pencil: *Lyonel Feininger
Possendorf IV 1953–54*
Estate of the artist

1955

559 EVENING HAZE
oil on canvas, 15×24″
upper left: Feininger 1955
on back of stretcher written in
charcoal: *Lyonel Feininger 1955
Evening Haze*
Andreas Feininger, New York
Plate 72

UNFINISHED WORKS
(oil on canvas)

A. 25½×20″   no title, unsigned
B. 24×16¾″   no title, unsigned
C. 15×24″   no title, unsigned
D. 14×20″   no title, unsigned
E. 15×27″   no title, unsigned
F. 27×22″   no title, unsigned
G. 32×22″   no title, unsigned
H. 25×36″   no title, unsigned
I. 39⅜×51″   no title, unsigned
J. 12×22″   no title, unsigned
K. 17×23¾″   no title, unsigned
L. 33×39″   no title, unsigned
M. 29¾×21″   no title, unsigned
N. THE OLD MAN IN THE
   WOODS
   27×22″
   upper left: Feininger
   after considering it completed,
   taken up again, painted over,
   but left in an unfinished con-
   dition (1955)

APPENDIX

CHRONOLOGY

1871   Charles Léonell Feininger born July 17th in St. Marks Place, New York City. First child of the violinist Karl Feininger and Elizabeth, née Lutz.

1873–77   Early years with his parents at 311 East 53rd Street, New York City, and with the Clapp family at Sharon, Connecticut.

1878   Summer with parents in North Adams, Massachusetts.

1880   Karl Feininger gives the first violin lessons to his son.

1883   Several weeks with grandparents in Columbia, South Carolina; summer visit with father to the St. Lawrence River.

1885   In the summer, a brief visit to Niagara Falls.

1886   Spends the summer with his sisters at Lake George, New York.

1887   While parents are on a concert tour in Europe, lives alone in New York City and in Plainfield, New Jersey. Works as errand boy for a firm of Wall Street brokers.
November 13th, sails for Hamburg, where he arrives November 25th. Stays with Miss J. Prealle, visits his parents in Berlin, obtains permission to study at the Kunstgewerbeschule, Hamburg.

1888   Thirteen works in the Easter Exhibition of the school; goes to Berlin to prepare for entrance examination at the Academy; passes examination October 1.

1889   Lives at Unter den Linden 16 in Berlin. First drawings for *Humoristische Blätter*; meets Fred Werner and Alfred Vance Churchill; summer at Harzburg.

1890   Illustrations for short stories, humorous drawings for Berlin papers.
Arrives September 2nd at the Collège St.-Servais, Liège; visits Brussels during the autumn.

1891   Leaves the Collège at Liège and begins study at the Studio Schlabitz, Berlin. During October Professor Woldemar Friedrich accepts him into the Higher Antique Class of the Academy; he meets Fritz Strothmann. Summer on the island of Rügen in the Baltic.

1892   Drawings for Berlin papers. During August and September at Rügen, visits Seedorf. Leaves the Academy. November 4, arrives in Paris, Rue Campagne Premier 9; works at the Atelier Colarossi.

1893   Leaves Paris on May 7; to Berlin, Schillerstrasse 16. Summer at Rügen.

1894   First drawings for Harper & Brothers; lives at Courbièrestrasse 12.

1895	Works for *Ulk*; further drawings for Harper's.
1896	Lives at Albestrasse 16 at home of Artur Berson, husband of Feininger's sister Helen.
1897	Drawings for *Lustige Blätter*. Staff cartoonist at *Ulk*.
1898	Drawings for *Narrenschiff*, *Lustige Blätter*; contract with *Ulk* terminated.
1900	Meets Clara Fürst in Berlin.
1901	Marries Clara Fürst; first daughter, Lore, born December 14th.
1902	Second daughter, Marianne, born November 18th.
1903	Exhibits drawings at the 8th Exhibition of the Berlin Secession.
1904	Caricatures and drawings exhibited in Berlin, Grosse Kunstausstellung.
1905	Meets Julia Berg (née Lilienfeld); leaves Clara. On July 24 to Graal on Rügen. Works for *Ulk* and *Lustige Blätter*. Lives in Berlin, Bambergerstrasse 44.
1906	Spends a few weeks in Weimar; first drawings of Gelmeroda. Early lithographs. In Berlin, contract with *Chicago Sunday Tribune*, in March; terminates contract with *Lustige Blätter*. Takes studio in Weimar, Kurthstrasse 7a. Goes to Paris with Julia, arrives July 24th. Takes studio at Boulevard Raspail 242. Works again at Atelier Colarossi, meets the German artists of the Dôme circle, Hans Purrmann, Rudolf Grossmann, Oskar Moll, Rudolf Levy. Drawings for *Le Témoin*, *Chicago Tribune*. During August and September in Normandy — Quiberville, Ouville, La Rivière. Friendship with Jules Pascin, Richard Götz, Paul Iribe; meets Robert Delaunay. First son, Andreas, born December 27th. Visits Arcueil, Meudon, Longueil.
1907	Contract with *Chicago Tribune* ends. April 7th begins to paint; first picture yellow porcelain monkey on colored ground. From Paris in the early summer to Güntherstal near Freiburg im Breisgau (Black Forest); paints after nature. During August to Baabe and Lobbe (Rügen); October back in Paris. Sees pictures by Van Gogh and Cézanne at Bernheim Jeune.
1908	Paris; during the spring to London, sees Turner's paintings; to Berlin. Paints grotesques — "Mummenschanz" pictures; figurative period. Works occasionally for *Ulk*, *Lustige Blätter*, *Sporthumor*. Fall to London, marries Julia; for several weeks in Paris, then settles in Berlin-Zehlendorf, Königstrasse 32.
1909	Paints first pictures in the new studio: *The Manhole I*, *Pink Street*. Second son, Laurence, born April 5th. Summer at Heringsdorf (Baltic Sea). Exhibits drawings in Berlin Secession.
1910	Third son, Theodore Lux, born June 11th. Summer Heringsdorf, Achterwasser (Baltic Sea). Beach scenes; September at Neppermin. First oil exhibited at the Secession.

1911   Spring in Weimar; May in Paris. Exhibits six paintings at the Salon des Artistes Indépendants. First acquaintance with Cubism. Summer at Heringsdorf; visits Benz, Zirchow. Drawings for *Licht und Schatten*.

1912   Friendship with Alfred Kubin; meets the Brücke artists, Erich Heckel and Karl Schmidt-Rottluff. New studio in Düppelstrasse (Zehlendorf). First architectural compositions: *High Houses I, Teltow I*.

1913   Berlin and Weimar (studio Kurthstrasse 7a). Explores the villages of Thuringia, among others: Hopfgarten, Dröbsdorf, Mellingen, Vollersroda, Possendorf, Klein-Kromsdorf and Gross-Kromsdorf, Nieder-Grunstedt, Legefeld, Eichelborn, Tiefurt, Gaberndorf, Kiliansroda, Öttern, Denstedt, Umpferstedt, and Zottelstedt. First painting of Gelmeroda. Invited by Franz Marc to exhibit with the Blue Rider group at the Erste deutsche Herbstsalon; represented there with five paintings. Bernard Köhler acquires *High Houses I*; Paul Poiret acquires *Teltow I*. Meets Herwarth Walden and the artists of the Sturm group.

1914   New studio, Potsdamerstrasse (Zehlendorf). During the spring in Weimar in his studio in the Kurthstrasse. Returns to Berlin at the outbreak of war.

1915   Berlin, *Self-Portrait*.

1916   Some weeks during the summer in Wildpark near Potsdam. Exhibition at the Sturm with Felix Müller.

1917   Summer in Braunlage, Harz; first one-man exhibition at the Sturm. Development of monumental style during the war years: *Zirchow, Vollersroda*.

1918   Summer in Braunlage, Harz. Joins the November Group; meets Walter Gropius. First woodcuts.

1919   Exhibition at J. B. Neumann; meets Alois J. Schardt. On May 18th with Gropius to Weimar. Foundation of the Bauhaus. Bauhaus manifesto appears with Feininger's woodcut *Cathedral of Socialism*. Attends his first meeting of Bauhaus Masters on May 30th.

1920   Weimar, Gutenbergstrasse 16. Drawings of Thuringian villages, among them, Gelmeroda, Vollersroda, Tiefurt, Umpferstedt, Eichelborn, Buttelstedt, Klein-Kromsdorf, Mellingen, Berka, Nieder-Grunstedt, Öttern, Nermsdorf, Possendorf, Lehnstedt, Süssenborn, Hayn. Visits Erfurt.

1921   Composes his first fugue. Late summer, Heiligenhafen, Lüneburg. Detroit Institute of Arts acquires *Side-Wheeler II*, first acquisition by an American museum.

1922   Composes fugues. Death of his father, February 1st. Visits during the summer Lüneburg, Lübeck, Neu-Brandenburg. At Timmendorf (Baltic) with Gropius and Kandinsky.

1923   Stays in Erfurt; studio at the Anger Museum.

1924   First summer in Deep (Pomerania), on the Baltic coast. From there visits Treptow. Architectural compositions and paintings of the Baltic.

1925	Summer in Deep, visits Cammin, Treptow, Greifenberg, Kolberg. End of the Bauhaus at Weimar.
1926	Moves to Dessau, Burgkühnerallee 3. Remains Master at the Bauhaus without teaching obligations. Summer in Deep. Foundation of the exhibition group, Blaue Vier (Blue Four): Feininger, Klee, Kandinsky, Jawlensky. Exhibition in the United States.
1927	Summer in Deep. Death of his mother, July 26th. Alfred H. Barr, Jr., and Jere Abbott visit Feininger in Dessau.
1928	Thirteen paintings in the National Gallery, Berlin (Kronprinzen-Palais). Exhibition of paintings from private collections in Berlin. Summer in Deep. Passes, on his return to Dessau: Swinemünde, Heringsdorf, Wolgast, Greifswald, Riebnitz, Brandenburg. Awarded gold medal and prize for *Architecture III* at Dusseldorf.
1929	Dessau. From May to June at Halle. Studio in the tower of the Moritzburg. Summer in Deep. Halle pictures.
1930	Dessau. Summer in Deep. Spends part of the year in Halle.
1931	Dessau. Spring in Halle. Visits Theodore Spicer-Simson in Bourron. Some days in Paris, Quimper, Tréboul, Concarneau. During August to Deep. In honor of 60th birthday, a large retrospective exhibition at the National Gallery, Berlin (Kronprinzen-Palais).
1932	Summer in Deep. End of the Bauhaus in Dessau.
1933	Leaves Dessau during March, in April to Deep. Fall and winter in Berlin-Wannsee in the house of friends.
1934	Summer in Deep. A few days during October in Kuhtz. Takes apartment at Lenthersteig 21, Berlin-Siemensstadt.
1935	Last summer in Deep. Receives invitation from Alfred Neumeyer to teach at Mills College, Oakland, California.
1936	Leaves Hamburg on May 6th; arrives at New York on May 14th; met by his old American friends. By boat through the Panama Canal to California. Arrives in San Diego June 12th, meets Emmy Galka Scheyer in Los Angeles. Summer course at Mills College. Visits San Francisco. August, Falls Village, Connecticut; revisits Sharon, Connecticut. In August to Stockholm via Hamburg. By the end of the year in Berlin. Decides to leave Germany. Last German paintings: *Vollersroda (Spring)*, *Gelmeroda XIII*. First one-man show in America at the East River Gallery, New York.
1937	Second invitation to teach the summer course at Mills College. Leaves Germany on June 11th, arrives in New York June 17th. From Mills College visits San Francisco. Arrives New York September 7th; stays at Hotel Earle, Washington Square.
1938	From now on at 235 East 22nd Street. Murals for New York World's Fair. Summer in Falls Village, Connecticut.

1939   New York. Summer in Falls Village. November 19th, Feininger paints for the first time in America.

1940   New York. Summer in Falls Village. Fall and winter New York. Manhattan pictures.

1941   New York. Development of the graphic style. Summer in Falls Village.

1942   New York. Summer in Falls Village. Wins acquisition prize for *Gelmeroda XIII* at the Artists for Victory exhibition, Metropolitan Museum of Art, New York.

1943   New York. Summer in Falls Village. Awarded Worcester Museum of Art prize.

1944   New York. Meets Mark Tobey, Fernand Léger. Large retrospective exhibition at the Museum of Modern Art, New York, with Marsden Hartley. Summer in Falls Village.

1945   New York. Summer course at Black Mountain College, North Carolina. Autumn in Stockbridge, Massachusetts.

1946   New York. Summer in Stockbridge.

1947   New York. Summer in Stockbridge; visits Alfred Einstein in Northampton, Massachusetts. Elected President of the Federation of American Painters and Sculptors.

1948   New York. Recovers from a serious operation at Stockbridge.

1949   New York. Summer in Center Moriches, Long Island. Autumn, a few weeks in Boston, Massachusetts. Exhibition with Jacques Villon at the Institute of Contemporary Art, Boston.

1950   New York. Mural for the liner *Constitution*. Summer at Cambridge, Massachusetts, at the house of Eric Schröder. Fall in Plymouth, Massachusetts.

1951   New York. Summer in South Lincoln, Massachusetts, in the house of Walter Gropius; late summer in Plymouth.

1952   New York. Summer in Cambridge; fall in Plymouth.

1953   New York. Summer in New Haven, Connecticut, in Albers' house; autumn in Plymouth.

1954   New York. July in Stockbridge. Mark Tobey visits Feininger.

1955   New York. Summer in Stockbridge; autumn in Plymouth. Elected Honorary Vice-President of the Federation of American Painters and Sculptors. Elected member of the National Institute of Arts and Letters.

1956   Dies in New York January 13th.

EXHIBITIONS

1910   BERLIN, Secession: *20. Kunstausstellung*. 1 oil.

1911   PARIS, Salon des Indépendants: *La 27ᵐᵉ Exposition 1911*. 6 oils.
BERLIN, Secession: *22. Kunstausstellung*. 2 oils.

1912   BERLIN, Secession: *24. Kunstausstellung*. 2 oils.
NEW YORK, Photographische Gesellschaft: *Deutsche Graphische Kunst*.
Group show.

1913   BERLIN, Galerie Der Sturm: *Erster Deutscher Herbstsalon*, 5 oils.

1914   DRESDEN, Galerie Ernst Arnold: *Die Neue Malerei*. 6 oils.
BERLIN, Freie Secession. Group show.
COLOGNE, Werkbundausstellung. Group show.

1916   BRÜNN, Group show.
BERLIN, Galerie Der Sturm: *42. Ausstellung*. Joint exhibition with
Felix Müller.
MUNICH, Neue Kunst Hans Goltz: *IV. Gesamtausstellung*. 5 oils; drawings.

1917   BASEL, Galerie Corray: *Sturm-Ausstellung*. 4 oils.
BERLIN, Galerie Der Sturm: *55. Ausstellung: Lyonel Feininger*. First one-
man show. 46 oils; watercolors, graphics, 111 works in all.
ZURICH, Galerie Dada. With Arp, de Chirico, Ernst, Kandinsky, Klee,
Kokoschka, Marc, Modigliani, Picasso, and others.

1918   MUNICH, Neue Kunst Hans Goltz. One-man show: 34 oils, also watercolors
and graphics.
HANOVER, Kestner-Gesellschaft: *Junge Berliner Kunst*. 3 oils.

1919   DRESDEN, Galerie Ernst Arnold: *Der Sturm*. 6 oils.
BERLIN, J. B. Neumann und Karl Nierendorf Galerie. One-man show.
BERLIN, Freie Secession: Summer exhibition.
DRESDEN, Galerie Emil Richter. One-man show. 38 oils, also watercolors,
graphics, 161 works in all.
DRESDEN, Secession: *Gruppe 1919*.
HANOVER, Kestner-Gesellschaft. Joint exhibition with Paul Klee. 36 oils,
51 watercolors, also graphics.

1920   ERFURT, Museum am Anger. One-man show.

1921   WEIMAR, Landesmuseum am Karlsplatz. Joint exhibition with Paul Klee.
BASEL, Kunsthalle: *Moderne Deutsche Malerei*. 5 oils. Exhibition was then
shown at: MAGDEBURG, Kunstverein.
BERLIN, *Grosse Kunstausstellung*, 2 oils.
GENEVA, *Internationale Kunstausstellung*. Group show.

1922 VENICE, *XIII. Biennale.* 2 oils.

BERLIN, Galerie Goldschmidt und Wallerstein. One-man show.

ERFURT, Kunstverein. One-man show.

MAGDEBURG, Kaiser-Friedrich Museum. One-man show.

1923 WIESBADEN, Städtisches Museum. Group show.

NEW YORK, N. Y., Anderson Gallery: *A Collection of Modern German Art.*
5 oils, also watercolors, drawings, and graphics.

1924 MUNICH, Graphisches Kabinett. Joint exhibition with Chagall.

DRESDEN, Neue Kunst Fides. One-man show.

BERLIN, *Grosse Kunstausstellung: Novembergruppe.* 2 oils.

1925 WIESBADEN, Nassauischer Kunstverein, Neues Museum. 8 oils, also watercolors and graphics.

DRESDEN, Galerie Hugo Erfurth: *Bauhaus Meister.* Fugues by Feininger
were played by Paul Aron (piano) at the opening.

DUSSELDORF, *Jahrhundert-Ausstellung Rheinischer Malerei.* Group show.

NEW YORK, N. Y., The Daniel Gallery, first exhibition of "The Blue Four,"
Kandinsky, Feininger, Klee, Jawlensky.

1926 DRESDEN, Neue Kunst Fides. One-man show.

HAMBURG, Kunstverein. Group show.

BERLIN, Galerie Goldschmidt und Wallerstein. One-man show.

BRUNSWICK, Gesellschaft der Freunde Junger Kunst. One-man show.
31 oils, also watercolors and graphics.

HANOVER, Kestner-Gesellschaft. 77th Exhibition: *Bauhaus Dessau.*

SAN FRANCISCO, Calif., OAKLAND, Calif., LOS ANGELES, Calif., Exhibition:
The Blue Four.

1927 ERFURT, Kunstverein. One-man show.

KASSEL, "Kunstverein der Städtischen Galerie." One-man show.

NEW YORK, N. Y., Grand Central Art Galleries. International group show.
2 oils.

1928 DUSSELDORF, Akademie: *Deutsche Kunst 1928.* Group show. (Gold medal
and prize for *Architecture III*).

DRESDEN, Neue Kunst Fides. One-man show. 28 oils, also watercolors and
drawings.

HALLE, Museum Moritzburg. One-man show.

BERLIN, National-Galerie: *Neuere deutsche Kunst aus Berliner Privatbesitz.*
13 oils.

BRESLAU, Schlesisches Museum. One-man show.

1929 BERLIN, Galerie Ferdinand Möller: *Die Blaue Vier.* 18 oils, also watercolors
and drawings.

DESSAU, Anhaltische Staatsgalerie, Palais Reina. One-man show.

BRESLAU, Altes Generalkommando-Gebäude. Joint exhibition with Erich
Heckel and Ewald Mataré.

BASEL, Kunsthalle: *Bauhaus-Meister.*

DUSSELDORF, Galerie Flechtheim. Joint exhibition with Paul Klee.

KIEL, Museum. One-man show.

KASSEL, Orangerie. Jubilee Exhibition of the Kunstverein and the Academy.

NEW YORK, N.Y., Museum of Modern Art: *Paintings by 19 Living Americans*. 7 oils.

1930   VENICE, *XVII. Biennale*. 1 oil.

COLOGNE, Kunstverein. Group show.

PRAGUE, Kunstverein. Group show.

BERLIN, National-Galerie. New acquisitions by Freunde der National-Galerie.

1931   DRESDEN, Neue Kunst Fides. One-man show in honor of Feininger's sixtieth birthday. Exhibition was then shown at ESSEN, Museum Folkwang.

BERLIN, National-Galerie (Kronprinzen-Palais). One-man show in honor of Feininger's sixtieth birthday. 72 oils, also watercolors, drawings, charcoal compositions, 137 works in all.

SAN FRANCISCO, Calif., California Palace of the Legion of Honor: *The Blue Four*. 7 oils, also watercolors and graphics. Exhibition was then shown at: MEXICO CITY, Mexico, Biblioteca Nacional.

1932   HANOVER, Kestner-Gesellschaft. One-man show. 50 oils, also watercolors, drawings, and graphics.

LEIPZIG, Museum der Bildenden Künste. One-man show. (Part of the National-Galerie exhibition, Berlin, 1931).

DESSAU, Kreis der Freunde des Bauhauses, Anhaltisches Landesmuseum. Group show.

KÖNIGSBERG, Kunstsammlungen der Stadt Königsberg und Kunstverein. Joint exhibition with Paul Klee.

HAMBURG, Kunstverein. One-man show. 55 oils, also watercolors and graphics.

HAMBURG, Kunstverein. First traveling exhibition. Group show.

OSLO, Kunstnernes. Modern German Art, painting and sculpture. 7 oils. Exhibition was then shown in COPENHAGEN with one additional oil.

1933   BERLIN, Galerie Paul Cassirer: *Lebendige deutsche Kunst*. 8 oils, also watercolors.

LOS ANGELES, Calif., Los Angeles Museum: *The Blue Four*. 11 oils, also watercolors, graphics, and 1 sculpture (wood).

1934   BERLIN, Galerie Karl Nierendorf. Joint exhibition with Georg Muche.

BERLIN, Galerie Ferdinand Möller. Group show.

1935   JENA, Prinzessinnen-Schlösschen. Group show.

BERLIN, Galerie Ferdinand Möller. One-man show. 67 watercolors; 33 pen drawings and charcoal drawings.

HAMBURG, Kunstverein: *Zeichnungen und Malerei als musikalischer Ausdruck*.

1936   BERLIN, Galerie Karl Nierendorf. One-man show. 28 oils, also watercolors and drawings.
HAMBURG, Kunstverein: *Malerei und Plastik in Deutschland*. 2 oils.
NEW YORK, N. Y., Museum of Modern Art: *Cubism and Abstract Art*. 3 oils.
OAKLAND, Calif., Mills College Art Gallery. One-man show. 16 oils, also watercolors, drawings, and graphics. Exhibition was then shown at:
SAN FRANCISCO, Calif., San Francisco Museum of Modern Art.

1937   NEW YORK, N. Y., Gallery Karl Nierendorf. One-man show.
OAKLAND, Calif., Mills College Art Gallery. One-man show. 35 oils, also watercolors, drawings, and graphics. Exhibition was then shown at: SEATTLE, Wash., SANTA BARBARA, Calif., LOS ANGELES, Calif., PORTLAND, Oreg.

1938   MINNEAPOLIS, Minn. One-man show. 33 oils, also watercolors and graphics.
ANDOVER, Mass., Addison Gallery of American Art, Phillips Academy. One-man show. 17 oils; 19 watercolors, drawings, and graphics.
PARIS, Musée du Jeu de Paume: *Trois Siècles d'Arts aux États-Unis*.
SAN DIEGO, Calif., Fine Arts Gallery of the City of San Diego. One-man show.
NEW YORK, N. Y., Mrs. Cornelius J. Sullivan and Karl Nierendorf Galleries. One-man show. 21 oils, also watercolors, drawings, and graphics.
CHARLESTON, S. C., Gibbes Memorial Art Gallery: *Solomon R. Guggenheim Collection of Non-Objective Paintings*. 5 oils.
LONDON, New Burlington Galleries: *20th Century German Art*. 2 oils.
NEW YORK, N. Y., Museum of Modern Art: *Bauhaus 1919–1928*. 7 oils.

1939   PITTSBURGH, Penna., Carnegie Institute: *The Pittsburgh International Exhibition of Contemporary Painting*. 1 oil.
LAWRENCE, Kans., Thayer Art Gallery, University of Kansas. One-man show.
BATON ROUGE, La., Louisiana State University. One-man show. 11 oils, also watercolors and graphics. Exhibition was then shown at: BEREA, Ky.
NEW YORK, N. Y., Museum of Modern Art. *Art in Our Time*. 1 oil.

1940   WELLESLEY, Mass., Farnsworth Museum, Wellesley College. One-man show. 25 oils, also watercolors and drawings.
KALAMAZOO, Mich., Kalamazoo Institute of Arts. One-man show.
NEW YORK, N. Y., Galerie St. Etienne. *American Abstract Art*. 3 oils.
LOS ANGELES, Calif., Dalzell Hatfield Gallery. One-man show.
CHARLOTTE, N. C., The Mint Museum: *Memories of Youth*. 8 oils, 8 watercolors.
NEW YORK, N. Y., Lilienfeld Galleries: *American Contemporary Paintings*. 6 oils.
NEW YORK, N. Y., Whitney Museum of American Art: *Contemporary American Painting*. 1 oil.

1941   NEW YORK, N. Y., Buchholz Gallery jointly with Willard Gallery. One-man show. 42 oils, also watercolors, 85 works in all. Exhibition was then shown at: GROSSE POINT, Mich., The Russel A. Alger House.

PROVIDENCE, R. I., Tilden-Thurber Gallery. One-man show.

WASHINGTON, D. C., Corcoran Gallery of Art: *17th Biennial*. 1 oil.

1942   NEW YORK, N. Y., The Metropolitan Museum of Art: *Artists for Victory*. 1 oil. (Purchase prize for *Gelmeroda XIII*).

1943   WORCESTER, Mass., Worcester Museum of Art. Group show. (Worcester Museum of Art prize).

NEW YORK, N. Y., Buchholz Gallery. One-man show. 16 oils, also watercolors.

NEW YORK, N. Y., Willard Gallery: *Fantasy in Feininger*. One-man show. 13 oils, also watercolors.

NEW YORK, N. Y., Lilienfeld Galleries: *A Group of American Artists*. 6 oils.

NEW YORK, N. Y., Whitney Museum of American Art: *Contemporary American Painting*. 1 oil.

WASHINGTON, D. C., Corcoran Gallery of Art: *18th Biennial*. 1 oil.

NEW YORK, N. Y., Museum of Modern Art: *Romantic Painting in America*. 2 oils.

SAN FRANCISCO, Calif., H. M. de Young Memorial Museum: *Meet the Artist* (exhibition of self-portraits). Exhibition was then shown at:

1944   PORTLAND, Oreg., Museum of Art; and then at: NEW YORK, N. Y., The American-British Art Center.

NEW YORK, N. Y., Buchholz Gallery: *The Blue Four*. 6 oils, also watercolors.

NEW YORK, N. Y., Museum of Modern Art. Joint exhibition with Marsden Hartley. 65 oils, also 77 watercolors, drawings, and graphics, as well as compositions for the murals at the New York World's Fair 1938–39.

LEICESTER, England, The Leicester Museum and Art Gallery: *Mid-European Art*. 4 oils, also watercolors and graphics.

1945   NEW YORK, N. Y., Whitney Museum of American Art: *Contemporary American Painting*. 1 oil.

POUGHKEEPSIE, N. Y., Vassar College. Joint exhibition with Marsden Hartley. 35 oils, 38 graphics. Part of the Museum of Modern Art exhibition, New York 1944. Exhibition was then shown at: BOSTON, Mass., AMHERST, Mass.; ST. LOUIS, Mo., St. Louis City Art Museum; ST. PAUL, Minn., St. Paul Gallery and Art School; SAN FRANCISCO, Calif., San Francisco Museum of Art; FORT WORTH, Texas; BUFFALO, N. Y., Albright Art Gallery; TULSA, Okla., Philbrook Art Center; LOUISVILLE, Ky.

1946   NEW YORK, N. Y., Buchholz Gallery. One-man show. 13 oils, also watercolors.

NEW YORK, N. Y., Willard Gallery: *Figures by Feininger*. One-man show. 9 oils, also watercolors.

1947   WASHINGTON, D. C., Cororan Gallery of Art: *20th Biennial*. 1 oil.

312

1948 VENICE, *XXIV. Biennale*. 1 oil.
NEW YORK, N.Y., Buchholz Gallery. One-man show. 17 oils, also watercolors.
NEW YORK, N.Y., Whitney Museum of American Art: *Contemporary American Painting*. 1 oil.

1949 BOSTON, Mass., Institute of Contemporary Art. Joint exhibition with Jacques Villon. 19 oils, also watercolors. Exhibition was then shown at: WASHINGTON, D.C., Phillips Gallery; and: WILMINGTON, Del., Delaware Art Center.
WASHINGTON, D.C., Corcoran Gallery of Art: *21st Biennal*. 1 oil.
NEW YORK, N.Y., Whitney Museum of American Art: *Contemporary American Painting*. 1 oil.

1950 NEW YORK, N.Y., Buchholz Gallery. One-man show. 20 oils, also watercolors.
HEMPSTEAD, N.Y., Hofstra College. One-man show. 8 oils, also watercolors and graphics.
PARIS, Galerie Jeanne Bucher. First one-man show in Paris. 40 watercolors. (Traveling exhibition of Kestner-Gesellschaft, Hanover).
MUNICH, Haus der Kunst: *Die Maler am Bauhaus (1. Internationale Kunstausstellung)*. 11 oils, also watercolors and graphics, 37 works in all.
PITTSBURGH, Penna., Carnegie Institute: *The Pittsburgh Exhibition of Contemporary Painting*. 1 oil. (2nd prize).
URBANA, Ill., University of Illinois: *Contemporary American Painting*. 1 oil.
HANOVER, Kestner-Gesellschaft. One-man show. 40 watercolors. Exhibition was then shown at: MUNICH, BRUNSWICK, MANNHEIM, DUSSELDORF, HAMBURG, BERLIN, and other German towns, and then at:

1951 YORK, CAMBRIDGE, LONDON.
MINNEAPOLIS, Minn., Minnesota University: *40 American Painters*.
NEW YORK, N.Y., Museum of Modern Art: *Abstract Painting and Sculpture in America*. 3 oils.
CLEVELAND, Ohio, The Cleveland Museum of Art: *The Work of Lyonel Feininger*. 44 oils, also watercolors and graphics. 247 works in all.
NEW YORK, N.Y., Whitney Museum of American Art: *Contemporary American Painting*. 1 oil.
WASHINGTON, D.C., Corcoran Gallery of Art: *22nd Biennial*. 1 oil.
SÃO PAULO, Brazil., Museu de Arte Moderna: *I. Bienal: Estados Unidos*. 3 oils.

COLOGNE, Galerie Ferdinand Möller: *Die alten Meister der modernen Kunst in Deutschland*. 4 oils.
KNOKKE- Le-Zoute, Albert Plage. *75 Œuvres du Demi-Siècle*. 1 oil.

1952 NEW YORK, N.Y., Curt Valentin Gallery (formerly Buchholz Gallery). One-man show in honor of Feininger's eightieth birthday. 26 oils, also watercolors and drawings.

313

PITTSBURGH, Penna., Carnegie Institute: *The Pittsburgh International Exhibition of Contemporary Painting*. 1 oil.

1953   LUCERNE, Kunstmuseum: *Deutsche Kunst. Meisterwerke des 20. Jahrhunderts*. 6 oils, also watercolors and drawings.
NEW YORK, N. Y., Whitney Museum of American Art: *Contemporary American Painting*. 1 oil.

1954   NEW YORK, N. Y., Curt Valentin Gallery. One-man show. 24 oils, also watercolors.
MUNICH, Bayerische Akademie der Schönen Künste. One-man show. 40 oils, also watercolors and drawings. 89 works in all. Exhibition was then shown at: HANOVER, Kestner-Gesellschaft and then went on to: AMSTERDAM, Stedelijk Museum with two additional oils.

1955   PITTSBURGH, Penna., Carnegie Institute: *The Pittsburgh International Exhibition of Contemporary Painting*. 1 oil.
MEMPHIS, Tenn., Brooks Art Gallery: *Three Modern Painters. Feininger, Hartley, Beckmann*. 6 oils.
SAN FRANCISCO, Calif., San Francisco Museum of Art: *Art in the 20th Century*.
KASSEL, Museum Fridericianum: *Documenta*. 9 oils.
BARCELONA, *III. Bienal Hispanoamericana*. 2 oils, also watercolors and graphics, 15 works in all. Exhibition was then shown at: FRANKFURT/M., *Moderne Kunst aus USA*, and then went on to:

1956   BELGRADE, THE HAGUE, PARIS, VIENNA, and: LONDON, Tate Gallery: *Modern Art in the United States*, with two additional oils.
CHARLOTTE, N. C., The Mint Museum. Joint exhibition with Andreas, Laurence, and Lux Feininger. Photographs, scores, and oils.
NEW YORK, N. Y., Willard Gallery. One-man show. 14 oils, 19 watercolors.
NEW YORK, N. Y., The Metropolitan Museum of Art: *Memorial Exhibition, Feininger, Kuhn, Kuniyoshi, Marin, Nordfeldt*. 10 oils, also watercolors, drawings, and graphics, 20 works in all.
FORT WORTH, Texas, Fort Worth Art Center: *Feininger: a Memorial Exhibition of His Work from Fort Worth Collections*. One-man show.
VENICE, *XXVIII. Biennale: American Artists Paint the City*. 3 oils.
CAMBRIDGE, Mass., Cambridge Art Association. Joint exhibition with Lux Feininger.
LONDON, Tate Gallery: *A Hundred Years of German Painting, 1850–1950*. 4 oils, also drawings.
NEW YORK, N. Y., Willard Gallery: *Gables*. One-man show. 8 oils, also watercolors, graphics, 32 works in all.
WOLFSBURG, Germany, Volkswagenwerk: *Deutsche Malerei. Ausgewählte Meister seit Caspar David Friedrich*. 3 oils.

1957   BOSTON, Mass., Museum of Fine Arts: *Gables*. One-man show.
BOSTON, Mass., Museum of Fine Arts: *European Masters of Our Time*.

NEW YORK, N. Y., Museum of Modern Art: *German Art of the 20th Century*. 4 oils, also woodcuts.

ROME, *Arte Tedesca dal 1905 ad oggi*. 1 oil.

1958   OGUNQUIT, Maine, Museum of Art of Ogunquit. 7 oils, also watercolors.

AMSTERDAM, Stedelijk Museum: *De Renaissance de XXe Eeuw*. 4 oils.

CAMBRIDGE, Mass., Busch-Reisinger Museum, Harvard University: *Lyonel Feininger, Paintings of Harbors, Ships, and the Sea*.

NEW YORK, N. Y., Willard Gallery. One-man show. 13 oils, also watercolors and graphics.

FORT WORTH, Texas, Fort Worth Art Center: *The Iron Horse in Art*. 1 oil.

NEW YORK, N. Y., Whitney Museum of American Art: *Nature in Abstraction*. 1. oil.

PITTSBURGH, Penna., Carnegie Institute: *1896–1955: Retrospective Exhibition of Paintings from Previous Internationals*. 4 oils.

MERANO, Italy, *Sala Esposizioni dell'Azienda Autonoma di Soggiorno*. 35 watercolors and drawings. One-man show.

TRENTO, Italy, Universita Popolare Trentina. One-man show. Watercolors and graphics.

1959   RALEIGH, N. C., North Carolina Museum of Art: *Masterpieces of Art*, memorial exhibition William R. Valentiner 1880–1958.

LONDON, Marlborough Galleries: *Art in Revolt: Germany 1905–1925*. 3 oils.

SAN FRANCISCO, Calif., San Francisco Museum of Art: *Lyonel Feininger Memorial Exhibition*. 71 oils, also watercolors and drawings, 137 works in all. Exhibition was then shown at:

1960   MINNEAPOLIS, Minn., Minneapolis Institute of Arts; and: CLEVELAND, Ohio, The Cleveland Museum of Art; and: BUFFALO, N. Y., Albrigt Art Gallery; and: BOSTON, Mass., Museum of Fine Arts.

YORK, England, The City Art Gallery: *Memorial Exhibition Lyonel Feininger*. 39 oils, 21 watercolors, 21 watercolor drawings, 6 drawings; also toys (wood). Part of the Cleveland Museum of Art exhibition, first shown at the San Francisco Museum of Art 1959; then shown at: LONDON, Arts Council Gallery; with additions at:

1961   HAMBURG, Kunstverein: *Lyonel Feininger 1871–1956 Gedächtnis-Ausstellung*. 62 oils, 157 watercolors, drawings, and graphics. Exhibition then at: ESSEN, Museum Folkwang; and BADEN-BADEN, Staatliche Kunsthalle.

Dessau, d. 9. Mai, 1928

Lieber Freund!

Zu Ihrem morgigen Geburtstage
wünschen wir Alle Ihnen viel Glück
und gute Gesundheit! Wir werden in
Gedanken bei Ihnen und Ihren Lieben
sein. Einliegend sind, nach 4=jähriger Pause,
endlich einmal wieder einige Holzschnitte, "Jahr=
gang 1928", die ich bitte, in Ihre Samm=
lung einzureihen.
Viele herzlichste Grüsse!
Ihr getreuer Lyonel Feininger
und Frau

Above: Letter to the collector A. H., Dessau, May 9, 1928

Opposite page: Letter to the artist's son Lux, New York, January 14, 1944

Friday, Jan. 14th, 1944

my dear Lux,

Manni has begun to
read to me while I stand
at my easel at work on
new paintings. She has been
reading "Airman's Odyssey", by
Antoine de St. Exupéry; a
book I hope you some day
will read, for its author is
a man of most exception-
ally exalted character and gifts. The series of Adven-
tures he describes are amazing, but more still
of importance is the spirit of his narrative. Besides
this book (which Manni is reading now for the
second time), we have had some of my old letters
from Weimar in 1925. Boy! I used to write a
lot when I was younger. Some days I wrote
two or even three letters to Manni, who was
for about 5 weeks away from home. And not
only did I write so much, but I did a lot of
work in the Bauhaus studio and attended to a
lot of other things in the course of my daily routine. I wonder where all this old-time zest +
energy has gone to? I expect it is due to
the life we are now leading, plus the increasing
years. But I think it is chiefly due to our isolated existence. Think of the surroundings in Weimar
and later, in Dessau, and the innumerable contacts
we had then. And most of all, we had you
three boys about us, and that is what is now
most lacking; that is what we feel the most.

My watercolor exhibition at the Buchholz Gallery
will be opened Feb. 1st. The other evening I
photographed all the drawings, and Wednesday I got

317

SIGNATURES

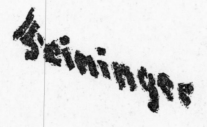

1891, from *Drapery Study*, p. 11
[reversed in color]

1907, from *L'Exode*, p. 34–35

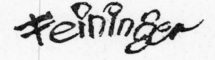

1909, from *Emeute*, p. 45

1915, from *Girl with Green
Stockings*, p. 182

1929, from *Gables III*, p. 210

1933, from *Bathers*, p. 215

1940, from *Manhattan I*, p. 145

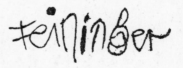

1955, from *Evening Haze*, p. 244

BIBLIOGRAPHY

This bibliography, which includes exhibition catalogues, is arranged in two parts, which correspond roughly to the two sections of the artist's creative life. Part One consists of European publications, chiefly in German, and was compiled by Dr. Annemarie Heynig. Part Two contains publications in English; it was compiled by Bernard Karpel, who also supplied the index (pages 341–44) for both parts. The two parts inevitably overlap to some extent; some cross references have been supplied in Part One to aid the English-language reader.

Part One. Publications from Europe (excluding England). Compiled by ANNEMARIE HEYNIG.

I. Writings by Lyonel Feininger

G 1   *From letters to Julia Feininger* (1910–1929). In catalog of Feininger exhibition, Amsterdam 1954–1955.

G 1 a   *Autobiographical article* in *Les Tendances Nouvelles*, no. 56:1338–40, ca. 1912, 6 reproductions.

G 2   *Letter to Paul Westheim*, Mar. 14, 1917. *Das Kunstblatt*, 15:215–220, Potsdam-Berlin, 1931.

G 3   *Zwiesprache Lyonel Feininger und Adolf Knoblauch.* *Der Sturm* (Berlin), 8 no. 6:82–86, 1917–18.

G 4   *From Letters by the Artist* (1925–1932). In: catalog Feininger exhibition, Munich, Bayerische Akademie der schönen Künste and Hanover, Kestner-Gesellschaft, 1954–55.

G 5   *Letters to a Friend.* Henner Menz: Letters and drawings by Lyonel Feininger 1932–1937. *Festschrift Johannes Jahn.* p. 331–336, Leipzig, E. A. Seemann, 1957.

G 6   *Lyonel Feininger on Georg Muche.* From a letter of Nov. 25, 1950. H. W. Wingler: Wie sie einander sahen. Moderne Maler im Urteil ihrer Gefährten. p. 94–95. Munich, Albert Langen – Georg Müller, 1957.

II. Graphic Editions

G 7   2 Lithographs in: *Zeit-Echo* (Munich – Berlin), vol. 2, no. 5:72; no. 9:130, 1915–16. A third graphic work, vol. 2, no. 2, Graphikverlag.

G 8   Etching: "Fischerboote im Regen" as supplement to a special edition of *Kunstblatt* (Weimar), vol. 1, no. 3, 1917.

G 9   Etching: "The Gate" in: *Die Schaffenden* (Weimar). Ed. Paul Westheim, vol. 1, portfolio 1, Kiepenheuer, 1918–19. Mentioned by Paul Westheim in: *Kunstblatt* (Weimar), 2:228–29, ill. p. 231, 1918.

G 10   Woodcut in the exhibition catalogue of the 48th Exhibition. [Lyonel Feininger], Neue Kunst, Hans Goltz, Munich, 1918.

G 11   Woodcut in: *Neue Blätter für Kunst und Dichtung* (Dresden), vol. 2, no. 7, 1919, Richter.

G 12   Woodcut: "Schiffe am Hafenquai" in: *Kunstblatt*, (Potsdam-Berlin), vol. 3, preceeding p. 32, 1919.

G 13   Woodcut: "Rathaus" in: *Ja! Stimmen des Arbeitsrates für Kunst in Berlin.* Berlin-Charlottenburg, Photographische Gesellschaft, 1919.

G 14   Woodcut: "Die Kathedrale des Sozialismus." Titlepage of the first manifesto of the Bauhaus in Weimar. 1919.

G 15   Woodcut in: *Das Kestnerbuch.* Ed. Paul Erich Küppers, pl. XI, Hanover, Heinrich Böhme, 1919–20.

G 16   Woodcut in: *Der Anbruch.* Graphisches Kabinett J. B. Neumann (Berlin – Vienna), vol. 2, no. II, 1919–1920.

G 17   Woodcut: "Zottelstedt" in: *Die Schaffenden.* Ed. Paul Westheim, vol. 2, 1st portfolio, Weimar, Kiepenheuer, 1920.

G 18   Woodcut: "Hansaflotte" in: Kurt Pfister: *Deutsche Graphiker der Gegenwart*, pl. 20, Leipzig, Klinkhardt und Biermann, 1920.

G 18 a   Woodcut: "Buttelstedt" in: *Jahrbuch der Jungen Kunst*, ed. Georg Biermann, following p. 204, Leipzig, Klinkhardt & Biermann, 1920.

G 18b   Woodcut: "Segelschiffe," in: Paul Westheim: *Das Holzschnittbuch* (issued in a special edition of 100), following p. 168, signed at lower left by the artist, Potsdam, Kiepenheuer, 1921.

G 19   *12 Woodcuts.* Bauhaus, Weimar. 12 plates in portfolio (each plate handprinted by the artist; issued in an edition of 10). 1st publication of: Staatliches Bauhaus, Weimar, May 2, 1921.

G 20   Woodcut in: *Die erste Mappe*, ed. Wolf Przygode. Signum of the plates and portfolios after design by Lyonel Feininger. Potsdam, Verlag der Dichtung, Kiepenheuer, printed by F. Voigt, 1921. Reviewed by: Heinz Lipmann and Paul Westheim in *Kunstblatt* (Potsdam – Berlin), 5:187–188, 1921.

G 21   *Meistermappe des Staatlichen Bauhauses Weimar.* Contains graphics by Lyonel Feininger. Design of portfolio by Feininger. Passim. Munich, Bauhaus-Verlag, 1923.

G 22   Woodcut: "Auf der Quaimauer" in: *Die Schaffenden*, ed. Paul Westheim, vol. 4, 1st portfolio, Berlin, Euphorion-Verlag, 1923.

III. General References

G 23   HERMANN, GEORG: Die deutsche Karikatur im 19. Jahrhundert. Smlg. Illustrierter Monographien. Vol. 2, p. 127, ill. 169–172, Bielefeld and Leipzig, Velhagen und Clasing, 1901.

G 24   *Der Deutsche.* Ed. Adolf Stein, vol. 2, no. 23, p. 727–729, Sept. 2, 1905. Berlin, Verlag des Deutschen.

G 25   KAHN, GUSTAVE: Europas Fürsten im Sittenspiegel der Karikatur. Ill. p. 98, 119, 138, 204, 212, 243. Berlin, Hermann Schmidts Verlag, 1908.

G 26   HALKE, PAUL: Der Karikaturist, *Die Kunstwelt* (Berlin), vol. 3, p. 667–70, 729–31, 3 ill. p. 729–31, Weise & Co., 1912.

G 27   *Dresslers Kunstjahrbuch.* Ed. Willy Oskar Dressler, vol. 7, p. 618, Rostock, 1913.

G 27 a *Maske und Palette.* Festalbum. Mar. 25 – Apr. 5, 1914.

G 27 b HAUSENSTEIN, WILHELM: Die bildende Kunst der Gegenwart, Malerei, Plastik, Zeichnung. Edition 1914: p. 304, 316; edition, 1920: p. 333, 347, Stuttgart–Berlin, Deutsche Verlagsanstalt.

G 28   THIEME–BECKER. Allgemeines Lexikon der bildenden Künstler. Vol. 11, p. 359, Leipzig, E. A. Seemann, 1915.

G 29   WESTHEIM, PAUL: Lyonel Feininger. *Das Kunstblatt* (Weimar), 1:65–70, 1917. 3 ill.

G 30   WESTHEIM, PAUL: Künstlerisches Denken – Feininger malt zwei Bilder. *Das Kunstblatt* (Weimar), 1 no. 12:353–60, 1917 (Feininger: p. 356–58), 2 ill.

G 31   FUCHS, EDUARD: Die Karikatur der europäischen Völker. Part II, p. 339, 2 ill. p. 328, 339, Munich, Albert Langen, 1918.

G 32   WESTHEIM, PAUL: Erinnerung an eine Sammlung. *Das Kunstblatt* (Weimar) 2:233–41, ill. p. 245, 1918.

G 33   Berlin, National-Galerie, Galerie der Lebenden. [New acquisition]. *Das Kunstblatt* (Potsdam – Berlin), vol. 3, p. 256, 1919.

G 34   *An alle Künstler!* Included one woodcut by Feininger, p. 21. Berlin, Kunstanstalt Willi Simon, 1919.
        ger, p. 21. Berlin, Kunstanstalt Willi Simon, 1919.

G 34 a DÄUBLER, THEODOR: Lyonel Feininger, *Das junge Deutschland*, vol. 10, 1919. Deutsches Theater (Reinhardt).

G 35   PASSARGE, WALTER: Die Stellung des deutschen Holzschnittes in der expressionistischen Kunst. *Der Cicerone* (Leipzig), 11 no. 15:480–86 (Feininger: p. 482), 1919.

G 36   PROBST, RUDOLF: Lyonel Feininger. *Neue Blätter für Kunst und Dichtung*, 2 no. 7:143–44, Oct. 1919, 4 ill., 1 woodcut (from original block), Dresden, Emil Richter.

G 37   COELLEN, LUDWIG: Lyonel Feininger. *Das Kunstblatt* (Potsdam – Berlin), 3:130–37, 1919, 8 ill.

G 37 a *Die Rote Erde* (Hamburg), no. 1, 1919.

G 38   *Der Anbruch* (Berlin – Vienna). 2 no. 2, 1919–20, Feininger: 1 woodcut (from original block), illustrations, Graphisches Kabinett J. B. Neumann.

G 39   SCHARDT, ALOIS J.: Lyonel Feininger. *Feuer*, Monatsschrift für Kunst und künstlerische Kultur (Saarbrücken), 1 no. 6:429–40, Mar. 1920, 7 ill., Gebr. Hofer.

G 40   HARTLAUB, GUSTAV F.: Die neue deutsche Graphik. Vol. XIV of the series "Tribüne der Kunst und Zeit", p. 84, Berlin, Erich Reiss Verlag, 1920.

G 41   *J. B. Neumanns Bilderhefte*, no. 5, May 1920, 4 ill. p. 66–7. Berlin, Graphisches Kabinett. J. B. Neumann.

G 42   *Die Rote Erde* (Hamburg), 1920, p. 348.

G 43   GRAUTOFF, OTTO: Die neue Kunst. In the series: "Die neue Welt." Ed. Alfred Manes, p. 133 and passim. Berlin, Karl Sigismund, 1920–21.

G 44   Auflösung des "Berliner Arbeitsrats für Kunst." *Der Cicerone* (Leipzig), 13:449, 1921, passim.

G 45   Detroit Museum. [New acquisition: "Raddampfer" (oil)]. *Das Kunstblatt* (Potsdam – Berlin) ,5:288, 1921.

G 46   *Das Graphische Jahr Fritz Gurlitt.* Introduction: Edwin Redslob, p. 14. Berlin, Fritz Gurlitt, 1921.

G 47   JUSTI, LUDWIG: Deutsche Malkunst im 19. Jahrhundert. Ein Führer durch die National-Galerie. p. 292–93, ill. no. 85. Berlin, Julius Bard, 1921.

G 48   DER SIEG DER FARBE. Ed. Adolf Behne. 40 plates. The first two editions include reproductions of Feininger oils. Berlin, Photographische Gesellschaft Charlottenburg. Reviewed in: *Das Kunstblatt* (Potsdam – Berlin) 5:192, 1921.

G 49   GLASER, CURT: Die Graphik der Neuzeit. p. 551–52. Berlin, Bruno Cassirer, 1922.

G 50   SCHMIDT, PAUL FERDINAND: Die Kunst der Gegenwart. Die sechs Bücher der Kunst, book no. 6, p. 95, ill. p. 92. Berlin-Wildpark-Potsdam, Akademische Verlagsgesellschaft Athenaion, 1922.

G 51   TIETZE, HANS: Deutsche Graphik der Gegenwart. Bibliothek der Kunstgeschichte, vol. 37, ill. no. 20. Leipzig. E. A. Seemann, 1922.

G 52   WOERMANN, CARL: Geschichte der Kunst. Vol. 6, 2nd ed. 1922, p. 504, illustrates Feininger. Leipzig, Bibliographisches Institut.

G 53   Mönchen-Gladbach, catalog of the Städtische Museum, 1922, no. 96 "Zirchow II," oil, ill.

G 54   BLÜMNER, RUDOLF: Kubismus, in: Jahrbuch der jungen Kunst. Ed. Georg Biermann. p. 337–42, ill. p. 34. Leipzig, Klinkhardt & Biermann, 1923.

G 55   PASSARGE, WALTER: Junge Kunst in Erfurt, in: Jahrbuch der jungen Kunst. Ed. Georg Biermann. p. 319–24 (Feininger: p. 323), ill. p. 325. Leipzig, Klinkhardt & Biermann, 1923. Also published: *Der Cicerone* (Leipzig) 15:1129–1134 (Feininger: p. 1134), ill., 1923.

G 56   Staatliches Bauhaus in Weimar 1919–1923. Walter Gropius: Idee und Aufbau des Staatl. Bauhauses. p. 139, 140. 2 ill. p. 182, 183. Weimar – Munich, Bauhaus-Verlag, 1923.

G 57   Die Blaue Vier. Feininger, Jawlensky, Kandinsky, Klee. [Mentions formation of the group for exhibition purposes in the States]. *Der Cicerone* (Leipzig) 16:385, 1924.

G 58   HILDEBRANDT, HANS: Die Kunst des 19. und 20. Jahrhunderts. Handbuch der Kunstwissenschaft, p. 383–84, ill. no. 416, Berlin-Wildpark-Potsdam, Akademische Verlagsgesellschaft Athenaion, 1924.

G 59   OSBORN, MAX: Geschichte der Kunst. 1st ed. 1910; 3rd ed. 1924, p. 480, ill. p. 478, Berlin.

G 60   ROH, FRANZ: Das Staatliche Bauhaus in Weimar. *Der Cicerone* (Leipzig) 16:367–69, 1924.

G 61 WALDEN, HERWARTH: Einblick in die Kunst. 3rd – 5th ed. 1924, p. 170, ill. p. 79, Berlin, Der Sturm.

G 62 WOLFRADT, WILLI: Lyonel Feininger, in the series: "Junge Kunst" vol. 47. 52 plates, frontispiece in color. Leipzig, Klinkhardt & Biermann, 1924.

G 63 WOLFRADT, WILLI: Lyonel Feininger. *Der Cicerone* (Leipzig) 16:163–173, 1924, 10 ill. on 5 sep. plates, 2 ill. in the text. Also published in: Jahrbuch der Jungen Kunst, ed. Georg Biermann, p. 63–9, Leipzig, Klinkhardt & Biermann, 1924.

G 64 *Europa-Almanach*, Eds. Carl Einstein, Paul Westheim. 6 ill.: p. 41, 88, 119, 194, 212, 217. Feininger composition: "Fuge VI für Orgel und Klavier zu 3 Händen," facsimile, supplement p. 88–89, Potsdam, Kiepenheuer, 1925.

G 65 Hellerau, Festspielhaus. Ständige Leihgaben lebender Künstler [including Feininger]. *Das Kunstblatt* (Potsdam – Berlin) 9:91, 1925.

G 66 EL LISSITZKY and HANS ARP: Die Kunstismen. Ill. p. 39. Zürich – Munich – Leipzig, Eugen Rentsch, 1925.

G 67 SPRINGER, ANTON: Handbuch der Kunstgeschichte. Vol. 5. 9th enlarged ed. 1925, p. 517, Leipzig, Alfred Kröner.

G 68 BREYSIG, KURT: Eindruckskunst und Ausdruckskunst. p. 103, Berlin, Georg Bondi, 1927.

G 69 SCHÜRER, O.: Neuerwerbungen der Mannheimer Kunsthalle. *Der Cicerone* (Leipzig) 19:412–14, ill., 1927.

G 70 SCHEFFLER, KARL: Geschichte der europäischen Malerei vom Impressionismus bis zur Gegenwart. II. vol. p. 216, Berlin, Bruno Cassirer, 1927.

G 70 a ESCHERICH, MELA: Das Bauhaus und seine Meister. *Individualität*. Book 3, p. 146. Dornach, Verlag für freies Geistesleben, 1928.

G 71 GRÖNING, RICHARD: Als Kunstsammler in Ostpreussen. *Das Kunstblatt* (Potsdam) 12:342–45, 1928.

G 72 Jüdisches Lexikon. Founded by Georg Herlitz & Bruno Kirschner, vol. 2. p. 615, Berlin, Jüdischer Verlag, 1928. [Feininger, however, was not Jewish. – Ed.]

G 73 Kassel, Städtische Galerie: Eröffnung einer modernen Abteilung der alten Gemäldegalerie. *Das Kunstblatt* (Potsdam) 12:254, 1928.

G 74 GROHMANN, WILL: Lyonel Feininger. *Deutsche Kunst und Dekoration* (Darmstadt) 65:413–14, 2 ill., 1929–30.

G 75 Redslob, Edwin: Het werk van Lyonel Feininger. *Wendingen* (Amsterdam) vol. 10, no. 7, 1929, illustrations.

G 76 Mönchen-Gladbach: Walter-Kaesbach-Stiftung. *Der Cicerone* (Leipzig) 21:81, 1929.

G 77 *Zeitschrift für Gestaltung* (Bauhaus, Dessau 1926–1931), illustrates Feininger: no. 1, p. 9, 1929.

G 78 Auftrag der Stadt Halle für Feininger [townscape of Halle for the magistrate of Magdeburg]. *Das Kunstblatt* (Potsdam) 14:256, 1930.

G 79 BOCK, ELFRIED: Geschichte der graphischen Kunst von ihren Anfängen bis zur Gegenwart. Propyläen-Kunstgeschichte, supplementary volume, p. 120, 702, ill.: p. 652, Berlin, Propyläen-Verlag, 1930.

G 80 Dresslers Kunsthandbuch. Vol. II, p. 244. Berlin, Karl Curtius, 1930.

G 81 SCHARDT, ALOIS J.: Die neuen Stadtbilder Lyonel Feiningers. *Kreis von Halle* (Halle), Monatsschrift für Kultur und den Sinn der Wirtschaft. No. 1, p. 21–25, ill. p. 3, Dec. 1930, Albert Neubert.

G 82 SCHARDT, ALOIS J.: Die Stadtansichten Lyonel Feiningers. *Der rote Turm*. Sammlung kleiner Schriften zur Kunst und Kulturgeschichte Halles. Ed. Kurt Gerstenberg. No. 12: Das Hallische Stadtbild. p. 57–61; 2 ill.: p. 58–9, ca. 1930–31. Titlepage of no. 12 in two different versions, one carries woodcut by Feininger.

G 83 SCHREYER, LOTHAR: Die bildende Kunst der Deutschen. Geschichte und Betrachtung. p. 141. Hamburg – Berlin – Leipzig, Hanseatische Verlagsanstalt, 1930.

G 84 Weimar, Schlossmuseum. [On instruction of the thuringian Volksbildungsministerium (Ministry for Public Instruction) the modern section, including Feininger, is relegated to storage]. *Das Kunstblatt* (Potsdam) 14:379, 1930.

G 85 EINSTEIN, CARL: Die Kunst des 20. Jahrhunderts. Propyläen-Kunstgeschichte, vol. XVI, 3rd ed., 1931: passim and p. 170, 4 illustrations: p. 466–469, 1 col. pl. no. XXIII. Compare 1st ed. 1926; 2nd ed. 1928. Berlin, Propyläen Verlag.

G 86 EWALD, AUGUST: Lyonel Feininger. *Der Querschnitt* (Berlin) 11:844–846, 2 ill., 1931.

G 87 HEIDEN, MARGARET: Neue Kunst in Detroit Institute of Arts. *Museum der Gegenwart*, Zeitschrift der deutschen Museen für neuere Kunst, 2 no. 1:13–22, ill. p. 16, Berlin, Ernst Rathenau, 1931.

G 88 JUSTI, LUDWIG: Deutsche Malkunst im 19. und 20. Jahrhundert. Von Corinth bis Klee. Ein Gang durch die National-Galerie Berlin. p. 168–69, 2 ill., plates 79–80, Berlin, Julius Bard, 1931.

G 89 READ, HERBERT: Moderne deutsche Kunst. From *The Listener* (London), translation: Max Sauerlandt. *Kreis von Halle* (Halle), p. 266–77 (Feininger: p. 272), Sept. 1931. Albert Neubert. Also in: *Der Kreis* (Hamburg), no. 6:324–32, 1932.

G 90 SCHARDT, ALOIS J.: Zum Schaffen Feiningers. Also a letter by Lyonel Feininger to P. Westheim of Mar. 14, 1917. *Das Kunstblatt* (Potsdam) 15:215–20, 9 ill., 1931.

G 91 SCHARDT, ALOIS J.: Beitrag zur Frage der Museumsgestaltung. *Kreis von Halle* (Halle), p. 122–129, ill.: p. 123, Apr. 1931, Albert Neubert.

G 92 SCHARDT, ALOIS J.: Feiningers Bilder der Stadt Halle. *Jahrbuch der Denkmalspflege in der Provinz Sachsen und in Anhalt*. Ed. by Hermann Giesau and Ludwig Grote. p. 48–59, 8 ill. and photographs after nature. Burg b. M., August Hopfer, 1931.

G 93 Frankfurt/M. Privatsammlung Harry Fuld [including works by Feininger]. *Das Kunstblatt* 16:16, 1932.

G 94 GROHMANN, WILL: Sammlung Ida Bienert (Dresden). [Including works by Feininger.] Potsdam, Müller & Kiepenheuer, 1932–33. Reviewed in: *Das Kunstblatt* (Berlin) 17:14–15, 1933.

G 95 KLUMPP, HERMANN: Abstraktion in der Malerei. Kandinsky, Feininger, Klee. Kunstwissenschaftliche Studien. Vol. XII. Feininger: 6 ill. Berlin, Deutscher Kunstverlag, 1932. Reviewed in: *Das Kunstblatt* (Potsdam) 16:88, 1932.

G 96 GOLLOB, HEDWIG: Die Entwicklungsgeschichte der modernen Kunst. Études sur l'art de tous les pays et de toutes les époques no. 11, p. 25, ill. 5 a. Strasbourg, J. H. Ed. Heitz, 1933.

G 97 HAMANN, RICHARD: Geschichte der Kunst von der altchristlichen Zeit bis zur Gegenwart. p. 876, ill. p. 879. Berlin, Th. Knaur Nachf., 1933. New edition: Munich, 1952.

G 98 Moderne Malerei vom Impressionismus zur Gegenwart. Ed. by Cigaretten-Bilderdienst Reemtsma. p. 51, ill. p. 50. Altona-Bahrenfeld, 1933. Reviewed in: *Das Kunstblatt* (Potsdam) 16:72, 1932.

G 99 REIMANN, HANS: Geschichte des deutschen Witzblattes. Von der Jahrhundertwende bis zum Krieg. *Der Cicerone* (Leipzig), 13:341–47, 1933, (Feininger: p. 346, ill. p. 347).

G 100 THEUNISSEN, G. H.: Der Romantiker Feininger. *Kunst der Nation* (Berlin), 2 no. 5:4, Mar. 1934, ill., 2 port.

G 101 HUYGHE, RENÉ: Histoire de l'art contemporain, la peinture. Passim and p. 436–437, ill. 568, Paris, Librairie Alcan, 1935.

G 102 SAUERLANDT, MAX: Die Kunst der letzten 30 Jahre. Eine Vorlesung aus dem Jahre 1933. 1st ed. Berlin, Rembrandt-Verlag, 1935. 2nd ed.: p. 150, ill. no. 60, Hamburg, Laatzen-Verlag, 1948.

G 103 HEUSS, THEODOR: Notizen zur Kunst. *Die Hilfe* (Berlin), Zeitschrift für Politik, Wirtschaft und geistige Bewegung, 42 no. 8, 188–190, 18 Apr. 1936, Bott-Verlag.

G 104 SCHWARZ, KARL: Die Juden in der Kunst. p. 167. Vienna – Jerusalem, R. Löwit-Verlag, 1936. [See note G 72.]

G 105 WILLRICH, WOLFGANG: Säuberung des Kunsttempels. Eine kunstpolitische Kampfschrift. passim and p. 75, J. F. Lehmanns, Munich – Berlin, 1937.

G 106 BURKHARDT, FRITZ: Die neue deutsche Graphik. *Prisma* (Munich), no. 2:20–22, Kurt Desch, 1946.

G 107 GEIST, HANS FRIEDRICH: Moderne Graphik – Franz Marc und Lyonel Feininger. *Hamburger Akademische Rundschau* (Hamburg), 1 no. 9:405–406, ill. p. 394, 1946–47. Hansischer Gilden-Verlag.

G 108 Kleines Lexikon abstrakter Maler. In the series: "Das Kunstwerk" (Baden-Baden), 1 no. 8–9, 53–56, 1946–47, 1 ill. on plate. Woldemar Klein.

G 109 HARTLAUB, GUSTAV F.: Die Graphik des Expressionismus in Deutschland. passim and p. 46, 58, ill. nos. 60–61. Stuttgart – Calw, Gerd Hatje, 1947.

G 110 LORCK, CARL von: Expressionismus. Einführung in die europäische Kunst des 20. Jahrhunderts. p. 57–58, ill. p. 51. Lübeck, I. M. Wildner, 1947.

G 111 TSELOS, DIMITRI: Review of: Dorothy C. Miller, Alois J. Schardt, Alfred H. Barr, Jr.: Lyonel Feininger and Marsden Hartley. New York, Museum of Modern Art, 1944. In: *Gazette des Beaux-Arts*, vol. 32, p. 190–91, 1947. See E 14, E 150.

G 112 HÄNDLER, GERHARD: Das Moritzburg-Museum in Halle. Zur Wiedereröffnung am 7. 10. 1948. (no pagination), titlepage: charcoal drawing by Feininger. Halle a. d. S., Friedrich.

G 113 Fibel der modernen Malerei In the series: "Das Kunstwerk" (Baden-Baden), 3 no. 6 and a special edition, p. 41, 1949.

G 114 GOERN, HERMANN: Das Moritzburg-Museum in Halle (Leipzig). *Zeitschrift für Kunst.* 3 no. 3:193–201 (Feininger: p. 193, 195, 5 ill. nos. 100–103, 105), 1949. E. A. Seemann.

G 115 RAVE, PAUL ORTWIN: Kunstdiktatur im Dritten Reich. passim and p. 57, 71, Hamburg, Gebr. Mann, 1949.

G 116 WINKLER, WALTER: Psychologie der modernen Kunst. passim and p. 106, Tübingen, Alma-Mater, 1949.

G 117 BÉNÉZIT, E.: Dictionnaire des Peintres, Sculpteurs, Dessinateurs et Graveurs. Vol. III, p. 700. Paris, Librairie Gründ, 1950.

G 118 Die abstrakten Künstler. In the series: "Das Kunstwerk" (Baden-Baden), 4 no. 8–9:87–96, (Feininger: p. 87, ill.), 1950.

G 119 ECKSTEIN, HANS: Das Bauhaus und seine Maler. *Zeitschrift für Kunst* (Leipzig) 4 no. 4:300–305 (Feininger: p. 305), 1950.

G 120 Moderne deutsche Graphik. In the series: "Das Kunstwerk" (Baden-Baden) 4 no. 2, 2 ill. p. 27, 1950.

G 121 RAYNAL, MAURICE, and others: Histoire de la peinture moderne. De Picasso au Surréalisme. passim and p. 160, ill. p. 158, Geneva – Paris, Albert Skira Ed., 1950. See E 40.

G 122 THWAITES, JOHN ANTHONY: Die Maler am Bauhaus. In the series: "Das Kunstwerk" (Baden-Baden) 4 no. 5:54, ill. p. 56, 1950. See E 149.

G 123 WILD, DORIS: Moderne Malerei. Ihre Entwicklung seit dem Impressionismus. p. 214. Zürich, Büchergilde Gutenberg, 1950.

G 124 *Documents.* L'Art allemand contemporain. Special edition publ. by: Bureau International de Liaison et de Documentation. Contains also: Grote, Ludwig: Du "Blaue Reiter" au "Bauhaus", p. 27–38 (Feininger: p. 34, ill. p. 37); Hartlaub, Gustav F.: L'art graphique moderne, p. 59–69 (Feininger: p. 63, ill. p. 61). Offenburg/Baden, 1951. See E 30.

G 125 KÜHNE: Lyonel Feininger 80 Jahre. Includes a poem by Edwin Redslob "Feininger". *Neue Bauwelt*, Zeitschrift für das gesamte Bauwesen (Berlin – Wiesbaden), no. 29, p. 120, 4 ill., 1 port., 1951.

G 126 Die Preisträger der Pittsburgh International [2nd prize: Feininger]. *Die Weltkunst* (München) 21 no. 4:3, ill., Feb. 15, 1951.

G 127 ESCHERICH, MELA: Lyonel Feininger. Zum 80. Geburtstag des Meisters. *Die Kunst und das Schöne Heim* (Munich), 50 no. 5:176, 2 ill. p. 177, 1952. F. Bruckmann.

G 128 GOMBRICH, E. H.: Die Geschichte der Kunst. London, Phaidon, 1950. German translation: p. 477:479, ill. no. 380, Cologne, Phaidon (Kiepenheuer & Witsch), 1952. See E 35.

G 129 SCHMIDT, PAUL FERDINAND: Geschichte der modernen Malerei. 1st edition 1952. 8th enlarged edition November 1957: p. 97, 152, 208, 254–256, 272, 304, 2 ill. p. 255–256. Stuttgart, W. Kohlhammer.

G 130 GROHMANN, WILL: Zwischen den beiden Kriegen. *Bildende Kunst und Architektur* (Berlin), Suhrkamp, 1953. 3rd vol. passim and p. 151–152, ill. no. 25. Letter by Lyonel Feininger of 14 Mar. 1917, first published in: *Das Kunstblatt*, 1931, (see bibl. G 90).

G 131 GROTE, LUDWIG: Deutsche Kunst im 20. Jahrhundert. p. 44–45, textillustration p. 43, 2 plates p. 44–45. Munich, Prestel, 1953.

G 132 SCHAPIRE, ROSA: Deutsche Expressionisten in Leicester. *Die Weltkunst* (Munich) 23:3, ill., Nov. 1, 1953.

G 133 BUCHNER, ERNST. Lyonel Feininger: Die Marktkirche in Halle a. d. S. Neuerwerbung der Bayerischen Staatsgemälde-Sammlungen, München. *Die Weltkunst* (Munich), 24 no. 10:2, ill., May 15, 1954.

G 134 HAFTMANN, WERNER. Malerei im 20. Jahrhundert. Text volume. 1st ed. 1954, 2nd ed. 1957, passim and p. 345–346, 496. Munich, Prestel.

G 135 HAZAN, FERNAND: Dictionnaire de la peinture moderne, p. 103–104, ill. Paris, 1954. See E 44.

G 136 Festgabe – Edwin Redslob zum 70. Geburtstag. Ed. George Rohde. Karl Hein Hering: [Record of the writings of Edwin Redslob and short biography], p. 381–402 (Feininger: p. 382). Berlin, Blaschker, 1954–55.

G 137 REIDEMEISTER, LEOPOLD: Berichte aus den Rheinischen Museen – Wallraf-Richartz-Museum. Museumsankauf. Wallraf-Richartz-Jahr-Buch, *Westdeutsches Jahrbuch für Kunstgeschichte*, vol. XVI, p. 225, ill. p. 224. Cologne, E. A. Seemann, 1954.

G 138 SCHREYER, LOTHAR: Ein Jahrtausend deutscher Kunst. p. 422–423, 2 ill. p. 424, 494. Hamburg, Christian–Wegner, 1954.

G 139 WALDEN, NELL, and SCHREYER, LOTHAR: Der Sturm. Ein Erinnerungsbuch an Herwarth Walden und die Künstler aus dem Sturmkreis. 3 ill. p. 87, 117, 171. Baden-Baden, Woldemar-Klein, 1954.

G 140 WINGLER, HANS MARIA: Der blaue Reiter, (No pagination). Feldafing, Buchheim, 1954.

G 141 Bauhaus 1919–1928. Editors: Herbert Bayer, Walter Gropius, Ise Gropius. passim and p. 18–19, 7 ill. Stuttgart, Hatje, 1955. German translation of the 1952 edition. See bibl. E 21.

G 141 a BOECK, WILHELM, and SABARTÈS, JAIME: Picasso. p. 255. Stuttgart, Kohlhammer, 1955. See E 26.

G 142 BUCHNER, ERNST: Amtliche Berichte der Staatlichen Kunstsammlungen – Bayerische Staatsgemäldesammlungen. [Acquisitions]. *Münchner Jahrbuch der bildenden Kunst*, 3rd series, vol. VI, p. 265–269 (Feininger: p. 269, ill. p. 268), 1955, Munich, Prestel.

G 143 HAFTMANN, WERNER: Malerei im 20. Jahrhundert. Volume of plates, p. 196, 286; ill. p. 176, 330, 331. Munich, Prestel, 1955.

G 144 Knaurs Lexikon moderner Kunst. p. 111–112, ill. Munich, Th. Knaur Nachf., 1955.

G 145 PRETZELL, LOTHAR: Pommersche Landschaft im Bilde der zeitgenössischen Kunst. Baltische Studien, ed. by: Gesellschaft für Pommersche Geschichte, Altertumskunde und Kunst, new series, vol. 43, p. 87–99 (Feininger: p. 89–90; 4 ill. p. 89, plates 9, 10, 11), 1955.

G 145 a STOREY, BENJAMIN: Lyonel Feininger. *Emporium*, Bergamo, 71:51–58, 9 ill, 1 port., 1955.

G 146 VOLLMER, HANS: Allgemeines Lexikon der bildenden Künstler des XX. Jahrhunderts, vol. 2, p. 85–86. Leipzig, E. A. Seemann, 1955. See E 66.

G 147 BARR, ALFRED H., Jr.: Meister der modernen Kunst. Munich – Vienna – Basel, Desch, 1956. German edition of: "Masters of Modern Art." p. 113, 1 col. pl. New York, The Museum of Modern Art, 1954. See E 19.

G 147 a BRION, MARCEL: Art Abstrait. Paris, Albin Michel, 1956.

G 148 GENZKEN-DRAGENDORFF, SIGRID: Zum Tode von Lyonel Feininger. *Der Kunsthandel* (Heidelberg), 48 no. 2:15, ill., 1956.

G 149 GEROLD, KARL GUSTAV: Deutsche Malerei unserer Zeit. p. 92–93, ill. no. 47. Vienna – Munich – Basel, Desch, 1956.

G 150 GÖPEL, ERHARD: Der deutsche Markt moderner Kunst. *Die Weltkunst* (Munich), 26 no. 12:11–12, ill., 1956.

G 150 a GROHMANN, WILL. Schmidt-Rottluff. Feininger passim. Stuttgart, Kohlhammer, 1956.

G 151 HÄNDLER, GERHARD: Deutsche Maler der Gegenwart. Vol. II: Die Kunst unserer Zeit, p. 24; 4 ill. p. 68–71. Berlin, Rembrandt, 1956. See E 39.

G 152 HENTZEN, ALFRED: Lyonel Feininger in memoriam. *Jahresring* (56–57). Ein Querschnitt durch die deutsche Literatur und Kunst der Gegenwart. p. 302–303. Stuttgart, Dt. Verlagsanstalt, 1956.

G 153 HESS, WALTER: Dokumente zum Verständnis der modernen Malerei. Rowohlt Taschenbuch no. 19, p. 127, 131. Hamburg, 1956.

G 154 MEHRING, WALTER: Nachruf Lyonel Feininger. *Neue Zürcher Zeitung*, Feb. 26, 1956.

G 155 MUCHE, GEORG: Nachruf auf Lyonel Feininger. Broadcast in: "Norddeutsche Rundfunk," Jan. 25, 1956. Printed in:

G 156 *Werk und Zeit* (Düsseldorf), 5 no. 2, 1956; and in:

G 156 a WINGLER, HANS MARIA: Wie sie einander sahen. Moderne Maler im Urteil ihrer Gefährten. p. 90–93. Munich, Albert Langen – Georg Müller, 1957; and also in:

G 156 b SCHREYER, LOTHAR: Dokumente und Visionen. p. 61–64. Munich, Albert Langen – Georg Müller, 1957.

G 157 Nachruf Lyonel Feininger. *Das Kunstwerk* (Krefeld, Baden-Baden), 9 no. 5:60, 1955–56, Agis.

G 158 Nachruf Lyonel Feininger. *Die Weltkunst* (Munich), 26 no. 3:12, 1956.

G 159 ROH, FRANZ: Der vierundachtzigjährige Feininger. *Die Kunst und das Schöne Heim* (Munich), 54:41–45, 7 ill., 1956.

G 160 SCHREYER, LOTHAR: Erinnerungen an Sturm und Bauhaus. p. 125, 131–141, 147, 176, 189, 197, 215, 219, 220, 245, 264, 272, 2 ill. p. 143, 144, 1 port. Munich, Albert Langen – Georg Müller, 1956.

G 161 TRIER, EDUARD: Zeichner des 20. Jahrhunderts. p. 101–102, ill. Frankfurt/M., Büchergilde Gutenberg, 1956.

G 162 ZAHN, LEOPOLD: Kleine Geschichte der modernen Kunst. Ullstein-Buch no. 92, passim and p. 100; ill. p. 101. Frankfurt/M., Das Goldene Vlies, 1956.

G 162 a *Die Bauhaus-Mappen*, Neue Europäische Graphik 1921–23: edited by: Peters, Heinz, p. 7–10, with catalog: p. 20–21; 6 ill. Cologne, Christoph Czwiklitzer, 1957.

G 162 b BRION, MARCEL: Meisterwerke der modernen Malerei. German translation from French pub. by Somogy, Paris: p. 24, 36, 90; col. pl. p. 76. Verlag Bertelsmann, 1957.

G 162 c FEININGER, LORE: Aus der Werkstatt Vater Lyonels. Ed. by: Rolf Röhnich, illustrated. Berlin, Arcivarion, 1957.

G 163 GÖPEL, ERHARD: Deutsche Holzschnitte des XX. Jahrhunderts. p. 53, 2 ill., p. 28–29. Wiesbaden, Insel-Verlag, 1957.

G 164 HESS, HANS: Dank in Farben. Aus dem Gästebuch Alfred und Thekla Hess. p. 39; ill. p. 28, col. plates: p 5, 17, 29 (also titlepage). Munich, R. Piper & Co., 1957.

G 165 Kaiserslautern, Katalog der Graphischen Sammlung der Pfälzischen Landesgewerbe Anstalt, 1950–57. Edited by: Ludwig-Hempel, Heinz. 1 ill.

G 165 a LANDOLT, HANSPETER: Die Sammlung Doetsch-Benziger. [Including works by Feininger.] Du (Zürich), Schweizerische Monatsschrift, 17 no. 6:9–10, 2 ill., 1 col., 1 col. pl., June 1957. Conzett & Huber.

G 166 MENZ, HENNER: Briefe und Zeichnungen von Lyonel Feininger. Festschrift Johannes Jahn (Leipzig), p. 331–336 with 2 letter-pages in facsimile and illustrations. VEB Seemann, 1957. See bibl. G 5.

G 167 PLATTE, HANS: Malerei. Die Kunst im 20. Jahrhundert. Ed.: Carl Georg Heise. p. 118–121, 212, 3ill.: p. 119, 121, 213. Hamburg, Standard-Verlag, 1957.

G 168 RÖTHEL, HANS KONRAD: Moderne deutsche Malerei. p. 60–61, 84, 2 ill.: p. 40, 42. Berlin – Darmstadt, Deutsche Buchgemeinschaft, 1957. See E 60.

G 169 SAUERLANDT, MAX: Im Kampf um die moderne Kunst. [Letters 1902–1933]. Ed. Kurt Dingelstedt. passim and p. 156–157. Munich, Albert Langen – Georg Müller, 1957.

G 170 SCHMALENBACH, WERNER: Grosse Meister moderner Malerei. p. 19, ill. p. 76–77. Lucerne, Kunstkreis-Verlag, 1957.

G 171 SCHREYER, LOTHAR: Lyonel Feininger. Dokumente und Visionen. 67 pages, 10 ill., 1 port. Includes also: Extracts of letters by Feininger (first published in catalog of Feininger exhibition, Munich-Hanover, 1954, [bibl. G 227]); Feininger letter of Mar. 14. 1917 (first publ.: Das Kunstblatt, 1931 [bibl. G 90]); "Zwiesprache Lyonel Feininger und Adolf Knoblauch" (first publ.: Der Sturm, no. 6, 1917–18 [bibl. G 3]); extract from Feininger obituary by Walter Mehring (first publ.: Neue Zürcher Zeitung, Feb. 26, 1957 [bibl. G 154]), obituary Lyonel Feininger by Georg Muche (first broadcast in "Norddeutscher Rundfunk." Jan. 25, 1956 [bibl. G 155]). Munich, Albert Langen – Georg Müller, 1957.

G 172 SECKEL, CURT: Zu dem Gemälde "Gelmeroda IX" im Museum Folkwang Essen. Der Kunsthandel (Heidelberg) 49 no. 5:19–20, ill.: titlepage, 1957.

G 173 BUSCH, KARL, and REUTHER, HANS: Welcher Stil ist das? p. 163, ill. Stuttgart, W. Spemann, 1958.

G 174 HARTLAUB, GUSTAV F., and WEISSENFELD, FELIX: Gestalt und Gestaltung. Das Kunstwerk als Selbstdarstellung des Künstlers. p. 119, 2 port. ill.: p, 126. Krefeld, Agis-Verlag, 1958.

G 175 HENTZEN, ALFRED: Lyonel Feininger – Aquarelle. 50 pages, 16 col. plates, 4 ill.: p. 37, 39, 45, 50. Munich, R. Piper & Co., 1958.

G 176 PLATTE, HANS: Robert Delauny und Lyonel Feininger. Zu zwei Bildern in der Hamburger Kunsthalle. Jahrbuch der Hamburger Kunstsammlungen, vol. 3, p. 39–46, 3 ill., one photo after nature. Hamburg, Dr. Ernst Hauswedell & Co., 1958.

G 177 SCHLEMMER, OSKAR: Briefe und Tagebücher. Ed. by Tut Schlemmer. passim and p. 103, 106, 152. Munich, Albert Langen – Georg Müller, 1958.

G 177 a SCHREYER, LOTHAR: Lyonel Feininger – Vom Erkenntnisbild zum Symbol. Christliche Kunstblätter (Linz a. d. Donau), 96 no. 4:18–23, 2 ill., 1958.

G 178 BUCHHEIM, LOTHAR-GÜNTHER: Graphik des deutschen Expressionismus. p. 59–60, 12 ill.: p. 60, nos. 26–35, 187. Feldafing, Buchheim, 1959.

G 178 a GROTE, LUDWIG: Erinnerungen an Paul Klee. Includes "Erinnerungen an Paul Klee," by (Julia and) Lyonel Feininger, p. 71–75. Munich, Prestel, 1959. See also bibl. E 2, E 3.

G 178 b JUNGHANS, FRITZ. Von der Einsamkeit des Schöpferischen. Zeitschrift für alte und neue Kunst (Zurich), pp. 20–23, 45–46, 48–49, ills., Dec. 1960.

IV. Chronological List of Exhibitions

One-Man and Two-Man Shows

1916

G 179 BERLIN, GALERIE DER STURM
42nd exhibition, June. Joint exhibition with Felix Müller.

1917

G 180 BERLIN, GALERIE DER STURM
55th exhibition, Sept.; all media. Catalog 4 p. passim.

1918

G 181 MUNICH, NEUE KUNST HANS GOLTZ
48th exhibition. Oct.; 34 oils, 34 drawings and watercolors. Catalog: 10 ill., 1 woodcut (after original block).

1919

G 182 BERLIN, GALERIE J. B. NEUMANN
June. Reviewed: Küppers, Paul Erich: Berliner Eindrücke. Feininger-Ausstellung im Graphischen Kabinett J. B. Neumann. Das hohe Ufer (Hannover). Editor: Hans Kaiser. 1:147, 2 ill.: p. 148, 151, 1919. Ludwig Ey; and by:
Schulte, Heinrich: Lyonel Feininger. Zu seiner Berufung an das Weimarer Staatliche Bauhaus und zu seinen Berliner Ausstellungen im Graphischen Kabinett J. B. Neumann und in der Freien Secession. Weimarer Blätter (Weimar), Zeitschrift des Dt. Nationaltheaters. Editor: Hans Esdras Mutzenbecher. no. 13:363–367, 1 ill., 1919. Bruno Wollbrück; and in:
Das Kunstblatt (Potsdam – Berlin) 3:224, 1919.

G 183 DRESDEN, GALERIE EMIL RICHTER
Sept. 38 oils, 25 watercolors, 27 drawings, 109 woodcuts. Catalog: 4 p., illustrations, passim. Reviewed: Kunstchronik und Kunstmarkt (Leipzig), vol. 55, new series XXXI, no. 9, p. 183, 1919. E. A. Seemann.

G 184 FRANKFURT/M., ZINGLERS KABINETT
Catalog: passim. Reviewed: Das Kunstblatt (Potsdam–Berlin), 3:384, 1919.

G 185 HANOVER, KESTNER-GESELLSCHAFT
29th exhibition. Nov.–Dec. 36 oils, 51 drawings and watercolors. Joint exhibition with Paul Klee. Catalog: Introduction by Paul Erich Küppers, 2 illustrations.

1920

G 186 ERFURT, STADTMUSEUM
Oils, watercolors, drawings. Reviewed: *Der Cicerone* (Leipzig), 13:723–724, 1921.

1921

G 187 WEIMAR, STADTMUSEUM
ERFURT, KUNST- UND BÜCHERSTUBE

1922

G 188 BERLIN,
GALERIE GOLDSCHMIDT-WALLERSTEIN
Reviewed: Schardt, Alois J.: Natur und Kunst in der neueren Malerei. Im Anschluss an die Feininger-Ausstellung bei Goldschmidt-Wallerstein. *Das Kunstblatt* (Potsdam–Berlin), 6:96–119, 1922, ill.: 8 oils, 10 drawings, 7 woodcuts.

G 189 MAGDEBURG, KAISER-FRIEDRICH MUSEUM
G 189 a ERFURT, KUNSTVEREIN

1923

G 190 WIESBADEN, STÄDTISCHE KUNSTGALERIE

1924

G 191 ERFURT, KUNSTVEREIN
Sept.–Oct. 100 watercolors, charcoal and pen drawings. Reviewed: *Der Cicerone* (Leipzig) 16:1033–1034, 1924.

G 192 MUNICH,
GRAPHISCHES KABINETT J. B. NEUMANN
Oils and graphic works by Lyonel Feininger and Marc Chagall. Reviewed: *Das Kunstblatt* (Potsdam – Berlin) 8:285, 1924.

1925

G 193 BERLIN,
GALERIE GOLDSCHMIDT-WALLERSTEIN
Nov.–Dec. Oils, watercolors, drawings. Catalog: 4 p., illustrations, passim. Reviewed: *Das Kunstblatt* (Potsdam – Berlin) 10:43, 1926, ill. p. 6.

G 194 DRESDEN, NEUE KUNST FIDES
Opening exhibition. Feb.–Mar. 18 oils, also watercolors, graphics and drawings. Catalog: 2 illustrations, passim.

1926

G 195 BRUNSWICK, GESELLSCHAFT DER
FREUNDE JUNGER KUNST. STÄDTISCHES
MUSEUM.
Mar.–May. 31 oils, 42 watercolors. Catalog: 5 p., illustrations, passim.

G 196 CHEMNITZ, KUNSTHÜTTE
G 197 DRESDEN, NEUE KUNST FIDES
Reviewed: *Das Kunstblatt* (Potsdam – Berlin) 10:284, 1926.

G 198 HANOVER, KESTNER-GESELLSCHAFT
69th exhibition, jointly with Christian Rohlfs (watercolors).

1927

G 199 ERFURT, KUNSTVEREIN
Mar. Review: *Der Cicerone* (Leipzig) 19:260, 1927.

G 200 KASSEL, KUNSTVEREIN DER STÄDTISCHEN
GALERIE

1928

G 201 BRESLAU, SCHLESISCHES MUSEUM
G 202 DRESDEN, NEUE KUNST FIDES
Feb.–Mar. 28 oils, also watercolors, charcoal and pen drawings. Invitation prospectus: 5 p., 2 illustrations.

G 203 HALLE, MORITZBURG-MUSEUM

1929

G 204 BRESLAU, GESELLSCHAFT FÜR KUNST-
FREUNDE
Jan.–Feb. Oils and watercolors.

G 205 DESSAU, ANHALTISCHE GEMÄLDEGALERIE
Mar.–Apr. Oils, watercolors, drawings.

G 206 DÜSSELDORF, GALERIE FLECHTHEIM
Aug.–Sept. Joint exhibition with Paul Klee.

G 207 ERFURT, KUNSTVEREIN
Jan. Drawings.
Reviewed: *Der Cicerone* (Leipzig) 21:143–144, 1929.

G 208 KIEL, MUSEUM
Oct. – Nov.

1930

G 209 DESSAU, BAUHAUS
G 210 ERFURT, KUNSTVEREIN
G 211 COLOGNE, KUNSTVEREIN
March.
G 212 PRAGUE, KUNSTVEREIN.

1931

G 213 DRESDEN, NEUE KUNST FIDES
Exhibition: "Lyonel Feininger zum 60. Geburtstag." 1st part: Mar. – Apr. Oils. Invitation and catalog passim. 2nd part: June–July. 60 watercolors and drawings. Catalog passim. This exhibition was then taken over by the Museum Folkwang, Essen, and then enlarged and shown at the National-Galerie, Berlin (G 214). On this: Grote, Ludwig: Lyonel Feininger zum 60. Geburtstag. Ansprache zur Eröffnung der Ausstellung in Neue Kunst Fides, Dresden. Werke von 1920–30. *Museum der Gegenwart* (Berlin). Zeitschrift der deutschen Museen für neuere Kunst, 2 no 2:41–49, 4 illustrations, 1931. Ernst Rathenau. Reviewed: Holzhausen, Walter: Zur Ausstellung in der Galerie Neue Kunst Fides. *Kreis von Halle* (Halle), p. 249–250, 2 illustrations p. 239, 249, August, 1931. Albert Neubert.

G 214 BERLIN, NATIONAL-GALERIE
Exhibition in honor of Feininger's 60th birthday. Catalog: Foreword by Ludwig Thormaehlen. 40 p., illustrations, passim. Reviewed: Bier, Justus: Lyonel Feininger. Zur Ausstellung in der National-Galerie zum 60. Geburtstag. *Die Kunst für Alle* (Munich), 41 no 8:224–229, 5 illustrations, 1931–32, F. Bruckmann.

G 215 ESSEN, MUSEUM FOLKWANG
Reviewed: Schardt, Alois J.: Zum Schaffen Feiningers. *Das Kunstblatt* (Potsdam – Berlin) 15:215–220, 9 illustrations, 1931.

1932

G 216 DESSAU, KREIS DER FREUNDE DES BAU-
HAUSES

G 217   HAMBURG, KUNSTVEREIN
55 oils, also watercolors and graphics. Reviewed: Holzhausen, Walter: Ausstellung Lyonel Feininger – 55 Ölgemälde, ferner Aquarelle und Graphik. *Der Kreis* (Hamburg), Zeitschrift für künstlerische Kultur. 9 no 4:241–242, 5 illustrations, 1932. Kreis-Verlag.

G 218   HANOVER, KESTNER-GESELLSCHAFT
118th exhibition. Jan.–Mar. 50 oils, 83 watercolors and drawings, also woodcuts (1918–1924). Catalog: 5 p., 3 ill., and letter by Lyonel Feininger to Paul Westheim of Mar. 14, 1917, first published in: *Das Kunstblatt*, 1931 (bibl., G 90).

G 219   HANOVER, STÄDTISCHES MUSEUM.

G 220   LEIPZIG, MUSEUM DER BILDENDEN KÜNSTE.

1934

G 221   BERLIN, GALERIE NIERENDORF
Joint exhibition with Georg Muche. Reviewed: *Die Weltkunst* (Munich), 8 no 10:4, 1934.

1935

G 222   BERLIN, GALERIE FERDINAND MÖLLER
Feb.–Mar. 100 watercolors, charcoal and pen drawings. Catalog: 5 p., illustrations, passim. Reviewed: Zeeck, H., in: *Die Weltkunst* (Munich), 9 no 11:2, ill., p. 3, 1935.

1936

G 223   BERLIN, GALERIE NIERENDORF
April. 28 oils, also watercolors and drawings. Catalog: 4 p., illustrations, passim.

1950

G 223 a   PARIS, GALERIE JEANNE BUCHER
May – June. 40 watercolors. Reviewed: J. A.: Les Expositions. *Art d'Aujourdhui*, May-June-1950, ill.

1950–1951

G 224   HANOVER, KESTNER-GESELLSCHAFT
40 watercolors. Catalog: Preface: Alfred Hentzen. 8 ill. and one detached double page with 3 illustrations. This exhibition of 40 watercolors then circulated in various towns, among others in:

G 225   MUNICH, BRUNSWICK, MANNHEIM, DÜSSELDORF, HAMBURG, BERLIN
Reviewed: Gerold, Karl Gustav: Lyonel-Feininger-Aquarelle in der Galerie Stangl, München. *Der Kunsthandel* (Heidelberg) 42 no 10:13–14, 1950. Geist, Hans Friedrich: Norddeutsche Kunstchronik – Braunschweig. *Das Werk* (Zurich) Vol. 38, 1951, appendix, p. 32.

1954

G 226   MUNICH, BAYERISCHE AKADEMIE DER SCHÖNEN KÜNSTE and

G 227   HANOVER, KESTNER-GESELLSCHAFT
Sept. – Nov. 40 oils, 49 watercolors and drawings. Catalog: Preface by Emil Preetorius and Alfred Hentzen. Feininger letters in extracts (1925–1932). 18 ill., 1 port. Reviewed: Hans Heilmaier. *Der Kunsthandel* (Heidelberg), 46 no 10:16–17, 1954. *Die Weltkunst* (Munich), 24 no 22:13, ill., 1954.

1954–55

G 228   AMSTERDAM, STEDELIJK MUSEUM
Dec. – Jan. 40 oils, 55 watercolors and drawings.

Catalog: Preface by Emil Preetorius; observations by Theo van Doesburg; Feininger letters to Julia Feininger in extracts (1910–1929); 18 illustrations. The same exhibition as bibl. G 226–227 but with 2 additional oils, cat. nos. 5 a, 6 a.

1955

G 229   DÜSSELDORF, GALERIE ALEX VÖMEL
Sept. [Watercolors].

1956

G 230   KAISERSLAUTERN, PFÄLZISCHE LANDES-GEWERBEANSTALT
Memorial exhibition. Jan. Graphics. Catalog: Obituary by C. M. Kiesel.

G 231   NEW YORK, METROPOLITAN MUSEUM
Memorial exhibition: Feininger, Kuhn, Kuniyoshi, Marin [see also bibl. E 326]. Reviewed: Kerrigan, Anthony: Crónica de Norteamerica. Conmemoraciones en el Museo Metropolitano: Feininger. *Goya* (Madrid), Revista de Arte, no. 13, p. 54–55, ill. p. 53, July–Aug., 1956.

1958

G 232   TRENTO, UNIVERSITÀ POPOLARE TRENTINA
Mostra retrospettiva di Lyonel Feininger. Feb. – Mar. Watercolors and graphics. Catalog: Preface by Giulio de Carli.

G 233   MERANO, SALA ESPOSIZIONI DELL'AZIENDA AUTONOMA DI SOGGIORNO
Mostra retrospettiva di Lyonel Feininger allestita da Emilio Dall'Oglio e Luigi Serravalli. May. 35 watercolors and drawings. Catalog: Preface by Gillo Dorfles in: Lyonel Feininger, no. 62 of the illustrated series: "All'Insegna des Pesce d'Oro", 15. ill., 1 col. pl., 1 port. Milan, Vanni Scheiwiller, 1958 [See also bibl. E 17. Reviewed in: *Emporium* (Milan), 64th year, 128 no 7:26–27, 1958. Luigi Serravalli: Lyonel Feininger a Merano. *le Arti*, May – June 1958.

Group Shows (Selected)

1903–04

G 235   BERLIN, 8. KUNSTAUSSTELLUNG DER SEZESSION
Zeichnende Künste. Winter. Feininger: 2 watercolors, 1 drawing.

1904

G 236   BERLIN, GROSSE KUNSTAUSSTELLUNG
Apr. – Oct. Feininger: 13 drawings (caricatures).

1909–1910

G 237   BERLIN, 19. KUNSTAUSSTELLUNG DER SEZESSION
Winter. Zeichnende Künste. Reviewed: Struck, Hermann: Die Schwarz-Weiß-Ausstellung der Berliner Sezession 1909–10. *Zeitschrift für Bildende Kunst* (Leipzig), new series, 21: 165–199 (Feininger: p. 178, ill. p. 196), 1910.

1910

G 238   BERLIN, 20. KUNSTAUSSTELLUNG DER SEZESSION
Summer. Feininger: 1 oil.

1910–1911

G 239   BERLIN, 21. KUNSTAUSSTELLUNG DER
        SEZESSION
        Winter. Zeichnende Künste. Feininger: 6 etchings,
        54 drawings, 3 gouaches.

1911

G 240   BERLIN, 22. KUNSTAUSSTELLUNG DER
        SEZESSION
        Summer. Feininger: 2 oils.

G 240 a PARIS, SALON DES INDÉPENDANTS 1911:
        SOCIÉTÉ DES ARTISTES INDÉPENDANTS,
        LA 27me EXPOSITION 1911
        Apr.–June. Feininger: 6 oils. Cat. p. 154 (cat. nos.
        2178–2183).

1912

G 240 b BERLIN, 24. KUNSTAUSSTELLUNG DER
        SEZESSION
        Summer. Feininger: 2 oils.

1913

G 241   BERLIN, GALERIE DER STURM
        Opening: Sept. 20. Erster deutscher Herbstsalon.
        Feininger: 5 oils (only 4 listed in catalog). Catalog:
        preface by: Herwarth Walden. Feininger: p. 2 (catalog
        nos. 131–134), 1 ill. Reviewed by: Behne, Adolf. Der
        erste deutsche Herbstsalon. In: *Die Neue Kunst*
        (Munich), Zweimonatschrift, editor Heinrich F. S.
        Bachmair. 1 no 1:223–225 (Feininger p. 224–225
        passim), 1913–14.

1914

G 242   BERLIN, 1. AUSSTELLUNG DER FREIEN
        SEZESSION
        Summer. Feininger: 2 oils.

G 242 a DRESDEN, GALERIE ARNOLD
        Die neue Malerei. Feininger: 6 oils.

1916

G 243   MUNICH, NEUE KUNST HANS GOLTZ
        Aug. – Oct. IV. Gesamtausstellung. Feininger: 8 oils,
        6 drawings. Catalog: 1 ill.

1917

G 243 a BASEL, GALERIE CORRAY
        Feb. – Mar. Der Sturm. Feininger: 4 oils.

G 244   BERLIN, GALERIE DER STURM
        III. Sturm-Gesamtschau. Feininger: 2 works.
        Reviewed in: *Das Kunstblatt* (Weimar) 1:256.

G 245   ZURICH, GALERIE DADA
        Feininger with Arp, de Chirico, Ernst, Kandinsky,
        Klee, Kokoschka, Marc, Modigliani, Picasso, and others.

1918

G 245 a HANOVER, KESTNER GESELLSCHAFT
        Dec. 1918 – Jan. 1919. Junge Berliner Kunst. Fei-
        ninger: 5 oils.

1919

G 246   BERLIN, SOMMERAUSSTELLUNG DER FREIEN
        SEZESSION.
        Feininger included. Reviewed: Ley, Walter: *Das
        Kunstblatt* (Potsdam–Berlin), 3:254, 1919. Schulte,

Heinrich: Lyonel Feininger. [On his appointment at
the Bauhaus, Weimar, and his Berlin exhibitions at
the Graphische Kabinett. J. B. Neumann and at the
Freie Sezession]. *Weimarer Blätter* (Weimar), Zeitschrift des Dt. Nationaltheaters, no 15:363–367, 1 ill.,
1919.

G 247   BERLIN, GALERIE PAUL CASSIRER
        Zeichnungen und Aquarelle unserer Zeit. Included
        Feininger. Reviewed: Wallerstein, Victor: Vom Wesen
        der Zeichnung. *Das Kunstblatt* (Potsdam – Berlin),
        3:147–154 (Feininger: p. 152, ill. p. 155), 1919.

G 247 a DRESDEN, GALERIE ERNST ARNOLD
        Apr. Der Sturm. Feininger: 6 oils.

G 248   MUNICH, NEUE KUNST HANS GOLTZ
        V. Gesamtausstellung. Feininger: 1 oil. Catalog: 1 ill.

G 249   MUNICH, GALERIE THANNHAUSER
        [Graphics]. Included Feininger. Reviewed: *Das Kunst-
        blatt* (Potsdam – Berlin), 3:255, 1919.

1920

G 250   BERLIN, KUNSTSALON HELLER
        Oct. [Graphics]. Included Feininger – woodcuts.
        Reviewed: *Das Kunstblatt* (Potsdam – Berlin), 4:352,
        1920.

G 251   COLOGNE, KUNSTHAUS GOYERT
        Dec. Included Feininger. Reviewed: *Das Kunstblatt*
        (Potsdam – Berlin), 5:32, 1921.

1921

G 252   BASEL, KUNSTHALLE
        Moderne deutsche Malerei. Sept. – Oct. Feininger:
        5 oils. Catalog: Preface by Alexander Zschokke. Before
        its dispersal this exhibition was shown in:

G 253   MAGDEBURG, KUNSTVEREIN
        Reviewed in: *Das Kunstblatt* (Potsdam – Berlin), 6:
        39, 1922.

G 254   BERLIN, GROSSE KUNSTAUSSTELLUNG
        Summer. Feininger: 2 oils. Reviewed: *Das Kunst-
        blatt* (Potsdam – Berlin), 5:222, 1921.

G 255   BERLIN, GALERIE PAUL CASSIRER
        [Watercolors]. Included Feininger. Reviewed in: *Das
        Kunstblatt* (Potsdam – Berlin), 6:38, 1922.

G 256   BERLIN, KUNSTSALON HELLER
        [Watercolors]. Included Feininger. Reviewed in: *Das
        Kunstblatt* (Potsdam – Berlin), 5:64, 1921.

G 257   GENEVA, INTERNATIONALE KUNST-
        AUSSTELLUNG
        Included Feininger. Reviewed by: Däubler, Theodor:
        Der Cicerone (Leipzig), 13:83–84, 1921.

1922

G 258   MUNICH, NEUE KUNST HANS GOLTZ
        Nov. – Dec. 68th Exhibition: 10 Jahre Neue Kunst in
        München. Part 1. Watercolors, drawings, graphics
        Feininger: 3 watercolors, 4 woodcuts.

1923

G 259   BERLIN,
        GALERIE GOLDSCHMIDT-WALLERSTEIN
        [Watercolors]. Reviewed in: *Das Kunstblatt* (Pots-
        dam – Berlin), 7:287, ill., 1923.

G 260   WEIMAR, STAATLICHES BAUHAUS
        Reviewed by: Passarge, Walter: *Das Kunstblatt* (Pots-
        dam – Berlin), 7:309–313, 1923.

1924

G 261 BERLIN, GROSSE KUNSTAUSSTELLUNG
[Feininger within the "Novembergruppe"]: 2 oils.
Reviewed in: *Das Kunstblatt* (Potsdam–Berlin), 8:221,
1924.

1925

G 262 BERLIN, GALERIE NIERENDORF UND
J. B. NEUMANN
[Watercolors]. Reviewed in: *Das Kunstblatt* (Potsdam–Berlin), 9:349, ill. 1925.

G 263 DÜSSELDORF, JAHRHUNDERT-AUSSTELLUNG
RHEINISCHER MALEREI
Included: Feininger. Reviewed in: *Das Kunstblatt*
(Potsdam – Berlin), 9:242, 1925.

1926

G 264 HANOVER, KESTNER-GESELLSCHAFT
77th exhibition. Bauhaus Dessau. Included Feininger.

1927

G 265 BERLIN, GROSSE KUNSTAUSSTELLUNG
Included: Feininger. Reviewed in: *Das Kunstblatt*
Potsdam – Berlin), 11:349, 1927.

G 266 BERLIN, NATIONAL-GALERIE
[Drawings].Included: Feininger. Reviewed by: Westheim, Paul: Die Zeichnung. *Das Kunstblatt* (Potsdam-Berlin), 11:321–325, 1927.

G 267 AUGSBURG, KUNSTVEREIN
Apr. Neuzeitliche Graphik und Aquarelle in Deutschland. Arranged by the Graphische Kabinett, Munich,
direction: Günther Franke. Catalog. Feininger:
2 woodcuts.

1928

G 268 BERLIN, NATIONAL-GALERIE
Apr. Neuere deutsche Kunst aus Berliner Privatbesitz.
Feininger: 13 oils. Catalog: 1 ill. Reviewed by: Thormaehlen, Ludwig: *Das Kunstblatt* (Potsdam), 12:131–136, 1928.

G 269 BERLIN, GALERIE NIERENDORF
[Watercolors]. Included: Feininger. Reviewed in: *Das
Kunstblatt* (Potsdam), 12:91, 1928.

G 270 DÜSSELDORF, DEUTSCHE KUNST 1928
Included: Feininger. Reviewed by: Cohen, Walter:
Der Cicerone (Leipzig), 20:437–446 (Feininger: p. 440,
ill. p. 445), 1928; Westheim, Paul: *Das Kunstblatt*
Potsdam), 12:181–184, 1928.

G 271 STETTIN, MUSEUM
May – June. Norddeutsche Ausstellungsvereinigung.
Included: Feininger

G 272 EAST PRUSSIA
Exhibitions in Gumbinnen, Insterburg and Tilsit. No
indication of dates, reviewed by: Gröning, Richard:
Das Kunstblatt (Potsdam), 12:341, 1928.

1929

G 273 BASEL, KUNSTHALLE
Apr. [Bauhaus Masters]. Reviewed in: *Das Kunstblatt*
(Potsdam), 13:124, 1929.

G 274 BERLIN, GALERIE FERDINAND MÖLLER
Oct. [Feininger, Kandinsky, Klee, Jawlensky]. Feininger: 18 oils, 20 watercolors, 10 drawings. Catalog:

Blätter der Galerie Möller, text by: Ernst Kállai. no. 5,
ill., p. 5, Oct. 1929.

G 275 BERLIN, RECKENDORFHAUS
50 ausgewählte Werke heutiger Kunst. Feininger:
1 oil. Reviewed in: *Das Kunstblatt* (Potsdam), 13:366,
1929.

G 276 KASSEL, ORANGERIE
May – Sept. Jubiläumsausstellung des Kunstvereins
und der Akademie. Included: Feininger.

G 277 COLOGNE, 25. AUSSTELLUNG DES KÜNSTLER-
BUNDES
Included: Feininger. Reviewed in: *Das Kunstblatt*
(Potsdam), 13:219, 1929.

G 278 MUNICH, DAS GRAPHISCHE KABINETT –
GÜNTHER FRANKE
Deutsche Landschaft. [Watercolors and drawings].
Included: Feininger. Reviewed in: *Das Kunstblatt*
(Potsdam), 13:188, 1929.

1930

G 279 BERLIN, NATIONAL-GALERIE
Ankäufe des Vereins "Freunde der Nationalgalerie."
Reviewed by: Ludwig Justi: *Museum der Gegenwart*,
1 no 1:17–29, (Feininger: p. 26–27, ill.), 1930; *Das
Kunstblatt* (Potsdam), 14:155, 1930.

G 280 BERLIN, GALERIE FERDINAND MÖLLER
Sept. Included Feininger: 1 oil. Catalog: "Blätter der
Galerie Möller," preface: Ernst Kállai: Vision und
Formgesetz. No. 8:5, Sept. 1930.

G 281 BERLIN, RECKENDORFHAUS
Oct.–Nov. Kunstblatt-Ausstellung: Kinder wollen
spielen. Reviewed by: Paul Westheim, *Das Kunstblatt*
(Potsdam), 14:289–292, 3 ill.: p. 303–304, 1930.

G 282 OSLO, KUNSTNERNES
Jan. [Modern Art in Germany, painting and sculpture]. Feininger: 7 oils. Catalog: preface by Thormaehlen, Ludwig. Feininger: 1 ill. Reviewed in: *Das
Kunstblatt* (Potsdam), 16:16, 27, 1932. The exhibition
was then circulated in various Scandinavian towns,
with slight variations, among others in: BERGEN,
STAVANGER, MALMÖ, and in:

G 282 a COPENHAGEN
May. Nyere Tysk, Maleri og Skulptur. Feininger: 8
oils. Catalog: preface: Thormaehlen, Ludwig. Feininger cat. nos. 42–49.

1933

G 282 b BERLIN, GALERIE PAUL CASSIRER
Dec. 1932 – Jan. 1933. Lebendige deutsche Kunst.
Feininger: 8 oils, 8 watercolors. Catalog: preface:
Ring, Grete.

1935

G 283 HAMBURG, KUNSTVEREIN
June. Zeichnungen und Malerei als musikalischer
Ausdruck. Included Feininger.

1936

G 283 a HAMBURG, KUNSTVEREIN
Malerei und Plastik in Deutschland. Feininger: 2 oils.

1937

G 284 MUNICH, HAUS DER KUNST
Entartete Kunst. Included Feininger. Catalog: edited

by Deutsche Reichspropagandaleitung Berlin. This exhibition was circulated in all the larger German towns.

1939

G 285 ZURICH – LUCERNE
May–June. Gemälde und Plastiken moderner Meister aus deutschen Museen. Feininger: 2 oils. Exhibition and auction catalog: Feininger: p. 24, ill. p. 25. Auction: Lucerne, June 30, 1939 (direction: Theodor Fischer).

1946

G 286 NEURUPPIN, KARL-MARX-HAUS:
GALERIE FERDINAND MÖLLER
Freie deutsche Kunst. Feininger: 1 oil, 6 woodcuts ill.

1950

G 287 DUSSELDORF, GALERIE ALEX VÖMEL
[Watercolors]. Included Feininger.

G 288 MUNICH, HAUS DER KUNST
May–June. Die Maler am Bauhaus. Feininger: 11 oils, 23 watercolors, 2 drawings, 1 woodcut. Catalog: preface: Ludwig Grote, Feininger: 6 illustrations, short biographical note, port. (cat. nos. 37–73), Munich, Prestel.

1951

G 289 DÜSSELDORF, GALERIE ALEX VÖMEL
Sept. [Watercolors]. Included Feininger.

G 289 a KNOKKE-LE-ZOUTE – ALBERT PLAGE July – Sept. 75 Oeuvres du Demi-Siècle. Feininger: 1 oil. Cat. no. 57, ill.

G 289 b COLOGNE, GALERIE FERDINAND MÖLLER
Nov. 1951 – Jan. 1952. Opening exhibition: Die alten Meister der modernen Kunst in Deutschland: Feininger: 4 oils. Catalog: "Blätter der Galerie Ferdinand Möller," new series, no. 1–2, ill., 1951.

G 289 c PARIS, BIBLIOTHÈQUE NATIONALE
Dec. Les peintres graveurs actuels aux Etats-Unis. Catalog: titlepage: Feininger, 2 graphics (cat. nos. 45, 46).

1952

G 290 COLOGNE, GALERIE FERDINAND MÖLLER
Die alten Meister der modernen Kunst in Deutschland II, "Brücke," "Blauer Reiter," "Bauhaus." Feininger: 6 watercolors, 3 woodcuts, 3 drawings. Catalog: "Blätter der Galerie Ferdinand Möller," new series, no. 6–7, ill., 1952.

1953

G 291 LUCERNE, KUNSTMUSEUM
Deutsche Kunst. Meisterwerke des 20. Jahrhunderts. Feininger: 6 oils, 2 watercolors, 1 drawing. Catalog: editors Ludwig Grote and Leonie von Wilckens. Feininger: p. 13, 29, 30, 49, 2 ill. pl. 44–45, Munich, Prestel.

1954

G 292 DARMSTADT, MATHILDENHÖHE
Ausstellung: Das Bild der Landschaft 1944–1954. Reviewed by: Robert Dangers in: Die Weltkunst (Munich), 24 no. 16:7, ill., 1954.

G 292 a LA NAPOULE. FONDATION HENRY CLEWS
July–Aug. 17 Aquarellistes Américains Contemporains. Included Feininger.

1955

G 292 b BARCELONA
Ausstellung: III. Bienal Hispanoamericana. Feininger: 2 oils, and watercolors and graphics. This exhibition was then circulated in: BELGRADE, THE HAGUE, PARIS and VIENNA.

G 293 KASSEL, MUSEUM FRIDERICIANUM
Ausstellung: Documenta. Kunst des XX. Jahrhunderts. Feininger: 9 oils. Introduction by: Werner Haftmann, ill. no. 6, Munich, Prestel. Reviewed in: Das Kunstwerk (Krefeld and Baden-Baden), Bilder aus der Documenta. 9 no. 2, ill., 1955–56 (no pagination).

1956

G 294 DUSSELDORF
Ausstellung des deutschen Künstlerbundes. Included Feininger. Reviewed by: Klaus J. Fischer, Das Kunstwerk (Krefeld and Baden-Baden), 10 no 1 – 2:67–68, ill., 1956–57.

G 294 a VENICE, 28TH BIENNIAL
Americans paint the City. Exhibition organized by: Art Institute of Chicago, Ill. Catalog: preface by: Lionello Venturi. Feininger passim. Text: Katherine Kuh, Feininger passim. 1 ill., p. 5, with caption by Mark Tobey. 3 oils. Reviewed in: Beaux-Arts (Paris), June 26, 1956.

G 295 WOLFSBURG, VOLKSWAGENWERK
Deutsche Malerei. Ausgewählte Meister seit Caspar David Friedrich. Feininger: 3 oils. Catalog: ill. 69.

1957

G 295 a HALLE, STAATLICHE GALERIE MORITZBURG
April–July. Von Menzel bis Picasso. Handzeichnungen und Graphik des 20. Jahrhunderts aus eigenen Beständen. Catalog: Schriftenreihe der Staatlichen Galerie Moritzburg in Halle, introduction by: Elisabeth Speer (Feininger: p. 23–24), no. 12, 1957. Feininger: 10 drawings, 1 watercolor, 4 ill., p. 90–93. Catalog contains list of all those watercolors, drawings and graphics lost in the action: "Degenerate Art," 1937–38. Feininger: cat. nos. 3–5; illustrations.

G 296 ROME
Arte Tedesca dal 1905 ad oggi. Feininger: 1 oil, 1 watercolor. Catalog: ill.

1958

G 296 a AMSTERDAM, STEDELIJK MUSEUM
July–Sept. De Renaissance van de XXe Eeuw. Feininger: 4 oils. Catalog: oil by Feininger reproduced on back cover.

G 297 BRUSSELS,
PALAIS INTERNATIONAL DES BEAUX-ARTS
Apr.–July. 50 Ans d'Art Moderne. Exposition Universelle et Internationale. Catalog: introduction by: Em. Langui (Feininger passim). Catalog: ill. p. 58. Feininger: 1 oil.

Part Two. Publications from the United States and England. Compiled by BERNARD KARPEL

I. Writings by Lyonel Feininger

E 1   *An interview with the artist*, in Addison Gallery of American Art. Lyonel Feininger. Andover Mass., Phillips Academy, 1938. Includes quotations from "an interview."

E 2   *Recollections of Paul Klee*, by Julia and Lyonel Feininger, in Paul Klee. p. [6–8] New York, Buchholz Gallery, 1940. Brief extract in Guggenheim, Peggy, ed. *Art of This Century*. p. 50 New York, Art of This Century, 1942. Also in:

E 3   *Recollections of Paul Klee*, by Julia and Lyonel Feininger, in Paul Klee. p. 7–8 New York, Museum of Modern Art, 1941. Second revised edition, 1945.

E 4   *From letters by the artist* (1906–1927), in Lyonel Feininger – Marsden Hartley. p. 18 New York, Museum of Modern Art, 1944.

E 5   *Comments by a fellow artist*, by Julia and Lyonel Feininger, in Paintings by Mark Tobey. p. [7–8] Portland Art Museum, 1945.

E 6   *Wassily Kandinsky*, by Julia and Lyonel Feininger. *Magazine of Art* 38:174 1945. Reprinted in:

E 7   *Concerning the Spiritual in Art* by Wassily Kandinsky. p. 12–14 New York, Wittenborn, Schultz, 1947.

E 8   *Perception and trust*, by Julia and Lyonel Feininger. *Design* (Ohio) 47 no. 8:6–7 Apr. 1946. "Impressions of Black Mountain College."

E 9   No problems. *Saturday Review of Literature* 32 no. 32:149 Aug. 6, 1949.

E 10   *From letters to Julia* p. [3–7], in Lyonel Feininger, drawings. New York, Curt Valentin, 1951. See E 12.

II. Graphic Editions

E 11   *Ten Woodcuts*. New York, Buchholz Gallery, 1941. 10 plates in portfolio (each signed by the artist) issued in an edition of 30.

E 12   *Lyonel Feininger Drawings*. New York, Curt Valentin, 1951. 7 p. plus 16 plates. Unpublished drawings in an edition of 1000. Includes "From letters to Julia, by Lyonel Feininger" (p. 3–7).

III. Major References: Monographs, Booklets, Important Catalogs

E 13   FEININGER, LYONEL. *Scrapbook* [of clippings, catalogs and reproductions]. ill. (pt. col.) New York, n. d. A continuing record assembled from documents in the Museum of Modern Art Library, including material from the artist. Supplemented by pictorial material on deposit in the photographic archive.

E 14   NEW YORK. MUSEUM OF MODERN ART. Lyonel Feininger – Marsden Hartley. 96 p. ill (port., col. pl.) New York, Museum of Modern Art, 1944. Joint exhibition and monograph: Feininger, p. 6-52. "With essays by Alois J. Schardt and Alfred H. Barr, Jr., and excerpts from the artist's letters. Edited by Dorothy C. Miller," also director of the exhibition. Includes chronology, list of exhibits, record of the artist's exhibitions, lists museums owning paintings, selected bibliography by H. B. Muller.

E 15   BOSTON. INSTITUTE OF CONTEMPORARY ART. Jacques Villon – Lyonel Feininger. 46 p. ill. (port.) New York, Chanticleer Press [1950]. "Published for the Institute of Contemporary Art, Boston; Phillips Gallery, Washington; Delaware Art Center, Wilmington" which displayed the exhibition. Foreword, J. B. Plaut, p. 6. – The pleasures of cubism, T. B. Hess, p. 24–27. – Lyonel Feininger, F. S. Wight, p. 29-30, 32. Also chronology, exhibitions, bibliography, p. 33–35. Catalogue, p. 45–46.

E 16   CLEVELAND. MUSEUM OF ART. The Work of Lyonel Feininger. 26 p. plus 18 plates Cleveland, The Museum, 1951. Preface by Leona E. Prasse, p. 7–8; "Lyonel Feininger in Lincoln" by Frederick S. Wight, p. 9-13. Exhibit of 247 works sponsored jointly by the Print Club of Cleveland.

E 17   DORFLES, GILLO. Lyonel Feininger. 24 p. plus 17 ill. (1 col.) Milan, All' Insegna del Pesce d'Oro, 1958. English edition, 500 copies; Italian edition, 500 copies. No. 62 of the miniature series (Pesce d'Oro). Includes chronology, bibliography. Also "catalogue of works exhibited" (Merano). See bibl. G 233.

E 17 a   SAN FRANCISCO. MUSEUM OF ART. Lyonel Feininger Memorial Exhibition 1959–1961. 20 p. ill. (4 col.) San Francisco [The Museum], 1959. Catalog of international circulating exhibition, first shown here Nov. 5 – Dec. 13. Assembled by Mrs. Lyonel Feininger, Marian Willard, Henry S. Francis. Introduction by Hans Hess, p. 9–12. For notes, see bibl. E 350.

IV. General References

E 18   BARR, ALFRED H., Jr. Cubism and Abstract Art. p. 68, 70, 153, 156, 209, 244 ill. New York, Museum of Modern Art, 1936. Exhibition and catalog.

E 19   BARR, ALFRED H. Jr., Masters of Modern Art. p. 113 col. pl. New York, Museum of Modern Art, 1954.

E 20   BAUR, JOHN I. H. Nature in Abstraction. p. 8, 35, 62 ill. New York, Whitney Museum of American Art, 1958. Exhibition and catalog; biographical note and colorplate.

E 21   BAYER, HERBERT, and GROPIUS, WALTER, GROPIUS, ISE, eds. Bauhaus 1919–1928. p. 19, 21, 79, 83, 86, 182–183, 199, 220, 222 incl. ill. New York, Museum of Modern Art, 1938. Issued on the occasion of the exhibition. Reprint issued by Branford, Boston, 1952.

E 22   BAZIN, GERMAIN. History of Modern Painting. p. 316, 361 ill. New York, Paris, London, Hyperion (distributed by Macmillan), 1950.

E 23   BERTRAM, ANTHONY. Contemporary Painting in Europe. p. 83 ill. London & New York, Studio, 1939. Special autumn number of *The Studio*.

E 24   BITTERMANN, ELEANOR. Art in Modern Architecture. p. 22-23 ill. New York, Reinhold, 1952.

E 25   BLESH, RUDI. Modern Art U.S.A. p. 127, 165, 183, 216, 225, 263, 294 New York, Knopf, 1956.

E 26   BOECK, WILHELM, and SABARTÉS, JAIME. Picasso. p. 255 London, Thames & Hudson; New York, Abrams, 1955.

E 26 a   BRION, MARCEL. German Painting. p. 133, 144, 155–156 ill. (col. pl.) New York, Universe, 1959. Also Editions Pierre Tisné.

E 27   BROWN, MILTON W. American Painting from the Armory Show to the Depression. p. 103, 116 Princeton, N.J., Princeton Unversity Press, 1955.

E 28   CHENEY, SHELDON. A Primer of Modern Art. p. 111, 206, 244 New York, Liveright, 1924. Other editions: 1927, etc.

E 29   CURRENT BIOGRAPHY YEARBOOK. 1955. p. 197 –199 port. New York, Wilson, 1956. Supplemental obituary in 1956 Yearbook p. 177.

E 30   DOCUMENTS (Periodical). German Contemporary Art. p. 7, 10, 26, 34, 39–41, 63, 65, 70, 102 ill. Offenburg-in-Baden, Dokumente-Verlag, 1952. Special issue, also in German and French (1951), edited by the Bureau International de Liaison et de Documentation.

E 31   GERTZ, ULRICH. Contemporary Plastik. Art 2. ed. (enlarged) p. IV Berlin, Rembrandt [1957?]. Second German edition, without English preface, issued 1953.

E 32   GIEDION, SIGFRIED. Space, Time and Architecture. p. 394 Cambridge, Harvard University Press, 1941. Other editions: 10th (1954).

E 33   GIEDION, SIGFRIED. Walter Gropius: Work and Teamwork. p. 13, 17, 27, 28, 34, 38 ill. New York, Reinhold, 1954.

E 34   GOLDWATER, ROBERT. Primitivism in Modern Painting. plate 57 New York, Harper, 1938.

E 35   GOMBRICH, E. H. The Story of Art. p. 436–437 New York, Oxford, 1950; London, Phaidon, 1950. Other editions: 19th (London, Phaidon, 1960).

E 36   GROHMANN, WILL. Paul Klee. p. 25, 63, 65 London, Lund Humphries, 1954; New York, Abrams [1955?].

E 37   GRUSKIN, ALAN D. Painting in the U.S.A. plates 18, 54 New York, Doubleday, 1946.

E 38   GUGGENHEIM, PEGGY, ed. Art of This Century. p. 50 New York, Art of This Century, 1942. Brief extracts from Feininger on Paul Klee.

E 39   HÄNDLER, GERHARD. German Painting in Our Time. p. 23–24, 68–71, 195 ill. (col.) Berlin, Rembrandt, 1956. Translated from the German.

E 40   HISTORY OF MODERN PAINTING. [VOL 3:] From Picasso to Surrealism. p. 10–11, 106, 116, 150–151, 156–158, 160, 195–196 col. pl. Geneva, Skira, 1950. "The painters of the Bauhaus," by Werner Schmalenbach. Chronological and bibliographical notes.

E 41   HITCHCOCK, HENRY-RUSSELL. Painting Toward Architecture. p. 70, 71 ill. New York, Duell, Sloan & Pearce, 1948. "The Miller Company Collection of abstract art." Text on Feininger by M. C. Rathbun.

E 42   JANIS, SIDNEY. Abstract and Surrealist Art in America. p, 31, 32, 35, 46, 49 ill. New York, Reynal & Hitchcock, 1944.

E 43   KUHN, CHARLES E. German Expressionism and Abstract Art: the Harvard Collection. p. 9, 11, 14–15, 22, 28, 33, 35 ill. Cambridge, Harvard University Press, 1957.

E 44   LAKE, CARLTON, and MAILLARD, ROBERT, ed. Dictionary of Modern Painting. p. 102–103 ill. New York, Paris Book Center, 1955. Translation from the French (Hazan, 1954).

E 45   LARKIN, OLIVER W. Art and Life in America. p. 351, 370, 409–410, 430 New York, Rinehart, 1956.

E 46   LOS ANGELES. UNIVERSITY OF CALIFORNIA. DEPARTMENT OF ART. Looking at Modern Painting. p. 82–84, 107, col. pl. Los Angeles, University of California, 1957.

E 47   McCURDY, CHARLES, ed. Modern Art: a Pictorial Anthology. p. 32, 139, 148 ill. New York, Macmillan, 1958.

E 48   MYERS, BERNARD, ed. Encyclopedia of Painting. p. 175–176 col. pl. New York, Crown, 1955.

E 49   MYERS, BERNARD S. The German Expressionists: a Generation in Revolt. p. 248–250, 378 et passim col. pl. New York, Praeger, 1957. European distribution: Thames & Hudson (London), DuMont Schauberg (Cologne).

E 50   NEW YORK. MUSEUM OF MODERN ART. Paul Klee. p. 7–8 New York, The Museum, 1941. Includes Feininger text. Second revised edition, ed. by M. Miller, issued 1945.

E 51   NEW YORK. MUSEUM OF MODERN ART. Painting and Sculpture in the Museum of Modern Art: a Catalog. p. 24–25 New York, Museum of Modern Art, 1958. Lists 5 works, "also prints and comic strips." 1948 edition edited by A. H. Barr, Jr. (p. 108–109, 307, 2 ill.); 1942 edition (p. 40).

E 52   PASADENA ART MUSEUM. The Blue Four: Feininger, Jawlensky, Kandinsky, Paul Klee – Galka E. Scheyer Collection. [32] p. ill. Pasadena, Cal. [1955]. Introduction by W. Joseph Fulton reports formal acquisition. Biographical note on Feininger; lists 45 watercolors and woodcuts (1916–1933), 4 ill.

E 53   PORTLAND ART MUSEUM. Paintings by Mark Tobey. p. [7–8] Portland, The Museum, 1945. Includes Feininger text (bibl. E 5) in catalog for Portland, San Francisco Museum of Art, Detroit Institute of Art, 1945–46.

E 54   PRAEGER PICTURE ENCYCLOPEDIA OF ART. p. 442, 466, 480, 486 col. pl. New York, Praeger, 1958. Various editors. English version prepared by the editorial staff of Thames & Hudson (London). German edition by Westermann Verlag (Brunswick).

E 55   PULITZER, LOUISE, and PULITZER, JOSEPH, Jr., COLLECTION. Modern Painting, Drawings and Sculpture. Catalogue by C. S. Chetham. v. 1, p.33–34, pl. 55; v. 2, p. 208–209, pl. 68 Cambridge, Harvard College, 1957–1958.

E 56   PUMA, FERNANDO. Modern Art Looks Ahead. p. 24, 26, 27, 40, 54. pl. 66 New York, Beechhurst Press, 1947.

E 57   RAYNAL, MAURICE. Modern Painting, p. 182, 231–232, 244, 301–302 col. pl. Geneva, Skira, 1956. Chronological and bibliographical notes similar to bibl. E 40.

E 57 a READ, HERBERT. A Concise History of Modern Painting. p. 174, 212, 214, 229, 2 ill. p. 175, 302, 1 colorplate p. 176. London, Thames & Hudson, 1959.

E 58 RITCHIE, ANDREW C., ed. Art of the Twentieth Century. p. 106, 108, 129, 210, 211–212, 232 ill. (col. pl.) New York, Museum of Modern Art, 1957. Texts by W. Haftmann, A. Hentzen, W. S. Liebermann in exhibition catalog "in collaboration with the City Art Museum of St. Louis, Missouri."

E 59 RITCHIE, ANDREW C. Abstract Painting and Sculpture in America. p. 33, 150 ill. New York, Museum of Modern Art, 1951. Exhibition catalog.

E 60 RÖTHEL, HANS K. Modern German Painting. p. 48–60, 87 2 col. pl. New York Reynal [1957]. Translated from the German.

E 61 ROTHENSTEIN, JOHN. The Moderns and their World. p. 19 pl. 76–77 London, Phoenix House, 1957.

E 62 SELZ, PETER. German Expressionist Painting. p. 64, 131, 137, 177, 266, 278–280, 313–315, 317 ill. Berkeley & Los Angeles, University of California Press, 1957.

E 63 SOBY, JAMES T., and MILLER, DOROTHY C. Romantic Painting in America. p. 42, 100, 135 ill. New York, Museum of Modern Art, 1943. Exhibition catalog.

E 64 THOENE, PETER. Modern German Art. p. 81–82 ill. no. 24, 25. Harmondsworth, Middlesex, Penguin Books, 1938. Pseudonym of Bihali-Merin.

E 65 WIGHT, FREDERICK S. Milestones of American Painting in Our Century. p. 52–53 ill. Boston, Institute of Contemporary Art; New York, Chanticleer, 1949. Exhibition catalog, preface by L. Goodrich.

E 66 VOLLMER, HANS. Allgemeines Lexikon der bildenden Künstler. Vol. 2, p. 85–86 Leipzig, Seemann, 1955. References include citations to material in English, although these are erratic in scope, and vary in significance.

E 67 WHO'S WHO IN AMERICA 1956–57. Vol. 29, p. 823 Chicago, Marquis, 1956.

E 68 WHO'S WHO IN AMERICAN ART. Ed. by Dorothy E. Gilbert. p. 133 New York, Bowker, 1953.

E 69 YALE UNIVERSITY. ART GALLERY. Collection of the Société Anonyme: Museum of Modern Art 1920. p. 53–54 ill. New Haven, Associates in Fine Arts, 1950. Text by A. Dorner; lists 6 works; biographical and bibliographical notes.

E 70 ZIGROSSER, CARL. The Expressionists: a Survey of their Graphic Art. p. 20–21, ill. New York, Braziller, 1957.

V. Articles and Reviews

E 71 Archives of American art: acquisitions; Feininger – Churchill collection. Art Quarterly (Detroit) 19 no. 2:174–175 1956.

E 72 Art at the Fair: part 1. Art News 37:7 ill. May 6, 1939. Includes Feininger's frescoes for the World's Fair, N.Y.

E 73 Bach in prisms [a review]. Time (New York) ill. Apr. 7, 1952.

E 74 BIE, OSCAR. Letter from Berlin. Apollo 10 no. 60:355–356 Dec. 1929.

E 75 B[IER], J[USTUS]. Feininger watercolors [Speed Museum exhibition]. Art News 36 no. 32:19 May 17, 1938.

E 76 BILL, MAX. The Bauhaus idea. In Architect's Year Book. no. 5, p. 29 ill. London, Elek, 1953.

E 77 BIRD, PAUL. Feininger to return [to the Nierendorf gallery]. Art Digest 11:18 port. May 1, 1937.

E 78 BREUNING, MARGARET. Staccato movements of Lyonel Feininger [at the Buchholz gallery]. Art Digest 22 no. 11:16 Mar. 1, 1948.

E 79 BREUNING, MARGARET. Feininger's infinite variety [at the Buchholz gallery]. Art Digest 24 no. 14:17 ill. Apr. 15, 1950.

E 80 BREUNING, MARGARET. [The Metropolitan shows Feininger, Kuhn, Kuniyoshi, Marin and Nordfeldt]. Arts (N.Y.) 30:46 Apr. 1956. Similar coverage in Art News 56:79 Apr. 1956; Art in America 4:56–57 Spring 1956.

E 81 Britannica Book of the Year. See bibl. E 138.

E 82 BROWN, MILTON. Three abstract painters [at the Buchholz and Willard galleries]. Parnassus 13:154 ill. Apr. 1941.

E 83 [Buchholz gallery catalogs: notes and introductions]. See index under Buchholz and Curt Valentin galleries.

E 84 [Buchholz gallery exhibition: a review]. Art News 47 no. 1:46 ill. Mar. 1948.

E 85 CATLIN, S. L. New paintings and watercolors for the permanent collection. Minneapolis Institute Bulletin 45:15, 20–21 Mar. 1956. Illustrates Feininger's "Hopfgarten."

E 86 CAUSTON, BERNARD. Art in Germany under the Nazis. London Studio 112 no. 524; 235–246 Nov. 1936. Illustrates Feininger's "Red Tower at Halle."

E 87 CHURCHILL, ALFRED V. Lyonel Feininger, woodcut artist. ill. American Art Student 7:18 Jan. 1924.

E 88 COATES, R. M. [Modern Museum's first big exhibit of the season]. New Yorker 20:50 Nov. 4, 1944. Review of Feininger-Hartley show at the Museum of Modern Art.

E 89 COATES, R. M. Art galleries: Exhibition at Willard gallery. New Yorker 31:98 Feb. 11, 1956.

E 90 COATES, R. M. Art galleries: Memorial to five American artists at the Metropolitan Museum. New Yorker 32:119–120 Mar. 10, 1956.

E 91 COE, N. Cathedral, Cammin, by Lyonel Feininger. Cleveland Museum Bulletin 44:67–70 Apr. 1957.

E 92 CUSTER, A. Feininger material for the Archives of American art. Detroit Institute Bulletin 35 no. 4:95–96 1955.

E 93 DAVIDSON, MARTHA. Crystal notes in Feininger's watercolors [at the East River gallery]. Art News 35:17, 23 ill. Dec. 26, 1937.

E 94 DAVIDSON, MARTHA. Lyonel Feininger in a comprehensive show [at Mills College Art gallery]. Art News 35:13 May 15, 1937.

E 95 DAVIDSON, MARTHA. Recent watercolors by Feininger, poet of abstraction [at the Sullivan Gallery]. Art News 37:13 ill. Nov. 19, 1938.

E 96 DERI, MAX. Principles of modern German art. International Studio 75:315–317 July 1922. Reproduces Feininger's "Windmill" (p. 316).

E 97 DEVREE, HOWARD. [Feininger at the Sullivan Gallery]. *New York Times* Nov. 13, 1958.

E 98 DEVREE, HOWARD. New York letter. *Magazine of Art* 34:209, 219 ill. Apr. 1941. Reviews Willard and Buchholz exhibition.

E 99 DEVREE, HOWARD. Lyonel Feininger dead [an obituary]. *New York Times* port. Jan. 14, 1956.

E 100 DORNER, ALEXANDER. Three newly acquired paintings. *Rhode Island School of Design Bulletin* 26 no. 2:8–11 ill. Apr. 1, 1938. Includes Feininger's "Church at Gelmeroda."

E 101 Exact fantasist. *Time* (N.Y.) 72:34–35 ill (port.) Dec. 29, 1958.

E 102 FARBER, MANNY. Feininger, Tack and Burlin. *Magazine of Art* 36 no. 3:108 ill. Mar. 1943. Reviews Buchholz-Willard shows.

E 103 FEININGER, T. LUX. Two painters. *Chrysalis* (Boston) 9 no. 9–10:[18 p.] 1956.

E 104 Feininger. *Current Biography* 16 no. 7:32–34 port. July 1955. Quotes reviews. Also published in bibl. E 29.

E 105 Feininger and Klee. *San Francisco Museum of Art edition – Magazine of Art* p. lvii – lxi ill. Apr. 1949. Includes text by Julia Feininger. "The present exhibition is his fifth at San Francisco since 1936."

E 106 Feininger and sons. *Life* (New York) 31 no. 20:89–96 ill (pt. col.) Nov. 12, 1951. Also portrait, 15:12 Oct. 25, 1943.

E 107 Feininger distills the essence of art. *Art Digest* 15:21 ill. Dec. 1, 1940. Acquisitions by Springfield and St. Louis museums.

E 108 Feininger: two angles in new painting. *Art News* 44:89 ill. Feb. 1946. Reviews Willard-Buchholz show.

E 109 Feininger without delusions or cramps. *Art Digest* 11:14 Aug. 1937. Quotes Dr. Alfred Newmeyer's foreword to the exhibit at Mills College art gallery.

E 110 Feininger watercolors [at the Speed Museum]. *Art News* 36:19 May 7, 1938.

E 111 Feininger watercolors. *Baltimore Museum of Art News* 14:5 ill. Jan. 1951. Quotes F. S. Wight on three acquisitions.

E 112 Focus on Feininger [at the Cleveland Museum retrospective]. *Art Digest* 26:12 ill. Nov. 15, 1951.

E 113 FRANKENSTEIN, ALFRED M. Lyonel Feininger. *Magazine of Art* 31 no. 5:278–283 ill. May 1938.

E 114 FRANKFURTER, ALFRED M. The chromium mean of American painting. *Art News* 40:8–9 ill. Apr. 1, 1941. Discusses his unsuccessful choice, Feininger's *Gaberndorf II*, at the Corcoran 17th biennial.

E 115 FRIEDMAN, B. H. The new collector: three typical collections. *Art in America* 46 no. 2:12-19 Summer 1958. Illustrates Feininger's "Lunar Web."

E 116 G[IBBS], J[OSEPHINE]. [The "Steamer Odin" acquired by the Museum of Modern Art]. *Art Digest* 18:13 Feb. 1, 1944.

E 117 GILBERT, CREIGHTON. The Feiningers of Louisville. *Allen H. Hite Institute Bulletin* (Louisville) 8 no. 2:[3–4] 1954.

E 118 GORDON, J. J. Recent accession: Feininger's *Zirchow V*. *Brooklyn Museum Bulletin* 15 no. 4:12 ill. 1954.

E 119 HALE, ROBERT B. The growth of a collection [by Edward Root]. *Metropolitan Museum Bulletin* (New York) 11:153–163 1952–53. Reproduces Feininger.

E 120 HAMILTON, CHLOE. Recent gifts: water color by Feininger. *Oberlin College Bulletin* 15 no. 1:17-19 2 ill. Fall 1957. Also including Feininger, 10:43–50 1952–53.

E 121 HESS, HANS. German expressionism. *Art* (London) 1 no. 8:5 Mar. 3, 1955.

E 122 HESS, HANS. Lyonel Feininger – a tribute. *Art* (London) 2 no. 6:2 Feb. 2, 1956.

E 123 HESS, HANS. Lyonel Feininger – obituary. *Burlington Magazine* 98:131 Apr. 1956.

E 124 HESS, THOMAS B. Feininger paints a picture. *Art News* 48:48–50, 60–61 ill (port.) June–Aug. 1949.

E 125 HESS, THOMAS B. Villon – Feininger: refining cubism. *Art News* 48:26, 160–161 ill. Nov. 1949.

E 126 HOFFMANN, EDITH. Feininger – Hartley. *Burlington Magazine* 87:207–208 Aug. 1945. Reviews Museum of Modern Art monograph.

E 127 KIENITZ, J. F. [Review of Feininger – Hartley, published by the Museum of Modern Art]. *College Art Journal* no. 4:237–239 1945.

E 127 a KORTHEUER, DAYRELL. In Memoriam Lyonel Feininger 1871–1956. *Art Life* (Charlotte, N. C.) 2 no. 1, 1 ill. Summer 1956.

E 128 LANE, JAMES W. Feininger's counterpoint in paint: Lyonel out of Johann Sebastian. *Art News* 40 no. 3:38–39, 51–52 ill. (port.) Mar. 15–31, 1941.

E 129 LIBERMAN, A. Feininger. *Vogue* 127:90–93 port., ill. (pt. col.) Apr. 15, 1956.

E 130 LIEBERMANN, WILLIAM S. One classic, one newcomer: Feininger, Baskin. *Magazine of Art* 54:28–31 ill. May, 1955. By the Curator of the Print Collection, Museum of Modern Art.

E 131 L[OUCHEIM], A[LINE]. Expressionist and cubist: America's vision. *Art News* 43:18 ill. Nov. 1944. Feininger-Hartley exhibition at the Museum of Modern Art.

E 132 LOUCHHEIM, ALINE B. Feininger looks back on 80 years. *New York Times* ill. Mar. 23, 1952. Not a review, but refers to the exhibition then showing at the Curt Valentin Gallery.

E 132 a Lyonel Feininger memorial exhibition. *Cleveland Museum Bulletin* 47:36–37 ill. Feb. 1960.

E 133 McBRIDE, HENRY. Feininger and Hartley [at the Museum of Modern Art]. *New York Sun* Oct. 28, 1944.

E 134 McHALE, JOHN. Gropius and the Bauhaus. *Art* (London) 1 no. 8:3, 10 Mar. 3, 1955. Reviews Gropius' recent book.

E 135 Meet the artist. *Art Digest* 17:8–9 Sept. 1943. Self-portraits show at the M. H. de Young Memorial Museum, San Francisco. Additional coverage: *California Arts and Architecture* 60:8 ff Sept. 1943.

E 136 Modern German art – till now. *London Studio* 16 no. 90:160–164 Sept. 1938. Reproduces Feininger.

E 137 MORLEY, GRACE L. McCANN. Contemporary art in local collections. *San Francisco Bulletin* 4:1–14 ill. 1955. Reproduces Feininger.

E 138 [Obituary: Lyonel Feininger. New York, 1956–57]. In addition to Devree, Hess and Kortheuer above, note: *American Annual* 1957 (p. 276–277); *Art News* 54:7 Feb. 1956; *Britannica Book of the Year* 1957 (p. 574); *Current Biography* 17:21 Mar. 1956 (also Yearbook 1957); *Time* 67:91 Jan. 23, 1956.

E 138 a A painting by Lyonel Feininger. *Currier Gallery of Art Bulletin* [p. 1–3] ill. May 1957. New acquisition: "The Mill in Spring (1935)."

E 139 PRASSE, LEONA E. Gelmeroda, a woodcut by Lyonel Feininger. *Cleveland Museum Bulletin* 45:237–238 ill. Dec. 1958.

E 140 PRASSE, LEONA E. A lithograph by Lyonel Feininger. *Cleveland Museum Bulletin* 38:216–219 ill. 1951. "Off the Coast," published by the Print Club of Cleveland; also refers to current exhibition.

E 141 PRESTON, STUART. Feininger survey [at the Buchholz and Schaefer galleries]. *New York Times* Apr. 16, 1950.

E 142 PUTZEL, HOWARD. Lyonel Feininger – an architectural expressionist. *The Argus* (San Francisco) 2:1–2 Feb. 1928.

E 143 PUTZEL, HOWARD. Lyonel Feininger. *St. Louis City Art Museum Bulletin* 25:53–54 ill. Oct. 1940.

E 144 RATHBONE, PERRY T. "The Glorious Victory of the Sloop Maria." *St. Louis City Art Museum Bulletin* 25 no. 4:54 ill. Oct. 1940.

E 145 RILEY, MAUDE. Feininger twice [at the Buchholz and Willard galleries]. *Art Digest* 17 no. 9:14 ill. Feb. 1, 1943. Also: "The modern shows Hartley and Feininger," 19 no. 3:6–7 ill. Nov. 1, 1944.

E 146 RUBIN, WILLIAM. Lyonel Feininger: a profile. *Art Digest* 28:8–9 May 1, 1954. Skyline [Feininger's first lithograph]. *Art News* 50:50 May 1951.

E 147 SWEET, FREDERICK A. Morris Graves and Lyonel Feininger. *Chicago Art Institute Bulletin.* 42:65–68 Sept, 1948.

E 148 TELLER, CHARLOTTE. Feininger – fantasist. *International Studio* 63 no. 249: suppl. p. XXV–XXX ill. Nov. 1917. Illustrates three works (1908–1909).

E 149 THWAITES, JOHN A. The Bauhaus painters and the new style epoch. Art Quarterly (Detroit) 14 no. 1:26–27, 31 ill. Spring 1951.

E 150 TSELOS, DIMITRIS. Feininger and Marsden Hartley [review of Museum of Modern Art monograph]. *Gazette des Beaux-Arts* 32 no. 969–70:190–91 Nov.–Dec. 1947.

E 151 TURKEL-DERI, FLORA. Berlin letter. *Art News* 29:18 Aug. 15, 1931; 30:19 Oct. 17, 1931. On the Essen exhibit at the Museum Folkwang, and the Berlin show at the National-Galerie.

E 152 UPTON, MELVILLE. Lyonel Feininger [at the Buchholz and Willard galleries]. *New York Herald-Tribune* Jan. 31, 1943.

E 152 a VALENTINER, WILHELM R. Expressionism and abstract painting. *Art Quarterly* (Detroit) 4 no. 3:210–239 ill. 1941. Fig. 21 (p. 231): Feininger.

E 152 b VAUGHN, M. [Feininger memorial exhibition]. *Connoisseur (American edition)* 145:287 ill. June 1960.

E 153 Water-colorist Lyonel Feininger [at the Willard Gallery]. *Architectural Record* 81:18–19 Jan. 1937.

E 154 Watercolors of Lyonel Feininger. *Milwaukee Institute Bulletin* 13:2 Nov. 1938.

E 155 Watercolors – U.S.A. [with list]. *Art Digest* (N.Y.) 20:17 June 1946. "Organized by the National Gallery and assembled by the Walker Art Center for a six months tour of Latin America. Reported 20:15 July, 1946 as a five-year tour sponsored by the State Department (Coordinator of Inter-American Affairs). Other

articles: *Antiques* Nov. 1946. *Museum News* June 1, 1946, *Art News* July 1946.

E 156 WATSON, JANE. News and comment [on "The Sloop Maria"]. *Magazine of Art* 33 no. 11:640–45, 649 ill. Nov. 1940.

E 157 WERNER, ALFRED. Lyonel Feininger and German romanticism. *Art in America* 44 no. 3:23–27 ill. Fall 1956.

E 157 a WERNER, ALFRED. Lyonel Feininger: Gothic to Bach. *The Painter and Sculptor* 2 no. 3:12–18 ill. Autumn 1959.

E 157 b WIGHT, FREDERICK S. Lyonel Feininger. *The American-German Review* (Philadelphia) 20 no. 6:18–19 Aug.-Sept. 1954.

E 158 ZABRISKIE, GEORGE. For Lyonel Feininger [a poem]. *Tiger's Eye* (New York) no. 7:64–65 ill. Mar. 1949.

VI. Chronological List of Exhibition

E 159 ANDERSON GALLERIES. A collection of modern German art, New York, 1923. Including 5 oils, 15 watercolors, 27 drawings and prints in first U.S. showing; introduction by W. R. Valentiner, shown "until Oct. 20."

E 160 DANIEL GALLERY. The Blue Four: Feininger, Kandinsky, Jawlensky, Paul Klee. New York, 1925. "Closing Mar. 10," brief foreword by C. Daniel; 50 works including 9 by Feininger (1 ill.). First American showing of the "Blue Four," introduced by Mme. Galka E. Scheyer, and subsequently shown cross-country, 1925–1934, with variations in catalogs and works.

E 161 GRAND CENTRAL ART GALLERIES. [Group show: Multi-national exhibition of works by American, British, French, German, Swiss and Mexican artists]. New York, 1927. Two oils by Feininger.

E 162 ELDER, PAUL, GALLERY. Graphic art of the Blue Four. San Francisco. Jan. 18–23, 1926. Announcement reports formal opening Jan. 16, with lecture by Mme. Scheyer.

E 163 OAKLAND ART GALLERY. The Blue Four. Oakland, Cal., May, 1926. 6 oils and 4 watercolors (1914–1924) by Feininger. Foreword by W. H. Clapp; 3 lectures by Mme. Scheyer advertised (May 2–31).

E 164 LOS ANGELES MUSEUM. The Blue Four. Oct. 1926. Nos. 1–15 by Feininger (1914–1924); all media. Probably shown later at the San Diego Fine Arts Society (1926? 1927?).

E 165 CALIFORNIA SCHOOL OF FINE ARTS. The Blue Four. San Francisco, University of California. Mar. 1–20 [1927?]. Undated announcement card.

E 166 SPOKANE ART ASSOCIATION. The Blue Four. Spokane, Wash., May 15–31, 1927. Nos. 15–25 by Feininger (1922–1924), including 4 oils, 5 watercolors, 2 wood blocks, at the Grace Campbell Memorial Bldg. Probably also shown at the Portland Museum of Art (1927?),

E 167 MINNESOTA UNIVERSITY GALLERY. Presenting Lyonel Feininger. Apr. 1928. Retrospective, with catalog foreword by Ruth Laurence.

E 168 MUSEUM OF MODERN ART. Paintings by 19 Living Americans. New York, Dec. 12, 1929 – Jan. 12,

1930. No. 19–25 by Feininger, 1 ill., biographical note.

E 169 OAKLAND ART GALLERY. Lyonel Feininger: block prints, etchings. Oakland, Cal., Jan. 1929. First one-man show at Oakland "through Jan. 31." His "first comprehensive American display" including oils and watercolors incorporated in the Blue Four 1931 show. The director, William H. Clapp, arranged the western tour of the Blue Four through the Western Association of Art Museum Directors, using material assembled by Mme. Scheyer in Germany "acting as our European representative."

E 170 BRAXTON, HARRY, GALLERY. The Blue Four. Hollywood, Mar. 1 – May 15, 1930. Feininger exhibited separately, Apr. 15 – 30. Nos. 1–63 includes all media. Illustration, portrait, biographical notes, press extracts (p. 9–11). Brief preface by Braxton.

E 171 ARTS CLUB OF CHICAGO. The Blue Four. Apr. 1–15, 1932. 36 Feininger works in all media; biographical note; prefatory quotations. Also reported elsewhere: 1932 "Blue Four exhibition at the Renaissance Society of the University of Chicago."

E 172 CALIFORNIA PALACE OF THE LEGION OF HONOR. The Blue Four. San Francisco, Apr. 8–22, 1931. 30 works by Feininger in all media; brief note.

E 173 OAKLAND ART GALLERY. The Blue Four. Oakland, Cal., Sept. 1931. "Exhibit closing Sept. 14"; brief foreword and biographical note; 35 works in all media.

E 174 MEXICO. BIBLIOTECA NACIONAL. Cuatro Azules. Nov. 24 – Dec. 1, 1931. Biographical and critical notes on Feininger; general introduction by Diego Rivera; rear-cover illustration by Feininger; no list of exhibited works in catalog (12 p.).

E 175 FAULKNER MEMORIAL ART GALLERY. The Blue Four. Santa Barbara, Cal., Mar. 3–13, 1932. 25 Feininger works in all media.

E 176 OAKLAND ART GALLERY. The Blue Four. Oakland, Cal., 1933 ? Reported indecisively by the director, W. H. Clapp. Possibly show later exhibited at Los Angeles, 1933.

E 177 LOS ANGELES MUSEUM. The Blue Four. Los Angeles, Cal., Oct. 1933. Important 40 p. catalog for "new collection assembled in Europe 1933," includes Feininger oils (no. 1–11), watercolors (no. 12–40), wood blocks, etchings, sculpture head.

E 178 HANSEN MUSIC CO. The Blue Four. Beverly Hills, Cal., Nov. 1934. Announcement card notes opening "Nov. 17, 1934."

E 179 MUSEUM OF MODERN ART. Cubism and Abstract Art. New York, Mar. 2 – Apr. 19, 1936. No. 69–71 by Feininger, 7 ill.

E 180 MILLS COLLEGE ART GALLERY. [Feininger]. Oakland, Cal., Summer 1936.

E 181 EAST RIVER GALLERY. Lyonel Feininger Aquarelles. New York, Dec. 7–21, 1936. 25 watercolors; introduction, probably first American one-man show in a commercial gallery. (East River Gallery later known as the Willard Gallery with shows in 1943, 1946, 1947, 1956, 1958, 1960).

E 182 FAULKNER MEMORIAL ART GALLERY. Lyonel Feininger. Santa Barbara, Cal., Free Public Library, Jan. 5–17, 1937. No. 1–30 (in the "Gallery"); no. 31–78 (in the "Print Room").

E 183 PHILADELPHIA ART ALLIANCE. Guggenheim Collection of Non-Objective Paintings. Philadelphia, Pa., Feb. 8–28, 1937. No. 162–165 by Feininger.

E 184 BROOKLYN MUSEUM. International Exhibition of Watercolors: 9th Biennial, Brooklyn, N.Y. May 8 – June 12, 1937. Two works by Feininger.

E 185 MILLS COLLEGE ART GALLERY. 2nd Feininger exhibition. June 27 – Aug. 7, 1937. 35 new paintings, 130 drawings and prints. (Also noted *Magazine of Art* 30:456 July 1937). Later shown at the San Francisco Museum of Art.

E 186 LOS ANGELES ART ASSOCIATION. UNIVERSITY GALLERY. [Lyonel Feininger]. Los Angeles Cal., 1937. Listed in bibl. E 14.

E 187 NIERENDORF GALLERY. [Lyonel Feininger]. New York, 1937. Listed in bibl. E 14.

E 188 PORTLAND MUSEUM OF ART. [Lyonel Feininger]. Portland, Ore., 1937. Listed in bibl. E 14.

E 189 SEATTLE ART MUSEUM. [Lyonel Feininger]. Seattle, Wash., 1937. Listed in bibl. E 14.

E 190 SAN DIEGO FINE ARTS GALLERY. [Lyonel Feininger]. San Diego, Cal., 1938. Listed in bibl. E 14.

E 191 EAST RIVER GALLERY. [Lyonel Feininger]. New York, Jan.–Feb. 1938. Listed in bibl. E 14.

E 192 ADDISON GALLERY OF AMERICAN ART. Lyonel Feininger. Andover, Mass., Phillips Academy, Feb. 19 – Mar. 20, 1938. 17 oils, 19 watercolors, drawings and woodcuts; biographical notes; quotations.

E 193 GIBBES MEMORIAL ART GALLERY. Solomon R. Guggenheim Collection of Non-Objective Paintings [3rd enlarged catalog]. Charleston, S. C., Mar. 7 – Apr. 17, 1938. No. 233–237 by Feininger; biographical note, p. 62–63.

E 194 J. B. SPEED MUSEUM. [Lyonel Feininger]. Louisville, Ky., Mar. 23 – Apr. 17, 1938. Exhibition by the University Art [Students] League; 23 watercolors, 13 woodblocks; chronology and translated excerpt from letter (1917). "First one-man modern show in Louisville." (The U.A.L. also organized a 1946 showing).

E 195 MINNEAPOLIS UNIVERSITY GALLERY. Presenting Lyonel Feininger: a retrospective. Minneapolis, Apr. 1938. 103 works (33 oils, 39 watercolors, 31 woodblocks); foreword by Ruth Lawrence; "first retrospective in America."

E 196 MUSÉE DU JEU DE PAUME. Trois Siècles d'Art aux États-Unis: Exposition organisée en collaboration avec le Museum of Modern Art, New York. Paris, May 24 – July 31, 1938. No. 57: *Steamer "Odin"* (1927). Catalog issued in two parts.

E 196 a NEW BURLINGTON GALLERIES. Exhibition of 20th Century German Art. London, July 1938. [Organized by a committee under the chairmanship of Herbert Read as an answer to the exhibition Entartete Kunst, Munich, 1937, (bibl. G 284)]. 2 oils, 1 watercolor, 1 drawing (cat. nos. 49–52) by Feininger.

E 197 SULLIVAN, MRS. CORNELIUS J., GALLERY. Lyonel Feininger: Paintings and Watercolors 1919–1938. New York, Nov. 7 (8?) – 26, 1938. Arranged by Mrs. Sullivan and Karl Nierendorf, supplemented by address by Dr. Alexander Dorner, Nov. 9;

21 oils, 24 watercolors and drawings; reviewed *Art Digest* 37:13 Nov. 19, 1938.

E 198 MILWAUKEE ART INSTITUTE. Watercolors of Lyonel Feininger. Nov. 1938. Article in its *Bulletin* 13:2 Nov. 1938; *Art News* 37:17 Nov. 12, 1938.

E 199 MUSEUM OF MODERN ART. Bauhaus 1919–1928. New York, Dec. 7, 1938 – Jan. 30, 1939. Seven oil paintings; seven reproductions; biographical note.

E 200 BROOKLYN MUSEUM. International Exhibition of Watercolors: 10th Biennial. Brooklyn, Mar. 18 – Apr. 30, 1939. No. 45–46 by Feininger (1 ill.).

E 201 MUSEUM OF MODERN ART. Art in Our Time. New York, May 10 – Sept. 30, 1939. One painting, one woodcut; two illustrations; brief note, p. 175, 251.

E 202 SOLOMON R. GUGGENHEIM FOUNDATION. Art of Tomorrow. 5th revised catalog. New York, 1939. Permanent collection opening June 1, 1939. No. 466–470 by Feininger, biographical note, p. 177–178.

E 203 CARNEGIE INSTITUTE. International Exhibition of Contemporary Painting. Pittsburgh, Oct. 19 – Dec. 10, 1939. No. 92 by Feininger.

E 204 INSTITUTE OF MODERN ART. Contemporary German Art. Boston, Nov. 2 – Dec. 9, 1939. No. 9–13 by Feininger; biographical note, p. 14.

E 205 THAYER ART GALLERY. [Feininger, one-man show]. Lawrence, Kansas, University of Kansas, 1939.

E 206 LOUISIANA STATE UNIVERSITY. DEPARTMENT OF FINE ARTS. [Feininger, one-man show]. Baton Rouge, La., 1939. Exhibition later sent to Berea Art College (Berea, Ky.).

E 207 MINT MUSEUM. [Lyonel Feininger, Josef Albers, Frank London]. Charlotte, N. C., 1940. "Memories of Youth," 8 oils, 8 watercolors.

E 208 FARNSWORTH MUSEUM. Paintings by Lyonel Feininger. Wellesley, Mass., Wellesley College, Jan. 10 – Feb. 3, 1940. No. 1–25 (oils), no. 26–41 (watercolors and drawings).

E 209 HATFIELD, DALZELL, GALLERIES. Fantasy in watercolor, by Lyonel Feininger. Los Angeles, Jan. 31 – Feb. 18, 1940. Biographical notes; 1 ill.

E 210 KALAMAZOO INSTITUTE OF ARTS. [Feininger]. Kalamazoo, Mich., Feb. 4, 1940. Listed in bibl. E 14; also San Francisco Museum of Art, 1940.

E 211 BUCHHOLZ GALLERIES. Landmarks in modern German art. New York, Apr. 2–27, 1940. No. 3–4 by Feininger works; preface by P. T. Rathbone.

E 212 STENDAHL GALLERIES. Feininger Watercolors. Hollywood, Apr. 22 – May 11, 1940. Announcement does not list works.

E 213 ST. ETIENNE GALERIE. American Abstract Art. New York, May 22 – June 12, 1940. No. 14–16 by Feininger; note by G. L. K. Morris.

E 214 LILIENFELD GALLERIES. American Contemporary Paintings. New York, Nov. 12–30, 1940. No. 8–13 by Feininger.

E 215 WHITNEY MUSEUM OF AMERICAN ART. Annuals [Contemporary American Painting and or Sculpture, Watercolors and Drawings]. New York, 1941–1955. Feininger continuously represented, e.g. Jan. 15 – Feb. 19 (2 works); Nov. 24, 1942 – Jan. 6, 1943 (1 work) etc. Also special shows, e.g. E 216.

E 216 WHITNEY MUSEUM OF AMERICAN ART. This is Our City. New York, Mar. 1941.

E 217 BUCHHOLZ and WILLARD GALLERIES. Lyonel Feininger. New York, Mar. 11–29, 1941. No. 1–42 (oils), no. 43–85 (watercolors); 8 ill.; preface by P. T. Rathbone; excerpts from letters (1905–1914); brief bibliography. Also "reported" but not in catalog: Arranged together with the Detroit Institute of Arts, July–August, 1941.

E 218 CORCORAN GALLERY OF ART. 17th Biennial. Washington, D. C., Mar. 23 – May 4, 1941. No. 17 by Feininger (ill.).

E 219 LA PINTURA CONTEMPORANEA NORTE AMERICANA. [Latin American circulating show]. May–Dec. 1941. An oil and watercolor by Feininger (1 ill.); organized by New York museums for the Coordinator of Inter-American Affairs, Washington, D. C.

E 220 KUH, KATHERINE, GALLERY. Lyonel Feininger. Chicago, Ill., May 5 (opening) 1941.

E 221 TILDEN-THURBER GALLERY. [Feininger Oils and Watercolors]. Providence, R. I., Oct. 27 – Nov. 1, 1941. Reported *Art News* 40:9 Nov. 15, 1941.

E 222 BUCHHOLZ GALLERY. Seventy-five Selected Prints. New York, Dec. 8–27, 1941. Included Feininger work or works, in this and successive "Christmas shows."

E 223 FEDERATION OF MODERN PAINTERS AND SCULPTORS. [Circuit Exhibition for the Southern States]. Jan. 1942. Reported to include Feininger.

E 224 JEWISH CLUB. [Group Show]. Detroit, Feb. 1942. Two oils by Feininger.

E 225 WORCESTER ART MUSEUM. [Decade of American Painting, 1930–1940]. Feb. – Mar. 1942.

E 226 WILDENSTEIN GALLERY. Federation of Modern Painters and Sculptors Second Annual. New York, May 21 – June 10, 1942. Plate 17: *Afternoon Light* by Feininger.

E 227 BUCHHOLZ GALLERY. Aspects of Modern Drawing. New York, May 5–30, 1942. No. 11–12 by Feininger.

E 228 METROPOLITAN MUSEUM OF ART. Artists for Victory. New York, Dec. 1942. Third purchase prize for *Gelmeroda XIII*.

E 229 BUCHHOLZ GALLERY. Seventy-five Selected Prints. New York, Dec. 8–26, 1942. No. 12–13 by Feininger.

E 230 BUCHHOLZ GALLERY. Lyonel Feininger: Recent Paintings & Watercolors. New York, Jan. 26 – Feb. 13, 1943. Paintings (no. 1–16), watercolors (no. 17–36); 4 ill. (drawings); collections.

E 231 WILLARD GALLERY. Fantasy in Feininger. New York, Jan. 26 – Feb. 13, 1943. 24 works (oils and watercolors); ill.

E 232 LILIENFELD GALLERIES. A Group of American Artists. New York, Feb. 1–27, 1943. No. 9–14 by Feininger.

E 233 CORCORAN GALLERY OF ART. 18th Biennial. Washington, D. C., Mar. 21 – May 2, 1943. *Cathedral* by Feininger.

E 234 PUMA GALLERY. Seven Moderns: Lyonel Feininger, Max Weber, Puma [etc.] New York, May 10 (opening), 1943.

E 235 WALKER ART CENTER. 92 Artists. Milwaukee, June 3 – July 1, 1943. *The Church* by Feininger (p. 15).

E 236 WILDENSTEIN GALLERY. Federation of Modern Painters and Sculptors Annual. New York, June 1943. 62 moderns including Feininger's "Mill in Spring."

E 237 M. H. de YOUNG MEMORIAL MUSEUM. Meet the Artist. San Francisco, 1943. Portrait (no. 62), ill., note (p. 54).

E 238 WHITNEY MUSEUM OF AMERICAN ART. Contemporary American Painting. New York, Nov. 1943. Included *Coast of Nevermore.*

E 239 NIERENDORF GALLERY. Feininger: Paintings, Watercolors, Drawings. New York, Nov. 1–20, 1943. 45 works.

E 240 BUCHHOLZ GALLERY. Early Works by Contemporary Artists. New York, Nov. 16 – Dec. 4, 1943. No. 12 by Feininger.

E 241 MUSEUM OF MODERN ART. Romantic Painting in America. New York, Nov. 17, 1943 – Feb. 6, 1944. Two works (illustrated).

E 242 CINCINNATI ART MUSEUM. Abstract and Surrealist Art in the United States. Feb. 8 – Mar. 12, 1944. No. 3 by Feininger. Shown at Denver (Mar. 26 – Apr. 23), Seattle (May 7 – June 10), Santa Barbara (June–July), San Francisco (July). Catalog published by the San Francisco Museum.

E 243 BUCHHOLZ GALLERY. Contemporary Prints. New York, Dec. 10–30, 1943. Included Feininger.

E 244 HATFIELD, DALZELL, GALLERIES. Fantasy in Watercolor by Lyonel Feininger. Los Angeles, Jan. 3 – Feb. 16, 1944. Lists 18 works (1 ill.), biographical note.

E 244 a LEICESTER MUSEUM AND ART GALLERY. Mid-European Art. Leicester (England), Feb. 5–7, 1944. Catalog preface, Hans Hess, mentions Feininger. Cover: woodcut by Feininger; 4 oils, 4 watercolors, 6 graphics (no. 1–14).

E 245 BUCHHOLZ GALLERY. Lyonel Feininger. Recent Watercolors and Drawings. New York, Feb. 8–26, 1944. 32 watercolors, 13 drawings (1940–1943); 4 ill.; collections.

E 246 MUSEUM OF MODERN ART. Modern Drawings. New York, Feb. 16 – May 10, 1944. Two works, 1 ill.

E 247 MUSEUM OF MODERN ART. Art in Progress. New York, May 24–Oct. 15, 1944. *Steamer "Odin"* (ill., p. 78); note (p. 220).

E 248 CARNEGIE INSTITUTE. Painting in the United States. Pittsburgh, Oct. 12 – Dec. 10, 1944. No. 112: *Dunes II.*

E 249 MUSEUM OF MODERN ART. Lyonel Feininger. New York, Oct. 24, 1944 – Jan. 14, 1945. See bibl. E 14. Museum exhibition (no. 264) included 65 oils, 77 graphics, with 8 works not listed in the catalog (9 oils and 26 graphics listed in the catalog were not exhibited). Also circulated (Feb. 1945 – May 1946) in available group of 35 oils and 38 graphics.

E 250 BUCHHOLZ GALLERY. The Blue Four: Feininger, Jawlensky, Kandinsky, Paul Klee. New York, Oct. 31 – Nov. 25, 1944. No. 1–19 by Feininger (1 ill.); quotes Jan. 13, 1924 letter.

E 251 CARLEN GALLERY. Watercolors by Feininger. Philadelphia, Dec. 1, 1944 – Jan. 11, 1945. Typewritten list of 53 works (1909–1944).

E 252 BROOKLYN MUSEUM. International Exhibition of Watercolors: 13th Biennial. Brooklyn, Mar. 8 – May 29, 1945. No. 48 by Feininger.

E 253 ST. LOUIS CITY ART MUSEUM. Lyonel Feininger. St. Louis, Sept. 1 – Oct. 14, 1945. One of the circulating versions of the Museum of Modern Art show, (bibl. E 249) with 14 paintings.

E 254 BUCHHOLZ GALLERY. Contemporary Prints. New York, Dec. 4–29, 1945. Included Feininger.

E 255 LOUISVILLE UNIVERSITY. ART STUDENTS LEAGUE. [Second Feininger Exhibition]. 1946. Details not known. The same group put on "the first one-man modern" at the Speed Museum, Louisville, Ky. in 1938.

E 256 BUCHHOLZ GALLERY. Lyonel Feininger: Recent Paintings, Watercolors, New York, Jan. 29 – Feb. 23, 1946. No. 1–13 (oils), no. 14–46 (watercolors); 5 ill. (drawings).

E 257 WILLARD GALLERY. Figures by Feininger. New York, Jan. 29. – Feb. 23, 1946. No. 1–9 (oils), no. 10–36 (watercolors).

E 258 BUCHHOLZ GALLERY. Carved in Stone. New York, May 27 – June 22, 1946. Part I: "Sculpture" (list does not include Feininger) – II: "Work by" includes Feininger but may not be solely sculpture.

E 258 a WALKER ART CENTER. Survey of Watercolor – U.S.A. from 1870 to 1946. [Latin America, Spring 1946 etc.]. Not an American show but prepared by the Walker Art Center for a circulating tour. Variously reported as a "six months" to a "five-year" tour sponsored by the Coordinator of Inter-American Affairs, Washington, D. C.

E 259 CARNEGIE INSTITUTE. Painting in the United States. Pittsburgh, Oct. 10 – Dec. 8, 1946. No. 120: *Moon in Dusk.*

E 260 BUCHHOLZ GALLERY. Contemporary Prints. New York, Dec. 10–28, 1946. Included Feininger.

E 261 WILLARD GALLERY. Selections. New York, Mar. 4–29, 1947. No. 1–2 by Feininger.

E 262 CORCORAN GALLERY OF ART. 20th Biennial. New York, Mar. 30 – May 11, 1947. Included a Feininger.

E 263 BROOKLYN MUSEUM. International Exhibition of Watercolor: 14th Biennial. Brooklyn, Apr. 16 – June 8, 1947. No. 18 by Feininger.

E 264 SEATTLE ART MUSEUM. [Paintings by Feininger?]. May 7 – June 1, 1947. Unclarified data on spring exhibition noted in 1947 annual report.

E 265 BUCHHOLZ GALLERY. Drawings by Contemporary Painters and Sculptors. New York, May 28 – June 21, 1947. No. 15–17 by Feininger.

E 266 CARNEGIE INSTITUTE. Painting in the United States. Pittsburgh. Oct. 9 – Dec. 7, 1947. No. 283 by Feininger.

E 267 CHICAGO ART INSTITUTE. Abstract and Surrealist Art. Chicago, Nov. 6, 1947 – Jan 11, 1948. Included a Feininger (reported Dec. 1947 *Bulletin*).

E 268 WILLARD GALLERY. Seven Years. New York, Dec. 6–31, 1947. No. 21 by Feininger.

E 269 BUCHHOLZ GALLERY. Lyonel Feininger: Recent Work. New York, Mar. 2–20, 1948. 17 oils, 23 watercolors (1945–47); 13 ill.

E 270 CINCINNATI MODERN ART SOCIETY. Abstract and Surrealist Art. Apr. 9 – May 2, 1948. Included a

Feininger watercolor. Exhibition circulated by the American Federation of Arts and previously shown at Chicago (Nov. 1947).

E 271 BUCHHOLZ GALLERY. Drawings and Watercolors from the Collection of John S. Newberry, Jr. New York, May 27 – June 11, 1948. No. 14 by Feininger (ill.).

E 272 ST. LOUIS CITY ART MUSEUM. St. Louis Collection. Sept. 20 – Oct. 25, 1948. Included Feininger's *Dunes* (Pulitzer Collection).

E 273 CHICAGO ART INSTITUTE. 59th Watercolor Biennial. Nov. 4, 1948 – Jan. 2, 1949. Included Feininger.

E 274 CORCORAN GALLERY OF ART. 21st Biennial: Washington, D. C., Mar. 27 – May 1, 1949. One work by Feininger.

E 275 SAN FRANCISCO MUSEUM OF ART. New Paintings by Feininger. Apr. 4 – May 1, 1949.

E 276 INSTITUTE OF CONTEMPORARY ART. Jacques Villon – Lyonel Feininger. Boston, opening Oct. 7, 1949. No. 45–63 (oils), no. 64–86 (watercolors); 17 ill. (port.). Also E 277. See bibl. E 15.

E 277 PHILLIPS GALLERY. Paintings by Jacques Villon – Lyonel Feininger. Washington, D. C., Dec. 11, 1949 – Jan. 10, 1950. See bibl. E 15. Later shown at Delaware Art Center.

E 278 HOFSTRA COLLEGE. Lyonel Feininger. Hempstead, N.Y., Feb. 16 – Mar. 4, 1950. Oils (8), watercolors (6), and graphics.

E 279 GREISS GALLERY. Woodcuts by Feininger [and works by Weber, Lorian, Pace]. [New York, 1950?]. Four graphics (1 ill.).

E 280 UNIVERSITY OF ILLINOIS. Contemporary American Painting. Urbana, Feb. 26 – Apr. 2, 1950. No. 40 by Feininger (plate 89), biographical note (p. 172–173).

E 281 BUCHHOLZ GALLERY. Lyonel Feininger. New York, Apr. 11–29, 1950. No. 1–20 (oils), no. 21–45 (watercolors), 12 ill. On cover: "A collection of drawings is shown at the Schaefer Galleries," see bibl. E 282.

E 282 SCHAEFER GALLERIES. Lyonel Feininger: Drawings. New York, Apr. 11–29, 1950.

E 283 VIRGINIA MUSEUM OF ART. American Painting 1950. Richmond, Apr. 22 – June 4, 1950. Included *Courtyard III* (ill.); exhibit and catalog by J. J. Sweeney.

E 284 METROPOLITAN MUSEUM OF ART. 100 Painters of the 20th Century . . . from the Collection. New York, Summer 1950. Colorplate of *The Church* (p. 94). Preface by R. B. Hale.

E 285 BUCHHOLZ GALLERY. Contemporary Drawings. New York, Sept. 26 – Oct. 14, 1950. No. 19–20 by Feininger.

E 286 POMONA COLLEGE. [Feininger Exhibition]. Claremont, Cal., Oct. 1950. Arranged by A. J. Schardt.

E 287 CARNEGIE INSTITUTE. International Exhibition of Paintings. Pittsburgh, Oct. 19 – Dec. 21, 1950. Plate 2: *Houses by the River*, awarded second prize at the first postwar international.

E 288 MUSEUM OF MODERN ART. Abstract Painting and Sculpture in America. New York, Jan. 23 – Mar. 25, 1951. Three oils (illustrated), biographical note.

E 289 UNIVERSITY OF ILLINOIS. Contemporary American Painting. Urbana, Ill., Mar. 4 – Apr. 15, 1951. No. 41: *Coast of Nevermore* (ill.).

E 290 CORCORAN GALLERY OF ART. 22nd Biennial, Washington, D. C., Apr. 1 – May 13, 1951. Included a Feininger.

E 291 MINNESOTA UNIVERSITY. ART DEPARTMENT. 40 American Painters 1940–1950. Minneapolis, May? 1951. Feininger illustrated; chronology. Review *Art Digest* Aug. 1951.

E 292 LINCOLN, MASS. [Reported as "a small improvised exhibition to celebrate Feininger's 80th birthday near Lincoln"]. July 1951.

E 292 a CITY OF YORK ART GALLERY. Feininger. An exhibition of forty Watercolors and Drawings. York (England), Oct. 1951. Catalog preface by Hans Hess, 1 col. ill. (titlepage): *Manhattan Tower*, 1948. This is the same exhibition that was organized by the Kestner-Gesellschaft, Hanover (bibl. G 242). Was later shown in Cambridge and at the A.I.A. gallery, London (Jan. 1952).

E 293 CRANBROOK ACADEMY OF ART MUSEUM. Mr. and Mrs. Harry L. Winston Collection. Bloomfield Hills, Mich., Nov. 8–25 1951. No. 6–7 by Feininger.

E 294 CLEVELAND MUSEUM OF ART. The Work of Lyonel Feininger. Nov. 2 – Dec. 9, 1951. Major retrospective of 247 works sponsored jointly by the Print Club. See bibl. E 16. 44 oils, 83 watercolors and drawings, 75 woodcuts, 1 portfolio ("12 Holzschnitte"), 19 etchings and drypoints, 11 lithographs, 2 comicstrips; 30 ill.

E 295 SÃO PAULO, MUSEU DE ARTE MODERNA. I Bienal. São Paulo, Brazil, fall, 1951–52. American section selected by A. C. Ritchie; included three oils by Feininger, no. 18–20.

E 296 MINNESOTA UNIVERSITY. German Expressionism. Minneapolis, 1951. No. 22–24 by Feininger, biographical note.

E 297 BROOKLYN MUSEUM. Revolution and Tradition. Brooklyn, N.Y., Nov. 15, 1951 – Jan. 6, 1952. No. 4 (ill.). 33 by Feininger; text by J. I. H. Baur.

E 298 BUCHHOLZ GALLERY. Sculpture by Painters. New York, Nov. 20 – Dec. 15, 1951. No. 31, *Angel*.

E 299 GALLERY OF CONTEMPORARY ART. Lyonel Feininger – John Tunnard. Bellevue, Washington, Mar. 8–30, 1952. Unsigned preface, 1 ill.

E 300 CURT VALENTIN GALLERY (formerly BUCHHOLZ). Lyonel Feininger. New York, Mar. 18 – Apr. 12, 1952. 80th anniversary show; 48 works (26 oils, 22 watercolors, 2 drawings; 16 ill.).

E 301 WALKER ART CENTER. Collection of Mr. and Mrs. Roy Neuberger. Minneapolis, May – Aug. 1952. Two Feiningers (1 ill.).

E 302 WHITNEY MUSEUM OF AMERICAN ART. Edith and Milton Lowenthal Collection, New York, Oct. 1 – Nov. 2, 1952. Also shown at the Walker Art Center, Minneapolis, Nov. 26, 1952 – Jan. 17, 1953. No. 28–30 by Feininger (1 ill.).

E 302 a CITY OF YORK ART GALLERY. The Expressionists. An Exhibition of Works by the German Expressionists from One Private Collection. York (England), Oct. 1952. 4 watercolors, 1 drawing, 12 graphics by Feininger. Was shown in several English towns and in Scotland with the same catalog.

E 303 CARNEGIE INSTITUTE. International Exhibition of Contemporary Painting. Pittsburgh, Oct. 6 – Dec. 14, 1952. No. 84 (ill.), biographical note.

E 304 PALMER HOUSE. Lyonel Feininger Watercolors. Chicago, Nov. 6 – Dec. 6, 1952.

E 305 BUCHHOLZ GALLERY (CURT VALENTIN). Drawings by Contemporary Painters and Sculptors. New York, Dec. 16 – Jan. 10, 1953. No. 16–17 by Feininger (1 ill.).

E 306 ALLEN MEMORIAL ART MUSEUM. Paintings from the College and University Collections. Oberlin, Jan. 20 – Feb. 15, 1953. Reproduces Feininger in *Bulletin* 10:43–50 (1952–53).

E 307 WILDENSTEIN GALLERY. Landmarks in American Art, 1670–1950. New York, Feb. 26 – Mar. 28, 1953. No. 47 by Feininger (ill.), brief note; benefit show for the American Federation of Arts.

E 308 METROPOLITAN MUSEUM OF ART. Edward Root Collection. New York, Feb. – Mar. 1953. Feininger reproduced in *Bulletin* 11:153–163 Feb. 1953.

E 309 BROOKLYN MUSEUM. International Exhibition of Watercolors: 17th Biennial. New York, May 13 – June 21, 1953. No. 123 by Feininger.

E 310 MARGARET BROWN GALLERY. Lyonel Feininger. Boston, Dec. 14, 1953 – Jan. 9, 1954. On announcement: Courtesy Curt Valentin Gallery, N.Y.

E 311 CURT VALENTIN GALLERY. Lyonel Feininger: Recent Paintings and Watercolors (1951–1954). New York, Mar. 30 – Apr. 24, 1954. No. 1–24 (oils), no. 25–55 (watercolors, 24 ill.) text by Mark Tobey.

E 312 BUCHHOLZ GALLERY (CURT VALENTIN). Contemporary Paintings and Sculpture. New York, Sept. 1954. No. 9 by Feininger.

E 313 CURT VALENTIN GALLERY (Formerly BUCHHOLZ). In Memory of Curt Valentin, 1902–1954: an Exhibition of Modern Masterpieces lent by American Museums. New York, Oct. 5–30, 1954. "The Bridge II," 1912 (ill.).

E 314 ALLEN H. HITE ART INSTITUTE. The Feiningers of Louisville. Louisville, Ky., Oct. 18 – Nov. 13, 1954. Watercolors (9), etchings (2), woodcuts (21), lithographs (1); text by C. G.; show held in the University Library (See bibl. E 117).

E 315 WHITNEY MUSEUM OF AMERICAN ART. Collection of Mr. and Mrs. Roy Neuberger. New York, Nov. 1954. No. 28–29 by Feininger; also shown at the Chicago Arts Club, University of California Art Gallery, San Francisco Museum, St. Louis Art Museum, Cincinnati Art Museum (Winter 1954 – Sept. 1955).

E 316 BUCHHOLZ GALLERY (CURT VALENTIN). Der Blaue Reiter. New York, Dec. 7, 1954 – Jan. 8, 1955. No. 4 by Feininger (ill.).

E 317 BUSCH-REISINGER MUSEUM. Artists of the Blaue Reiter. Cambridge, Mass., Jan. 21 – Feb. 24, 1955. No. 4–5 by Feininger (1912–1914).

E 318 ASSOCIATED AMERICAN ARTISTS GALLERIES. Federation of Modern Painters and Sculptors: Painting Section. New York, Feb. 14–26, 1955. No. 31: *Weird Moon* (ill.), biographical note.

E 319 BROOKLYN MUSEUM. International Exhibition of Watercolors: 18th Biennial. New York, May 4 – June 12, 1955. No. 172 by Feininger.

E 320 SAN FRANCISCO MUSEUM. Art in the 20th Century. San Francisco, Cal., June 17 – July 10, 1955. Four works by Feininger.

E 321 CARNEGIE INSTITUTE. 40th International Exhibition of Contemporary Painting. Pittsburgh, Oct. 13 – Dec. 18, 1955. No. 99 (plate 31), biographical note.

E 322 MUSEUM OF MODERN ART CIRCULATING EXHIBITION: Three Modern Painters: Feininger, Hartley, Beckmann. Nov. 1955 (etc.). Included 6 Feininger paintings and toys Started Nov. 7 at Brooks Art Gallery, Memphis, Tenn., subsequently North Carolina, Texas, Kentucky, New Hampshire, Florida, Virginia, Minnesota, Florida, Georgia, Tennessee.

E 323 RIVERSIDE MUSEUM. Federation of Modern Painters and Sculptors: 14th Annual. New York, Dec. 1955. No. 31 by Feininger (ill), biographical note.

E 324 AMERICAN FEDERATION OF ARTS. Pioneers of American Abstract Art [a Circulating Exhibition]. Dec. 1955 – Jan. 1957. No. 11–12 by Feininger, biographical note. Shown at Atlanta Public Library, Dec. 1955; then Louisiana State Museum, J. B. Speed Museum, Lawrence Museum, G. T. Hunter Gallery, Rose Fried Gallery, N.Y.

E 325 WILLARD GALLERY. Lyonel Feininger Exhibition. New York, Feb. 1 – Mar. 3, 1956. No. 1–14 (oils), no. 15–33 (watercolors) from 1940–1955; 4 ill., preface.

E 326 METROPOLITAN MUSEUM OF ART. [Memorial Exhibition]: Feininger, Kuhn, Kuniyoshi, Marin, Nordfeldt. New York, Feb. 24 – Apr. 29, 1956. Including oils (10), watercolors (2), lithographs (3), drawings (3), etchings (2). Reviewed *New Yorker* 39:119-120, Mar. 10, 1956.

E 327 FORT WORTH ART CENTER. Feininger: a Memorial Exhibition of his work from Fort Worth Collections. Ft. Worth, Tex. Mar. 6 – Apr. 1, 1956. Oils, watercolors, woodcuts (4 each).

E 327 a TATE GALLERY. Modern Art in the United States. A selection from the collection of the Museum of Modern Art, New York, London, Jan. 5 – Feb. 12, 1956. Arranged by the Tate Gallery and the Arts Council of Great Britain in collaboration with the Museum's international program. Introduction and preface by John Rothenstein and Philip James. Text by René d'Harnoncourt and William S. Liebermann. Feininger p. 14–15, 41–42 passim. 4 oils and 5 graphics by Feininger, no. 11–13, 130–134.

E 327 b TATE GALLERY. A Hundred Years of German Painting 1850–1950. London, Apr. – June 1956. Arranged by the government of the Federal Republic of Germany. Preface by John Rothenstein, introduction by Alfred Hentzen. Feininger: p. 12. 4 oils and two drawings by Feininger, no. 36–40. Front cover illustrates Feininger *Church of the Minorites II*, in color. Reviewed by Hans Hess, *Burlington Magazine*, 98 no. 639:204, June 1956.

E 328 AMERICAN FEDERATION OF ARTS. German Watercolors, Drawings and Prints [a Circulating Exhibition]. New York [etc.], 1956. Sponsored by the

Federal Republic of Germany, preface by L. Reygers; no. 19–21 by Feininger (1 ill.). Shown in New York at the Borgenicht and Weyhe Galleries (reviewed *Art News* 55:54, June 1956).

E 329 WALKER ART CENTER. Expressionism, 1900–1955. Minneapolis, 1956. Illustrates *Trumpeter in the Village* (1915). Also circulated to Boston, San Francisco, Cincinnati, Baltimore.

E 330 WILLARD GALLERY. Gables by Lyonel Feininger. New York, Nov. 27 – Dec. 29, 1956. Based on one theme (1921–1954); 32 works in all media; "pencil sketches" (1921–1922); text by Julia Feininger.

E 331 ROSE FRIED GALLERY. Pioneers of American Abstract Art. New York, Dec. 1956 – Jan. 9, 1957. No. 11–12 by Feininger.

E 332 WORLD HOUSE GALLERY. The Struggle for New Form. New York, Jan. 22 – Feb. 23, 1957. No. 23 by Feininger.

E 333 CHICAGO ART INSTITUTE. American Artists Paint the City. Feb.(?) 1957. Reviewed by A. S. Weller in *Arts* 31:3–14 Feb. 1957: "American show at the Institute combined with the 'City' exhibit from the Venice Biennial (bibl. G 294 a)."

E 334 KNOEDLER & COMPANY. [The Louise and Joseph Pulitzer Collection]. New York, Apr. 9 – May 4, 1957. Later exhibited at Fogg Art Museum, Cambridge, Mass., May 16 – Sept. 15. (see bibl. E 55).

E 335 MINNEAPOLIS INSTITUTE OF ARTS. Gables by Lyonel Feininger. Apr. 10 – May 12, 1957.

E 336 SÃO PAULO. MUSEU DE ARTE MODERNA. IV Bienal. O Arte do Bauhaus, Exposição oficial da Alemanha. São Paulo, [Fall 1957]. Preface by L. Grote, 1 ill., biographical note.

E 337 MUSEUM OF MODERN ART. German Art of the Twentieth Century. New York, Nov. 1957. No. 37–42 by Feininger, 3 colorplates, 1 ill. (see bibl. E 58).

E 338 FORT WORTH ART CENTER. The Iron Horse in Art. Fort Worth, Tex., Jan. – Mar. 1958. *Locomotive with the Big Wheel*, 1915 (ill.).

E 339 WHITNEY MUSEUM OF AMERICAN ART. Nature in Abstraction. New York, Jan. 14 – Mar. 16, 1958. *Lunar Web*, 1951 (col. pl. 62), biographical note (p. 35); preface by J. I. H. Baur. Also shown 1958: Phillips Gallery, Fort Worth Art Center, Los Angeles County Museum, San Francisco Museum, Walker Art Center; and in 1959: St. Louis City Art Museum.

E 340 BUSCH-REISINGER MUSEUM. Lyonel Feininger [paintings of harbors, ships and the sea]. Cambridge, Mass., Oct. 6 – Nov. 8, 1958.

E 341 WILLARD GALLERY. Feininger. New York, Mar. 6 – Apr. 12, 1958. 25 watercolors, 1939–1953, 4 ill. Also Dec. 1958.

E 342 CARNEGIE INSTITUTE. 1896–1955: Retrospective Exhibition of Painting from Previous Internationals. Pittsburgh, Pa., Dec. 5, 1958 – Feb. 8, 1959. Four paintings (1 ill.); biographical note.

E 343 DEUTSCHER KUNSTRAT. German Graphic Art of the 20th Century. Canada, 1958–1959. A circulating exhibition for Canada arranged by the Federal Republic of Germany and the Deutscher Kunstrat. Feininger, no. 18–20 (woodcuts), brief note, Catalog (32 p.) has preface by D. N. Buchanan & A. Jarvis (National Gallery of Canada), and by Alfred Hentzen.

E 344 ADDISON GALLERY OF AMERICAN ART. The American Line: 100 Years of Drawings. [Andover, Mass., Phillips Academy, 1959]. Catalog for exhibit circulated by the American Federation of Arts. No. 92 by Feininger (ill.); brief note.

E 345 MARLBOROUGH GALLERY. Art in Revolt. Germany 1905–1925. London, opening Oct. 1959. Preface by Will Grohmann. 3 oils by Feininger, no. 44–45 a, 3 ill. p. 110–112.

E 346 SAN FRANCISCO MUSEUM OF ART. Lyonel Feininger Memorial Exhibition. Opening in San Francisco, Nov. 5 – Dec. 13, 1959. Exhibition arranged by the Cleveland Museum of Modern Art. See E 350.

E 347 WILLARD GALLERY. Lyonel Feininger. Watercolors, from the Collection of Mrs. Julia Feininger. New York, Feb. 2 – Feb. 27, 1960. 25 watercolors, 4 ill., dating from 1922.

E 348 AMERICAN ACADEMY OF ARTS AND LETTERS – NATIONAL INSTITUTE OF ARTS AND LETTERS. A Change of Sky: Paintings by Americans who have worked abroad. New York, Mar. 4 – Apr. 3, 1960. No. 10 by Feininger (ill.).

E 349 FAIRWEATHER HARDIN GALLERY. Feininger watercolors. Chicago, Apr. 5–30, 1960. Illustrated announcement refers to works from the Willard Gallery and the Reverend Laurence Feininger ("exhibited for the first time").

E 350 CLEVELAND MUSEUM OF ART. Lyonel Feininger Memorial Exhibition 1959–1961. For catalog see bibl. E 17 a. Shown at Cleveland: 72 oils, 53 watercolors, 12 drawings, over 100 prints and watercolor drawings. Also in educational corridor: The relief print with special reference to the work of Feininger. Material specially selected "as not exhibited before." Shown (with same catalog): San Francisco (Nov. 5 – Dec. 13), Minneapolis (Jan. 5 – Feb. 7), Cleveland (Feb. 18 – Mar. 20), Buffalo (Apr. 8 – May 8), Boston (May 19 – June 26). A section of this exhibition consisting of 39 oils, 21 watercolors, 6 drawings shown in England at York (Oct. 6 – Nov. 5) and London (Nov. 16 – Dec. 17), with reduced catalog. Catalog nos. 1–2 shown only in England. Also shown: 2 oils, 1 watercolor, 21 watercolor drawings and toys not in catalog. Also in Germany, enlarged exhibition: 62 oils, 157 watercolors, drawings and graphics, at Hamburg (Jan. 21 – Mar. 15, 1961), Essen (Mar. 15 – May 7), and Baden-Baden (May 14 – June 26), with new catalog.

340

Index to the Bibliography

344

LIST OF ILLUSTRATIONS

Text Illustrations

346

PHOTOGRAPH ACKNOWLEDGMENTS

Amato, Washington 282; Angle, Montgomery 286, 482; Annau, Glasgow 98, 150, 230; Arni Studio, New York 195; Baker, New York 23, 25, 32, 44, 53, 65, 70, 84, 99, 110, 112, 118, 119, 127, 129, 135, 136, 141, 143, 144, 147, 160, 169, 173, 177, 182, 189, 197, 204, 211, 229, 235, 238, 239, 240, 241, 243, 244, 256, 269, 276, 290, 292, 293, 294, 296, 304, 315, 330, 331, 354, 355, 356, 357, 362, 371, 377, 378, 381, 385, 386, 393, 397, 401, 402, 403, 409, 410, 411, 414, 418, 419, 420, 421, 423, 427, 428, 432, 434, 490, 497, 500, 502, 512, 518, 539; Bayerische Staatsgemäldesammlungen, München 327; Borg, Öreboro 300; Brugger, Stuttgart 196; Burstein, Boston 101, 113; Byers, New York 285; Catcheside, New York 96; The Art Institute of Chicago 509; Cleveland Museum of Art, Cleveland 425; Commercial Photographie Studio, Toronto 178; Danz, Halle 333, 339; Detroit Institute of Arts 117; Engelskirchen, Krefeld 170, 236, 384; Epha, Duisburg 200; Erfurth, Gaienhofen 61; Feininger, Andreas, New York 365; Feldweg, Stuttgart-Degerloch 369; Fine Arts Associates, New York 298; Fischer, Düsseldorf 139; Flude Studio, Irwin, Pa. 132; Frequin, Den Haag 220; Graves, Columbus, Ohio 443; The Solomon R. Guggenheim Museum, New York 146, 289, 363, 368, 373, 376; Guniat, Zürich 307; Halbach, Ratingen 156; Hess, Pittsburgh 57; Hessisches Landesmuseum, Darmstadt 302; Hirsch, München 40; Juley, New York 228; Keysselitz Foto-Werbung, München 317; Kittel, Quedlinburg 14, 15, 36, 37, 38, 55, 106, 152, 250; Kleinhempel, Hamburg 335; Klima, Detroit, Mich. 214; Köster, Berlin-Lichterfelde 305; Krütgen, Halle 345; Lerner, New York 528; Lessinger, Brooklyn 114, 252; Moholy, Dessau 270, 288; Molzohn-Foto, Altheim 45; Museum of Fine Arts, Boston 322; Museum of Modern Art, New York 101, 124, 194, 210, 219, 246, 247, 248, 351; The North Carolina Museum of Art 163; Obermire, Cincinnati 380, 451, Öffentliche Kunstsammlung, Basel 251, 262, 352; Paramount, Springfield, Mass. 343; Phillips Studio, Philadelphia, Penna. 309; Plaget Studio, St. Louis 100; Rainford, New York 366; Rheinisches Bildarchiv, Köln 174, 254, 341; Rosenblum, New York 171, 323; Savage, St. Louis 109; Serisawa, Los Angeles 115; Schiff, New York 162, 537; Schuch, Charlottenburg 199, 216, 358; Soame Studio, Toronto 172; Staatliche Museen zu Berlin 93, 179, 185, 186, 258, 295, 348; Stern, New York 249; Steves, M.-Gladbach 267; Studly, New York 52, 140, 154, 157, 176, 233, 242, 275, 281, 283, 312, 324, 353, 389, 391, 396, 438, 460, 463, 464, 465, 467, 468, 470, 476, 479, 481, 484, 485, 487, 489, 493, 504, 515; Taylor and Dull, New York 458; Toledo Museum of Art, Toledo, Ohio 477; Tweedy, London 79; Van Diemen-Lilienfeld Galleries, New York 435, 440, 462; Wachsmann, New York 49, 75, 77, 83, 93, 95, 99, 111, 125, 145, 149, 151, 155, 161, 165, 167, 169; Witzel, Essen 97, 116, 263.

FOOTNOTES

Childhood in America (pages 1–5)

1. Letter from Karl Feininger, Dec. 12, 1909.
1a. Letter from Julia Feininger to the American publisher, July 13, 1961.
2. Letter from Lyonel Feininger to Alfred H. Barr, Jr., p. 3, in answer to a questionnaire, Aug., 1944 (hereinafter referred to as Barr Q).
3. Letter to Julia, Dec. 9, 1905, from Berlin. Translation.
4. Barr Q., p. 3.
5. Letter to Julia, Jan. 18, 1906, from Berlin. Translation.
6. Letter to Lux, June 27, 1953, from New Haven, Connecticut.
7. Barr Q., p. 1.
8. Letter to Theodore Spicer-Simson, Sept. 18, 1937, from New York.
9. Barr Q., p. 1.
10. Communication from Francis H. Kortheuer, Mar. 3, 1958, to the author.
11. Letter to Lux, Apr. 14, 1943, from New York.
12. Kortheuer, op. cit.
13. Ibid.
14. Letter to Alfred Vance Churchill, June 11, 1890, from Berlin.
15. Barr Q., p. 2.

The Years of Study (pages 6–11)

1. By Fred S. Cozzens.
2. Letter to Lux, July 26, 1948, from Stockbridge, Massachusetts.
3. Letter to Kortheuer.
4. Letter to Lux, July 2, 1946, from Stockbridge, Massachusetts.
5. Letter to Lux, July 26, 1948, from Stockbridge, Massachusetts.
6. Letter to Churchill, May 20, 1890, from Berlin.
7. Letter to Fred Werner, Feb. 23, 1946, from New York.
8. Nov. 16, 1890, from Liège.
9. Edouard Riou, 1833–1900, illustrator of Jules Verne.
10. Oct. 7, 1890.
11. Letter to Churchill, Nov. 16, 1890, from Liège.
12. Churchill Collection.
13. Letter to Churchill, Nov. 24, 1890, from Liège.
14. Ibid.
15. Ibid.
16. Ibid.
17. Letter to Churchill, from Liège.
18. Feb. 23, 1946, from New York.
19. Letter to Churchill, Oct. 6, 1891, from Berlin.
20. Letter to Churchill, Jan. 12, 1892, from Berlin.
21. Ibid.
22. Letter to Churchill, Feb. 17, 1892, from Berlin.

23. Letter to Churchill, Oct. 6, 1891, from Berlin.
24. Ibid.
25. Letter to Churchill, Jan. 12, 1892, from Berlin.
26. Letter to Churchill.
27. Letter to Churchill, June 24, 1893, from Berlin.
28. Ibid.
29. Ibid.

The Caricaturist (pages 12–26)

1. 1894, from Berlin.
2. Feb. 23, 1946, from New York.
3. April 2, 1894, from Berlin.
4. Hermann, p. 123. Translation.
5. Letter to Kortheuer, Apr. 15, 1898, from Berlin.
6. Hermann, op. cit.
7. Letter to Kortheuer, Jan. 30, 1898, from Berlin.
8. Letter to Kortheuer, Feb. 23, 1898, from Berlin.
9. Letter to Churchill, June 24, 1893, from Berlin.
10. April 6, 1894, from Berlin.
11. Post card to Kortheuer, Mar. 10, 1894, from Berlin.
12. Letter to Julia, Feb. 9, 1906, from Berlin. Translation by Julia Feininger. Published in catalogue of Feininger exhibition, Mar. 11–29, 1941, Buchholz Gallery, New York.
13. "Animierkneipe," *Lustige Blätter*, vol. XVII, no. 4.
14. *Lustige Blätter*, vol. XXII, no. 24.
15. Autograph letter of Jan. 19, 1924, sold at Gutekunst & Klipstein, Bern, as Lot 34, Auction 89, May 14, 1958. Translation.
16. Letter to Churchill, April 36 [sic], 1896, from Berlin.
17. Letter to Kortheuer, May 12, 1899, from Berlin.
18. Post card to Kortheuer, Jan. 11, 1903, from Berlin.
19. Post card to Kortheuer, Nov. 28, 1903, from Berlin.

The Emerging Painter (pages 27–43)

1. Letter to Julia, Oct. 8, 1905, from Berlin. Translation.
2. Letter to Julia, Oct. 11, 1905, from Berlin. Translation.
3. Letter to Julia, Oct. 14, 1905, from Berlin. Translation.
4. Letter to Julia, Oct. 16, 1905, from Berlin. Translation.
5. Letter to Julia, Nov. 7, 1905, from Berlin. Translation.
6. Letter to Julia, Oct. 30, 1905, from Berlin. Translation.
7. Letter to Julia, Nov. 1, 1905, from Berlin. Translation.
8. Letter to Julia, Nov. 2, 1905, from Berlin. Translation.
9. April 29, 1906.
10. Letter to Lux, July 2, 1946, from Stockbridge, Massachusetts.
11. Dec. 25, 1912, from Berlin. Translation.
12. Letter to Churchill, June 24, 1893, from Berlin.
13. Ill. in Alfred H. Barr, Jr., *Matisse, His Art and His Public*, New York, 1951, p. 309.
14. Letter to Julia, Aug. 25, 1907. Translation.
15. Letters to Julia, Aug. 27, 28, 29, 1907, from Baabe (Rügen). Translation.

16. Letter to Julia, Sept. 2, 1907, from Baabe or Lobbe (Rügen). Translation.
17. Letter to Lux, July 2, 1946, from Stockbridge, Massachusetts.

New Perspectives (pages 44–58)

1. Letter to Julia, July 4, 1908, from Berlin. Translation.
2. Letter to Julia, Aug. 11, 1909, from Berlin. Translation.
3. Letter to Julia, Aug. 15, 1909, from Berlin. Translation.
4. Letter to Julia, Sept. 2, 1910, from Neppermin.
5. Letter to Julia, Sept. 13, 1910, from Neppermin (Feininger calls it "Nevermind").
6. Letter to Julia, Sept. 14, 1910, from Neppermin.
7. Letter to Julia, Sept. 19, 1910, from Neppermin.
8. Letter to Churchill, Mar. 13, 1913, from Berlin.
9. May 11, 1911. Translation.
10. Letter to Julia, May 12, 1911, from Paris. Translation.
11. Letter to Julia, May 14, 1911, from Paris. Translation.
12. Cf. Hans Platte, "Robert Delaunay und Lyonel Feininger," in *Jahrbuch der Hamburger Kunstsammlungen*, vol. 3, 1958.
13. *Les Tendances Nouvelles*, No. 56. Translation.
14. Ibid.
15. Letter to Julia, Aug. 14, 1912, from Benz. Translation.
16. Letter to Julia, Aug. 16, 1912, from Heringsdorf or nearby. Translation.
17. Letter to Churchill, Mar. 13, 1913, from Berlin.
18. Ill. in Will Grohmann, *Karl Schmidt-Rottluff*, Stuttgart, 1956, p. 195.
19. Dec. 27, 1953, from New York. Translation.
20. Nov. 27, 1912, from Berlin. Translation.
21. Chap. 3. Translation.
22. Possibly *Street in Paris (Pink Sky*, cat. 43).
23. No. 56. Translation.
24. The International Exhibition of Modern Art in New York at the 69th Regiment Armory, 1913.
25. Letter from Ed. A. Cramer, Mar. 2, 1912, from New York.

The Mature Painter (pages 59–86)

1. Letter to Julia, Aug. 20, 1908, from Berlin, Translation.
2. June 4, 1914, from Weimar. Translation.
3. June 15, 1913, from Weimar. Translation.
4. Letter to Julia, May 30, 1913, from Weimar. Translation.
5. Letter to Julia, May 18, 1913, from Weimar. Translation.
6. Ibid.
7. Letter to Julia, Apr. 3, 1913, from Weimar. Translation.
8. Quoted by Feininger in letter to Julia, Sept. 29, 1931, from Deep. Translation.
9. Letter to Mark Tobey, Dec. 2, 1952, from New York.
10. Letter to Julia, Aug. 21, 1913, from Weimar. Translation.
11. Letter to Julia, undated, postmark: Aug. 26, 1913, from Weimar. Translation.
12. *Salons des Indépendants 1911: Société des Artistes Indépendants, Catalogue de la 27me Exposition 1911, Quai d'Orsay Pont de l'Alma, du 21 Avril au 13 Juin* (Published by L'Emancipatrice, Paris). P. 154: "Feininger (Lyonel), né à New York (Etats-Unis).
– – 32, Königstrasse, Zehlendorf – Berlin (Allemagne).
2178 Emeute; 2179 Le pont vert; 2180 Longueil (Nor-

mandie); 2181 La locomotive ancienne; 2182 Le vélocipédistes; 2183 Fin de séance."
13. Received July 17, 1913, from Sindelsdorf, Upper Bavaria. Translation.
14. Letter to Kubin, Sept. 17, 1913, from Weimar. Translation.
15. From "Die Presse und der Herbstsalon," *Sturm*, 1913, pp. 114–115. Translation.
16. Letter to Julia, Sept. 13, 1913, from Weimar. Translation.
17. Letter to Kubin, Oct. 5, 1913, from Berlin. Translation.
18. Letter to Julia, Sept. 15, 1913, from Weimar. Translation.
19. Letter to Kubin, Oct. 5, 1913, from Berlin. Translation.
20. Ibid.
21. Letter to Kubin, Dec. 23, 1913, from Berlin. Translation.
22. Letter to Kubin, Oct. 5, 1913, from Berlin. Translation.
23. Jan. 21, 1913 (letter completed Feb. 8, 1913), from Berlin. Translation.
24. Letter to Julia. Translation.
25. Letter to Julia, June 11, 1914, from Weimar. Translation.
26. Letter to Julia, Sept. 2, 1917, from Berlin. Translation.
27. Lothar Schreyer, *Dokumente und Visionen*, Munich, 1957, p. 25. Translation.
28. From Berlin. Translation.
29. May 14, 1928, from Dessau.
30. "Lyonel Feininger," *Der Cicerone*, vol. XVI, 1924, No. 4, p. 168.
31. Schreyer, op. cit., pp. 19–20. Translation.
32. May 4, 1913, from Weimar. Translation.
33. Letter to Julia, Aug. 15, 1917, from Berlin. Translation.
34. Letter to Kubin, Sept. 28, 1916, from Berlin. Translation.
35. Jan. 15, 1915, from Berlin. Translation.
36. June 21, 1914, from Weimar. Translation.
37. Letter to Julia, Sept. 1, 1917, from Berlin. Translation.

The Bauhaus Years – Weimar (pages 87–107)

1. *Staatliches Bauhaus Weimar, 1919–1923*, Bauhausverlag, Weimar–Munich, 1923. Translation.
2. Letter to Julia, May 19, 1919. Translation.
3. Ibid.
4. Letter to Julia. Translation.
5. Letter to Julia, Oct. 5, 1922, from Weimar. Translation.
6. Ibid.
7. Letter to Julia, from Weimar. Translation.
8. Autograph letter sold at Gutekunst & Klipstein, Bern, as Lot 72, Auction 89, May 14, 1958. Translation from the French.
9. Letter to Julia, Aug. 12, 1922, from Lüneburg. Translation.
10. The A-major fugue for organ. Ed. Peters; Vol. II.
11. Prelude and fugue in B minor.
12. Letter to Julia, May 18, 1920, from Weimar. Translation.
13. "Nos. 1, 2, 3 for piano, 5 was never finished (but also for piano); all the others for organ: 4, 6 ... (the fugue is of 1922) ... 7 ("Trauerfuge," written at the death of his father, on the inverted subject of fugue no. 1), 8 – two versions –, 9, 10 (two versions), 11, 12, and 13 (this is really the second version of fugue 8)." Communication from Laurence Feininger to the author, Apr. 11, 1958.
14. *Europa*, no. 7, Gustav Kiepenheuer Verlag.
15. Letter to Julia, May 7, 1913, from Weimar. Translation.
16. Barr Q., p. 2.

17. Letter to Julia, Aug. 18, 1924, from West-Deep. Translation.
18. Letter to Julia, July 7, 1924, from West-Deep. Translation.
19. Letter to Barr, May 14, 1928, from Dessau.
20. Letter to Julia, Dec. 11, 1925, from Weimar. Translation.
21. Letter to Julia, May 30, 1919, from Weimar. Translation.
22. Letter to Julia, July 28, 1923, from Weimar. Translation.
23. Letter to Julia, Aug. 1, 1923, from Weimar. Translation.
24. Letter to Stefan Pauson, Nov. 26, 1925, from Weimar. Translation.
25. Letter to Julia, Mar. 9, 1925, from Weimar. Translation.
26. Georg Muche, obituary of Lyonel Feininger in Hans Maria Wingler, *Wie sie einander sahen. Moderne Maler im Urteil ihrer Gefährten*, Munich, 1957. Translation.
27. Walter Gropius, communication to the author, Mar. 5, 1959.
28. Muche, op. cit.
29. Letter to Julia, Feb. 13, 1925, from Weimar. Translation.
30. Letter to Julia, Feb. 21, 1925, from Weimar. Translation.
31. Letter to Julia, Oct. 17, 1925, from Weimar. Translation.

The Bauhaus Years – Dessau (pages 108–29)

1. Letter to Julia, July 30, 1926, from Dessau. Translation.
2. *Zeichner des XX. Jahrhunderts*, Frankfurt, 1956.
3. *Lyonel Feininger Aquarelle*, Munich, 1958.
4. Letter to Julia, Feb. 25, 1927, from Dessau. Translation.
5. Letter to Julia, Sept. 20, 1927, from Dessau. Translation.
6. Letter to Julia, Sept. 27, 1927, from Dessau. Translation.
7. Letter to Julia, Sept. 28, 1927, from Dessau. Translation.
8. Letter to Julia, Sept. 24, 1927, from Dessau. Translation.
9. E. Martin Browne, foreword to *Penguin Plays*.
10. Wilhelm Boeck and Jaime Sabartés, *Picasso*, New York, 1955, p. 255.
11. Letter to Julia, July 25, 1927, from Deep. Translation.
12. Jere Abbot.
13. Letter to Julia, Dec. 6, 1927, from Dessau.
14. June 30, 1928, from West-Deep.
15. Letter to Barr, July 5, 1928, from West-Deep.
16. Letter to Julia, July 14, 1928, from Deep. Translation.
17. Letter to Julia, Mar. 22, 1931, from Halle. Translation.
18. *Stadtkirche* rather than *Marktkirche* appears in the catalogue of the National Gallery exhibition, Berlin, 1931.
19. Letter to Schardt, July 4, 1929, from Deep. Translation.
20. Letter to Julia, Jan. 22, 1931, from Halle. Translation.
21. Letter to Julia, Jan. 23, 1931, from Halle. Translation.
22. Letter to Julia, May 16, 1931, from Halle. Translation.
23. John R. Spencer, "Rhetorica Pictura: A Study in Quattrocento Theory of Painting," *Journal of the Warburg and Courtauld Institutes*, 1957, vol. XX, nos. 1–2, pp. 26–44.
24. Letter to Julia, May 26, 1929, from Halle. Translation Julia Feininger.
25. Letter to Julia, Mar. 22, 1929, from Halle. Translation.
26. Letter to Julia, Apr. 16, 1929, from Halle. Translation.
27. Letter to Julia, Apr. 19, 1929, from Halle. Translation.
28. Letter to Julia, Apr. 22, 1929, from Halle. Translation.
29. Letter to Julia, from Berlin.
30. Letter to Julia, July 1, 1930, from Deep.
31. Letter to Julia, May 31, 1929, from Halle.
32. Letter to Julia, June 9, 1931. Translation.
33. Letter to Spicer-Simson, June 23, 1931, from Quimper.
34. Letter to Julia, Sept. 9, 1931, from Deep. Translation.
35. Letter to Julia, Apr. 11, 1931, from Halle.
36. Letter to Julia, Sept. 16, 1931, from Deep.
37. Letter to Julia, Sept. 18, 1931, from Deep. Translation.
38. Ibid.
39. Letter to Julia, Dec. 10, 1931, from Dessau. Translation.
40. Letter to Lux, Aug. 27, 1932, from West-Deep.

Withdrawal from the German Scene (pages 130–38)

1. Letter to Lux, Dec. 17, 1934, from Berlin.
2. Letter to Julia, Mar. 29, 1935, from Berlin.
3. Letter to Julia, Sept. 14, 1935, from Deep. Translation.
4. Barr Q., pp. 3–4.
5. Ibid., p. 4.
6. May 31, 1937, from Berlin.

Return to America (pages 139–47)

1. To Schardt, Feb. 3, 1942, from New York.
2. Sept. 9, 1937, from New York. Translation.
3. Letter to Spicer-Simson, Sept. 18, 1937, from New York.
4. Ibid.
5. Karl Gustav Gerold, Vienna, 1956. Translation.
6. Letter to Jawlensky, July 23, 1938, from Falls Village, Connecticut. Translation.
7. Letter to Schardt, Nov. 8, 1940, from New York. Translation.
8. Letter to Lux, July 11, 1940, from Falls Village, Connecticut.
9. Letter to Schardt, Aug. 16, 1940, from Falls Village, Connecticut. Translation.
10. Letter to Schardt, May 15, 1941, from New York. Translation.
11. Undated letter, probably December 1941, from New York.
12. Letter to Schardt, Feb. 3, 1942, from New York.

Manhattan (pages 148–59)

1. Letter to Schardt, Feb. 3, 1942, from New York.
2. Ibid.
3. Letter to Lux, Dec. 6, 1942, from New York.
4. Letter to Lux, Mar. 31, 1943, from New York.
5. Letter to Lux, Jan. 28, 1945, from New York.
6. Foreword, Catalogue of Lyonel Feininger exhibition, Mar. 30–Apr. 24, 1954, Curt Valentin Gallery, New York.
7. Letter to Lux, July 24, 1945, from Black Mountain College, North Carolina.
8. Letter to Marcks, Dec. 31, 1948, from New York. Translation.
9. Letter to Lux, Mar. 31, 1943, from New York.
10. Letter to Lux, July 2, 1946, from Stockbridge, Massachusetts.
11. Letter to Schardt, Apr. 7, 1946, from New York.
12. Letter to Schardt, Jan. 7, 1952, from New York.
13. Letter to Lux, Sept. 6, 1952, from Plymouth, Massachusetts.
14. Letter to Lux, Sept. 17, 1951, from Plymouth, Massachusetts.

The Last Years (pages 160–70)

1. Letter to Tekla Hess, July 15, 1951, from Lincoln, Massachusetts.
2. Letter to Lux, May 21, 1954, from New York.
3. Letter to Erlo van Waveren, Aug. 6, 1953, from New Haven, Connecticut.
4. Letter to Lux, Oct. 6, 1953, from Plymouth, Massachusetts.
5. Letter to Lux, Nov. 29, 1953, from New York.
6. Letter to Lux, Nov. 1, 1953, from New York.
7. Fritz Strich, *Deutsche Klassik und Romantik*, Bern, 1949.
8. Letter to Lux, from Stockbridge, Massachusetts, undated, 1955.
9. Letter to Lux, Sept. 12, 1955, from Stockbridge, Massachusetts.
10. Letter to Marianne Noack, née Feininger, from New York. Translation.
11. Letter to Lux, May 27, 1954, from New York.
12. Letter to Van Waveren, July 18, 1955, from Stockbridge, Massachusetts.
13. Letter to Lux, Jan. 3, 1954, from New York.
14. Letter to Karl Schmidt-Rottluff, Jan. 3, 1956, from New York. Translation.

INDEX